HEROIC HEARTS

HEROIC
HEARTS

*Sentiment, Saints, and Authority
in Modern France*

Jennifer J. Popiel

UNIVERSITY OF NEBRASKA PRESS

Lincoln

Parts of chapters 2 and 3 previously appeared as "St. Philomena('s) Remains: Religion, Sentiment, and Patriarchy Undermined in Post-Revolutionary France," in "Faith in Revolution," *Age of Revolutions*, January 2020, https://www.ageofrevolutions.com. Parts of chapter 4 previously appeared in French as "Virginité et sacrifice de soi: Philippine Duchesne, Euphrosine Perier et la vocation religieuse au XIXe siècle," in *Écrire le mariage des lendemains de la Révolution à la Belle Époque: Discours, idéologies, représentations*, ed. Stéphane Gougelmann and François Kerlouegan (Publications de l'université de Saint-Étienne, 2017), 95–108. All rights reserved.

Publication of this volume was assisted by the Saint Louis University Research Institute and the Saint Louis University Department of History.

Library of Congress Cataloging-in-Publication Data
Names: Popiel, Jennifer J., author.
Title: Heroic hearts: sentiment, saints, and authority in modern France / Jennifer J. Popiel.
Description: Lincoln: University of Nebraska Press, [2021] | Includes bibliographical references and index.
Identifiers: LCCN 2020038657
ISBN 9781496219619 (hardback)
ISBN 9781496227201 (epub)
ISBN 9781496227218 (mobi)
ISBN 9781496227225 (pdf)
Subjects: LCSH: Catholic women—France—History—19th century. | Sentimentalism—France—History—19th century. | Women—Identity—History—19th century. | Religion—Social aspects—France—History—19th century. | Church and the world—History—19th century.
Classification: LCC BX1530 .P596 2021 | DDC 282/.4408209034—dc23
LC record available at https://lccn.loc.gov/2020038657

Set in Arno Pro by Mikala R. Kolander.

To Kate, Molly, and Lucy,
each a world-changing hero
in her own right

Contents

Illustrations

Preface

When I see a bumper sticker or T-shirt with the phrase "Well-behaved women seldom make history," a part of me immediately responds to the underlying truth of the statement. Social and cultural change hasn't been a gift for asking nicely; it is hard-won by people who are willing to struggle, suffer, and fight. And yet when Laurel Thatcher Ulrich penned that phrase in her 1976 article, "Vertuous Women Found," she did not mean that females should be rebellious to guarantee their relevance as historical actors. In fact, she was reminding readers that, while historians prefer aberrational and insubordinate women, there are also other important historical actors, including "pious matrons [who] have had little chance at all . . . against Antinomians and witches."[1] Even though the history of women, gender, and sexuality has changed dramatically in the intervening years between Ulrich's article and this book, devotion and conformity continues to exclude women from consideration unless the women have, by definition, become aberrational.[2]

The underlying assumption that religious practice is private and feminine—and therefore historically insignificant and unrelated to the public sphere—is nowhere more true than in France, where conflicts between devout belief and anticlericalism rose to fever pitch with the French Revolution. From the nineteenth century forward, public debates and important texts tied women and religion to the home. For example, Jules Michelet, the most significant French historian of the nineteenth century, offered throughout his body of work one of the clearest modern discourses about masculine Republicanism, by which women were to be private, emotional, and religious and men public, scientific, and political.[3] Joan Scott has explained how even today the discourse articulating a separation of church and state relies on gender inequality for much of its force.[4] As Carol Harrison has also noted, scholars coming from a "postreligious vantage point" have often replicated Michelet's anticlerical conventions in their own work, assuming that religion stands in opposition to modernity.[5] As Charles Taylor has explained, in the modern world the public was "allegedly emptied of God, or of any reference to ultimate reality," becoming a wholly secular space.[6] While religious faith and practice have not necessarily decreased, their functions have been moved to the domestic sphere.[7] For women's historians, the problem of cultural conventions about women's lesser value is compounded by scholarly assumptions that religion is irrational and was necessarily relocated away from public life.[8] Religious belief becomes indicative of a life of limited horizons for women, imposed from outside and depriving them of authentic agency. Accordingly, though "the feminization of religion" is invoked time and again, religious sources are rarely read as sources important to women's intellectual and moral formation. Historians almost always see nineteenth-century women as religious, but rarely by intentional choice or avocation.

Much of my career has been spent in researching well-behaved women, or at least the discourses surrounding them. For me, too, this did not extend to religion. In my first book, *Rousseau's Daughters*, I explored how Rousseauean ideology used a language of self-control and moral formation to highlight women's domestic roles. I argued that the shift away from hierarchy and toward individuality provided women with a language and framework for increased agency, one that encouraged promoted the value of women's roles and highlighted the importance of their civic participation.

When I turned to a second project, I looked to take the implications of my argument forward. If the domestic revolution was not merely part of a repressive sexual contract, women, influenced by the new ideals, should have been seen exercising new authority or independence. Were there later historical records that demonstrated that women, rather than being more sequestered, had become more engaged with public life, using new ideas of moral autonomy and individualism? This book's research grew out of my desire to answer that question. I looked for locations of post-Revolutionary women's action. I also examined how women seized upon new cultural ideals. The deeper I dove into the research, the more I found that the cultural discourse of sentiment—Rousseau's language of the heart—quickly became aligned with another set of discourses that had also been marked as feminine: those tied to Catholic belief and practice. This included devotions such as the Sacred Heart but also the increasingly significant presence of women religious who ministered to the sick, the young, and the poor. Thus, women who used sentimental language—marked as "feminine" in the early nineteenth century—were not always, or even primarily, traditionally domestic or nurturing. In fact, large numbers of them were celibate and independent.

The contradictions inherent in our assumptions about these cultural discourses are at the heart of the book. On the one hand, sentimental and devout women were generally "well-behaved." They were pious, subordinate to authority, and law-abiding. On the other hand, despite their obedience and the popularity of sentimentalism, these women struck a nerve. At the time writers, artists, and even their own parents decried the women's independence, their activism, and their agency. Responses to sentimental art were also conflicted. Like the women, the art was often unassuming at first glance, but forceful and even aggressive underneath the surface. Modern forms of communication were also at the center of women's worlds, both in the ways they offered their ideas to the public and in their own consumer choices. The culture of sentiment demonstrates how well-behaved women existed not in opposition to prevailing ideals but because of them. It also demonstrates how, like Ulrich's pious matrons, important swaths of society have been waiting for us to understand their significance, not because they didn't make history, but because we accepted cultural descriptors of "feminine" forms of expression as illegitimate and weak. As you encounter the culture of sentiment and read the words of its proponents, I hope that you will come to know them as they so often saw themselves: women on a mission to change the world.

Acknowledgments

By the time that an academic monograph is finished, every author owes a debt of thanks to more people than can possibly be mentioned. Given the time that has elapsed between my first monograph and this one, I owe more debts than the average. It should go without saying that none of the errors are the fault of anyone but me. Similarly, these acknowledgments only begin to touch the surface of the debts that I owe.

I became a French historian in large part because of the joys of the city of Paris. Research in Paris has only become more and more wonderful over the past twenty years, thanks to the helpful and kind staff of the Bibliothèque Nationale de France (BnF). For this book I have used BnF collections located at Arsenal, Tolbiac, and Richelieu. I owe a particular debt of thanks to the staff at Richelieu. Despite various construction projects, I have always been able to find some portion of the project to research, and their willingness to help me think creatively about access—and to supervise my forays into the depths of storage—has made it a particular pleasure. The staff at the Départment des Estampes has been particularly wonderful; they facilitated my discoveries and seemed to find almost as much joy in some of my sources as I did. I am also indebted to the BnF's new copyright policy, which meant that I had to make far fewer Solomonic choices when deciding on illustrations for this book. The Bibliotheque Historique de la Ville de Paris has also been a lovely place to work; I appreciate their librarians and the peace of the reading room. When I began this project, the sources at the Archives Nationales were in Paris; by the time I completed the work, my resources had moved to Pierrefitte-sur-Seine. Each staff made sure that I had the resources that I needed. I am grateful. For more than one summer, Dominique Martineau has shared her airy and light apartment; it has become a home away from home, and I am glad to know her! (Many thanks to Nina Kushner for introducing us, and I am also glad for Nina's company climbing all those stairs!)

Despite the joys of Paris, when I began research on this project, I realized that a year in Paris with four children would be an intimidating prospect at best. I am grateful to Denise Davidson for talking me through the possibilities of research in Lyon—as well as encouraging me in the idea that I could take all the children abroad for a year without losing my mind. While I owe the Fulbright Commission Franco-Américaine the greatest thanks for offering me both funding and time, I owe Denise gratitude and appreciation for the initial inspiration (as well as her kindness to me from my first year as a graduate student until the present day!). Laura Talamante shared her contacts, which made my Fulbright application possible, and her generosity of spirit as well as joy in French experiences is always an inspiration. In Lyon I am grateful to Jacques Guilhaumou, Claude Gautier, and Anne Verjus for engaging with my work and facilitating my stay. Anne has become a friend well beyond Lyon; I appreciate her joie de vivre, her challenge for me to see the world in a new way, and her willingness to discuss ideas that go beyond history. The archivists and librarians of the Archives Municipales de Lyon, the Bibliotheque Municipale de Lyon, and the Oeuvres Pontificales Missionare (Lyon) provided resources that were crucial to shaping this project during my research stay in Lyon.

The Archives of the Carmel de Lisieux and the University of Dayton both provided access to important material that deepened my understanding of the history of sentimentality and consumerism in the nineteenth century. I am grateful for their archivists and staff.

The Doussin family responded to an importunate email with generosity of spirit, opening up their collection and their home. Jean-Pierre and Jacqueline offered me unlimited access to their incredible collection of religious material culture. They patiently answered every question and encouraged wide-ranging conversation over food and wine. Mitsi welcomed me as one of her people. I could hardly imagine a more idyllic setting for research, and I hope for many more visits with them.

In St. Louis, the Jesuit Archives and Research Center (JARC) offered assistance and time. Their new facility is a researcher's dream; I am already thinking up projects that will use more of it. The Archives of the United States–Canada Province of the Society of the Sacred Heart were not only small and quiet, but Lyn Osiek, their archivist, went out of her way to meet with me and to email me documents that were related to my project, even when I wasn't entirely sure what I was looking for. Their archives are also a treasure trove; I hope to have a long enough career to fulfill all the plans I have for them, too! The librarians at Saint Louis University were as important as anyone. Everyone, from the check-out desk to ILL (Interlibrary Loan) has been central to the success of this project. They found books, purchased resources, facilitated research, and were unfailingly helpful . . . with far fewer resources than they ought to have. Particular thanks to Jamie Emery, who is hands-down the best subject librarian around.

I love the collegiality of French historical studies. My undergraduate and graduate mentors—Gary Kates and Lynn Hunt—still generously offer their time and share their excitement about ideas, whether critiquing or praising. Words are insufficient to thank them or to tell them what they mean to me. I wouldn't be a historian—French or otherwise—without the model that Gary provided. The guidance and kindness that Lynn has offered and the vibrant intellectual community that she shaped are crucial to my scholarship today. In that vein, I have debts to Lauren Clay, Denise Davidson, Suzanne Desan, Paul Hanson, Jeff Horn, Sheryl Kroen, Gene Ogle, Jeff Ravel, David Smith, Tip Ragan, Jen Sessions, Victoria Thompson, and many others for their criticisms, kindnesses, drinks, and good restaurant recommendations. Suzanne read portions of the work and was willing to offer significant feedback, even though she likely feared my (sentimental?) tendency toward tears! I appreciate all of you. (I owe Jeff H. more drinks than most . . . almost as many as Lynn. This is a public acknowledgment of that debt. I have no doubt he'll collect.)

Rachel Fuchs left her mark on this project in many ways; her presence is missed. Danna Kostroun's writing support and encouragement were central to the project, especially the completion of chapter 5. Other women in the field, such as Joelle Neulander, Leslie Tuttle, Naomi Andrews, and Carolyn Eichner, have been great conference buddies. I count on them to push me on my blind spots, to support me when I need it, and not to back away from hard questions or conversations about conflicted topics. I love who they are, and I value what they bring to the world. Kristen Wood and Ellen Amster, the same goes for you. I'm glad we shared graduate school; I'm even happier that we're past tenure together. Thanks for allowing me to see the world with you. This is equally true of people who I've gotten a better glimpse of through social media: Jen Sessions, Julie Hardwick, Judith Miller, Robin Mitchell, and Meghan Roberts. Social media has its faults, but at its best it makes us more humane and helps us share our expertise so that we don't keep reinventing the wheel. As I moved into religious material, Sarah Curtis and Carol Harrison were both extremely generous with their time as well as references and recommendations. Sarah has read material, talked about ideas, and helped me think through problems. I'm so grateful! At conferences, Daniel Watkins and Tom Kselman engaged ideas and posed questions and concerns. This book is better for their work as well as their comments on my own. Dana Sanchez, Juan Alonzo, Vivian Dzokoto, and Tom Levine have shaped the final stages of this work and projects to come; I am grateful for their example and the occasional nudge in the direction of work-life balance.

The University of Nebraska Press has been a welcoming and interested home for this book since before I was entirely certain of what I wanted it to be. Alisa Plant said that she was interested and kept touching base, even when service obligations threatened to derail my writing. Matthew Bokovoy and Heather Stauffer took over when Alisa returned to LSU and they have been wonderful shepherds, with a great vision for the book. Similarly, Jane Curran has been a great copyeditor. If errors remain, I'm sure I introduced them on the sly!

Saint Louis University (SLU) has been a source of many kinds of support. Grants from the College of Arts and Sciences and the Office of the Vice-President for Research facilitated two summer trips to Europe and made the book possible through a subvention. Greg Beabout and Fr. David Meconi keep reminding me of many of the things I value about

Jesuit education . . . and of the reasons that I joined a Jesuit university. I appreciate their commitment to higher things and their love for the mission. The Department of History also provided research and publication funding as well as graduate student research assistants whose work allowed me to move this project along. (Thanks to those graduate students, who include Nick Lewis, Matthew Morgan, Eric Sears, Meg Smith.) My colleagues at Saint Louis University were also a source of support, inspiration, copyediting, and motivation. They pushed me to clarify where I was obscure, celebrated little victories, and had faith in me and this project. Katrina Thompson and Heidi Ardizonne offered both cheer and energy. Fr. Steven Schoenig, Damian Smith, Thomas Finan, and Doug Boin joined in the faculty seminars organized by Silvana Siddali. Our conversations pushed me to think comparatively. They also were up for the occasional coffee, willing to read pieces, and commiserated when necessary. Hal Parker, Mark Ruff, Claire Gilbert, and Fabien Montcher covered similar territory, shared readings, and had faith in the project. Two grants, one from the SLU Women's Commission and a SPARK grant from the office of the Vice President for Research, provided the opportunity for monthly lunches with female faculty. These were a great opportunity to think through interdisciplinary approaches, research problems, and issues of work-life balance; they also allowed me to get to know Pauline Lee better, something that has made time on the third floor of Adorjan Hall much better. I am grateful for the Women of Adorjan lunch group and the grants. Chris Pudlowski and Kelly Goersch are unfailingly funny, kind, and helpful, not only great resources, but wonderful friends. Pearl Ewing is an incredible woman; she meets the challenges of each day with a smile. I am so glad that she is in my life. Teresa Harvey rounds out this group as someone who is full of joy and love for others. I love seeing all these women's smiles in the morning. COVID made it clear just how much I count on them each day. My job is half as good without them nearby. Flannery Burke is a better teacher than anyone I know. I'm lucky to be in the same department with her. She also let me borrow her wonderful dog for a year . . . which led to our family's adoption of two of the best dogs ever. Our family is happier for it. Torrie Hester is kind and brilliant, and

I have the great good fortune of being in the same department as her so that some of her excellent personal and collegial qualities might rub off on me (maybe, eventually). She recommended the lifechanging National Center for Faculty Development and Diversity (NCFDD) to me. Lorri Glover's entry into the history department as the Bannon Chair was a blessing. I admire her immensely and am grateful for her humor, good advice, and common sense. She has read every word of this manuscript and taught me to celebrate every milestone.

We met Laurie and Craig Anzilotti in Los Angeles in 1999. They and their children are chosen family, plus it's a party once the Anzilottis arrive! Thérèse ardently desired to be ordained a priest; I'm sure that she would have been an interested party to many of our conversations and shared moments over the past twenty years.

The women of this book were excited by the possibilities of new media. Similarly, when I was a young mother and graduate student, researching and writing a dissertation, I found a group of women online. They weren't all (or even mostly) academics, but they shared a lot of the struggles that I had. All of my kids grew up with the women and children of "the board"; it feels normal to them, and the advice and companionship of these women has helped me more than I can express.

Kasey Walker and Kathy Marty have both been my friends for a long time. They are strong and faithful women who have changed the world for the better. More than one woman in these pages reminds me of them. I hope they see the resemblance.

My sister and my mother live thousands of miles away. Frequently when I read Philippine Duchesne's letters, I thought about how much she loved her family, and how little she saw them. "Philippine probably did a better job keeping in touch," I hear them thinking. (Perhaps it should go without saying that she was a saint, so she was better at a lot of things.) I love both of you and am glad you are my family, even if I don't say it enough. Thanks for being strong women who gave—and give—me examples of how to face the world.

Zélie Martin wrote about her sister-in-law with effusive and sentimental words. I'm not quite as prone to gushing, but I am grateful for the love and grace that my in-laws, especially Elmer and Dottie Borgmeyer, have shown to me for more than twenty years. Their support and faith has been a foundational part of my life since college. Though Elmer passed away as this book was being completed, my love and appreciation for both of my in-laws continues.

The women of this book said that marriage and childhood were a distraction from world-changing work. They weren't wrong. The offspring on the other side of that equation could complain as well, I'm sure. Jeanne Chantal's son grumbled about abandonment. My kids—James, Kate, Molly, and Lucy—have been told to be quiet after I got home but still needed to claw my way out of the past. At dinner I've been known to make them listen when I had to share the day's cool finding . . . even when they did not think it was nearly so neat. I've missed milestone events because I was in France for research. Through it all, they've been at least passingly interested and always supportive of the fact that my work needs to get done, too. I love the people that they are, and I am so proud of them. My dissertation was dedicated to David and James (the only child we had at the time); this one is for all of the girls.

Last but not least, there's my husband. At some point in this research project, Dave turned to me and said, "Your last book was all about raising children, even as we had small children. This one is all about how terrible marriage is for women. If the first had substantial overlap with our life, maybe I should ask some questions about this one?" So, now's as good a time as any to go on record saying that Dave is the reason that I can do the things I do. Marriage in this book is frequently a nightmare, "all servitude," and often to untrustworthy and controlling men, but that's not my life. My husband is my intellectual cheerleader, an excellent reader, a talented cook, a loving dad, a clever gift-giver, a terrible punster, and someone I hope that I never have to share a home office with again. Dave, I love you; let's keep doing this for a long time.

HEROIC HEARTS

Introduction

Pastel Saints and Powerful Women

The classic image of the frail woman known as Thérèse of the Child Jesus and the Holy Face (née Thérèse Martin) shows a young girl, in the habit of a nun. She is serene, with a small smile on her rounded face that invites the viewer to contemplate her further. She also holds a crucifix nearly covered in roses, literally dripping with flowers and petals. Because the image was intended for veneration, multiple elements remind the viewer of Thérèse's sanctity. Her halo indicates that she is in heaven; the omnipresent roses represent suffering and trials borne patiently for and offered to Christ. The flowers are also iconographically central to the name most commonly given to the young woman: Thérèse, the Little Flower (see figure 1). This was, for the twentieth century, the principal portrait of Thérèse and, as her sister said, "the Portrait of the saint published everywhere."[1] It was ubiquitous, popularized on small holy cards as well as on china, in books, and other consumable products.[2] The image bears visual witness to its sentimental and bourgeois roots; it owes its construction to the most commercially popular European style of Catholic art in the second half of the nineteenth century, Sulpician art.[3] Products from the Rue Saint-Sulpice in Paris featured hearts, lace, gilt, flowers, and an androgynous, even feminine, Jesus (see figure 2).[4] Sulpician statues and images evoked emotion and emphasized spiritual practices that were intended to produce an intimate connection to God. Sulpician images were also sentimental in other ways, as they situated believers within narratives of heroism, martyrdom, and suffering and cultivated the idea that proper emotional responses, born from the heart, were a central part of moral improvement.[5] The sentimental and Sulpician image of Thérèse was centered in the mass consumption preferences of the nineteenth century, which highlighted emotion, suffering, and the power of individual contemplative piety.[6]

The Little Flower's fame is obvious to even a casual observer. Globally, an estimated thirty million photographs of Thérèse had been produced by the time of her canonization in 1925, less than thirty years after her death.[7] Additionally her autobiography was massively popular, and holy cards, biographies, and other books offered further entry into her world. Thérèse's writings, as well as works about her, were purchased by believers and unbelievers alike, often without regard to gender or political affiliation.[8]

However, even among her admirers, many, especially intellectuals, were turned off by the feminine, bourgeois, and sentimental nature of her cult. As one of Thérèse's early biographers, Henri Ghéon, complained, "[T]he tinseled and sugary appearance of the devotion to the 'little saint' (the abuse of this diminutive drove me mad) had successfully concealed from me the definite greatness and perhaps originality that was certainly hers. Too many roses! Too many flowers! I could see nothing but roses."[9] In the early twentieth century, Vita Sackville-West also complained about the saccharine language and imagery that surrounded Thérèse, which was "as nauseating as a surfeit of marshmallows" and detracted from understanding her true character.[10] At midcentury Thomas Merton's autobiographical masterpiece explained how Merton had been inclined to see Thérèse as a "mute pious little doll in the imaginations of a lot of sentimental old women."[11] This was not merely the fault of other people's representations; Thérèse's propensity to keep "everything that was bourgeois about her" reinforced that perception. Merton explained that throughout her life, Thérèse maintained "her taste for utterly oversweet art, and for little candy angels and pastel saints playing with lambs so soft and fuzzy that they literally give people like me the creeps."[12] These criticisms continue today; modern feminist writers often see the Theresian cult of submission as effeminate and weak; they therefore seek a "more virile postVatican II spirituality."[13]

From the nineteenth century until today, feminized sentimentality has been a barrier to comprehension, something that subjugates rather than empowers, sickens instead of strengthens. Today calling something sentimental implies that it is trivial and characterized by an excess of emotion, appropriate only for women.[14] Similarly, dripping flowers, rhapsodies about nature, and diminutive language set teeth on edge long before the twentieth century; complaints about syrupy and maudlin images began not long after they rose to popularity. In that context it is not surprising that Ghéon and Sackville-West had to look beyond Thérèse's facade to understand the power of her vision. Like them, Merton also detested what he saw as the bourgeois smugness of nineteenth-century French Catholicism, but he eventually discovered that "the Little Flower really was a saint . . . a great saint, one of the greatest: Tremendous!"[15] To Merton and many others Thérèse was heroic, even though she had the unfortunate fate of existing within a consumerist devotional culture that masked her greatness through simpering ugliness.[16] In this same vein, scholars have complained about the heavy-handed curation of Thérèse's image after her death and implied that heavily retouched photographs and dripping sentimentality do not offer a "true" portrait of the saint's strength.[17]

However, Thérèse was not only accidentally consumerist or sentimental. In a way that was unusual for a cloistered nun, Thérèse communicated her ideas to others, using sentimental language and ideas in her poetry, plays, letters, and autobiography.[18] She has even been declared a Doctor of the Catholic Church—only the third woman to be so declared—because of her exceptional ability to offer the "science of love" to the believing public.[19] Thus even as she laid claim to greatness, the Little Flower situated herself in both mass culture and a language of sentiment, not incidentally but by her choices and as a central part of her appeal. Certainly her image was heavily curated and successfully calculated to appeal to bourgeois tastes. Even so, it was, as Merton notes, not an unfamiliar or hostile idiom for Thérèse. On the contrary she embraced sentiment. This included the hearts, flowers, and syrupy sweetness of visual culture; it also was grounded in her belief that proper emotional disposition, including an open heart, offered a foundation for individuals to become exceptional.

Thérèse's sentimentalism, her immediate fame, and her placement in a vibrant consumer society highlight the need for further attention to the culture of sentiment. On the one hand, as William Reddy has clearly explored, by the mid-nineteenth century, sentiment was culturally marked as feminine, weak, antimodern, and private, a state of affairs that is also reflected in modern attempts to see past sentiment's feebleness to an individual's strength.[20] On the other hand, for most of the nineteenth century, French sentimentalism was popular, compelling, and commercially successful; its ideas of martyrdom and heroism surrounded women and encouraged them to see themselves as capable of changing the world.[21] The paradox between these two poles is made evident by the varied interpretations of the popular Catholic devotion to the Sacred Heart of Jesus. Some historians have interpreted it as feminine because of its emotional and sentimental nature while others argue that it should be seen as masculine because of its political resonance and emphasis on combat.[22]

A closer look at the culture of nineteenth-century sentiment indicates that Thérèse was not alone in being both sentimental and authoritative. In the decades before Thérèse, other women were shaped by sentimental language and used it as a path to autonomy and worlds of heroic action. For example, Rose Philippine Duchesne and Pauline Jaricot both devoted their lives to public service. Duchesne traveled the globe as a missionary nun. Jaricot wrote sentimental theological treatises—widely published in the first half of the century, though virtually unknown today—and established religious foundations. Both women corresponded with popes, bishops, and diplomats. Each of them also used a sentimental understanding of the world to shape others. Even Thérèse's mother, Zélie Guerin Martin, subscribed to a worldview in which she was called to be religiously heroic, a saint, though she contextualized small, often domestic choices as central to a valiant life. Though she was married, with family and work obligations, Martin immersed herself in contemporary culture and purposely shaped others. Women such as these could see and use a language of emotion, nature, and the heart as empowering, rather than weak.[23]

Perhaps this should not surprise us. Historically, sentimentality was not always negative. In the mid to late eighteenth century, sentimentality and sensibility were highlighted in philosophy and novels, with Jean-

Jacques Rousseau serving as one exemplar for the idea that emotional responses were the basis for virtuous behavior and had moral implications for all humans.[24] The cultural practices tied to sentimentality were not only feminine nor were they private, even as they privileged individual reflection. Sentiment, politics, and culture were intertwined. Even as sentimentality was closely tied to ideas about private virtue, it also "gave political actions their emotional significance" and "linked individual bodies to the national body."[25] Sentimental novels, objects, and theological constructs certainly intended to evoke emotional responses, but they did so to raise political and social questions, to contest oppression, and redefine politics. Sentimentality might have been emotional, but that did not mean that it was weak.

However, in the early nineteenth century, femininity became linked with sentimentality. This, combined with the sexist nature of the modern public sphere, produced a tautological rhetoric that marked women as sentimental, antimodern, and fit primarily for domestic labor.[26] By the mid-nineteenth century, a language of the heart was linked to women, who were believed to be dominated by their emotions. Though emotional outpourings had served masculine political functions during the French Revolution, gendered cultural constructs eventually undergirded a sense that women were not appropriate modern actors because the source of their knowledge was emotional rather than rational, driven by hearts and not heads.[27] Sexual and social norms that had been somewhat malleable became more fixed, and increasingly strict lines were drawn between them.[28] In a very modern way, then, it makes sense that sentimentality—religious or otherwise—came to be seen as lacking in strength. It does not, however, as clearly follow that nineteenth-century women experienced sentimentality as weak or disempowering.

The fact that sentiment came to be opposed to virility but remained tied to religion also fits with the fact that the nineteenth-century French Catholic church became "feminized" or "feminine."[29] Religious practice emphasized individual devotion, and piety increasingly highlighted emotional responses over rational ones, both cultural signals that accentuated Catholicism's nonmasculinity.[30] Additionally the Catholic Church looked more and more female centered. Women attended more Masses than men, mothers managed the religious education of their children, and intellectuals coded religion as feminine and domestic.[31]

Devotional culture was only one part of a feminizing tendency in religious life. Cadres of women joined active religious orders in France after the Revolution, engaging in teaching, social work, and hospital work.[32] While the male hierarchy had dominated religious orders before the Revolution, outnumbering women by more than two to one, women's religious orders exploded in number after the Revolution.[33] By 1861 women accounted for more than half of the religious personnel of the Church, and the number continued to grow. In 1808 there were at least 13,900 vowed women religious in France. Seventy years later that number had climbed to over 127,000.[34] These women were no longer primarily cloistered nuns, as they had been after the Council of Trent and before the Revolution. Instead, they were almost all sisters who belonged to active orders. This resulted in the ubiquitous and vigorous presence of women religious in public works. Both in terms of devotional practice and the bodies who represented the Church on the streets, the French Church looked feminine.

At the same time, no Catholic woman could preach or be ordained to the priesthood. Clerical leadership was entirely off limits. Theological debates and spiritual direction were driven by clerics and therefore rarely accessible to women. Despite a long-standing tendency to refer to the Church by a feminine pronoun, its pronouncements were made by bishops and popes: all men. In this context, one might ask how truly feminine the Church was. Men directed the Church; women adopted its doctrines, echoed its words, and followed in clerical footsteps. Even opponents of the Church saw religious men as leaders and women as followers. For example, Jules Michelet, fervently anticlerical and one of the most influential French writers of the nineteenth century, explained at midcentury, referring to the priests, "Our wives and our daughters are raised and ruled by our enemies."[35] Across the political spectrum, men tended to see women as subordinate and unable to form their own ideas about the world, let alone determine the course of the Catholic Church.

How then did a language linked to women come to predominate in religious discourse? Historians have often seen the exclusion of women from secular institutions—and their importance in religious ones—as a likely cause. They posit that, as Revolutionary language and practices defined women's natural role as private, the only place that remained for them was the Church, even if it too was patriarchal.[36] Given the dearth of other possibilities, perhaps women chose to work within—and even accept—the confines of a controlling and patriarchal discourse. This explanation cannot be entirely satisfactory, however, as it fails to explain why a discourse controlled by men would emphasize femininity.[37] Joan Scott's recent work has offered context for this analysis, explaining that Western secular and masculinist norms tied religion, emotion, and passivity together to eliminate women from influence in a modern world.[38] Scott demonstrates how Western narratives of political masculinity attempted to excise women from public life, making Christian women morally and sexually subservient to men.

This book accepts Scott's argument but also demonstrates the simultaneous existence and appeal of a powerful and competing cultural discourse. Sentimentality offered a world in which religion and emotion were indeed feminine and redemptive but more than passive and domestic. In this way *Heroic Hearts* takes a lead from postsecular theory and suggests that to begin with a question of exclusion and norms is misleading. Theorists such as Saba Mahmood have reminded us that our distinctions of "secular" and "religious" are themselves products of assumptions that arise from the hegemonies of modernity.[39] Though "we tend to translate religious truth as force, a play of power that can be traced back to the machinations of economic and geopolitical interests," the reality is not always so clear. Further, "acts of resistance to relations of domination . . . do not exhaust the field of human action."[40] Devout Catholic women could embrace Catholicism for reasons that were about neither oppression nor liberation. A feminized church might be one in which the hierarchy was male, but women demonstrated by their presence and actions that they found the ideas to be persuasive, useful, and worth promulgating in "religious" arenas as well as "secular" ones.[41]

Regardless, by embracing a patriarchal Church and promoting a devotional culture that many saw as weak and feminine, women placed themselves into what has since become a complicated narrative. As Sarah Curtis has explained, French women religious "sometimes acted in ways that modern feminists would recognize—traveling widely, exercising authority, speaking out." At the same time, they also "were seeking simultaneously to subjugate themselves to what they saw as God's will."[42] This conjunction is sometimes problematic for those who see contradiction between feminist authority and a subordination of will that appears antimodern, especially in its emphasis on emotion.[43] As Phyllis Mack reminds us, feminist theorists have often been tempted to negate the agency in religious women's choices, even to the point of claiming that joining a religious order is "an example of the wrong use of agency."[44] Mack, like Mahmood, reminds us that this is "an avoidance of our responsibility not only to look for strategies of self-assertion in a patriarchal, class-based culture, but to look steadily at women's (and men's) own ideas about ethics, autonomy, and spirituality."[45] It is also consonant with a sexuality that cannot be fully disciplined by marriage, one that is at odds with the parceling out of political power to heads of families.[46] Nor did nineteenth-century French Catholic women see their religious choices or their adherence to sentimental ideals as a negation; a devout female could reconcile being a discerning subject in charge of her destiny with being an obedient Christian, subjecting herself to suffering—and the dictates of the Catholic Church—because of her heart's response to God's will.

Though scholars of modern Europe have explained how women's public behavior in the later nineteenth century, including labor agitation and suffrage movements, grew out of feminist opposition to the limitations of biological determinism, they have been slower to investigate the relationship between "weak," feminized, or exclusionary discourses and women's own sense of authority.[47] For example, as Ruth Harris points out, scholars have sought to explain why feminism failed to find a large audience in France. This research often begs the question of agency in its assumptions that a language of political demands was the correct way for women to have exercised authority. Even when historians use religious sources and tropes to inquire about the importance of female relationships and the inspirational power of faith in relation to the domestic sphere, they rarely inquire into women's—frequently religious—construction of their behavior and experiences.[48] Because religious devotion is sometimes hostile to women's intentional construction of themselves and limits their ability to act as social and civic beings, much modern scholarship acts as if it must always be so.[49] Indeed, when devout women, like these nineteenth-century French Catholics, become actors, at least in part by recourse to a religious narrative, studies frequently treat them as aberrations, some of the rare few who resisted patriarchal religious or domestic ideologies.[50] Social service work, motivated by religious impulses, is sometimes an exception, though it, too, is frequently discussed as an outgrowth of domestic nurturing and separate spheres ideology.[51]

However, some scholars, especially those informed by postsecular theory, have offered signal examples of how to investigate binary and sectarian assumptions. The work of these theorists cuts across historiographical divisions, including the traditional separation of "religious" from "secular" inquiries.[52] In their work one sees an articulation of how implicit links between modernization and secularization have shaped theological, sociological, political, and religious categories of analysis. Postsecular cultural theories trace out new ideas about autonomy, including a demand for the integration of experiences of religious vitality.[53] For example, Charly Coleman's work on the Enlightenment has demonstrated that claims about the transcendent have been a central part of modern understandings of the self.[54] Mahmood and Brent Nongbri have both argued that "religious" and "secular" are not universally opposing paradigms and indeed that it is to everyone's benefit to understand the different ways that religious practices have functioned in the context of pluralistic societies.[55] Carol Harrison's and Amanda Izzo's work attests to the ways in which women's religious beliefs operated in the same context as secular principles.[56] Similarly, Raymond Jonas's work on the Sacred Heart demonstrates how a religious symbol was an important modern signifier, rather than publicly irrelevant, and Thomas Kselman's examination of conversion demonstrates how the nineteenth century opened up religious choices in new ways.[57]

Postsecular studies question scholarly assumptions in a number of areas: whether or not there was a modern shifting of religion to private life, how society came to differentiate religious practices and transcendent beliefs from rational and instrumentalist reasoning, and if religious institutions and norms were removed from secular ones.[58] In this context a study of sentimentalism in the lives of devout Catholic women of the nineteenth century, who contemporaries often saw—and many modern theorists have seen—as antimodern, private, and irrational, is an ideal research arena. Claims about the feminization of religion in the nineteenth century, coded as emotional and separate from secular institutions, sit at the intersection of all of these formerly assumed "secularities." Even as the culture of sentiment went beyond "sacred" and "profane," it shaped women's worldviews.[59] An "unsectarian" examination of sentimental language and constructs will therefore help us understand French Catholic women's religious beliefs as enmeshed in the same discursive structures as secular principles, both capable of serving as a foundation for how these women engaged the world.[60]

Jurgen Habermas's early work offered theoretical underpinning to much of the scholarly work that divided the modern male and nonmodern female, rational and irrational.[61] Craig Calhoun, however, explains that Habermas now argues that "finding ways to integrate religion into the public sphere is a vital challenge for contemporary society and theories of contemporary society."[62] Even so, it has not always been clear how Habermas's revised understanding of practical modernity can be brought into conversation with the theories behind postsecular studies writ large. This is especially true given that much of the Habermasian understanding of religion and the public sphere prioritizes rationalist discourse. It is an unfortunate fact that a scientific-naturalistic worldview that refuses to engage irrational components of religion also excludes other nonrational aspects of human experience.[63] Confining reason to empirical and "scientific" boundaries produces a world that cannot adequately understand or incorporate emotion.[64] The result is a modernity in which neither emotion or transcendent beliefs can have explanatory force, offering an incomplete view of the range of lived realities.[65]

An overreliance on reason excludes the full range of society in other ways, too.[66] Because reason demands generality, it "must reduce all the human varieties of existing to experiences that are neither particular, individual, or unique, nor subjective, exceptional, or profound, but instead average and universally human."[67] Given that the default object of study is—still—masculine, an equalizing and normative philosophical apparatus is deeply problematic for understanding the history of women.[68] Finding ways to incorporate difference, including the nonrational, offers more space for engagement with people's own ideas about ethics and autonomy.

Literary scholars such as Margaret Cohen and David Denby have rethought the place of feminine sentimental writing in the social order, and historians such as William Reddy and David Andress have explained why emotional outpourings could be deeply political but were eventually coded as private and feminine.[69] Studies like these point to the ways in which sentiment, femininity, and devotion can be integrated into our understanding of the modern world, such that a woman might achieve "definite greatness" even as—or because—she identified with a language of suffering and weakness that was irrational and tied to the heart rather than the head.[70]

This work therefore seeks, within a framework of postsecular women's history, to problematize metanarratives of rational autonomy and of religion's historical relationship to modernity and secularization. It takes its initial cues from Habermas's work on the public sphere, in which he described how novels and mass print culture encouraged and informed a discourse of agency and judgment. By tracing the rising self-consciousness of a culture-consuming class, Habermas demonstrated some of the modern practicalities that expanded the public body.[71] Even as the nineteenth-century expansion in communication technologies often resulted in a depoliticization of content, the process of culture consumption continued in such a way that "[t]he experience of privacy made possible literary experimentation with the psychology of the humanity common to all, with the abstract individuality of the human person."[72] A modern project of self-assertion intersected with a commercially fostered consumer attitude. It assumed that deeply personal ideas were meant to be shared and consumed by others who were also engaged in self-shaping enterprises.

Though in his early work Habermas claimed that the creation of this consuming public resulted in the subordination and exclusion of women, he also believed that the content under consideration was easily divided out, with the private concerns of family life and religious belief and public concerns of a secular nature (sports events, corruption, etc.) existing separately. His twenty-first-century insistence on postsecular corrections now pushes us to find a more complete picture of "the humanity common to all."[73] One possible response is to set a path that resituates assumptions about emotion and normative behavior.

Heroic Hearts takes up the challenge in its exploration of how nineteenth-century females both consumed and produced sentimental material. Its sources range from catechisms, novels, and personal letters to pious images, games, and autobiographies. Closer examination of these sources and the lives of nineteenth-century women, some all but forgotten today, demonstrates that the language of sentiment shaped women's vision of the world and authorized threatening forms of independence. Letters "created spaces of spiritual liberty between people, beyond the constraints of daily life and distance."[74] Autobiographical writing allowed for the presentation of oneself as authoritative and heroic.[75] Similarly engagement with visual culture was subject to a reflexive process whereby the writer shaped and was shaped by community ties.[76] Literary and material objects demonstrate how the spaces of women's identity construction existed not only in family and home but also in schooling and charity work, the communicated and published word, and consumer culture.[77]

For these reasons, in its use of "modern" this work emphasizes not acceptance of a particular political position or vision of the world, but instead, like Rousseau, an adherence to ideals of self-governance and self-construction, to philosophical modernity. As philosopher Jeffrey Bloechl explains, "The modern subject does not govern its actions with reference to some external norm, be it natural or supernatural. As moderns, we can no longer say our private discernment is clearly the proximate norm of a life seeking salvation, but must affirm that discernment as something closer to the ultimate norm of such a life."[78] In other words the modern subject is one who seeks to mold her life according to a vision that she authorizes as authentic. Even though she, like any premodern agent, continues to be shaped by her cultural milieu and invisible discourses, she now understands her life as embedded in an autonomous sense of ethics.[79] This can be true across the political spectrum and without regard for the religious content of the material that she marshals toward this shaping of judgment.

While this description is similar to other postsecular treatments of "modern" subjects, such as Bruno Latour's "Modern" or Talal Asad's "conscious agent-subject," this book does not prejudge what a modern subject ought to desire, whether it be freedom, pleasure, or something else.[80] Instead, the primary test is of the subject as a thinker who claims to order her life by a rationale that she upholds as normative because of her own discernment, not an external standard. She claims authority over the construction of her identity even as she is deeply embedded in the modern processes that shape her vision of the world and allow her to attempt to shape others.[81]

Using this criterion, *Heroic Hearts* reorients our understanding of the gendered and sentimental authority that led young French women to fashion lives of heroic self-abnegation. It accomplishes this by examining the artifacts that they used, read, and left behind, many of which have never been considered: spiritual autobiography and other religious treatises, sentimental novels, printed games, holy cards, hagiographic legends, and family correspondence. In the analysis of these materials, this book demonstrates that, in nineteenth-century France, religious and nonreligious tropes were often interchangeable. Perhaps most importantly, by juxtaposing narratives that we would define as either secular or religious and examining them across an era of exploding production and consumption, the book demonstrates how French idioms of sentimentality produced an unsectarian and authoritative language of heroism, martyrdom, and virtue. Discourses surrounding Catholicism, love, and marriage encouraged women to see themselves as individuals whose primary obligation was to take their place in conversation with and in service to the community at large, becoming heroes who would save the world by their love. Like Thérèse's strength and her sentimentality, these phenomena were mutually constitutive rather than at odds with one another.

By looking at the role of sentiment in the cultural shaping of vocational identity, as well as women's individual responses to these ideas, *Heroic Hearts* engages current debates about the history of religion, emotion, and modernity. Unlike studies of the meaning of the Sacred Heart or the Catholic Church's enunciation of the spiritual meaning of the sacrament of marriage, it is not concerned with theology in and of itself, nor centrally with discourses beyond France's borders.[82] Instead, it investigates the conceptual apparatus that framed the lives of French Catholic women.

Although speculative reason and patriarchal politics increasingly relied on narratives of secular rationality, a great deal of practical reason continued to be shaped by nonrational ideas and symbols and embraced qualities that would quickly be cast as merely feminine, religious, or weak. Devout nineteenth-century Catholic women who used the language of sentiment did not agree that their perspective was antimodern, nor did they limit their demands for social reconstruction to a private and domestic sphere. Instead, like many Revolutionary women, they assumed that their vision of the world should extend to territory outside of the conjugal family, and they sought to influence others with their vision. In their manipulation of modern consumer culture, women further demonstrated that this nineteenth-century discourse was not limited to the private sphere but was critical and audience oriented, both important qualities for Habermasian modernity.[83]

It is true that, in the nineteenth century, nurturing domesticity, centered in the home, became the most prominent cultural ideal for Western European women, and that many of the bourgeois artifacts related to that ideal today strike us as effeminate and weak.[84] Additionally, as cultural and intellectual trends argued for the relegation of women to the home as wives and mothers, France and other Western nations experienced the feminization of religious practice. Nineteenth-century French women operated in a world that increasingly argued that religion was private, in opposition to the political and public. Both Catholics and anticlericals also perpetuated the idea that there was a "wrong" form of Catholicism, which was emotional, uncontrolled, and ultimately dangerous.[85] The rhetoric of political masculinity and secularization described by Joan Scott was an unavoidable part of women's lives.[86] This intellectual current in culture and society reinforced that women were "naturally" religious and emotional and that these qualities were therefore particularly appropriate to women.

However, the sources of this book remind us that cultural and theological practices of the post-Revolutionary era reinforced the value of sentiment and religious devotion in ways that contradicted an assumption of the privacy of domesticity or the irrevocable authority of husbands or fathers. Girls and young women consumed religious and secular books, images, and ideas, whose messages were mutually supportive. These cultural artifacts did not assume that emotional engagement and religious practice limited women to the home or that asceticism removed women from the world. Instead, a culture of sentiment offered women ways to see themselves as heroes, ready to fight valiantly for their ideals and the creation of a new world. Their devotions, such as dedication to the Sacred Heart of Jesus, emphasized love and emotion even as they also stood for demands that their Christian life be central to public life.[87] Women's religious understandings and practices were not isolated, household bound, or private but took place within a shared community where devotion, even when it was derived from the heart, was not only a matter of private feeling.[88] Belief demanded action on the part of the believer and could not be separated out from other forms of daily life.[89]

In a world that emphasized interiority and sentimental constructs, it was the heart that was one's moral center.[90] To be sentimental was to judge correctly, both in thought and feeling. Tears might accompany proper feeling and could serve as evidence that one was experiencing emotion that was significant and true.[91] As the sentimental novel maintained, "[F]eelings . . . were more important than wealth or honor."[92] Even the popular languages of mysticism and asceticism, which seemed to reinforce the separateness of religious belief, did not truly accentuate common distinctions between public and private, emotion and reason. In their claims that believers should serve as public witnesses and discipline their bodies, ascetic ideas and practices underlined the Christian's responsibility to change the world.[93] Ascetic theology also explicitly confronted the relationship of women's sexuality to freedom and explained how mastering one's own desires or submitting to suffering could help shape an entirely new culture.[94] Even when it rejected the world as it currently existed, these forms were communal and idealistic, seeking to create a society transformed for the better. The nexus of sentiment, devotion, and nineteenth-century women's agency therefore demands further study.

Even a brief overview of the relevant history of piety and devotion demonstrates the ways in which common assumptions about femininization and Catholicism do not sit neatly with the facts of women's historical experiences. Though they were excluded from the clerical hierarchy, seventeenth-century women had important roles in the Catholic Church. Private devotion, especially veneration of the Sacred Heart, promoted the idea of God as gentle, loving, and directly accessible. After the Council of Trent, the Church reinforced demands for cloistering women religious, and conjugal spirituality also became a point of focus.[95] However, even as both cloister and marriage increased in theological emphasis, seventeenth-century piety offered numerous models of saints who were religiously active outside of convents or families. *Beatés* and laywomen could be involved in local social work, join confraternities and lay societies, and take part in religious processions.[96] These trends emphasized women's spiritual responsibilities and endowed them with power in both a personal and a social sense.[97]

The eighteenth century continued to emphasize the theological implications of marriage, including the use of language that recognized the spiritual dimension of human sentiments.[98] At the same time, the Church also pulled back from some of the emotional language and individuality of popular Catholic devotions, instead reinforcing the hierarchical and patriarchal authority of clerics. This included a redirecting of attention back to the Mass and sacraments and the promotion of standard forms of catechism.[99] These changes were intended to limit popular expressions of religious fervor because of their link to superstition, but the emphasis on hierarchy and the Eucharist rather than popular piety also highlighted masculine authority.[100]

The Revolutionary era saw a profound shift in religious influence, with women able to exercise more authority than ever before. The Revolution asked clerics to swear an oath of loyalty to the Revolution, which resulted in the dismissal of those who would not take the oath and their replacement with constitutional priests, who were often boycotted by the local faithful. When priests who refused the oath were declared traitors by the state, those who didn't flee were arrested.[101] Once dechristianization got underway, the law suppressed the priesthood and attempted to end the practice of Catholicism entirely.[102] Without a clerical hierarchy or churches, individuals could secretly perform some rites such as baptisms, "white" Masses with unconsecrated hosts, and catechesis of children, but much else had to be abandoned.[103]

Women's participation then took on a particularly prominent role, and their adherence to sentiment and the Church became a way to promote and maintain their faith in the face of state hostility.[104] Women replaced the local priest as the primary teachers of catechism.[105] The Sacred Heart became a sign of opposition to the Revolutionary government, and the emotion that it stood for not only took a larger role in piety but also had political implications.[106] Devotional practices such as processions to sites of reported apparitions, veneration of the Sacred Heart, and recitation of the rosary became a way to maintain faith in a time of repression. Even if the hierarchy had wanted to discourage popular religious practices, it would have been difficult, given that there were few clerics, and those were in hiding.

In the Revolutionary era, religion was often experienced in private or small communities, and individual piety was mediated through the family setting, with catechism learned from mothers, rosaries said *en famille*, and religious reading offered orally, for the benefit of the family.[107] However, this did not mean that devotion was apolitical or socially disengaged, and clerics did not discourage emotional practices in the Revolutionary era. The practices were hidden of necessity, given the fact that Catholicism had been outlawed. Still, just as the church building combined both sacred and profane purposes before the Revolution, so too, did religion continue to play a role in the whole fabric of life. Religious emblems—the Sacred Heart in particular—were useful for rallying and identifying counter-Revolutionary forces. Taking the side of the Church did not mean that all female activists were opposed to liberal politics, but no matter what their response to the new political ideas, when women defended Catholic prerogatives, they claimed moral authority for their right to practice the faith they chose and to do so openly, something that placed religion firmly into a public context.[108] Additionally, religious belief and practice authorized women to see themselves as actors in a communal enterprise. Women took on public roles through their activism, a position facilitated by the destruction of the hierarchical and masculine institutional structure of the Church. Women were publicly engaged because of their religious commitments, not in spite of them.[109]

By the mid-1790s, it became clear that the French population "did not want a republic if the price was to be a continued assault on Catholic Christianity," but that the people could accommodate a nonroyalist state that did not disallow religious practice.[110] The Directory did not wholly heed this lesson; Napoleon did. Soon after Napoleon rose to power, priests who had fled from France for safety began to return in great numbers.[111] Seeing the social utility of the Church as well as the necessity of breaking the alliance between counter-Revolutionary agitation and religious adherence, Napoleon regularized the position of the Church. The Concordat of 1801 reinstated a hierarchical Church in France. Though it was a Church with a shortage of clerics and little chance of offering the same pervasive approach to life and faith that it had only thirty years before, it was certainly not "private."

An acceptance of a public role for the Catholic Church was problematic from the same Revolutionary perspectives that had tried to abolish saints' days and root out Catholic "superstition," with the issue made more urgent given that religious practice increasingly appeared to be feminine and irrational. However, not only dechristianizers but also some Catholics were troubled by the authority that devout women now wielded. As the bishop of Mâcon complained in 1801, "How does it come about . . . that women, whom the Apostle has commanded to learn their duties in silence, dare to permit themselves to influence the doctrine and conduct of those given to them by the Lord to lead and teach them?"[112] Religious women had lost sight of their own limitations.

Nowhere was this picture clearer than in the image of the celibate religious. Both male and female celibacy had been questioned throughout the Enlightenment and Revolution, with *philosophes* and Revolutionaries seeing the failure to procreate as a marker of poor citizenship rather than a holy or sacrificial act.[113] While none of the foundresses of the orders that came into being after the Revolution would have self-identified as radical, most rejected marriage and maternity, choosing to devote their lives to strangers, often in opposition to their families' wishes. The orders they founded were active in the world and global in reach. Some regions of France saw as many as one in ten women of marriageable age take the veil.[114]

From numerous perspectives women's devotion to celibacy was intolerable. Politicians worried about the impact on the already worrisome birth rate. One liberal Catholic reformer claimed that nuns were a threat to both home and nation, as celibate religious life "murder[ed] in one's breast the generations to come."[115] If woman as ideal citizen was shaped by her destiny to be a mother, then women who rejected both motherhood and home were unnatural and threatening.[116] The increasingly large number of women who became vowed religious demonstrated that religion authorized women to view themselves within too large of a sphere of action. As Judith Surkis has noted, married heterosexuality was a metaphor and the source of social integration; in this context chosen celibacy was a rejection of social integration.[117]

Jules Michelet was particularly obsessed with the liberating potential of religious and emotional discourses, especially what he saw as women's tendency to reject the attractions of hearth and home because of mis-guided religious adherence.[118] His most focused treatment of this topic was found in his massively popular work *Priests, Women, and Families.* The first edition was printed in 1845, though there were multiple reprint-ings, translations, and new editions in the years that followed. Michelet's writings are exceptional for pinpointing exactly what worried many nineteenth-century men about women's devotion. Women's sexuality was supposed to be disciplined by marriage; this was not possible if religion liberated them from men's authority.[119] Michelet's language also contin-ues to echo in twentieth- and twenty-first-century claims about a natural opposition between a secular public life and a religious private life.[120]

Michelet describes the ideal social order as one where women are emotional and private, acting not as rational and scientific citizens but as lovers and mothers.[121] Women were not meant to be independent think-ers; they needed a husband to guide them. While some nuns, such as those of Philippine Duchesne's order, the Religious of the Sacred Heart, had assumed authority over women, this was a particularly unnatural act that needed repudiation.[122] Following a cleric was only slightly better. In short, women's exposure to religious ideas threatened their biologi-cal femininity. Some refused to procreate, becoming lifeless and unnat-ural nuns. Others adopted forms of religious belief that were "trifling, romantic, and false," supported by novels and encouraged by priests in confessionals rather than the direction of their husbands.[123]

The solution for this problem lay in an insistence that women follow their husbands, being proud to say, "I am the wife of a strong man."[124] As Michelet explained, the wife ought to internalize her husband's guidance rather than offering a conflicting vision of the world, based on a hostile religious ideology. He said, "This home must truly be our home, and this table our table. We must not find at home the old dispute that has already been settled in science and the world, with our wife or child tell-ing us on the pillow a lesson learned from the words of another man."[125] Women were meant to be subordinate to men in this vision of the world, and Michelet's ideal women were no exception. Instead of creating their own identity, they accepted their husband's direction.

Michelet claimed that women's piety was particularly dangerous because clerics used the natural language of women, speaking to their hearts, and this allowed priests to usurp the husband's authority. Further, the nineteenth-century devotions that appealed to women were, Michelet argued, founded in and linked to nonrational practices that could be traced back to the seventeenth century. Priests as well as modern consumer culture had valorized and popularized these emotional forms of piety, appealing to women and subverting the headship of husbands.

Devotion to the Sacred Heart typified the problem. Claiming that its success was due to the fact that it appealed to women's carnal and sensual side, Michelet insisted that the Sacred Heart offered emotional and spiritual union that had sexual overtones and served to cuckold the husband who should be served instead of the priest.[126] Michelet's complaints, then, were not that religion's sentiment encouraged women to be emotional—he believed that was in keeping with their nature—but it allowed them to become intellectually and sexually independent of the masculine heads of household. Michelet assumed that women were attracted to sentimental language. Their tendency to rely on emotion was part of the reason that they needed the guidance of a secular man.[127] As Carol Harrison explains, "His dire warnings of female vulnerability to Catholicism were the corollary of his celebration of male autonomy and republican citizenship."[128] Women's sentimentality was exactly why they needed trustworthy husbands.

Michelet's description of the public sphere as masculine and rational, truly exclusive of sentiment and religion, was a piece of wish fulfillment, an attempt to write active and energetic women into a limited family life, away from the influence and threatening authority offered by the unsectarian—but emotional and heroic—language of sentimentality.[129] As Michelet understood well, sentimental domesticity and popular religiosity were part of a larger cultural presence that liberated women and encouraged independent judgment.[130] Attempts to underline secularization and dismiss the relevance of emotion and religious devotion were about diminishing women's independence and reducing their influence;

they were not the result of an already-accomplished and "natural" retreat of religion and emotion into the home.

Nineteenth-century religious discourse complicated bourgeois domestic rhetoric and offered an antidomestic current for "respectable" women, something scholars have not yet fully understood.[131] The women who chose to become nuns were, on the one hand, traditional and obedient. Their expressions of belief were frequently sentimental; religious and emotional were both "natural" things for women to be. They also operated within Catholic religious norms, including seeking and obtaining hierarchical approval for their activities. Like most women, they were not political radicals or even reformers; they were often hostile to Revolutionary change.[132] On the other hand, by living under the control of neither father nor husband, they revealed a deep chasm between patriarchal and domestic assumptions and their devout—but threatening—sense of individual, authoritative, feminine vocation. The eruption in public and active women's religious orders, similar to post-Reformation vocational shifts, also calls into question the argument that religious practice was a default position left to women once they had been written out of public relevance.

The fact is, while celibate and active religious sisters were numerous and visible in France, devout Catholic women in France complicate our understanding of the nineteenth century. Some French women who didn't join religious orders also rejected marriage, not because of an inability to find a husband, but because of a desire to remain single.[133] These celibate women—who, in Michelet's vision, would die "without protection and home"—also used a religious language of sentiment to justify action in the world.[134] Like the sisters in religious orders, they claimed both emotional and physical independence. They didn't procreate, and they worked outside of family contexts, in opposition to the rhetoric that limited them to the home and to physical maternity.

Even women who married might do so with an understanding of their vocation—both within the home and without—as fashioned in a way that would set them at odds with the prevailing (masculine) culture. As Michelet noted in *Priests, Women, and Families*, the married woman who allowed herself to be shaped by religion would end up turning against her secular husband. He described the husband's unfortunate position in the following terms: "The husband finds the house larger and more empty. His wife has become entirely another being . . . everything has changed in their intimate habits, always for a good reason: 'Today is a fast-day'—and tomorrow? 'It is a holy day.' The husband . . . would consider it very wrong to trouble this exalted devotion; he is sadly resigned: 'This becomes embarrassing,' says he. 'I had not foreseen it; my wife is turning saint.'"[135] Michelet's language could aptly be described as hysterical; it certainly betrays the fact that he and many of his contemporaries were terrified by women's insistence on their right to order their lives according to a heroic vision of the world, a demand that threatened patriarchal control.

Michelet thus offers us crucial insights about nineteenth-century Catholic women's belief and practice in France. Devout women were immersed in a culture of sentiment that allowed them to bypass rationalist and secular understandings of the world, even as they understood their identities in modern ways. Equally, these women entered the public sphere as they not only were shaped by but also influenced and engaged the cultural and intellectual ideas that surrounded them. Exploring religious sources, secular literature, and imagery in ways that Catholic young women would have found sensible untangles the complicated affinities between sentiment, femininity, and modernity.

Heroic Hearts examines the material that surrounded girls to better understand the cultural and intellectual connections between religion, emotion, and women's sense of themselves as heroic actors in the world. The first three chapters describe and analyze the burgeoning consumer culture that shaped French women's assumptions about love, marriage, and religious vocation, while the last three chapters use the writings of young French women from the nineteenth century—often preserved for hagiographical reasons—to explore the communication and reception of these ideas.

The first half of the book understands the intersection of sentiment and devotion as offering authority to individuals. It engages post-

Revolutionary religious formation, early nineteenth-century didactic reading and novels, and the post-1830 explosion of images and objects. Together these sources serve to draw an unsectarian picture of the terminology that surrounded French women as the century progressed. They demonstrate the cultural currency of martyrdom, heroism, and sacrificial love as well as the central intellectual role played by imagery of the heart, all connected to the language of sentiment in a growing consumer culture.

Chapter 1 studies the literature and practices that shaped Catholic girls' ideas of individual spiritual destiny, including what it meant to accept one's place in a patriarchal society. In particular it examines the complicated nature of religious belief in Revolutionary and post-Revolutionary France. While catechisms and hagiographies reinforced gendered hierarchies and reminded readers of seventeenth-century forms of piety, changing practices also promoted women's importance as catechists and encouraged private devotions such as an emphasis on the Sacred Heart. The literature offered religious idealism and even a rejection of biological fathers' plans for those who obeyed God first. These ideas dovetailed with messages of heroic piety—even to the point of martyrdom—and a mistrust of marriage, messages that would also be found in secular novels. Because new ideals of domesticity highlighted female moral and emotional agency, the ideas worked together to provide an image of powerful women, tasked with fighting against terrible odds for the creation of an ideal world.

Chapter 2 examines these same themes in the educational and novelistic literature that surrounded French girls in the post-Revolutionary era. Didactic tales, the first independent reading for adolescents, intended to shape well-behaved young people through moral stories wrapped in a language of autonomy and self-determination. The models from didactic literature were further replicated in the highly popular sentimental novel. Though the novels were emotional and idealistic, they were far from sparking, as Gustave Flaubert claimed, a "revitalized cult of love." Instead, they presented domestic trials as a microcosm of social upheaval. These novels, ranging from Bernadin de St. Pierre's *Paul et Virginie* and

Chateaubriand's *Atala* to Cottin's *Claire d'Albe* and Staël's *Corinne*, under-scored the trials of marriage and the transience of love even as they encouraged protagonists to imagine themselves as both independent and in exile from their contemporary world.

Chapter 3 analyzes how an explosion in print culture offered images that expanded the reach of a rhetoric that was ambivalent about marriage and home life. French culture valorized motherhood, which is not to say it emphasized or prioritized companionate relationships between men and women. In the broad circulation of images, many of which remain unexplored by scholars, love and marriage were a trap, a temptation rather than a path to success. A continuing emphasis on sentiment, religion, and the importance of following one's heart, set into a context of embattled Christianity and the necessary rejection of contemporary values, autho-rized more and more female consumers to work for the creation of a better world, but not necessarily under the guidance of a husband or a father. The Sacred Heart, as a sentimental and political image, demonstrates the intersection and prominence of these devotional norms.

Taken together, these first chapters thus serve to illuminate the intel-lectual and cultural formation of nineteenth-century girls from the Rev-olution well into the second half of the nineteenth century. The evidence reveals no generally positive emphasis on secular or married love but instead a widespread understanding of male-female love relationships as disempowering and even threatening. Girls also learned that fidelity and other virtues were easiest to accomplish without a spouse. Reli-gious tropes were often identical to secular ones. While sentiment was highlighted far more often than reason, it was a source of strength, not a detriment, and a rhetoric of struggle and sacrifice gave meaning and purpose to this vision.

The final three chapters examine French women from each "state" in life: dedicated religious life, single life, and married life. In each of its chapters, the self-fashioning and reflections of three devout women paint a picture of how young Catholic women of the nineteenth century—whether religious, single, or married—situated themselves within the framework of post-Revolutionary French society. The second half of the book explores the objects and language that surrounded and shaped these women as well as the women's attempts to mold the world around them. A language of heroism and martyrdom formed the basis of their demands for the centrality of following their hearts, even as they communicated those ideas to others, using autobiography and letter writing, theological treatises, and everyday objects of consumption.

Frequently documents for each of these women are available because of the Church's claims about their sanctity, the sense that they were women of heroic virtue in a Catholic context. Sometimes, the women themselves mixed hagiography with autobiography as they wrote about their extraordinary responses to God and to the world.[136] While sources arising from such contexts are not unproblematic, hagiography—whether true or not—demonstrates how and why people who lived in nineteenth-century France promoted a vision of these women's reported behavior as heroic, indicative of their ability to do extraordinary things.[137]

Chapter 4 shows how the earliest cultural influences come to life in the story of Rose-Philippine Duchesne (1769–1852), a nun who joined the Religious of the Sacred Heart and became a missionary to North America. Personal letters and a spiritual autobiography reflect on autonomy and emotion not only through Duchesne's life and words but also through that of Duchesne's niece, Euphrosine, who joined her aunt's order under the name Sister Aloysia. Both women were part of the influential order that Michelet decried; their letters demonstrate how religious vocation encouraged women, using sentimental language, to reject biological family in order to fulfill the destiny that they believed had been written on their hearts.

Chapter 5 examines the early writings of a wealthy woman, Pauline Jaricot (1799–1862), who took a vow of perpetual virginity but refused to enter any order to preserve independence of action. Jaricot's influence extended far beyond her family and native city of Lyon, though she is virtually unknown today. She fundraised for overseas missions, founded a global missionary organization, promoted veneration of St. Philomena, and attempted to start a workers' commune. Jaricot's multifaceted demonstration of her piety reveals how sentimental language and a reliance on the heart inspired women to work in the world, without regard to political boundaries.

Chapter 6 analyzes marriage, child-rearing, and vocation through the life of Zélie Guérin Martin (1831–1877). Like Duchesne and Jaricot, Martin was shaped by sentimental domestic ideology. Unlike both of them, she married and bore nine children before dying at the age of forty-five. After her marriage Zélie continued to run her lace-making business, a venture in which her husband Louis joined her, though he had to give up his own work to do so. The letters show how a married woman, steeped in sentimental language and heroic virtue, was both a creator and a consumer, one who demanded autonomy for her everyday decisions about sex, marriage, and family, choices that underline her modernity in both a philosophical and a Habermasian sense.

The Martins' letters remain for us to read because of the extraordinary renown of their youngest daughter, St. Thérèse, the Little Flower. The book returns to Thérèse in the conclusion in order to examine her spirituality and popularity as an outgrowth of sentimental constructions. It again takes up her image, which was, as Ghéon and Merton note, heavily influenced by heroic sentimentalism and embedded in self-conscious bourgeois consumption. Thérèse's popular vision resonated across the world, and examining it in conjunction with earlier uses of sentimentality opens new vistas on religious responses to modern consumer culture.

Through the women of the second half of the book, the sources of the first half are made tangible, allowing us to see how devout young women, shaped by sentimental language and constructs, sometimes envisioned their spiritual and communal lives. Like their more well-studied male contemporaries, they situated themselves—and were situated—within narratives where "victimization, heroic suffering, [and] supposedly 'natural' social relationships" had a place of prominence.[138] Ideas of martyrdom and heroism encouraged women to see themselves as capable of changing the world, making it possible for them to demand greatness not in opposition to prevailing religious or cultural ideals but because of them. Emotional experiences, including martyrdom, suffering, and exile, could serve as heroic inspiration rather than pejorative descriptors.

Historical studies of devout women, especially in the premodern era, have indicated that religion serves as a location for women to exercise authority.[139] The cultural formation and individual responses of the women who are the concern of this work further demonstrate that religious ideas enabled and encouraged French women's action in the world. Though they are now seen as weak, marginal, and intellectually impoverished, they were vibrant, influential, and based in categories that were shared across the culture. Nineteenth-century sentimentality authorized demands for world-changing independence.

< 1 >

Shaping the Sentimental Order

Martyrdom, Marriage, and Catholic Heroism

[N]othing is more likely to inspire young ladies to love religion and Christian virtues. Each of these lives is a charming painting, made to touch hearts and to fill them with the most generous sentiments. The tender age of the heroines makes the examples of piety and charity that they offered to their families and cities even more interesting.

—Review of Carron's *Three Christian Heroines*
in the *Année Littéraire* (1785)

At the middle of the nineteenth century Jules Michelet lamented the influence of priests over women.[1] Men had a political and social problem, he said, because women were tied to the Catholic Church. Michelet believed that improper novel reading was a significant part of the problem. He explained that the wrong kind of literature, "the sickening half-worldly and half-devout productions . . . will find readers among these poor women, the martyrs of *ennui*. Such delicate and sickly forms can support a nauseous dose of musk and incense, which would turn the stomach of any one in health."[2] Religious reading would engrave the tabula rasa, "write in this book of blank paper whatever they will! And to write what will last forever!"[3] Reading had not made French women more progressive and liberal but instead confirmed them in superstition, promoting a devout Catholic identity that was, from an anticlerical point of view, "fundamentally irreconcilable with liberalism's notion of religiously neutral citizenship."[4] Women's reading was dangerous.

Michelet's emphasis on uncritical visions influencing easily manipulated women evidences one form of a patriarchal fear of reading. As both literacy and book production increased, readers had become less subject to earlier limitations on literature. Instead of relying on a limited number of texts, shared orally in groups, individuals progressed from one book to another without oversight.[5] Increased access and literacy allowed the consumption of more and more texts, including not only the reading of novels but also heroic tales of missionaries and the *Genius of Christianity*.[6] Reading without guidance from men was dangerous; the solution was for wives, daughters, and mothers to read fewer books, but to read chosen works more carefully and deeply. Martin Lyons has explained that "[t]he anxious dreams of the nineteenth-century bourgeois were peopled by all those who threatened his sense of order, restraint and paternal control," especially those who gave women ideas that broke apart carefully constructed hierarchies.[7] There was a battle to control women's thoughts, emotions, and futures.

But who was this generic "bourgeois" demanding paternal control? The nineteenth-century order was notoriously conflicted; regime change was more a matter of course than an aberration. In this context, indiscriminate reading was threatening to men on both left and right. Honoré Daumier used political cartoons to publicize the problem of a reading wife, one who left household chores untended while she read novels. However, the Catholic Church also launched a crusade against bad books in the first third of the nineteenth century. Clerics were also concerned about the temptation that novels could pose to otherwise religious women.[8] They feared that women might search for books that offered "erotic desire and impossible romantic expectations. [Women] would read superficially instead of purposefully without meditating and digesting their texts."[9] In other words, Michelet's midcentury panic was hardly unique; men of all sorts worried that increasingly accessible reading could encourage women's natural tendencies toward romantic and sensual notions. Men who hoped to maintain their hold on power or increase their share of influence wanted to take charge of reading.[10] Women's autonomy—for reading as elsewhere—was not a masculine goal.

However, if reading had destructive force, it also had productive force. This power—and the threat inscribed in its potential—was particularly important for women's reading, a fact that was implicit in an emphasis on women's reading under the guidance of men. By the early nineteenth century the most prominent elite ideals assumed that women were uniquely capable of helping children develop into moral adults, and an explosion of published material rose to lead women to—and through—their obligations.[11] Advice manuals gave mothers and daughters a "proper" approach to the sundry tasks of their lives. Women's journals, devotional works, and the periodical press offered women useful advice and provided them with models by which they could judge their femininity and place in the world. Catechisms, parish participation, and stories of saints' lives emphasized the spiritual side of narratives about ideal womanhood.[12] Women's reading would mold sons and daughters and, by extension, the future of the nation.[13]

While the political and social authorities of post-Revolutionary France may have fretted about women's reading and attempted to provide literature that would help readers develop the "proper" points of view, historians recognize that readers were not actually tabulae rasae. We know that their malleability is limited and that one cannot always predict a reader's response to a work. As Michel de Certeau has explained in *The Practice of Everyday Life*, consumers of culture "go poaching." By this, he means that they not only take bits and pieces to use as they will, but also that they change the meaning in the process, reading it in ways that are personally meaningful but could not be predicted by the author.[14] Thus, even if we know that men were concerned about women's reading and wished to control what women read, we also realize that the didactic lessons in the canons upon which these men relied were not, in and of themselves, fully constitutive of the readers' values. Historians cannot always draw a direct line from the messages found in catechisms or novels to the ideals that the readers held. We can, however, see what women and children were supposed to learn and what ideas surrounded readers, what values and concepts were available for them to "poach from" as they thought about their position in the world. This chapter therefore explores the messages in early nineteenth-century catechisms and popular hagiographic literature, the formational books that Catholic men hoped would offer responses to the danger of bad or indiscriminate reading by Catholic women.[15]

The Catholic Church believed that much of post-Revolutionary French society had strayed from the fold because of the eighteenth century's philosophical and rationalist influence.[16] In fact, though many reform-minded clerics had been deeply engaged with Enlightenment ideas, the Civil Constitution of 1791 crystallized clerical opposition to the Revolution, especially within the hierarchy.[17] After the Bourbons returned to power, priests attempted to reconvert and to welcome back those who had been lost. In addition to burning *mauvaise livres*, books seen as responsible for influencing ideas of revolution, Catholic publishing companies, with the approval of local ordinaries, produced their own works to educate and convince. Catechisms, hagiographies, and other forms of moral reading were produced by the Society for Good Books, so that all portions of society could benefit.[18] Other publishers took secular material and abridged it to provide unthreatening but morally uplifting reading for girls from the French classics (Racine, Molière, and Madame de Sévigné, for example).[19] While Michelet blamed sentimental and gothic literatures for women's superstitious tastes, he could equally have found the targets of his vitriol—celibacy, seventeenth-century theology, and an emphasis on the independence of women's souls—in literature that was written for far more impressionable ages, those with an even more blank slate.

At the most basic level, the Catholic framework for understanding the world was found in the catechism. Those who could not read would have learned catechism lessons by rote, something made easier by the question-and-answer format.[20] As literacy expanded, children and women encountered more books than before, but catechisms remained centrally significant as the "the first book, in schools and in families, that one gives to children for reading."[21] Catechisms were an important part of how small children were taught to organize, understand, and approach their world.

Nineteenth-century publishers were concerned about the abundance of different catechisms available for religious instruction. "[B]y 1800, the total stood at 181 catechisms published in 102 dioceses," and some bishops worried that parents would become confused about the basics of Christian belief and sacramental life.[22] The significance of the catechetical model and the multiplicity of available catechisms continued to be subjects of intense interest even as Napoleon's *Imperial Catechism* was published in 1806. Though it is likely that few parishes saw the new book in that year, the letters to the faithful that accompanied the new catechisms indicate the importance that the national government placed on offering a uniform religious instruction. The archbishops and bishops who wrote accompanying letters used them to confirm Napoleon's right, through the Concordat, to see to the formation of the faithful. They argued that offering a single national teaching would create a unified religious education for the French church, in the Gallican tradition.

Some bishops, however, contested the emperor's right to provide a catechism for children. They complained about the imprecision of the work and suggested that, as bishops, they were better placed to approve catechetical works and thereby offer lessons in theology.[23] As these bishops recognized, the power struggle was not only one between Napoleon and the Roman church, as represented by the papacy. Napoleon's *Imperial Catechism* followed the traditional format in the ways it emphasized the sacraments and Christian doctrine, but it also affirmed the Christian obligation of obedience to the ruler.[24] Catholics, brought back into the fold by the Concordat but still potentially fractious, would be reminded from a young age that the emperor's authority derived from the same place as the authority of a father. The catechism thereby affirmed both patriarchy and secular authority, making it a political and social tool as well as a religious one.

However, despite official interest in producing a single religious model for the entire nation, early nineteenth-century religious teachers generally had access to more, not fewer, catechisms. If parishes had relied on multiple versions of books in the eighteenth century, by the middle of the nineteenth century, they were almost inundated with catechetical possibilities, including catechisms that remained in use from the preceding century. For example, one French catechism of 1734, *Catechism or Familiar Instruction on the Principal Points of the Christian Religion,* was signed in 1821 by a young reader with his name and the date. This book had not only made it through the Revolutionary and Napoleonic upheaval but was still being used by students during the Restoration, nearly one hundred years after its initial publication.[25] Many dioceses also continued to edit, revise, and produce catechisms for the use of their faithful. Often the versions that remain in archives and libraries today are annotated with childish scribbling, indicating in real ways how children were exposed to the catechetical teaching at a parish level.[26] Additionally, publishers offered catechisms "for the use of every church in France" or "useful to people, children, and to those who are charged with their instruction." The fact that these were sold in multiple-volume sets and printed in numerous editions indicates that there was money to purchase catechisms on both national and local levels, with an interest that went beyond the parish.[27]

Catechisms varied in style, though they emphasized the particulars of Catholic devotional practice in their inclusion of daily prayers and Mass parts. In the nineteenth century the prefaces of catechisms often addressed the parents or teachers directly, with discourses on the importance of catechesis and rebirth in belief.[28] However, while some catechisms included historical (biblical) content, others contented themselves with a brief overview of the Ten Commandments, laws of the Church, and the sacraments. One "catechism" on the importance of spiritual formation even left out the sacraments entirely, as it was a foundation for understanding the "Interior Life of a Christian," rather than a book intended to introduce students to the most basic elements of faith and doctrine.[29]

Despite the diversity of books available for religious instruction, the century's most commonly printed catechism was Claude Fleury's *Historical Catechism*.[30] Multiple editions of Fleury's work were published during the Empire, a process that continued during the Restoration and into the last half of the century. The *Historical Catechism* shared a common set of goals with most other catechisms, including discussion of the Ten Commandments, Church laws, and the sacraments. Fleury's work also included some biblical exegesis and highlighted important points of Christian doctrine, which underlined its similarity to other commonly used pedagogical texts, offering an inclusive approach that helps explain its popularity.[31]

Additionally, nineteenth-century prefaces to the work usually sidestepped the question of politics entirely, instead calling for the contextualizing of Christianity for those ignorant of the basics of the faith, an ever-larger portion of the population since the Revolution. Post-Revolutionary editions of this work did not highlight problems with obedience to the Emperor, nor did they claim that the politics of the era had been allowed to corrupt doctrine. Instead, Fleury's *Catechism*, itself originally a product of the later seventeenth century, claimed that its current utility lay in combatting the ignorance of Christians, even devoted ones, who knew how to practice superstitiously but had no deeper understanding of the basic tenets of the faith.[32] Claiming that "[i]gnorance [of the essentials of religion] is one of the principal sources of the corruption of morals,"[33] it promised to offer an overview of biblical history as well as Christian doctrine. Despite—or perhaps because of—its stated purpose, this work did not provide the words of the Ave Maria or Pater Noster, unlike many of the diocesan catechisms.[34]

In the post-Revolutionary context, the immense popularity of a catechism that went beyond recitation of prayers makes sense. During the Revolution, religious instruction had often been haphazard. Children—and even young adults—could know their prayers but still lack important context. In its desire to reconstitute "true" belief, Fleury's *Historical Catechism* offered instruction in what it saw as the heart of the matter, the deepest meaning of Church teaching and religious life. The work began with biblical history and then proceeded to Christian doctrine, offering a higher order of instruction than the memorization and recitation of prayers. Additionally, nineteenth-century introductions to the *Historical Catechism* echoed the contemporary concern with popular reading and demonstrated how a seventeenth-century work could provide children with the catechetical teaching that they needed to fully enter into Christian life, without being led astray by incorrect ideas.[35]

The *Historical Catechism* was divided into a Small and Large Catechism. The Small Catechism was sufficient to prepare a child—either male or female—for First Communion, an important sacrament of initiation, while the Large Catechism could provide a more extended religious education. The Small Catechism emphasized the necessary knowledge for a young student and offered an abbreviated version of biblical history, along with the lessons that were fundamental for all Catholic Christians, even those unlikely to proceed further in their theological studies. This was a catechism in the usual sense of the word, intending to educate those who had not yet fully entered into the practices of the Church. Additionally, however, it would help children and adolescents understand their world as shaped by God in all ways, with a divinely ordained historical order that had resulted in the Catholic Church.

To make the story clear and compelling, this catechism emphasized narrativity, the stories of miracles and the engagement of God with humans. This would, the publisher argued, speak to peasants, working women, and children.[36] He explained that everyone, reading or not, could "hear and remember a story where the sequence of events proceeds imperceptibly and captures the imagination . . . Hence the curiosity for news, novels and fables. Above all, children are the most eager for this, as everything is for them the pleasure of novelty."[37] Thus, these stories, especially when combined with engraved images, would solve the usual problem of the dry dullness of catechisms and the fact that they were unlikely to be picked up for pleasure reading. It would satisfy the natural taste of the uninformed for novels and profane stories. "Images are very appropriate to strike children's imagination and to help them memorize. This is the writing of the ignorant."[38] Of course, it was obvious to the writer that the catechism would still not just be placed into the hands of an untutored child. The stories would be taught, in context, ideally by a priest, who would instruct the children through the use of images and events, but certainly not expect children to read and draw the proper lessons on their own.[39]

This struggle for the proper molding of children's minds was not without its moral lessons for parents, especially fathers. The preface frequently reminded parents about the importance of personal instruction. Patriarchal control demanded that parents not abdicate their responsibility, leaving moral teaching entirely to priests and those outside the family circle. Fathers, as the heads of families, ought to use their natural authority to teach their children and servants. Mothers might also be able to use the material to teach daughters, though of course, "few fathers and mothers would wish to take this effort," choosing instead to "put daughters in a pension and boys in a collège."[40] This was not a neutral statement. "It should not be shocking," he added, "if children have little love or even respect for their parents, and it's a great happiness when they manage to become honest men and good Christians. On the contrary, one often sees success when the fathers are virtuous, capable, and careful to instruct them well."[41] While the priest could use a child's natural inclination for the marvelous and the novelistic to some success, the father, a natural figure of respect within the home, could do more than amuse with stories of the miraculous. For example, when a father taught his own children, the story of Abraham's sacrifice and the importance of the patriarchs were cast into relief. Family context would offer the most solid authority to the lesson, pairing biblical and familial authority.[42]

This concern over patriarchal authority is present even in the basics of Fleury's work. The first lesson of the Small Catechism was on the creation of the world as found in Genesis. This section not only briefly explained how God made the world, but drew the concrete point that that when He formed man and woman, He instituted marriage.[43] From the very beginning of human relationships, sexual difference and, as a result, marriage existed. While the catechism reminded readers of the biblical injunction whereby man was to love woman as he loved himself, the Small Catechism had a decidedly mixed view of women's destiny in her relationships with men. Woman was one flesh with man, made from his side, but her worldly example was as likely to corrupt as to save, especially when the flesh and its desires were involved. Lesson 2, on the first sin, reminded students that it was woman who ate of the forbidden fruit and gave it to man to eat.[44] Lesson 10 recounted how Solomon lost his wisdom in giving himself over to pleasure with women. The women, whom he loved passionately, trapped him in idolatrous practices.[45] Lesson 27, which recounted the fall of Jerusalem and the revolt of the Jews, explained the horror of the situation by explaining that "Jerusalem was besieged. The resulting famine was so terrible that there were mothers who ate their own children,"[46] a story that was reinforced in the question and response section of the catechism. The only woman of virtue mentioned in the Small Catechism was "a girl of excellent holiness, named Mary, who had resolved to remain a virgin, though she had been affianced to a holy man named Joseph."[47] If stories were to strike children's imaginations and help them memorize the truths of the faith, including the destiny of Catholic Christians, the Catholic girls who heard these stories would find only one female model to emulate, and one who had, thorough her holiness, rejected becoming one flesh with a man.

The Small Catechism drew children in with stories. The second part of the work then led them through an abridgement of Christian doctrine, including an explanation of Trinitarian doctrine and a recounting of the Ten Commandments. Church laws, including fasting and the keeping of Holy Days, were followed by a series of lessons on the sacraments. In the Small Catechism, the overview of the sacraments said that marriage's central importance lay in the fact that it "furnishes the Church with subjects so that she will endure as long as does the world."[48] The catechism linked the institution of marriage to the creation of the first man, given a woman for his companion and helper, and for the birth of all other men.[49] Lesson 29, "Of Marriage," hastened to add, "Though marriage be very holy, the state of perfect continence is more excellent. Married persons are divided between God and the world, by the care of their family. Virgins and widows are free to give themselves entirely to God."[50] The sample question and answer did not actually emphasize marriage so much as the state of celibacy; it noted that not all were capable of the perfection of perfect continence, as it was a singular gift from God.[51]

Nothing about this understanding of the sacrament of marriage was exceptional or even unexpected.[52] As Agnès Walch has argued, conjugal spirituality had been emphasized to a greater degree after the Council of Trent, including in sermons that accompanied a reading of the biblical text of the wedding feast at Cana. The homilies emphasized marriage as a sacrament and a path to sanctity.[53] Despite this fact, the post-Revolutionary era saw little change in the language of conjugal spirituality. Sermons and prayers continued to use pre-Revolutionary language that emphasized chastity, obedience, and a sentimental but mystical alliance between the souls of spouses.[54]

For catechetical teaching in particular, this meant that an emphasis on the specific meaning and importance of marriage was an exception rather than the rule. For example, the 1804 *Catechism of the Diocese of Saint-Claude* devoted ten lessons to the sacrament of penance and only one to the sacrament of marriage.[55] The *Catechism of the Diocese of Poitiers* had a similar balance and included, in its single page, a long reminder that fast days and times of penance were not appropriate for celebration of the sacrament of marriage.[56]

An emphasis on celibacy and the downplaying of marriage followed the historical teaching of the Church. The preference of celibacy to marriage followed the Pauline injunctions found in First Corinthians, which emphasized the single-minded devotion that the celibate could harness in the service of God; unity with God alone was clearly preferable to even a blessed union with man. Marriage could be a path to heaven, but the Bible also reminded the faithful that "the married man is anxious about the affairs of the world, how to please his wife, and his interests are divided."[57] Catechisms recognized this tension.

Marriage was not forbidden, and it was good insofar as it resulted in the sanctification of man and women and the production of children raised in the faith. However, it was not the highest calling, which was devotion entirely to the things of the Lord. Additionally, religious teaching remained mostly unaffected by the flowering of domesticity in the early nineteenth century. Catechisms rarely emphasized preparation for the sacrament of marriage beyond, perhaps, respect for one's parents in the choice of spouse and solemnity in an approach to the altar.

Notable for its uniqueness is the long section on marriage found in the *Dogmatic and Moral Catechism*, a four-volume set that devoted nearly seventy pages of the final volume to the question of marriage. This work never mentioned the higher calling of celibacy, though it did take care to emphasize that the purpose of marriage was mutual assistance and the raising of holy children. The pages devoted to marriage included some unique material, including a defense of the idea of marriage as a sacramental pact, possible impediments to contracting a marriage, and an outline of qualities that one should avoid in a spouse (especially the problem of finding girls who were not so worldly as to attend dances or to seek to "make others talk about them").[58] A significant portion of this section on marriage was dedicated to a retelling of the story of Tobias and Sarah, found in the book of Tobit, which demonstrated the proper attitude that one ought to have with respect to marriage itself and one's spouse in particular.[59]

The story offered an instructive narrative to emulate. Tobias, Tobit's son and the hero of the story, was a righteous Jew. He wanted to marry the beautiful Sarah, but she came with a problem. She had been married seven times, but before any marriage could be consummated, the demon of lust, Asmodeus, had killed every man who wished to marry her. Tobias, however, prevailed against the demon because he had both the supernatural guidance of the Archangel Raphael and righteousness on his side. After defeating the demon, Tobias made this point explicit. He knelt with Sarah and prayed for God's blessing on his wedding night, saying, "Lord, not out of lust do I take this kinswoman of mine."[60] The author emphasized that the Bible thus offered an emphatic lesson against concupiscence in marriage, which instead should be a site of mutual sacrifice. The story continued to be prominent throughout the century (figure 3).[61]

Rather than being an outlier, the *Dogmatic and Moral Catechism* is best understood as offering the reverse image to Fleury's *Historical Catechism*. Both provided narrative lessons that delineated the ways in which marriage and worldly relationships were to be mistrusted and how spiritual life always offered greater happiness and success than merely seeking after physical satisfaction. Frequent quotations from and references to seventeenth-century works about self-discipline were common.

Even the *Catechism for the Interior Life*, which primarily emphasized spiritual formation, was predicated on the basic moral principles taught to all young Christians. Those who cared about their salvation should discipline themselves and become removed from all particular desires;

they should "bind, strangle, and suffocate inside all impure and disordered desires that come from the flesh."[62] A reader of any of these catechisms would recognize that the highest calling was to holiness and that marriage might help achieve that end, but it was equally likely to serve as a distraction. In the worst cases, when one married for the wrong reasons, "Marriage will be an anticipatory hell that will lead you to another Hell," with jealousy and fighting preventing the establishment of a harmonious household.[63] As explained in a quotation from the seventeenth-century Francis de Sales, one of the principal advocates for the importance of the marriage vocation, inappropriate affection for one's spouse was like "a worm that forms in the best fruit, devouring the unfortunate hearts that it has bitten, corrupting even the most beautiful unions, exciting suspicion, coldness, disgust, separation, divorce, and even murderous attacks between the affected spouses who have been offended."[64] The catechetical literature emphasized the inculcation of self-discipline and, ultimately, keeping one's eyes fixed on heaven, so as not to end up in hell—both on earth and after death.

Of course, catechisms did not intend to offer guidance for marriage, given that the primary readers of the catechisms were preparing for their First Communion. Instead, advice about marriage would have to be found in manuals that addressed conjugal life, books that were intended for the already-married. However, conjugal manuals for marriage had decreased in popularity in the eighteenth century and all but disappeared from view in the nineteenth.[65]

Thus, as nineteenth-century children were beginning to think about their potential vocation or place in the world, religious formation emphasized individual service to God and careful development of one's spiritual life. Both boys and girls received basic instruction out of the same catechisms, and the lessons themselves emphasized the similarity of spiritual duties, not a gendered set of obligations. Even when particularly gendered examples were provided, they may have led to the conclusion that a holy soul had no sex.

At least two prominent traits from catechetical teaching were also evident in religious reading designed for early nineteenth-century Catholic girls. First, discussion of love encouraged readers to direct their love appropriately and emphasized disregard for the world. Secondly, the words and theology of Frances de Sales, an important exemplar in conjugal spirituality, found pride of place in many works. Both of these facts encouraged readers to hearken back to the spirituality of the seventeenth century.

De Sales's writings were particularly popular and were published and republished during the century, especially his *Introduction to the Devout Life*, which was written for lay readers. *Spiritual Combat*, one of de Sales's favorite books and one that he had frequently recommended to those for whom he provided spiritual direction, also remained fashionable.[66] Devotional and literary works of the seventeenth century were central to the revamping of French *bons livres*, and the saints they emphasized were also often of that era.[67] Martin Lyons has argued that the Catholic desire to revisit the seventeenth century, including its heavy emphasis on Salesian devotion, was a response to the upheaval of the Revolutionary era. He explains, "A return to the sermons and morality of the seventeenth-century literary classics could restore the faith and fortify wavering souls in the true doctrines of the Church."[68] Books were chosen to avoid the taint of rationalist philosophy altogether by sending readers back to the time when Catholicism was transcendent in France. Returning to the period of Bossuet, Francis de Sales, and the Edict of Nantes contextualized appropriate belief.[69]

In fact, de Sales was such a paragon of nineteenth-century religious thought that Michelet made his life and work a special target, devoting the first two chapters of *Priests, Women, and Families* to a condemnation of seventeenth-century spirituality in general and Francis de Sales in particular. Francis, who served as a confessor to many laywomen and had praised women as the "devout sex," argued that charity was a better means of achieving spiritual progress than individual penance and retreat from public life. Some of the most prominent women linked with him, such as Jeanne de Chantal and Marie Guyard, took his advice and became known for their devotion to the forgotten, sick, and abandoned. As Michelet recognized, this emphasis on the seventeenth century symbolized more than a return to earlier forms of devotion; it encouraged women to leave their domestic obligations for emotional and even physical autonomy.

According to Michelet, Francis de Sales advised Chantal in a way that left "her entirely free, with no obligations, save that of Christian friendship."[70] He further claimed that Sales used his hold on Chantal to convince her to abandon her family, "those two old men, her father, her father-in-law, and her own son, who, they say, stretched himself out on the threshold to prevent her passing."[71] From Michelet's perspective, this spirituality co-opted women's nurturing tendencies in service to God while keeping them away from men. Married women might even begin to detach themselves from their husbands, "turning saint," an outcome that the husband could not challenge.[72] Seventeenth-century devotional forms could be very dangerous.

Similarly a return to the seventeenth century meant more than merely reprinting older devotional literature; as both Michelet and the clerics in charge of *bons livres* understood, it also intended to capture and even shape the minds of women.[73] Fleury had emphasized a narrative approach in early catechesis, but an opening remained for more advanced reading. Religious publishers stepped in to answer the call, producing collections of saints' lives and stories of good Catholics who succeeded in living holy lives even when facing unimaginable odds.[74] The holy models could capture a reader's imagination, relying on an intellectual and spiritual return to the past even as they encouraged nineteenth-century action. Of course, if the stories followed the lessons of the catechisms, "domestic fulfillment" might look very different than expected, given that marriage and mutual spousal affection were not always an obvious destination.

Nowhere is the popularity of new stories and heroic models for emulation, drawn from older models, more apparent than in hagiographic collections of the first half of the century. Popular books written by a prominent émigré priest, Guy-Toussaint-Julien Carron, typify this development. Abbé Carron was born in a region that was notable for both high levels of illiteracy and antiliberalism. As a young priest, he was deeply interested in social reform, especially poverty and reform in the textile industry. In 1792 he was imprisoned for refusing to swear the constitutional oath of loyalty to the Revolution. He escaped to England, where he opened schools for male and female émigré Catholic children and wrote books, published in France and England, to defend Catholicism and inculcate traditional beliefs in his readers. He returned to France in 1814, where he continued to write prodigiously for an appreciative audience.[75] The titles of his books, targeted at children and young adults, betray their clear moralizing purpose. We see such names as *Young Christian Heroines, or Edifying Lives and Historical Treatises Dedicated to Young Girls*, or *The Lives of the Just in the State of Marriage*.[76] Despite—or perhaps because of—their didacticism, these works were immensely popular, many works being republished more than ten times by a single publisher, with multiple publishers across France producing the works to respond to national demand. Not all were targeted at young women, but books directed at young men and priests were in the minority of Carron's oeuvre. Instead, the great majority of his works told stories that engaged issues of vocation and devout practice for young women.

Over and over again Carron's books held up the lives of Christians who triumphed against society and themselves, practicing the virtues of chastity, poverty, and charity. As Carron was an émigré and a member of the generation that had come through the Revolution, it is perhaps understandable that his books, marketed to post-Revolutionary parents, invoked an embattled Christianity. On the other hand Carron's first book of emulation, *Three Christian Heroines, or Edifying Lives of Three Young Women*, was published in 1782, long before the outbreak of revolution and nearly a decade before the expulsion of nonjuring priests from France.[77] This means that its initial impulses can best be read in a line that developed alongside the catechisms that had offered narrative emphases to provide models of behavior and encourage self-abnegation. While these characteristics were useful to post-Revolutionary purposes, they also provided continuity with sentimental and novelistic discourses that had developed well before the Revolution itself.

Additionally Carron was not merely reactionary. He remained in France until 1792, leaving only when his refusal to swear the oath made it impossible for him to remain. Upon his return from England, Carron continued to be interested in education and social reform, and he circulated in a wide literary circle. He was close to the literary giant Chateaubriand and counted Lamennais, who engaged the theological and intellectual implications of liberalism, among his friends.[78] In short, it is not self-evident that his writing grew out of a desire to avoid the modern world or to transform the post-Revolutionary world back into the seventeenth century.

Instead Carron began with a Rousseauean vision of the world. He believed that a girl, who might be a future mother, was the ideal reader for his moralistic writing.[79] In its dedicatory preface to *Three Christian Heroines*, Abbé Carron addressed his own mother. He said that he had "never forgotten the moment where, upon beginning to think, I conceived for the first time the happiness I had received in having you [as a mother] from the beginning."[80] He gave particular thanks because "your care, your concerns, your sorrows and your efforts with your child, your touching lessons and affecting examples, all of these told me that heaven had granted to me the most tender and best of mothers."[81] He also claimed that the idea of his mother had inspired him to write. As her virtue had shaped him, so he too wished to cause these virtues to be multiplied across the earth. As she had given him, through her example and her teaching, a taste for Christian piety and of disgust for vice, he said, "I offer this to you, I dedicate this book to you, as a good to which you are due, all the more insofar as it emphasizes the virtues that you have caused to be born."[82] The girls who read his work were to be, like Carron's mother, young Christian heroines, using an ideal model to themselves grow in virtue and good works.

Despite the fact that the dedication was to a grown woman, Carron's mother, the ideal reader was not an adult, already molded by the world. Instead, adolescents would read these stories at an impressionable age, and rather than being lost or corrupted, they would internalize holy models, full of piety and self-abnegation, which would inspire them as they entered adulthood. The multiple editions of the works bear witness to the intended audience and the high hopes that the stories would inspire virtuous imitation of the holy behavior in the stories. A review of the third edition of *Three Christian Heroines* exulted: "Nothing is more edifying than this little work, nothing better calculated to inspire young ladies to love religion and Christian virtues. . . . The tender age of these heroines makes for even more interesting examples of piety and charity, beyond that which they have given to . . . the cities in which they were born."[83] The seventh edition emphasized its intended readership by its epigraph, Ecclesiastes 12:1, which reminded the reader to "Remember your creator in the days of your youth."[84] This version also lauded the possibilities provided by the models, explaining that it included new stories, "no less interesting than the first ones, no less appropriate for inspiring a lively emulation in the young reader who wishes to begin a noble career by the taste of good things and especially by the study of the triumph of religion."[85] The stories that children had read would act as a "manual for the different ages that one must travel through here on earth" and would thus "protect them from the pitfalls of the world," which would otherwise call to them like a siren.[86] Carron, Lamennais, and other prominent Catholic social critics wanted to offer an antidote to the emptiness, the "isolation in which both man and society have been left by eighteenth-century philosophy—man struggling against the hazards of life with no help to sustain him, no torch to guide him, and society struggling against revolutions with no public faith."[87] Boys and girls were the hope of the future, but they themselves needed a guide to appropriate behavior, and these stories would offer them just that.

The books offered opportunities to contemplate one's response to God's call, not only through a series of life stages, but also through the contemplation of different vocations. The *New Christian Heroines* offered *Edifying Lives of Young Girls*, but there were also similar works that recounted the *Lives of the Just in the State of Marriage* and the *Lives of the Just among Christian Virgins*.[88] (In keeping with the nineteenth-century emphasis on post-Reformation spirituality, the holy models had disproportionate representation from the seventeenth century.)[89] These stories were to be direct instruments in the creation of a new, heroically Catholic individual, especially a female one. Readers were reminded that these were real lives and not "an imaginary painting, and these beautiful morals and holy unions of the early Christians can be your own, if you read with reflection."[90] Here, diligent and meditative reading was a solution to disorder, like that described at the beginning of the chapter. The books thus offer us insight into not only the characteristics of the ideal individual but also the obstacles that were likely to keep individuals from becoming paragons of virtue.

And yet, even as "the world" was invoked as a threatening external presence, the models were almost entirely drawn from aristocratic families or bourgeois families of substantial means. Young people of privilege were the intended audience for these books. The families who provided these books to their children were not workers or artisans but wealthy and well-educated families, the same ones who were struggling over control of the political landscape in the first half of the century. The philosophical content would help determine the social content. The struggle for women's hearts and minds was part and parcel of the fight for political ascendancy.

Given that the books were written to create Christian citizens through the inculcation of the proper values in impressionable readers, one might well expect that religious devotion would be used as a buttress to reinforce women's domestic obligations.[91] The *Lives of the Just in the State of Marriage* initially seems to fit this mold, as it opens with a dedication to Christian spouses that affirmed some of the new companionate ideals. It cast marriage into the context of mutual happiness and reminded both spouses to "still make a rule of showing yourself to each other in the same lovable exterior by which you came to please each other initially."[92] Even as it reminded the wife to pay attention to her appearance, it admonished the husband to remember that "Heaven gave you a companion, a friend, and not a slave."[93] The home was to be a source of strength, a union in the middle of society, for mutual and social benefit.[94]

However, these stories echoed both Fleury's *Historical Catechism* and the *Dogmatic and Moral Catechism* in their emphasis on restraint and the higher calling of faith in God. The dedication also emphasized that happiness was not about passion or sentiment but was based on self-control.[95] It was clear that "bonheur" to which it referred was ultimately divine happiness, or the wisdom of salvation. Two persons became one flesh, praying together, going to Church together, and giving alms together. In the end, the lives of emulation offered to privileged young readers looked substantially more like the catechisms than what is typically understood as nineteenth-century domestic ideology of affection, caretaking, and nurturing spirituality. The catechisms had emphasized disinterested self-giving, continence in marriage with a preference for complete celibacy, and devotion to spiritual life and one's obligations to the Lord. So too did the lives of married persons as recounted by Abbé Carron.

A closer look at the recurring themes in the *State of Marriage* makes the point explicit. In this work, Carron recounted twenty-seven lives of holy people, nearly all drawn from other published collections and most echoing well-known and popular stories from centuries past.[96] Despite the overwhelming number of female lives—nearly 90 percent were women—not a single life met a "typical" domestic model where a woman married her husband and then spent her life in service to her family, loving her husband, nurturing and educating her children, and making her home a haven. More than half of the stories focused on the life of a widow after the death of her spouse and emphasized that the woman under consideration was, like the widows of the Bible, charitable and devoted to the world. Many of the stories told how the widows became consecrated nuns at some point before death.

Most of the stories noted, in their recounting of a woman's life, that she had been attracted to religious life as a young girl but was persuaded—against her will—to marry. Louise de Marillac "wanted to consecrate herself to God and spend her days in the cloister," but her confessor convinced her that God had other plans for her, so she agreed to marry.[97] Jeanne Pinczon du Hazay aspired to the religious life and was even tormented by her stepmother for refusing to marry her stepbrother.[98] However, "despite her ardent desire to only marry the cross, and her lack of desire for marriage, as she had demonstrated a thousand times to her father, she was forced to give her hand to a gentleman named M. du Houx de Forsantz. Heaven blessed her obedience."[99] Barbe Acarie was even held up as an example for all states of life, as she had been a virtuous girl, a virtuous wife, and then a model nun. Despite that, she was "called to the state of marriage against her heart; she had wished at least to imitate the purity of the virgins of the Lamb by practicing conjugal chastity in the most perfect way."[100] Many of these women, the stories explained, loved the solitude of the cloister but agreed to marry at the insistence of parents or family members. Marriage was not the ideal; it was a practical concession to family and social expectations.

Almost universally, family demands for marriage grew out of pragmatic interests. Political and social connections that were related to family well-being were often at stake. Jeanne Françoise Frémiot refused to marry a man who would endanger her faith but agreed, at her father's urging, to marry the Baron of Chantal, who offered not only personal advantages but also a distinguished pedigree.[101] Marie-Félice des Ursins, born in Rome, wanted to enter religious life, a desire that grew as she did. However, her father told her that she would marry. As a girl who knew her duty, she agreed to marry; "this news afflicted her without finding her unwilling to comply."[102] At fourteen she married Henry, the Duke of Montmorency, and was brought to France, where she transferred her love to her husband, as expected. Even men could be called to the religious life but end up married, as one of the three male examples of holy married men was Anne-François, Marquis de Beauvau, who wished to join the Jesuits as a young man and had a "strong attraction to the religious life. His father opposed this plan, which he regarded as the effect of a passing fervor," and the father sent his son to Paris, where Beauvau embarked on a worldly life and forgot the initial call, though it never truly left his heart.[103] Though all of these people found happiness and spiritual fulfillment in some way before their death, marriage was a hindrance, not a help, for their salvation.

In fact, most of the young women who actively wished to marry did so because they had already lost a single-minded attraction to virtue. For example, Madeleine Robineau married a baron who allowed her to indulge her love for jewels and adornment. Early in her marriage she had what Carron termed an "irregular life," though the late hours, amusements, and games he described sound like typical aristocratic diversion of the seventeenth century.[104] Robineau adored her spouse "with a form of idolatry," until his early demise, six years into their marriage.[105] She was pregnant at the time, and the loss sent her into labor. Her child was born dead, and she lost her mother and brother soon after; these losses became the catalyst for her deeper faith and active charity. Similarly, Marie-Elisabeth Tricalet succumbed to self-indulgence, including the desire for ornaments and frivolous living. She accepted the suit of M. LeBoeuf, secretary to the king, and after her marriage, she continued to spend great amounts of time and money on her appearance and other worldly attractions, including the reading of novels and other fictitious books that led her astray. Only after the death of her husband did she begin to think seriously about her place in the world and become inclined toward religion.[106] After her conversion, Tricalet even kept her change of heart secret from her family until she entered the convent so that her family would not have the opportunity to oppose her decision. While marriage might offer the opportunity for a change of heart and a turn toward God, husbands—except by their death—were rarely the cause of the conversions previously described. Love for a spouse or children was immoderate, and families preferred their financial and political contacts to the girls' faith preferences.

The relationship between Marguerite de Ragecourt and her husband, the aforementioned Marquis de Beauvau, is an interesting exception to the general story of trials and conversion after the death of a spouse. Ragecourt, married to Beauvau at an early age, was worldly and loved the distinctions of privilege. While she was "very exact in her conduct, one could not say that she was as a result particularly Christian; the motives that drove her were too human and her thoughts too worldly."[107] As her spouse developed a deeper understanding of his calling, however, she began to follow his example and saw "what a difference there was between an honest woman according to the world, and a holy woman before God."[108] In an attempt to become truly virtuous, she acted as a widow instead of a married woman. The couple took a vow of temporary celibacy within marriage and soon thereafter made a perpetual vow to live as brother and sister.[109] Eventually her husband sought and was granted permission to be ordained a priest. He then consecrated his life to service and gave most of his wealth away, leaving her and the children little on which to live. Marguerite was left to raise the children by herself, though her husband often wrote to her to offer advice. Marguerite then tried to establish each of the children in religious life or marriage so that she would be free to enter a convent. M. Beauvau, who had himself rejected the tears of his spouse and held to an unbreakable resolve for the religious life, offered pointed thoughts on a proposed marriage for a daughter, writing, "For your sex, every engagement is servitude, and once it has been undertaken, there is no going back. That is why one can hardly contemplate too much when a girl still has her freedom."[110] Marriage might, fortuitously, lead to conversion, but it was more likely to result in dissipation and distraction.

Beauvau was not alone in this view. To a person, the holy women who were widowed refused to remarry. After her husband died, Marie Lumague devoted herself to raising her daughter and, with the advice of Vincent de Paul, made a perpetual vow of chastity.[111] Marie Guyard, widowed at nineteen, was left pregnant, with few worldly resources. She could have remarried in order to fix her position and offer a better existence to her son, but she would not consent to a second marriage.[112] Madame de Miramion, also widowed at nineteen, was pressed to remarry, but she also would not agree and instead "listened to the interior voice that called her uniquely to the service of God."[113]

Remaining widowed was often a choice with a great personal cost. Jeanne Chantal, whose husband was shot while hunting, wished to remove herself to religious life thereafter, but like Ragecourt, she needed to establish her children. Because she did not set up a new household, she had to live with her irascible father-in-law in order to make ends meet. This situation was nearly untenable, as Chantal was tyrannized by both the old man, who regularly threatened to disinherit her, and his housekeeper, who refused her access to necessary items.[114] Even so, Chantal preferred this situation to remarriage.

Chantal's and Guyard's stories demonstrated how even privileged women could end up impoverished if they did not have the protection of a husband. This shows in concrete ways how important marriage was as a family strategy and the level of pressure that could be brought to bear on a young woman who wished to remain unmarried. In this context these women's insistence on their vocation and appeals to conscience appeared doubly heroic. Not only did they devote themselves to Christ, but they did it in opposition to their families and social circles.[115]

Recent studies on domestic life and nurturing motherhood in the nineteenth century might lead one to suppose that family life would be a source of strength and wholeness. However, the stories of these young women did not emphasize a happy domestic life. Quite the opposite, in fact, as many of the stories mention that the young woman under consideration lost her biological mother at a young age. Louise Marillac never knew her mother, and Jeanne Chantal lost her mother when she was only eighteen months of age. Marie Bonneau de Miramion and Jeanne Pinczon du Hazay had no mothers to protect or defend them. These girls were useful insofar as they could help cement family connections, and the fact that they were pressed to marry was a consequence of their vulnerability. If the absence of a mother did not hurt them spiritually, it certainly contributed to their defenselessness.

One might think that these women would build on their experience of loss and make the care of their children a priority. However, one of the most well known of the women mentioned was known not only for her holiness and position as the foundress of Congregation of the Visitation, but also because of the child abandonment that she resorted to in order to pursue her religious vocation. As Michelet had reminded his readers, Chantal had famously stepped over the body of her son, who laid himself across the doorstep to prevent his mother from leaving for the monastery; she did not allow this to stop her, but walked over him and continued on her way.[116] Chantal was a spiritual giant and would have been easily recognized by Catholic readers of the early nineteenth century, as would her fellow religious, Marie Guyard (also known as Marie de l'Incarnation). Guyard, like Chantal, entered the convent against the protests of her child. Guyard's eleven-year-old son came to the convent with his schoolmates and tearfully pleaded for his mother to be returned to him, but she persisted in her vocation, even to the point of leaving France to found the Ursuline order in New France. She compared this decision, supported by her confessor, to Abraham's sacrifice of Isaac.

In these stories the abandonment of children was a sacrifice to the higher calling that the woman heard from God and fit with a dynamic where children and families were almost always a threat to the heroic self-abnegation of virtuous men and women. Just as some women loved their husbands immoderately, Charlotte Marguerite de Gondy loved her children too much. Her experience with them was both a source of pain and a distraction from her higher calling. As a result Gondy began to be removed from the bonds of the world after her son died, an experience that broke her heart but left her reliant only on God.[117] Suzanne de la Pommélie was tormented by her family and husband because of her conversion from Calvinism to Catholicism; her in-laws and even her children were a cause of suffering like that experienced by Job.[118] Mothers were often absent, and children and spouses were the source of trials. The primary lesson was that only in God could women really find true fulfillment.

Even those who waited to pursue religious life until their children were grown engaged in a battle between spiritual desires and their family's needs. Though both eventually found the freedom to join religious orders, Barbe Acarie and Louise Marillac struggled to balance their familial and spiritual obligations. Acarie made sure that her works of piety and charity did not allow her to neglect her obligations within the home, and the story leaves the impression that her family obligations forced her to abandon her spiritual preferences. For example, Carron writes that Acarie could not read religious works because she would fall into a trance and neglect her domestic chores. He also recounts how Acarie obeyed her husband above all, even leaving Mass at the moment of Communion because her husband called.[119] It is little surprise that the state of marriage was "against her heart." Louise Marillac was even less obviously content with the price that she paid as a married woman; she submitted to married life because of the advice of her confessor and financial exigencies after the death of her father, but she continued to doubt that she had made the right choice, until a vision assured her that eventually she would be able to make the vows she desired. Her husband's ill-health and poor humor likely did not add to her happiness on earth.[120]

For all these women, everything eventually came right after the death of their spouses. Acarie was able to use her high position and alliance with Francis de Sales to introduce the Carmelites into France. She also used her social contacts to solicit financial support for the foundation of the Ursulines. Marie Guyard was not only a foundress but also a missionary and the adoptive mother of natives in New France. Jeanne Chantal founded the order of the Visitation and received spiritual direction from Francis de Sales, who eulogized her as the perfect woman, the one for whom Solomon searched in vain.[121] Louise Marillac connected with Vincent de Paul and helped to found the Daughters of Charity, becoming a model for all women as not only a wife and mother but also as a teacher, nurse, social worker, and religious foundress.

It came right, from their perspective, because they were able to move outside of their physical families, "vanquish nature," and instead form bonds of service to Christ with a spiritual family.[122] In many cases this involved a new intellectual relationship between important men and these women, but it also involved finding an adoptive family, mothering the poor and neglected, Christ in others. This change not only necessitated a rejection of any special ties to their children, but also involved transferring their feminine and maternal loyalty to Christ.

To demonstrate the change in circumstances, more than one story overturned the traditional hierarchy of family in a very literal sense. For instance, Barbe Acarie entered the convent after her daughters, by which time one of her daughters was the superior for the community. Acarie submitted to her daughter willingly, recognizing the child's spiritual authority over the mother. Anne-François Beauvau also joined the Jesuits after his oldest, who was by then the novice-master. Beauvau, like Acarie, submitted without hesitation to his son. Natural ties could—and even should—be overcome, allowing for detachment from the world and wholesale devotion to God. The heroic achievements enabled by self-abnegation ranged from the simple, such as care of individual orphans, to the globally significant, such as the founding of institutions and the spread of Christianity across the globe.

These narratives about married women featured heroines who were already well known to French audiences, but they also found good company in other hagiographical works, which emphasized the heroic nature of other virtuous (and mostly celibate) women. Despite the exemplary behavior of its protagonists, the dedication of the *Lives of the Just among Christian Virgins* struck a defensive note. It began, "To offer the models of all virtues in a group of virgins who have given honor to their sex and glory to religion, as well as happiness to humanity, isn't that to, at the same time, present an apologia for celibacy? . . . In preference of divine vocation, celibacy is still better, as Saint Paul has declared in formal terms, and the tradition of the Church has never strayed from this point."[123] Consecration to God was the best path to heaven, and the stories of the young women eulogized in the *New Christian Heroines* further proved the argument. The seventeen girls under consideration were models of virtue, and almost all were celibate.

In only two stories did the young women marry. As was typical, they only married under pressure from their families, as they wished to be nuns and consecrate themselves entirely to God. Both women died shortly after marriage. The first, Catherine de Harlay, got pregnant and quickly fell ill. She embraced sickness and died after giving an inspiring lecture on love and charity to her family. She never became a mother and only lived on as a model wife in the memory of her family.[124] The other, the Indian Princess Vobalamma, converted to Christianity after hearing the message of a missionary, but her family, who had not converted, opposed her decision. She wanted to remain celibate but agreed to marriage with the promise of baptism and freedom of religious practice in her new home. It was soon clear that the promise was insincere; her in-laws had no more intention of allowing her to be baptized and live as a Christian than did her family of origin. She remained faithful to her belief and continued to agitate for fulfillment of the promises. As a result, she was surrounded by hostility in her new home and soon died.[125]

In point of fact, the celibate women had a far greater maternal impact than either Harlay or Vobalamma. They were able to mold their communities and the young people around them, providing charity, educating children, especially in religious doctrine and catechism, and offering moral models that were recognized by entire cities. Like the holy widows discussed in the *Lives of the Just*, the young women in these stories rejected the attractions of the world, dressing modestly and without adornment in service of the neighbor. Jeanne Anne Marie Poulain de Corbion, who lost her mother at a young age, devoted her life to a new family, first adopting the servants as a new family and soon becoming a "mother to the poor," a title with which the entire community lauded her.[126] Anne-Marie Gilbert Auverger was a similar paradigm of virtue who became a "good mother" to the poor.[127] Her charity led to her early demise; during a local epidemic, she cared for the sick without regard for her own health. She took ill and died of a fever, though her death contributed to the moral health of the town of Châteaugiron, as they spoke of her holy memory and took her virtue as an inspiration for their future behavior.[128] Anne-Jeanne Victoire de la Fosse Moisson gave alms, instructed orphans, and committed other works of mercy designed to bring her closer to God. Her virtue led the entire city of Caen to honor her after her death.[129] Anne-Félicité Hay des Netumières, who took the name of Marie de Chantal when she became a nun, was an example to all girls, whether they would marry or join religious orders. "The faithful recitation of the actions of Mother Chantal proves that the religious profession, far from making itself useless to the neighbor, instead consecrates itself to the neighbor's happiness in all its works."[130]

Mlle des Netumières should even be seen as the ideal model to the reader, insofar as the single engraving that adorned the second volume of stories was one of her teaching young children. The image demonstrated her great impact on the community, and the caption helped the reader who might miss the point, explaining that "Felicity gathered them together on Sundays and feast days . . . she gave them an exhortation and then a spiritual reading."[131] These women's larger communities were the beneficiaries of their nurturing and good works, making it clear that the mission to serve the family of God was a calling with a far greater impact than that of marriage to an individual.

Not only was consecrated celibacy likely to have greater social importance than becoming a wife and mother, but it was also a vocation that was often lived out in opposition to the preferences of birth families, who fought the girls' religious vocations or even Christian belief. Vobolamma's family made promises that they never intended to keep, and the family of Catherine Tegahkouita (Kateri Tekakwitha) opposed her commitment to Christian celibacy.[132] Both were persecuted and found their greatest peace in death. The Calvinist parents of Esther Leggues were so appalled by their daughter's conversion that they threatened to kill her. She was unbreakable in the face of their hostility and continued to demonstrate her love for them in ways that did not violate her conscience. When accused of being a disobedient child, Leggues insisted that God had a higher authority than her mother, saying "God will inspire in my mother the desire to save herself, and as for me, I do not want to lose myself."[133]

The call to individual conscience and spiritual health as a more powerful responsibility than earthly obedience to parents was made explicit in other stories as well. Marie-Anne Fitch, an English convert to Catholicism, loved her family deeply and knew that her conversion would wound them. She sought protection from Mary as her heavenly mother and argued that true love of God made her a better child to her parents in the end. In all religious things, however, she continued to insist on the primacy of her own belief and her need to care for her spiritual health first and foremost.[134] As she said to her mother, "Oh, mama! I feel for you the most vivid tenderness, but it is necessary for me to follow my conscience, to avoid the depths of hell."[135] When Marie-Anne's steadfast faith converted her own mother, Mr. Fitch protested against the disobedience of these women in his house. Mrs. Fitch echoed Marie-Anne in saying that Mr. Fitch would not prevent her from becoming Catholic. "You don't have that power . . . my soul is my own, I want to save myself . . . no one has the rights to my conscience."[136] Marie-Anne eventually received permission to spend some time at a convent in order to recover her health after a sickness. After seeking the Lord's advice, she made a decision to never leave the convent.[137] Predictably, her father was opposed to this plan, though a visit to the convent convinced him of the goodness of the nuns and the beauty of his daughter's vocation and was the vehicle for his own conversion to Catholicism. The story ended by comparing Marie-Anne to St. Francis de Sales, the bishop of Geneva and the catalyst for many conversions from Calvinism to Catholic Christianity. Family in this instance meant, first and foremost, obedience to God's plans and a return to Mother Church.[138]

The independence of thought and freedom of action that seemed to be part and parcel of being a "Christian heroine" were exemplified in the life of Catherine Henrici, an engraving of whose life was featured at the front of volume 1 of these lives (figure 4).[139] Henrici, an educated and brilliant Venetian woman, was engaged to a Venetian lord chosen for her by her father. Before they could marry, however, the island on which they lived was attacked by Mahomet II. Catherine inspired the women of the island to fight, exhorting them to die rather than to be captured alive by the Turks. The island was besieged, and her fiancé was killed in defending against the Turks. Henrici's father would have been killed as well if his daughter had not parried a saber stroke aimed at his head. Eventually the Turks overtook the island, and Catherine and her father were captured. Her beauty appealed to Mahomet II, who wished to take her as his wife. Following the example of the captured women, the "Christian amazons who had so courageously defended their country," Catherine refused to give in.[140] She was persuaded neither by Mahomet's promises of riches nor his threats of force. When Mahomet brought in her father and threatened his life, parent and child stood firm, which frustrated Mahomet and resulted in the death of both. This is, the reader is told, the best model of all. While Catherine might have married her fiancé, "these two loves would not offer to us by that a more beautiful model" than did their virtuous death.[141] She was not converted by the world but died faithful to virtue.

This message was, Carron explains, designed to encourage young women to "call Jesus Christ to their marriage," to suggest that they should not look for riches but for character.[142] However, these stories subverted the message Carron promoted. For example, the moment depicted in the engraving of Henrici's life was the moment not where Catherine confronted Mahomet II and died in defense of Christian virginity, but one taken from the middle of the battle for control of the island. In this moment Catherine's fiancé is dying at her side. Meanwhile she reaches for the saber that is about to strike at her father. This engraving seems to reinforce the overall thrust of the models found in the stories: women who follow Christ are not ones in happy domestic situations, but ones who follow their individual consciences and heroically demand autonomy, even at great cost to themselves.

One of the few non-European women featured in the *Lives of the Just in the State of Marriage* was Madame Candide Hiu, a woman who lived chastely and converted her pagan husband and his family to Christianity. As a widow she gathered funds to support the Jesuits and enabled the spread of the Gospel in China. In his reflective lesson at the end of the story, Abbé Carron demanded of his readers, "Christians of the nineteenth-century Church, you who were born in the heart of the truth . . . compare your belief, your morals, and your actions, to those of this generous neophyte!"[143] Carron's call made explicit what readers would have understood throughout the work: these stories were for emulation. Each story depicted a woman of destiny who invited the reader to respond emotionally, choosing to ignore rational criteria of personal gain or family obligation and instead devote herself to Christ. By joining these women in heroic behaviors, the readers could both be "Christians of faith and action, all at once."[144] Just as young girls rejected adornment and once-married women became brides of Christ, the reader could herself become a heroine. The narrative approach offered young women ways to imagine their own lives, including the chance to embrace a destiny in which they resisted their natural inclinations—and even the limitations of sex—in order to become Christian heroines. The lives of the holy models would not be without trials, but the burdens were of their choosing. Jesus was a perfect, if demanding, spouse, and with Him, one expected the cross but was rewarded with eternal life.

As Allan Greer has noted in his examination of hagiographies, "the stories of saintly lives deserve examination in their own right as sites where notions of gender difference and . . . hierarchy were enunciated, qualified, challenged, and inverted."[145] Carron's books demonstrate that the nineteenth-century hagiographies certainly intended to offer models for behavior even as they displayed alternatives to traditional gender roles and social hierarchies. These works emphasized the sphere of action open to women and encouraged them to remake society.

Michelet, who understood the primary currents of mid-nineteenth-century Catholicism as much as he despised them, attacked celibacy as unnatural and, in fact, argued that contemporary woman should never be celibate. He explained: "[I]n our modern harmony what is this but a barbarous contradiction, a false, harsh, grating note? What I then beheld before me was to be defended neither by nature, nor by history. . . . it reminded me much less of chastity than of sterile widowhood, a state of emptiness, inaction, disgust."[146] And yet, Catholic readers could agree that celibacy was "unnatural" but see its very rejection of the physical self as the justification for such a vow. In fact, from the Catholic perspective, marriage was more likely to be a state of emptiness and inaction than was widowhood or religious life, and the active, creating, nurturing woman might be the best version of herself when she rejected family and social expectations. Even more significantly, the first third of the century had seen a widespread promotion of this view through catechism and hagiography, promoted in an engaging style and authorized by organizations such as the Catholic Church or the Society for Good Books. By the time that Michelet complained about women's reading at midcentury, the horse may have already been out of the barn, insofar as girls had already been encouraged to claim the authority that God offered. Furthermore, the religious message of heroic self-abnegation seen in early nineteenth-century catechetical teaching dovetailed with early nineteenth-century sentimental discourse, as is seen in the next chapter.

< 2 >

Contesting Oppression

Love, Suffering, and Sentimental Literature

> Do you know the heart of man, and could you reckon upon the incon-
> stancies of his affection? . . . Eve had been created for Adam, and Adam
> for Eve. If they, nevertheless, could not remain in that state of happiness,
> what couple after them could do so?
>
> —Chateaubriand, *Atala*

Early nineteenth-century works intended for religious formation were
not alone in positing a contrast between human obligations and those
from a higher authority. The idealism and tropes of post-Revolutionary
sentimental novels also rejected physical self in answer to an emotional
duty.[1] Furthermore they offered spaces for powerful female agency by
the "defiant and self-affirmative spirit" that they presented to the world.[2]

However, the force of this language and style has been obscured from
view. Novelists such as Balzac, Stendhal, and Flaubert discredited sentimental novels as overly emotional and feminine, not only because they
were so often written by women but because sentimental writing privileged uncompromising approaches to the world that these writers saw
as naive.[3] Similarly, a "long-standing poetic preference for realism . . .
and the power of realism in other media and genres" has blinded many
contemporary readers to the importance of the language and concepts
found in the sentimental novel.[4] This is not because it was secretly sub-
versive or unorthodox, *pace* Joan Stewart, but because its idealism and
material details had their own importance that do not speak to most
scholars and readers today.[5] Until recent Anglo-American criticism began
to investigate these works more closely, neither traditional literary read-

ings nor feminist criticism had seen the tropes in sentimental literature as a space for powerful female agency.[6] The novels still are not part of the literary canon.[7]

However, rather than accept mid-nineteenth-century social norms—or impose modern standards that would have been unfamiliar to the writers of sentimental novels—we can understand the force and vocabulary of the novels in their own time. While literary scholars have primarily looked at the sentimental novel within a literary trajectory—one that ceded to realism's method—this chapter works within a different signifying chain. As a work of cultural history, it offers a reading of the novels that contextualizes the popularity and language of didactic and sentimental literary productions before the rise of midcentury realism. It also charts a rising hostility to their discourse, much of which continues to the present day. The nineteenth-century construction of sentimental novels not as products for emulation and formation, but as an emotional, social, and sexual threat, demonstrates how changing historical realities were culturally "digested."[8]

Sentimental novels belonged to a literary genre first popularized in France through Jean-Jacques Rousseau's *Julie, or the Nouvelle Heloise* (1761). They drew readers in with their vivid depiction of the contrast between the demands of social obligations and individual choice.[9] Readers responded passionately to scenes of emotional distress and tenderness. They wept at the death of heroines, a frequent occurrence in novels' plots.[10] Though the sentimental genre had eighteenth-century origins, it exploded in popularity with the French Revolution and was wildly popular for decades, only being supplanted by realist novels around midcentury.

Margaret Cohen has argued that the genre struck a perfect tone for the years following the Revolution, allowing those who had experienced Revolutionary events to work through their anxieties about tyranny, liberty, and social organization.[11] While the first years of the Revolution had lauded the rights of man and individual agency, the Terror emphasized the general will and collective responsibility. The popular sentimental novel offered readers a way to confront the tensions that arose over which to prioritize: free choice or the public benefit. By dramatizing conflicts between collective welfare and individual choice in intimate settings, sentimental novels dealt with the question of how to accommodate positive and negative rights in liberal society.[12] Through marriage dramas or family conflict, readers confronted the struggle between two goods in a personally manageable and coherent way.

At least one author was explicit about this function of sentimental work. In *Literature Considered in Its Relation to Social Institutions* (1800), Mme de Staël argued that the novel offered the best form of instruction for people to understand themselves, their relationships with others, and their communities.[13] She said that sentimental fiction provided a more complete vision of human nature than either politics or law. Staël explained: "All political power is instituted against crime; virtue makes power useless, and power causes virtue to wither. All that men establish in common are negative forces: do not harm, do not steal, do not destroy."[14] Political force was limited to preventing misconduct and therefore useless for understanding virtuous behavior.

The novel, on the other hand, delivered an important form of active moralizing that used women's influence as authors, readers, and heroines to change society.[15] Staël also claimed that women spoke an emotional language that did not come naturally to men.[16] Sentimental stories, increasingly seen as the realm of women and the feminine, were implicitly didactic.[17] They helped each reader come to terms with what was good and what was bad. "Novels can paint characters and feelings with such power and detail, that there is no other reading that will produce such a deep imprint of hatred for vice and of love for virtue ... [because] of the truth of the representation."[18] From Staël's perspective, women's private and sentimental voices, even as they existed apart from politics, were not silenced or alienated but exercised important functions.

The novel's importance and popularity was not only for elite readers. Most of the popular authors of sentimental literature were women, and consumers ranged across social class. Publication and distribution of novels after the Revolution marked "one of the first stages in the development of a 'mass' culture in which the cultural cleavages between the bourgeoisie and the *menu people* began to disappear."[19] Servants and elites could hear a novel declaimed as the emotional focus of an evening's entertainment.[20] The stories appeared at the top of print runs and in the most-desired titles for lending libraries.[21] Their broad influence in a shifting moment of commercial culture was also reflected in the fact that popular novels made their way onto other items for consumption as well. Clocks, plates, vases, and fabric prints all depicted scenes from the most popular novels; fashion plates offered styles inspired by heroines. The aesthetic communities of the sentimental novel were available for purchase, not just so one could own a piece of *Atala* or *Paul et Virginie*, but because a great number of people were eager to incorporate the ideals into their own lives.[22]

The force of the sentimental vision was also threatening. The lessons of sentimental novels harnessed emotion and order to make sense of the world. In doing so, they authorized readers, including women, to engage the conflict between individual liberty and the welfare of all.[23] Like religious works, sentimental plots and narrative structures used a language of martyrdom and emotion to confirm that women's actions could be heroic, religious belief was a stronger support than faith in human men, and a new world could only be created when women offered models of sacrifice by holding fast to their principles. These idealistic values, consonant with religious explanations of the world, authorized women to act. The power and logic of these works also offered women access to social criticism and a vision of the world as it might be, rather than as it was.

One response to this threat can be seen in Gustave Flaubert's novel *Madame Bovary*, from 1856, which offered a stereotypical formula for the nineteenth-century attack on girls' reading. The protagonist, Emma Bovary, had a religious and sentimental literary formation. Her early reading revolved around the catechism and pious images.[24] Sermons and passages from Chateaubriand's *Genius of Christianity* (1802) impressed Emma with the "sonorous lamentations of . . . romantic melancholies reechoing through the world and eternity!"[25] Her senses absorbed the excitement and passion of these examples; she looked to make sacrifices for Christ. The nuns began to think that Emma might have some vocation to religious life, but instead Emma developed a taste for novels, which encouraged her fantasies of exoticism in everyday life.[26] Emma soon dreamed of sultans, doves, and men on balconies and longed to be swept off her feet. When she got married, her stable, dull husband could not compete with the novels' heroes. In fact, her husband Charles is a picture of the prosaic, only reading medical journals. He is therefore someone that Emma, who "detested commonplace heroes and moderate sentiments, such as there are in nature," could never love.[27]

As Flaubert's defense attorney explained at his trial for obscenity, Flaubert did not just create a fictional reader; he also offered a warning to the world. Sentimental novels would allow women to construct an individual and emotional ego that was based on devotion and illusion.[28] Emma's sense of self, shaped by reading, was unrealistic and threatening. She did not merely look for a man who was romantic; Emma wanted to build her life as a romance where she was the hero. Marie-Antoine Jules Sénard, Flaubert's defense attorney, argued that *Madame Bovary* was a new and a better moral tale, a warning against letting girls remain irrationally sentimental and religious: "[T]he author places before [the reader] this question: 'Have you done what you ought for the education of your daughters? Is the religion you have given them such as will sustain them in the tempests of life, or is it only a mass of carnal superstitions which leaves them without support when the storm rages? Have you taught them that life is not the realization of chimerical dreams, that it is something prosaic to which it is necessary to accommodate oneself? Have you taught them that?"[29] Sénard demonstrates how girls were imagined as victims of their sentimental formation, because it made them unable to see clearly the realistic—and masculine—limits of their worlds.[30]

Within Sénard's testimony—and the construction of religion as the foundation of Emma's missteps—one sees the power and threat in Catholic girls' reading of sentimental literature. Emma Bovary encapsulates men's midcentury fears not only about sentimental reading but also religion's ability to subvert men's authority over women.[31] The devout female reader would be ruined by books and the images contained therein, because both her faith and novels would encourage her to want more than life had in store.[32] Rather than the ordinary, she would seek the extraordinary.

Hostility to sentimentality was not only an elevation of the matter-of-fact over the idealistic but also included a positivistic hostility to Christianity and the miraculous. Sentiment, along with Christian belief, was "an established form of fantasy, a system of wish-fulfilment, a deluding myth," and "the deflation of Christianity was part of the deflation of Romanticism."[33] To be deeply religious and emotional ran in the same vein, and both belief systems needed to be destroyed so that men could exert proper authority over women.

But what of the nearly four million nonfictional female readers in France?[34] What were their relationships to books, sentiment, and religion? Over the course of the eighteenth and early nineteenth centuries, female literacy grew faster than male literacy.[35] As already discussed, more books were entering homes as prices fell, and young women, like other readers, changed their reading practices from intensive reading of a few books, including the Bible, to extensive reading of a greater number of books, a process that not only allowed for more material but also more possible interpretations of the books that were being read.[36] Reading aloud continued to be popular throughout the early part of the century, and both short texts and prose fiction were read in groups for entertainment.[37] Of course, both girls and young women were frequently limited in their reading material to what they could find at home or what they were given, which meant that topics in the books were restricted by each girl's position in society, her family's wealth, and the choices of the male readers or book collectors.[38] As girls began to enter schools in greater numbers after the Revolution, their reading material may have increased, but conservative pedagogical messages that emphasized religion, domesticity, and Christian virtue were still the norm.[39]

Scholars have reconstructed publication records as well as lending library directors' requests for popular novels.[40] These demonstrate that sentimental novels, especially those written by women, were exceedingly popular in the first half of the nineteenth century. Given that men's purchases were central to what was available for women's reading, those novels had to have been generally licit. Indeed, for much of the first half of the nineteenth century, sentimental novels were seen with approbation, though there were of course complaints about novel-reading in general.[41] Additionally young women began their reading with catechisms and religious material before moving to novels. Females also read explicitly didactic moral literature, alone and in groups, in their formation as readers. Thus, although Flaubert's careful construction of Emma's fictional reading list produces an image that is consonant with what we know of popular works for female readers, the moral weight attached to such reading would not have been clearly negative in the first half of the century.[42]

Despite some masculine concern about the evil influence that literature—especially novels—might wield, numerous women claimed that reading was an authentic source of self-improvement.[43] From their perspective, feminine reading would enlighten the reader and offer her examples that would inspire her to be the best version of herself. The reading act was not political but neither was it private. Instead, it existed in a social context where proper reading enabled women to be autonomous and moral social beings.[44] Given that women were increasingly imagined as the "primary consumers of novels, it seems reasonable to speculate that there was something about stories of female self-sufficiency and virtue that [women] found particularly appealing and inspiring. Their enthusiasm may well have been based on this image of empowering virtue, so unlike the modest and self-effacing virtues typically attributed to or preached to women."[45] Instead of a "chimerical dream," where young men in soft leather boots might carry the reader away, the reader was encouraged to create an authentic and active path to happiness, one that did not emphasize romantic love.[46] Rather than finding that novels taught them to be masculine, female readers argued that women learned about honesty, self-control, and feminine virtue. Additionally, as much reading was done aloud, in semipublic spaces of the home, we should also see reading for virtue and improvement as a communal task from the outset, one in which moral tales were digested together, for both individual and general improvement.[47]

Thus, the path to self-improvement began with the first steps of read-ing, not only religious material, but also the didactic material that intended to help readers and listeners internalize proper values. In previous work I have examined the late eighteenth- and early nineteenth-century liter-ature of childhood. *Rousseau's Daughters* emphasized the ways in which children's books prioritized self-discipline as a primary component of childhood education.[48] An important corollary to the expectation of self-control was an emphasis on moral autonomy. Certainly didactic tales attempted to condition children so that they would behave in unambig-uous (and often gendered) ways.[49] However, to be "self-controlled," an adolescent had to not only internalize proper values but then also actively replicate the principles in everyday life. As a result, the themes and struc-tures of didactic tales, or literature of the "second age," emphasized the development of moral autonomy. A description of sentimentalism as vapid and uncritical may have appealed to midcentury men fearful of the possible corruption engendered by women's reading, but the mor-ally active narrative of the didactic tale presented a remarkably different structure to its consumer, though one that was likely no less frighten-ing to men who feared a novelistic loss of control over women's lives.[50]

In didactic tales the adolescent consumer was, quite importantly, no longer a small child, under the intellectual and physical control of others. Madame de Genlis, one of the most popular sentimental novelists, also wrote stories for children. Her *Tales of the Castle* spent much of its preface explaining why there was a particularly pressing need for appropriate lit-erature for adolescents. Genlis argued that stories like hers, intended for older children, inspired virtuous behavior.[51] She claimed that ideal educa-tional tales would not rely on artifice or manipulation but would present the material with moral force and engagement, so that children learned appropriate behavior.[52] Genlis presumed that the child had moved past the stage where she could be directed by others and exist only within their orbit; a different educational approach was both necessary and fitting. Other popular books also made the link between the reader's advanc-ing capacity and greater moral agency explicit. For example, Berquin's *The Friend of Adolescents* introduced one of the protagonists as a young man who had just made the transition to knee breeches.[53] Both the text and an accompanying illustration demonstrated that his mother and sister were surprised and impressed by his newly adult presence. They remarked on the fact that the young man knew many things and that he had arrived in their presence already comporting himself like an adult.[54]

Berquin and Genlis were not alone in signaling the second age as a period of impending physical and moral independence for readers. *Evenings of Adolescence*, *Stories of Adolescence*, and *Morals of Adolescence* were just three of the popular didactic books of the period, all of which used their titles to indicate the reader's approaching adulthood. Similarly, Sophie Renneville's *Correspondence of Two Little Girls* was designed to form "the heart and spirit" of "young girls leaving childhood" through moral lessons that they could read as guides to behavior as they formed their own households.[55] Though each of these books regarded the reader as not yet an adult, the book itself was intended to play an important part in the development of emotional maturation, as it would inculcate an active process of reading and response by which readers would be prepared to enter the world.[56] As with Carron, some of these works also cited Proverbs 22:6: "Teach a young man in the way that he should go; even when he is old, he will not depart from it."[57] This was explicitly a method intended to produce adults who would make proper choices on their own.

There was not a single style that was most appropriate for this process; didactic books took many different forms. For example, Berquin focused on a single story filled with examples from the natural world. Renneville offered her readers an epistolary novel that emphasized emotional relationships, while Genlis, Edgeworth, and many others offered collections of novellas, each having a unique plot and emphasizing single vices or virtues.[58] While the novella-style collection of moral tales may have been the most popular type, insofar as numerous editions of stories were produced in this style, even the many collections of stories were dwarfed in number by Laurent Bérenger's *Morality in Action*, the most popular of all didactic books of the first half of the nineteenth century.[59] Bérenger's multivolume collection offered numerous short tales, each with its own protagonist and virtue of note. While *Morality in Action* also relied on an assortment of interesting tales, its anecdotes were only a few paragraphs each, far shorter than the tales of Genlis and others. This made them particularly easy to assign in snippets or to read aloud, like earlier anthologies.[60] They also were based in history rather than being completely fictional.

Despite these differences, Bérenger's subtitle and preface pointed to the same approach found in other didactic works. He offered an active process of reading that would shape a morally responsible young person. The subtitle of Bérenger's work reminded the reader that the *Selection of Memorable Facts and Instructive Anecdotes* [were] *Appropriate to Make One Love Wisdom, to Train Young People's Hearts with Examples of All the Virtues, and to Adorn Their Spirits with the Memories of History*.[61] In his preliminary reflections on the work, Bérenger also explained, "A child raised with the precautions that we desire will soon seek, by a noble emulation, to equal the models that we present to him. He will feel how appealing virtue is, he will do good without end, and find his own most pure happiness in the happiness of others."[62] Genlis, too, sought to improve readers "through striking examples, scenes designed to touch and imprint on the imagination: that is Morality put into action."[63] Yet another author noted that didactic books shared a "common goal, [which was] to inspire the same social virtues and to guard against the same vices."[64] In each of these cases, then, the books were constructed with the expectation that young readers would soon be making their own choices. The books were to offer adolescents patterns of behavior so they would be able to emulate excellent models and reject poor examples. These stories were not to be consumed passively, as escapist literature. Like hagiographies, the narratives were a method to condition one's heart and mind; they offered warnings as well as good companions and positive influences to fall back on when one might otherwise be led astray. Also like hagiographies, the stories found in *Morality in Action* offered "true" stories from the past, often emphasized young protagonists, and demonstrated individual heroism against great temptation or odds. Readers were to become courageous actors after being formed by the stories in the books.

There was a large market for these didactic tales, not only for the numerous and varied *Stories*, but especially the collections of anecdotes, like Bérenger's, that were used time and again to reward schoolchildren for good behavior and performance.[65] While these books were rarely required reading in schools, they were part of a large market formed by the institutional possibilities of prize books for a growing number of schools and by affluent parents looking for books that would cross the divide between toy and educational object.[66]

While all didactic tales intended to offer readers stories in which they could place themselves, Bérenger's *Morality in Action* was unique in several ways. First, it had an enviable popularity, nearly cornering the market on prize books and inspiring imitators who hoped to cash in on its popularity.[67] Second, its approach relied not just on literary or sentimental appeal but on the appearance of fact as provided by the retelling of numerous "historical" events.[68] The anecdotes, whether true or literary, gave the appearance of verisimilitude. Not every hero was rich and noble, but most them were, and the conflict of many of the stories grew out of the sense that nobles had the obligation to care for the poor, to use their wealth to diminish the suffering of others. In the stories, life offered a constant conflict between good and evil, and evil could be as simple as being willfully blind to the privilege of one's life.

Stories offered themes of sacrifice, obligation, and freely offered generosity, including actual hagiographic stories where saints' lives were retold to reinforce self-sacrifice and Christian piety.[69] In other, less familiar histories, noble men used their positions as scions of powerful families not to prey upon others but to assist them. For example, M. Armand de Brezé, nephew of Cardinal Richelieu, used his influence and a great deal of his own money to secure a fair trial for a destitute widow. The grateful woman, having no way to repay him for his efforts on her behalf, offered him her daughter in return. M. de Brezé was revolted by the implication that he would be so base as to take advantage of the girl's virtue, or that he would require payment for an act of charity, but he spoke to the girl in order to warn her about her mother. When it turned out that the young woman wished to become a nun, Brezé took her to a nearby convent and paid her dowry so that she could join. Brezé himself died in battle within a few years, before reaching the age of twenty-seven.[70] Other stories offered similar inspiration. Young brothers, fleeing the lava, ash, and fires of the Aetna explosion, left behind the worldly treasures of their home and instead walked through the flames carrying their mother and father, who were unable to escape on their own.[71] A young man was promised the hand of a beautiful and destitute young woman. Upon learning that she also wanted most of all to be a nun, he paid her dowry to the convent but still supported her parents, who needed the help to live.[72]

Not all attributes were gendered, nor was heroism limited to men.[73] Women were portrayed as heroically self-abnegating.[74] One married woman, for example, hid her husband (and eventually twin children) from the Roman authorities to keep them safe, despite the toll that it took on her.[75] Another, the wife of a judge, interceded on behalf of a poor peasant woman. Because she could not change the outcome of a lawsuit, she gave up all her discretionary funds, claiming that it was to purchase a beautiful jewel, but in fact she secretly orchestrated the purchase of land on which the peasant could live.[76] These tales shared an emphasis on how a single person, even one who was quite young, could make a difference, "turn the course of history after his own fashion."[77]

Didactic literature thus offered its readers, including girls, tales of heroism, self-sacrifice, and social responsibility. Most had settings that would have been both familiar and idealized for readers of hagiographic material. Readers were reminded of many possible life paths, but most of all, they were supposed to learn that "[w]e are not in the world to amass riches, to lead a life of pleasure; we are not there to fill our intellect with scientific inquiry, to write poetry, to trace lines, etc. Our primary vocation is to work to make ourselves worthy of the heavenly inheritance through a truly Christian life."[78] What a "truly Christian life" would look like had been modeled by the anecdotes and was supposed to be internalized by the reader. Adolescents would remember the stories as they made their way into the world.

Sentimental novels offered readers the next step toward becoming moral agents who would shape the world. These stories, entirely fictional, moved past historical narrative and moral platitudes to engage problems of modern liberal society. These included the confrontation of social inequality and construction of a just moral order as an autonomous agent, all concerns implied by the stories of the didactic tales but addressed less directly. The four novels under consideration in the remainder of this chapter, two authored by men and two by women, were chosen because of their broad influence across the Revolutionary era.[79] Though they have different approaches to narration and argument, there are powerful similarities in each heroine's understanding of her own agency and voice.

Some of the most popular plots imagined the creation of new worlds. By setting their action in exile from the civilized world, the narratives explored how the protagonists, freed of "civilized" expectations, might construct new social contracts with one another. One such novel, seen by contemporaries as "without rival in bringing hearts to virtue," was *Paul et Virginie* by Bernardin de Saint Pierre.[80] This colossal best seller, first published in 1788, was widely available and popular for children as well as adults throughout the later eighteenth century and first half of the nineteenth century.[81]

The story told of Paul and Virginie, who were raised as brother and sister on an island in the Indian Ocean, off the coast of Africa. Both of their mothers took refuge there after bad experiences in France. Virginie's mother, Mme de la Tour, married for love but beneath her social class. She was rejected by her family, so she and her husband went to the Ile de France to make a new life together. Her husband died shortly thereafter. Paul's mother, Margaret, was betrayed by a man in Brittany who promised her marriage but abandoned her when she became pregnant; she fled to the Ile de France to salvage her reputation. Both women were therefore impoverished and wounded by their experiences with civilization; their differing social class was of little importance in their friendship. They shared everything in common—even their slaves were married to one another. In most ways their homesteads on the Ile de France were a refuge from much social inequality and misogyny, a reconstituted family.[82]

Virginie's impending adolescence disturbs the peaceful idyll. Virginie starts to become sexually aware and realizes that she has disturbing feelings for Paul. To make the literary point clear, at the same moment that she becomes conscious of herself as a sexual being, a hurricane lashes the island and destroys much of the peaceful oasis that Paul and Virginie had created.[83] Readers could understand this lesson much as didactic literature of the second age had: adolescence carried with it great risks, as children became more independent (figure 5).

However, despite the impending threat, Mme de la Tour and Margaret fail to take action. Though they discuss the possibility of marrying Paul and Virginie to each other as a solution to the problem, they ultimately decide that Paul and Virginie are still too young for this kind of responsibility. In the meantime Mme de la Tour's Parisian aunt, a woman of wealth and power, demands that Virginie be sent to France to be educated and civilized in preparation for marriage and inheritance. Virginie agrees to go, both in deference to her mother's wishes and with the hope that with the sacrifice of a few years in France, she will secure everyone's fortunes forever. Her adolescent formation will not be natural, but worldly.

Virginie does indeed become civilized; she learns to read and write and behave in polite society. However, upon learning that her aunt intends not to let her return to the island, but plans to marry her off to a nobleman, Virginie resists, only to be summarily dismissed as a silly, overly romantic girl. She is eventually disinherited and sent back at the height of hurricane season.[84] Her ship is struck by a storm while within sight of the harbor, and Virginie drowns rather than remove the clothing that would weigh her down. Her death marks the end of this paradise; soon the entire family passes away.

Margaret Cohen has noted that critics of sentimental novels saw *Paul et Virginie* as offering a natural pathway to emotionality and hypersensibility, rather than a fruitful exploration of the rational social contract.[85] Additionally, this tale was predicated on a vision of spontaneous moral feeling that was religious in inspiration and not reflective or rational.[86] Later writers believed that, instead of being formed to become responsible adults, young readers of these novels would cement a turn down the wrong path when they chose this vision of exotic retreat.[87]

Perhaps it is unsurprising that critics were horrified by a story that offered idealism and tragedy in its contrast of the "prejudices of the world" with the "happiness that belongs to nature and virtue."[88] The sentimental code took as a given the conflict between social expectations and individual desire and, in *Paul et Virginie*, used something akin to a biblical ideal, a retelling of the creation story, to explore the problems that adults inherently faced in resolving contradictory duties.[89] The spiritual concerns of Christianity and sentimental novels also overlapped, insofar as they heightened an emphasis on passion and the miraculous.[90] In its setting—with the created family not only separate from society but threatened by everyday civilization outside the island—*Paul et Virginie* certainly failed to encourage readers to "accustom themselves to the prosaic," offering neither compromise nor concession.[91]

Paul and Virginie, a new Adam and Eve, lived in a natural paradise, as close as two children possibly could be. The reader was encouraged to identify with the exotic locale, the happiness of childhood, and the threats inherent in adult responsibilities, especially those linked with civilization.[92] Self-knowledge in the form of Virginie's emergent sexuality was particularly dangerous, announcing itself alongside a hurricane, the same force that ultimately destroyed Virginie herself. This last component was particularly troubling for critics; Balzac and Lamartine characterized *Paul et Virginie* as dangerous reading for girls because of the potential that it had for awakening passion in young women.[93] To be sure, as Flaubert himself emphasized when describing Emma Bovary's development as a self-indulgent reader, it was not primarily exposing women to a language of passion that caused problems. Rather, it was the fact that passion, exoticism, and sensuality were tied to religion, modesty and virtue, which allowed a progression from mysticism to hedonism.[94]

Detractors were not the only ones to see virtue and religious emotion as a central part of the message of *Paul et Virginie*. Chateaubriand also saw these characteristics, though he explained them in far more positive terms. To Chateaubriand, exile was central to the meaning of the story, as it emphasized the Christian's distance from the corruption of the world. Reflecting on the importance of *Paul et Virginie* in his *Genius of Christianity*, Chateaubriand explained:

> We also discover the Christian in those lessons of resignation to the will of God, of obedience to parents, charity to the poor, strictness in the performance of the duties of religion,—in a word, in the whole of that delightful theology which pervades the poem of Saint-Pierre. We may even go still farther and assert that it is religion, in fact, which determines the catastrophe. Virginie dies for the preservation of one of the principal virtues enjoined by Christianity. It would have been absurd to make a Grecian woman die for refusing to expose her person; but the lover of Paul is a *Christian* virgin, and what would be ridiculous according to an impure notion of heathenism becomes in this instance sublime.[95]

Virginie refused to remove her clothing because she insisted on complete and uncompromising innocence. For Chateaubriand, this was a powerful and inspiring lesson.

For the critic, however, being moved by this Christian sentiment was more than quixotic; it was irrational and dangerous. Virginie's head may not have been turned by novel-reading, but she was certainly otherworldly and therefore not a fit example for female readers. Indeed, nineteenth-century critics are not alone in their hostility to Bernardin's tale, which persists to this day. Numerous modern readers also find it hard to imagine the novel as inspiring, given its patriarchal overtones and acceptance of slavery. Lieve Spaas calls it a "monstrous idyll" because Paul and Virginie are "condemned to chastity."[96] Naomi Schor points out how, even as *Paul et Virginie* critiques patriarchy on one level ("better dead than seduced and abandoned"), it simultaneously underscores "patriarchy's censure of female sexual activity—better dead than troubling the homosocial order."[97] "Serious scholars freely state their lack of sympathy . . . for the heroine's state of mind."[98] For modern critics Virginie's death seems to affirm a repressive sexual ethics. Equally, the underlying Christian demand of innocence, purity, and "strictness in the performance of the duties of religion" is also tied to the exotic locale of the novel, which affirms the exclusion of women from civilized and public spaces.[99] Women cannot exist in men's spaces and must die to confirm that they are Other.

Nineteenth-century men and modern scholars are dissatisfied with the sexual politics of *Paul et Virginie*, albeit for different reasons. However, typical readers of the early nineteenth century, who had themselves read hagiographies and didactic literature before moving on to *Paul et Virginie*, adored sentimental novels.[100] To them the religious interpretation was not a weakness of the novel, but a strength. The death of the heroine was ordained from the beginning of the novel and confirmed the double bind of social expectations versus individual desires being resolved most easily through religious belief; or "that life without belief in the Divinity is empty, and that God . . . offers consolation to those who suffer on earth."[101] Further, they were persuaded that the novel showed Virginie "deliberately choosing to die and choosing to die untainted *because* she has reserved her love for God alone. She prefers the purity of divine love to the imponderable nature of human, sexual love for Paul."[102] This interpretation was consonant with their worldview and formation; it also likely appealed to them.

While this version of the story might not charm a modern female reader, many women of the eighteenth and nineteenth centuries were religiously devout, and a typical female response in deeply Catholic families was to reject both political activism and Revolutionary ideology.[103] Being excluded from politics, whether by the Civil Code or by novelistic convention, was a description of fact, and in this context political invisibility was not necessarily an obvious problem. Many women did not read or seek "alternate" intellectual outlets because political speech was forbidden to them, but because "reading was perceived as the primary activity by which women's self-education would take place."[104] Christian women were concerned with virtue and the state of their souls, and literature addressed itself directly to those questions.

It is in that vein that sentimental reading, which offered important material for reflection and formation, was significant. "Since 'right' reading was neither a passive nor mechanistic skill, but rather an active construction of the mind, women who read novels could see its primary purpose as education and the improvement of the moral self."[105] Novels intersected the problem of the active construction of one's self at the point of virtue. *Paul et Virginie* is particularly relevant to both questions of virtue and women's self-construction against a hostile society. For example, the Old Man not only reassured Paul that Virginie would be faithful when Paul suspected that she had abandoned him, but also affirmed female readers' intellectual and bodily independence. When the Old Man says that each person is adapted perfectly to live within the world, he is quick to add that the individual's heart is reserved to God as the author of life.[106]

Chastity—even chastity to the point of death—should thus be understood in the context of the readerly desire to control one's own destiny. Rather than serving to narrowly emphasize women's sexual difference or exclude women from sexual pleasure, chastity demanded bodily integrity and denied men the right to tyrannize over women. The conversation between the Old Man and Paul demonstrates this:

> THE OLD MAN. Women are false in those countries where men are tyrants. Everywhere, violence produces a disposition to deceive.
> PAUL. How can men tyrannize over women?
> THE OLD MAN. By marrying them off without consulting them; by marrying a young girl to an old man, or a woman of sensibility to an indifferent husband.[107]

Given the sinfulness of humanity, liberation for women might necessitate total rejection of the world, including forceful rejection of men's possession of women's bodies. The sentimental project, which set problems of the collective (society, public good, general welfare) against problems of the individual (free choice, privacy, erotic love, nature) thus recognized women's predicament even as it offered them an opportunity to work through the implications and contextualized the solutions in ways that were consonant with their understanding of the world.[108]

Paul et Virginie was not the only novel to use virtue, celibacy, and exile to free women from the impossible demands of the world, nor was it alone in using moral language to examine social conflict. Chateaubriand was inspired by Bernardin de St. Pierre's story to create his own version of a mythic creation tale, called *Atala*, after the female protagonist. Similarly, the story was set in an exotic locale, this time North America of a time long past. The setting, inaccessible to the reader by time and space, offered an image of a new paradise.[109]

In *Atala*, a very old native man, Chactas, a member of the Natchez tribe, tells the story of his youth. He recounts his exile from home and capture by an enemy tribe, the Muscogees, who intend to kill him. The chief of the Muscogees has an adoptive daughter, who is a Christian, named Atala. Atala sets Chactas free so that he will not be executed by her tribe, and the two run away together. As they travel, Atala falls in love with Chactas. However, she is not free to marry him because she has sworn perpetual virginity as a promise to her mother. Despite this pledge Atala grows closer and closer to Chactas and fears that her passion will lead her astray; she takes poison and dies rather than betray her vows. A Eucharistic miracle accompanies her death; Chactas understands that all that has transpired is the will of God.

This novel was an immediate success when it was published in 1801. *Atala, or the Loves of Two Savages in the Desert* was wildly popular, appearing in six editions in the first year and sixteen or more translations within a few years of publication.[110] The novella was intended to be part of *The Genius of Christianity* and was republished with the longer, more philosophical work in 1802. While some clerics found the inclusion of novels within the *Genius* to be inappropriate, their view was certainly a minority view with respect to the general population.[111] Both works were especially well liked by women, which cemented Chateaubriand's reputation as a writer. Chateaubriand claimed that soon after their publication, people clamored around him, especially "the young women who cried at the novels, the crowd of Christians and the other enthusiasts for whom honorable action makes the heart beat."[112]

Atala shares several characteristics with *Paul et Virginie*, including the linking of exile and virtue in a story with a female hero.[113] Both stories took place outside of everyday locations, and the religious sentiments and passionate feelings were predestined to end tragically. The feminized religion that shines through both novels links women and Christianity with "faithfulness and honour, with emotion and with love, and with yearning and with hope."[114] Though this was inspirational, it was also subject to the criticism that these ideals were unrealistic and unsustainable in the world, that novels such as these failed to teach young women how to adapt themselves to the sphere in which they would have to live. For example, Emma Bovary's bad foundation through reading was linked to Chateaubriand not only through the *Genius of Christianity* but specifically through the novella. When Emma gave birth to a daughter, she contemplated naming her "Atala," offering the reader of the novel another link between sentimental reading and inappropriate formation.[115] Girls who read and cried and sighed over Atala's death were not fit to live in an ordinary world.

Atala also has modern points of criticism in common with *Paul et Virginie*. Some of this is because, like *Paul et Virginie*, much of *Atala* has not aged particularly well. Critics are frustrated by *Atala*'s politics, both its imperialist undertones and its exclusion of women from participation in public life. Through the combination of exoticism and the necessary death of the heroines, both novels exclude women and native peoples from incorporation into the body politic. Even as the publication dates of the two novels cross the Revolutionary era, a moment in which women's actual participation in public life exploded, their plots serve to underline the ways in which women are always foreign and never citizens. In *Atala*, for example, the characters "are never united with the *patrie* that ... seems tantalizingly to surround them. The very sublimity of the wilderness becomes the index of its inhumanity, or conversely, of their estrangement from it."[116] From this critical perspective, the wandering of the native and the woman seems to make it clear that there is no home for them; Atala's aimlessness demonstrates how ill-fitted women are to incorporation into civic life. Thus, "[t]he presumption of progress, of some sort of liberation of and for women fostered by the macro-narrative of the revolution is denied by the seemingly ritualistic sacrifice of the eternal female protagonist, as well of course as by the historical record."[117]

Most frustrating of all, to modern critics, is the fact that Atala must die to protect her body. As Naomi Schor notes, *Atala* is not alone in this literary approach, but the novella's organization and design sets an important precedent. "Atala, whose access to sexuality is barred by the vow her mother made at her birth committing her to virginity, is but the first of a long line of nineteenth-century French heroines denied *jouissance*."[118] Schor is not making a simple argument about women's right to claim sexual pleasure. She and other critics recognize that the destruction of a heroine who has been fashioned in this way seems to signal that women may be virtuous only when the threat posed by their independent existence has been permanently removed by their death. Women were often forceful agents during the French Revolution; the novel's writing of women into exile is one way of removing women from public life.[119] From this perspective, exoticism and the virtuous death go hand in hand, as exclusion from the world of politics and civilized society is naturally, even necessarily, linked to death. Femininity is strange and foreign and must be relegated to a strange land, along with the savage.[120] Using the philosophy of Michel de Certeau, one critic argues that "feminine exoticism, like the exoticism of the savage, is always, in the end, the story of an execution, of a sacrificial putting to death."[121] Women are allowed tombstones, memorials, and allegorical power, but not bodily force or even physical integrity.

Equally importantly, modern critics link religious language and virtue to oppressive gender exclusion in the sentimental novel. For example, Naomi Schor says that the novel's brilliance can be found in its ability to mobilize both religion and gender, but to oppress rather than to liberate. She explains: "This then is what I will not hesitate to call Chateaubriand's brilliant innovation in *Atala*: in the guise of rehabilitating Christianity in the wake of the secularizing trends of eighteenth-century philosophy and the dechristianization promoted by the revolution, Chateaubriand unites to stunning effect the categories of gender with those of religion."[122] She claims that the "language of [Atala's] mother is coextensive with that of the Christian apologist: the key words in her vocabulary are persecution, salvation, and damnation."[123] For Schor, like many other critics, *Atala* serves to legitimate the exclusion of women from participation in civic life through the fusing of a language of martyrdom and sentiment, with the "usual consequences for the woman: silence, immobilization, and ultimately, death."[124]

While this modern critique is both powerful and significant, the nineteenth-century situation demonstrates in important ways that female readers did not internalize sentimental novels as exclusionary and immobilizing. Instead, the gendered call to exile and virtue that the novels outlined may have been part of a "sophisticated and psychologically astute choice in the [reader's] struggle for legitimacy," especially given the value accorded to the outsider in Romanticism.[125] Additionally, the sacrifices and authority of the female protagonist in *Atala* had meaning and power for Chateaubriand's woman readers; they laid particular claim to Atala's voice.[126] For example, Chateaubriand also published a second linked novella, excerpted from the *Genius of Christianity*. This story, *René*, shared *Atala*'s North American setting as well as a tragic ending, though it acted through a male protagonist. In the second tale, the central character, René, tells Chactas of the Natchez about his past. He describes a lonely life in which he has been perpetually unsatisfied and wandered from place to place. He once decided to put an end to his sorrow by killing himself, but his beloved sister learned of his plan and came to stop him. She, however, would not stay with him but left to enter a convent. René later discovered that she chose to become a nun to conquer her forbidden passion for him. René was shattered by this revelation and left for Louisiana, where he received a letter that told him of his sister's death. The novella ends by reporting that René himself died in a battle between the Natchez and the French shortly after recounting his tale for Chactas.

René was deeply popular with young men, who styled themselves after the protagonist. Its narrative, however, was not nearly as popular with females. "Whereas *Atala* and *Génie du Christianisme* were championed primarily by women, *René* was largely taken up by men."[127] There was, then, something particularly appealing to young women about the story of a virginal maiden, as protagonist, actively and centrally sacrificing herself for the sake of chastity.

Additionally, given Chateaubriand's reputation as a Catholic writer who had suffered during the Revolution, the women who "clamored around him" surely knew that much of Chateaubriand's work was influenced by his own exile from France during the Revolution.[128] The prospectus for *Atala* claimed that it had been written while Chateaubriand was "in the huts of savages" in North America. As his literary voice highlighted the experience of an exile, at odds with his *patrie*, it also could reinforce the experiences of those who had found themselves at odds with their nation during the Revolution, even if they had not been physically displaced. Historical scholarship has demonstrated that it was common—though not universal—for devout women to reject the Revolution.[129] Given that, one should not assume that a literary otherness that denied the "macro-narrative of revolution" would be problematic to most female readers, as it could speak to a feeling of estrangement from the current world and even reinforce their sense that a virtuous woman belonged only in a remade society. Thus, young women who read and wept and sighed for sentimental novels like *Paul et Virginie* and *Atala* could indeed be celebrating chastity, through which they were also endorsing "their genuine belief in female worth and their determination to demonstrate that value," including not an exhortation to be "demure, retiring, or uncoy, but . . . courageous, resolved, and responsible."[130] Nineteenth-century female readers could embrace the martyrdom and exclusion found in *Atala* and see it as a form of liberation rather than imprisonment, a demand for a new society that would allow their moral integrity to remain intact.

Some concrete examples from the novel make this point particularly clear. As Atala and Chactas wander in the wilderness, they get caught in a massive storm, which, as with the storm in *Paul et Virginie*, symbolizes the growing, dangerous, and destructive passion between the two lovers. They hear a bell from the mission and head toward its refuge, finding along the way a hermit, Père Aubry, who has already headed out to save anyone who might be in need. Atala throws herself at his feet, saying that heaven has sent him to save her.[131] Aubry offers a refuge to both Atala and Chactas. Once they are safe, they see the impact of the storm: "[T]he fires of the conflagration caused in the forests by the lightning were still shining in the distance; at the foot of the mountain an entire pine-wood had been thrown down into the mud, and the river was charged pell-mell with molten clay, trunks of trees, and the bodies of dead animals and of dead fishes, floating upon the still agitated surface of the waters."[132] The storm reminds the reader of the danger and destructiveness of desire. While the hermitage, representing Christian devotion, is a place of peace, a relationship with Chactas would force Atala away from the retreat, into a passionate and erotic love affair. That might sound positive to modern ears, but in the novel it is a significant threat to Atala's own self.[133]

Consequently, while Aubry contemplates blessing the marriage of Atala to Chactas, when he finds out that she has poisoned herself and will die rather than marry, he consoles her with some hard truths about marriage between men and women, including that men and women are not really made to be happy together. He says that the "soul of man becomes weary, and never loves the same object long and fully. There are always some points upon which two hearts do not agree, and in the end those points suffice to render life insupportable."[134] *Atala* reminded its female reader that chastity was safety and that the moral imperative of the Christian religion, which also demanded suppression of sexual drives, would protect a woman's truest self.[135] A rejection of domesticity and maternity was offered as explicit protection of women from men's faithlessness, as men were described as fickle, jealous, and forgetting even their mothers' deaths.[136]

An emphasis on exile and chastity served to redefine both women's potential and the ultimate direction of their fulfillment. The aesthetic of Christianity that emerged from the sentimental novel persuaded by the heart, not reason. Chactas, for example, was not swayed to the truth of Atala's faith by intellectual argument, nor was he consoled by it. Instead, "[h]e prostrates himself before the sublime and supernatural images of God and angels, transfixed and convinced. This, indeed, is the beauty of religion, a religion 'which has made a virtue of hope.'"[137] The source of support for Christian belief now found its greatest depths in an emotional, energetic, and feminine virtue.[138] *Atala* in particular is an "exemplary [illustration] of the aesthetic of Christianity," as it offered a vision for human identity that reinforced emotion, femininity, and individual agency (Atala suicides rather than betray her vows) even as it highlighted removal from the world.[139] Women who read and admired these novels embraced an image of the world in which idealism, independence, and exile—including by martyrdom or celibacy—were linked.

Although women had been written out of politics by many of the concrete decisions of the Revolutionary era, "the Revolution bequeathed them a moral identity and a political constitution. Gender became a socially relevant category in post-Revolutionary life."[140] Sentimental novels, in both their plots and structures, fit with the exile of women from politics even as the stories underlined the importance of feminine emotion, moral agency, and distance from a corrupting world. As a contemporary review of sentimental novels explained, "natural affections, tender sentiments, and moral and pious thoughts ... satisfy the tastes of many" because they mark "the return of opinion toward healthy ideas and conservative principles. We must be grateful to novelists for having given an asylum to truth when false politics and false philosophy have proscribed it."[141] Moral agency did not have to be centered in political participation.

Of course, sentimental literature was not truly removed from all politics nor from social considerations. Instead, the formative reading of women was idealistic and virtuous, set in a context in which it confronted the problems of the political moment. This was true even though the novels used, not political language, but a language of family and domesticity to address tensions between individual freedom and collective welfare. The domestic, utopian, and even exiled space thus serves as a "microcosm of the liberal public sphere where unity takes the form of debate and conflict."[142] The tensions of the sentimental novel demonstrate no blind acceptance of the idea that women should be deprived of rights, nor was a setting of "exile" equivalent to silencing or setting aside.

The sentimental novel's function as a microcosm of collective life is even more clear in some of its less overtly religious expressions. Sophie

Cottin's *Claire d'Albe* (1799) was the best-selling novel of the first years of the Restoration, and Sophie Cottin one of the most lauded authors of the early nineteenth century.[143] Unlike the novels of Christian virtue, *Claire d'Albe*'s setting, while idyllic, is not paradisaical, and the morals appear to repudiate traditional values—the heroine is both virtuous and adulterous. Despite these differences, the messages of independent moral judgment and exile from civilized society wind through the novel and offer a heartbreaking outcome for a situation in which freedom and choice have been pitted against social order. While *Claire d'Albe* differs greatly from *Paul et Virginie* or *Atala*, readers appropriated it to the same effect.

As an epistolary novel, *Claire d'Albe* works on the same model as Rousseau's *Julie*, the prototypical sentimental novel.[144] Most of the letters are from the heroine, Claire, to her best friend, Elise, described as the "dearest portion of [Claire's heart]."[145] Through the letters we learn that Claire is twenty-two and has been married for seven years to a man who is nearly forty years older than she; the couple has two children, a boy and girl. Claire initially describes her marriage as predetermined for her by her father, but ideal. Her husband is a loving and wonderful man, and they live in seclusion on a country estate, far from the disruptions of worldly society in the city.

Unlike *Julie*, Cottin's narrative soon offers troubling hints that disrupt the happy domesticity: M. d'Albe is jealous, has a quick temper, and places his own desires first.[146] Claire feels unfulfilled and restless, even if she claims that she is resigned to her lot in life.[147] With poor judgment M. d'Albe brings a young cousin, Frédéric, into their lives to help with the factory that M. d'Albe owns. Not just any young man, Frédéric is as fresh and original as the first man, Adam, and as physically glorious, with "the head of Antinous on the body of Apollo."[148]

Claire and Frédéric spend a great deal of time together. Initially, there is distance between the two. Frédéric is uncultivated and impolite to Claire. He looks suspiciously at her, because he assumes that a young woman who marries an old man must have done so for her own interests and with guile. Eventually, he notices her charity and goodness, the fact that she has a tender heart and cares for others without looking to be rewarded for it.[149] The two fall in love. While Claire admits that she loves Frédéric, she resists her emotions and sends him to live with Elise.[150] M. d'Albe persuades Elise to write—falsely—that Frédéric has given his heart to another. Claire nearly dies of a broken heart because she believes that she has so badly misjudged Frédéric's virtue and honesty.[151] Frédéric, however, hears of the plot and returns in time to make passionate love to Claire on her father's tomb, just before she dies. The final letter, from Elise, recounts these events, ostensibly to reinforce virtue, though the actual message seems more mixed, given that Claire prefers illicit love to virtue and death to life with her husband and children.[152]

Claire d'Albe was set within the context of the Revolutionary experience even as it was opposed to it. At least one other sentimental author, Mme de Genlis, condemned the novel for the immorality of its heroine and its frank depiction of mutual passion.[153] Genlis ascribed the tone of Cottin's novel to the period of its writing, during the reign of Robespierre. Genlis said that Cottin's "pen, dipped in blood, could only describe false and frightening pictures."[154] Mme de Genlis claimed *Claire d'Albe* was the "first novel in the Romantic genre." She argued that it "was the first of them to represent delirious, furious, and ferocious love, and a heroine who was virtuous, religious, angelic . . . giving herself up without restraint and without shame to all the eruptions of an unrestrained and criminal passion."[155] Genlis feared that this novel would lead the reader astray by offering her freedom from prevailing values. Genlis's language seems to confirm Sénard's argument that such novels, whether by themselves or on top of religious sentiment, provided a vision of extraordinary color, rather than commonplace expectations.

It is true that Claire ultimately is unable to accustom herself to everyday life. She dreams of "a better ideal . . . [in order to] find the happiness that the heavens have refused me."[156] Like Atala and Virginie, Claire (and Emma) prefers death to the tyranny and complacency of marriage. Unlike in the Christian novels, Claire tastes illicit passion with a devoted lover, one who nearly dies himself rather than forsake her and is, it is hinted, not long for this world without her.[157] Where Atala and Virginie use exile to demand independence, Claire is willing to accept death as the punishment for tasting passion and autonomy.

However, Claire's emotional struggle arises not because of a feminine misunderstanding of the real demands of the world, but as a result of a conflict between negative and positive rights. Claire has been given no choice in her marriage; her dying father, anxious to provide a secure future for her, arranged a marriage to his best friend. Claire had a "worthy husband" "chosen for [her]," rather than having her own choice in the matter.[158] Claire recognizes that she has a moral responsibility to her husband, and "Claire would die rather than be guilty."[159] At the same time, her exile has been invaded by "a charming young man, endowed with all that is greatest in virtue, most congenial in wit, most captivating in candor," and she has fallen in love against her own will.[160] When she finally commits adultery, she does indeed experience passion, but also her prediction is true: Claire will die as a result of the conflict between duty and desire.

It is for this reason that another contemporary review of Cottin's work argued that it was neither immoral nor removed from religious beliefs. It agreed with Genlis that *Claire d'Albe* was a product of Revolutionary conflict, but rather than seeing love, adultery, and death as an immoral sequence, the anonymous reviewer argued that the novel's emphasis on sentiment and passion was an important corrective to the Revolutionary weight on the good of all. The reviewer explained that there was a pressing need for novels such as this that would highlight individual agency in a despotic world: "Thus, when the bloody tyranny of the praetorium oppressed the universe, ardent love and ardent Christianity, which, truly understood, is love itself, consoled the coming generations for their catastrophes, and the fervent novices of both sexes encouraged each other to gather the palms of martyrs."[161] This reviewer saw the conflict between duty and desire as like that experienced under Roman oppression, with martyrdom and necessary Christian love demonstrating the important sacrificial context. The sentimental novel thus reminded its readers that the ultimate cause of a heroine's death was the conflict between collective responsibility and individual agency, weighted not only against women but against all free individuals.

Claire's death was the result of a terrible collision of untenable choices that echoed the problem of social organization. Even without the paradise of Chateaubriand or Bernadin, the microcosm of the collective took on deeply religious meaning. Woman martyred herself because conflict between the collective and individual left her no other resolution. The domestic unit existed not in opposition to but as a representation of the whole, subject to the same unresolvable conflicts found in public life.[162]

Sentimental literature's emphasis on women as moral agents in exile was nowhere more clear than in the writings of Mme de Staël. Staël's works, including sentimental novels, linked emotional experience (including religious belief) with social critique. Her novel *Corinne* (1807) was incredibly popular. It went through multiple editions and was deeply influential in its tale of the battle between a masculine emphasis on law and separate spheres versus openness to feminine artistic, cultural, and emotional influences.[163] Staël's other works also demonstrate that the literary use of emotion was intended to serve as a corrective to power imbalances. Staël herself was deeply engaged with liberal politics and attracted the ire of Napoleon for daring to insist on women's capacity for intellectual and social influence. Additionally, as a product of French salon culture, Staël recognized that both public life and love relationships were places where women could exercise individual autonomy.[164]

However, as a disciple of Rousseau, Staël also accepted that, to a large extent, "public liberty and order are in solidarity with domestic peace and order," which was a general affirmation of theories of complementarity and privacy.[165] Staël thus argued that emotion and private life were key for public virtue. Despite her high profile and widespread influence, modern critics often find this portion of Staël's thought frustratingly anti-feminist, even reactionary.[166] Staël's writings are therefore a particularly useful way to work through both contemporary and modern approaches to sentimentality and to examine how feminine emotion and religious belief might have facilitated women's understanding of their exclusion from the masculine rationality of post-Revolutionary politics.[167]

Staël, who saw the novel as more formative than political discourse, argued that political life was not the central location of moral activity. In fact, at times of political imbalance, the highest duty of all persons might be to avoid politics. "The old legislators made it a duty for the citizens to take part in political interests. The Christian religion must inspire a disposition of a completely different nature, that of obeying authority, but keeping away from affairs of the state when they compromise the conscience."[168] This was an observation that grew out of political experience during the Terror or under the authoritarianism of Napoleon; politics might leave no space for truly authentic action. In those moments, a retreat from the political would be more useful than remaining within it.[169] Private action carried a greater moral weight and had more resonance than legislative activism, not only for women, but also for men. Whereas older—ancient—models assumed that politics was the center of all formation, didactic literature, including sentimental novels, offered instruction in how to be a complete person. Making oneself "worthy of [a] heavenly inheritance" did not demand changing the world through legislation, especially at times when politics itself was suspect.[170]

Given this critique, Staël's most successful sentimental novel, *Corinne*, reveals itself as a highly intentional depiction of the limits of early nineteenth-century women's agency as well as an examination of the creative power of woman as a moral agent out of step with her moment. The protagonist, Corinne, is a beautiful, mysterious, and celebrated Italian artist, excellent at improvisation, writing, and drawing. As Corinne is being crowned in triumph in Rome, she meets a British peer in mourning: Oswald Lord Nelvil. The two are deeply and inexplicably drawn to each other, even though Corinne's mysterious past haunts her and Oswald disapproves of her public use of her talents. Once they become lovers, he is jealous of the general adulation for Corinne; he wants her to perform only for him. Oswald hopes that his love for her will encourage her to abandon Italy and to prefer domestic life to the "luster" of her genius.[171] For her part Corinne is torn; she wishes to please Oswald, but she still enjoys the "lively and flattering homage of the Italians."[172]

Eventually, they divulge their secrets to one another.[173] We discover that Corinne is tied to Oswald by more than their experiences in Italy; she was intended as a wife for him, until Lord Nelvil's father rejected her as inappropriate, due to her vivacity and refusal to submit to English norms. Oswald is now intended to marry Corinne's half-sister, Lucile, whose charms are described as fully English (traditionally domestic and submissive).[174] Oswald is unable to reconcile his dead father's disapproval of the woman he loves with his own feelings; when he is called back to England with his regiment, he returns to the views that surround him and marries Lucile. Corinne is heartbroken by his betrayal, and her health persistently declines. Hearing of Corinne's illness, Oswald returns to Italy with Lucile and their daughter, Juliette. Corinne passes on her artistic talents to Juliette and offers relationship advice to Lucile before she dies. Before that death, however, a final public performance of her poetry reminds everyone of her glory, as well as its destruction by Oswald.

Like all sentimental novels, *Corinne* focuses on the conflict between social expectations and individual choice. The novel's themes of autonomy, exile, and repressive social norms emphasize the central conflict, which is the battle between patriarchal law (typified by control of women and rigid enforcement of sex roles) and feminine emotion and the leadership of the heart (exemplified by Corinne's improvisatory genius). As in *Paul et Virginie, Atala*, and *Claire d'Albe*, the male protagonist is depicted as a new Adam, but his desire to create a new society, with a more egalitarian social contract, cannot solve the problem of the oppression that women experience. The story culminates in the death of the heroine, who is the moral force behind the narrative. Corinne's death comes about because the man with whom she falls in love, the only man who can understand her genius and touch her heart, is also unable to "see in a woman who would be his wife anything other than the faithful and discreet guardian of the family home."[175] Oswald is both guilty and inferior to Corinne because he cannot abandon patriarchal assumptions about women's natural submission to men. There is no happy ending possible for this heroine, no creation of a new society.

Corinne's demand for intellectual autonomy serves to emphasize that she stands outside crucial norms of society. She refuses to live by her stepmother's dictum that a woman's only role is to care for her husband and children.[176] Ultimately, Corinne abandons England for Italy and argues for Italy's superiority as a locale for women, saying "domestic virtues are the glory and happiness of women in England, but if there is one country where love subsists outside of the sacred bonds of marriage, among those countries, the one which pays most attention to women's happiness is Italy."[177] While Corinne does not violate the norms of female chastity, she cares little for appearances.[178] For example, when she leaves for Naples with Oswald, she argues that her happiness and behavior is her concern, not that of others.[179] Corinne claims the right to act as a free moral agent, not in order to pointlessly defy social norms, but to behave according to the necessary dictates of individual self-determination, just as men do. As Corinne asks Oswald, "If society did not bind women with all manner of chains while men go unshackled, what would there be in my life to keep anyone from loving me?"[180] She intends to choose her own destiny, even if that choice leads to suffering and death.

As a woman and an independent agent, Corinne is set apart from her contemporary society in more ways than one. *Corinne*'s setting is Italy; the protagonist lives in voluntary exile from England. This exile emphasizes the denial of separate spheres that has been central to Corinne's life. Italy exists as a place where Corinne's talent—and Corinne herself—can flourish in ways that would be unthinkable in England. Corinne's choices to embrace her ambition and artistry, and to emphasize emotion rather than rationality, are all unwelcome in England. Her resettlement in Italy under a single name, without any patronymic, similarly demonstrates her rejection of the ideal of private domesticity, subsumed under masculine control.[181]

Exile and a rejection of domesticity and separate spheres are tied to the broader political and social context of the novel. Corinne's artistry and influence is recognized and lauded in Italy, which, not coincidentally, is itself a state under siege, in political exile. While Napoleon's conquest of Italy does not figure in the novel, it would have been impossible for readers not to hear the Italian travelogue without thinking of the subjugated political status of the peninsula. Corinne's first artistic improvisation in the book is on the theme of the "glory and welfare of Italy."[182] Corinne represents the woman of genius and Italy itself; both representations are historically powerful but no longer hold power in their own right. The reader is driven to see the elision between genius and political oppression. "Corinne incarnates the soul of a country which does not yet exist, and which has also been reduced to silence and mediocrity, just as the Revolution has reduced every woman who wants to be useful to the nation by her spirit."[183] Corinne can prosper in Italy, which not only exists in a metaphorical sense to emphasize the qualities that make Corinne heroic, but also reminds the reader that sentimental relationships mediate between public and private for communities as well as individuals.[184]

Thus, when Corinne succeeds in Italy, with the adulation of crowds, but does not have individual love, she is not flourishing, a fact that she recognizes when she encounters Oswald. Though the narrator of Corinne recognizes that "Corinne was blind to her own welfare, in attaching herself to a man likely rather to repress than to excite her talents,"[185] it also seems inevitable that Corinne will fall for a man who cannot appreciate her. Corinne serves as an arbitrating force between the law and patriarchal society and emotion and genius, even as that negotiation causes her to lose her own artistic presence and, ultimately, destroys her.[186] Given the fact that a reconstituted domestic life is the model for a new social order, the reader comes to understand that when domestic peace is impossible, it is a sign of something deeply amiss in the public order as well. Corinne needs to be loved on her own terms to be fulfilled, but in society as it exists, there is no existing person who can respond to the needs of her heart. In the end, the novel proposes religious belief and love for Christ, rather than romantic love, as the only force that can allow for the emotion and life of the protagonist to be fully experienced without repression.

While Corinne initially resists this answer—early on, she has a sense of foreboding at seeing women in a convent—over the course of the novel, it becomes clear that human society is too limited for women; it tyrannizes over them and crushes their freedom of expression. Religious life, perhaps counterintuitively, is opposed to patriarchal norms. Both Corinne's and Oswald's words demonstrate this sense. Early in the novel Corinne takes Oswald on a tour of Rome. They see Saint Peter's Basilica, which represents not only Italy but also the ability to achieve a balance between opposites, something that the plot of the sentimental novel seeks to do. "Eternal motion and eternal rest" are united in the square of St. Peter, and Corinne explains how contrasts are resolved in Christian belief. She says that the figures that surround them "recall immortality even on the altar of death" and explains further that the church is a mix of powerful opposites. It "perfectly characterizes a mixture of obscure dogmas and sumptuous ceremonies . . . severe doctrines, capable of mild interpretation: Christian theology and Pagan images; in fact, the most admirable union of all the majestic splendors which man can give to his worship of the Divinity."[187] Similarly, the glittering sunlight on the plaza gives way to the dark interior, even as both work together to release death into life, resolving the contradictions that hold men's souls to earth. Oswald sees the appeal, but he resists, pointing to Italy's political disorder as a reason to reject the obvious charm.

Oswald's masculine rationality is unable to see the true value of what is set before him, especially in the context of the renunciation of the world. This is an ongoing theme. For example, Oswald goes to the Sistine Chapel to hear Allegri's *Miserere*, but first he sees Michaelangelo's paintings of the Last Judgment, with the Sibyls bearing witness on the ceiling, surrounded by a crowd of angels.[188] Oswald finds this scene of heaven gloomy and frightening, but if we see Corinne as a modern Sibyl—as she is referred to in the novel multiple times—his gloom is based in foreboding at seeing the image of her glory and his separation from her. Corinne, for her part, hears the music and is called to heaven. "It seemed to her it was in such a moment of exaltation that one would want to die . . . if an angel suddenly came and on its wings carried away feeling and thought, those divine sparks which would return to their source. Death would then be, as it were, only a spontaneous act of the heart, a more fervent, better answered prayer."[189] While Oswald fears losing Corinne, in her best moments Corinne recognizes that renouncing the world is a better choice, one that is full of God's mercy. In this way Corinne's spiritual experience during Holy Week further confirms her experience of life as a young English woman. She says that the domestic separation and lack of animation that is expected of women in England was stultifying; "I had been in Italian convents; they seemed to me full of life in comparison with this circle."[190]

Ultimately, when Oswald is unable to move past his desire to own Corinne, to possess her genius entirely for himself, he confirms that the masculine community is unable to accommodate feminine voices in the world.[191] Corinne's final poetic presentation serves as a witness to the fact that God and religious belief are the safe havens against the limits placed on women by patriarchy: "You do not reject, my God, the tribute of talents . . . There is nothing narrow, nothing enslaved, nothing limited in religion. It is the immense, the infinite, and the eternal; far from taking away from genius, imagination from its first impulse goes beyond the bounds of life, and the sublime of all kinds is a reflection of divinity. Ah! if I had only loved the divine, if I had placed my head in the sky, safe from stormy affection, I would not be broken before my time."[192] When Corinne removes the miniature of Oswald and replaces it with a crucifix, she reminds the reader that Jesus came "not for the powerful, nor the inspired," but for "the sufferer, the dying."[193] She thus completes her withdrawal from the world and her liberation from social oppression. Like the other sentimental heroines who reject the world, she is not accepting her erasure but trumpeting her unwillingness to be limited to a role in which she is oppressed.

Modern critics do not find Corinne's death or the invocation of religion and women's difference inspiring. Deborah Heller, for example, argues that the "tragedy of a woman's misplaced affections and her betrayal by an unworthy man [is a] more conventional as well as a conceptually less interesting plot than other possibilities."[194] Lori Marso finds Staël's Rousseauan overtones odd and ironic.[195] Ellen Peel argues Oswald ends up in a better place than Corinne because, unlike her, he falls in love again. He survives the end of the affair. However, Peel also notes, "It is true that he is never contented, but his separation from Corinne does not ravage him as it does her."[196] These readings, while potentially consonant with a modern vision of the world, misunderstand the context in which readers and listeners would have digested the plots of sentimental novels. It is true that Oswald lives, but he lives unable to forget Corinne and unable to pardon himself for her death.[197] Corinne's life was passionate, honest, and total. Her death is liberatory; her divine spark has returned to its source. Oswald's living, on the other hand, is both incomplete and punitive. He has Lucile and Juliette, who echo Corinne, to remind him of the genius that he destroyed. While a contemporary reader would weep at Corinne's death, she would be unlikely to think that Oswald had been the lucky one.

The contemporary fervor over the novel accentuates this point. *Corinne* was an immediate success both inside France and out. Elizabeth Barrett Browning wrote that "*Corinne* is an immortal book and deserves to be read three score and ten times—that is once every year in the age of man."[198] Contemporary French readers admired both the character and the novel, claiming, for example, that all of Paris was in love with Corinne, just as Oswald had been.[199] Staël's vision of the world offered emotion renewing society, selfishness and patriarchy condemned. The people who wrote to Staël to applaud her novel claimed ownership in her vision, not only because they wanted to acknowledge that they, too, recognized Corinne's exceptional nature, but because in that recognition they shared in Corinne's genius.[200]

The didactic and sentimental literature that surrounded young women offered them an opportunity to critique the existing social order. While the stories took place in exile, supported religious belief, and ended in death—components that have little appeal for either mid-nineteenth-century critics or modern ones—those pieces enabled critique of the world as well as its reenvisioning. The message that young women received—and by all accounts, welcomed—was that they were moral agents in exile who would find true fulfillment not through lives of pleasure or wealth but through chastity and devotion to Christian virtue. Ultimately relationships with men would disappoint, as all that men could offer was selfishness, misunderstanding, or tyranny. Women, who had the supreme capacity of love, would be able to regenerate the world and thereby triumph over it, a claim that shared significant characteristics with religious formation and, as the next chapter demonstrates, mass visual culture.

Fig. 1. (*left*) Thérèse of Lisieux (Bousse-Lebel, 1910). Courtesy of BnF, photo by Jennifer Popiel.

Fig. 2. (*below*) "I accept your offering. May your heart always remain in this blessed state" (Bouasse-Lebel, 1856). Courtesy of BnF, photo by Jennifer Popiel.

S. ANGE RAPHAËL & LE JEUNE TOBIE

Fig. 3. (*left*) "The Angel Raphael and the Young Tobias" (Bouasse-Lebel, 1855). Courtesy of BnF, photo by Jennifer Popiel.

Fig. 4. (*below*) "Henrici would have been killed if his daughter had not blocked the saber stroke leveled at him by an infidel." Frontispiece from vol. 1 of Carron's *New Christian Heroines* (1817). Courtesy of BnF, photo by BnF.

Fig. 5. Adolescence of Paul and Virginia (Pellerin, ca. 1810).
Courtesy of BNF, photo by Jennifer Popiel.

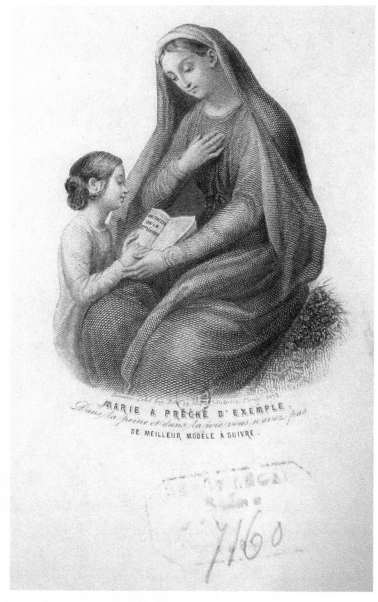

Fig. 6. "Mary Preached by Example. In sorrow and in joy, you have no better model to follow" (Bouasse-Lebel, 1886). Courtesy of BnF, photo by Jennifer Popiel.

Oh comme la souffrance
rapproche et unit....

Fig. 7. "Oh! How suffering brings us together and unites us" (Letaille, 1846). Courtesy of BNF, photo by Jennifer Popiel.

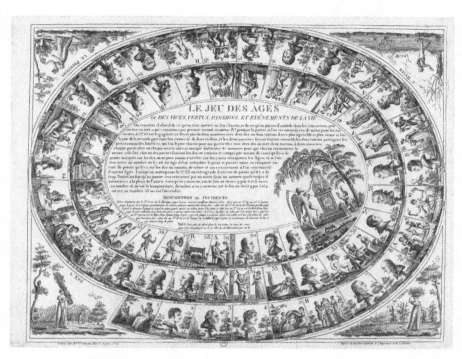

Fig. 8. The *Game of Life Stages* (1810). Courtesy of BnF, photo by BnF.

Fig. 9. Details: boxes 1, 6, 12, and 19 (Infidelity, Marriage, Divorce, and Love). Courtesy of BnF, photo by BnF.

Bouasse-Lebel, Paris.

Ste PHILOMÈNE.

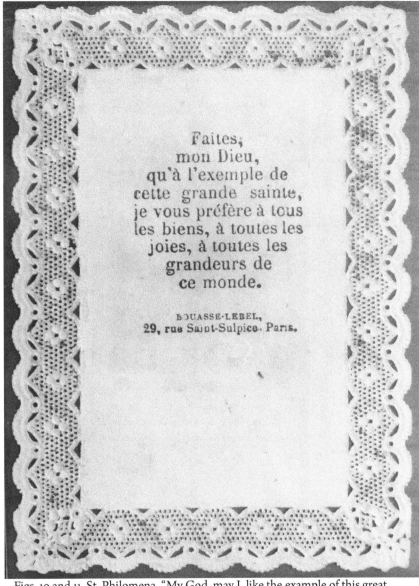

Faites,
mon Dieu,
qu'à l'exemple de
cette grande sainte,
je vous préfère à tous
les biens, à toutes les
joies, à toutes les
grandeurs de
ce monde.

BOUASSE-LEBEL,
29, rue Saint-Sulpice. Paris.

Figs. 10 and 11. St. Philomena. "My God, may I, like the example of this great saint, prefer you to all the goods, all the joys, all the greatness of this world" (Bouasse-Lebel, ca. 1845). Courtesy of Jean-Pierre and Jacqueline Doussin, photo by Jennifer Popiel.

Fig. 12. St. Philomena, Patroness of Persevering Souls. "To taste the joys of heaven, voluntarily sacrifice the joys of the earth" (Letaille, 1852). Courtesy of BNF, photo by Jennifer Popiel.

Fig. 13. "When the Holy Chalice sets my heart free, I no longer wish for the joys of the earth" (Bouasse-Lebel, 1854). Courtesy of BnF, photo by Jennifer Popiel.

Fig. 14. "In the Heart of Jesus, serene and solitary, I lose myself!" (Letaille, 1842). Courtesy of BnF, photo by Jennifer Popiel.

Là, recueillie et solitaire, dans
le sein de Jésus je me perds!...

Fig. 15. "Heart to Heart with Jesus. Charity is not a sterile word; it's a holy zeal to do good." (Bouasse-Lebel, 1862). Courtesy of Jean-Pierre and Jacqueline Doussin, photo by Jennifer Popiel.

Fig. 16. "I was lost in the sea of this world, but Jesus touched my heart and I saw the light" (Letaille, 1842). Courtesy of BnF, photo by Jennifer Popiel.

Fig. 17. Morning Star / Most chaste Mother (Bouasse-Lebel, ca. 1860). Courtesy of BnF, photo by Jennifer Popiel.

Fig. 18. What God Wants (Bouasse-Lebel, 1849). Courtesy of BNF, photo by Jennifer Popiel.

Figs. 19 and 20. "When will I see Heaven, my well beloved fatherland?" (Bouasse-Lebel, 1862). Courtesy of Jean-Pierre and Jacqueline Doussin, photo by Jennifer Popiel.

Fig. 21. "Entry Ticket for Heaven, earned in the Divine School of Patience" (Letaille, ca. 1840). Courtesy of Archives Nationales (France), 2019 F/19/5434, photo by Jennifer Popiel.

Fig. 22. "Love one another as I have loved you. Propagation of the Faith. This is the Heart that loved you so much" (Letaille, before 1848). Courtesy of BnF, photo by Jennifer Popiel.

< 3 >

Seeing the Path to Heaven

Sentimental Virtue and Visual Culture

MY HEART IS READY! Blessed is he whose heart submissively yields to
trials and tribulations; *he is becoming like his master!* Oh! If Christ cruci-
fied entered our hearts, we would soon know all that it is important for
us to know! Because Jesus has many who love his kingdom, but few who
love his cross, *and yet salvation is in the cross.*

—Bouasse-Lebel Holy Card (1868)

Sentimental themes emphasizing women's authority did not disappear or
even diminish in force after 1830. Rather, access to visual resources of all
kinds expanded, and consumers became surrounded by images for play
and recreation in addition to religious pictures.[1] Visual culture affirmed
women's placement into communities of belief and treated domesticity
with suspicion. Even as images of all sorts became more firmly knit into
the fabric of French lives, resistance to marriage and valorization of the
role of the heart continued to be central to the prevailing cultural discourses of French lives. Furthermore, in their evocation of sentimental
models, engravings and pictures made use of and promulgated a language
of emotional authority. Indeed, a closer look at the culture of nineteenth-
century images indicates that mass-produced works, whether secular
or religious, encouraged women to trust themselves and to act independently. The proliferation of these images, as well as their underlying
messages, further complicate any narrative that understands religious
sentiment as private, removed from a mainstream "secular" culture, or
lacking in authority.

For example, an 1848 image offered by the Parisian company Bouasse-Lebel, one of the most popular nineteenth-century producers of Catholic iconography, depicted a mother and daughter embracing in their home as Jesus hovered behind them. The touching scene was captioned: "You owe to [Jesus] the joy that floods your hearts; let recognition [of that fact] inspire your love."[2] At first glance, the tableau seems both domestic and loving, reinforcing the sense that religious belief, emotional outpourings, and exclusion from public life might go hand in hand. However, a closer look complicates this interpretation. The mother holds four laurel wreaths and a stack of books, signs of the daughter's accomplishments at school. While the daughter has returned home, her prizes—and the return to her mother's arms—are not entirely a product of a nurturing mother, but of someone else's investment in the daughter's formation. Additionally, in the context of the mass production of pious images, a domestic setting and motherhood were aberrational; only a tiny fraction of this work dealt overtly with either domesticity or maternity. In fact, holy cards that were set in a home usually depicted a child praying in front of a personal altar, with no other people around, and images of maternity held up the Virgin Mary as an ideal mother, standing in for all mothers (figure 6).[3] Religious images did not emphasize home or marriage; instead, like other sentimental constructs, they emphasized exile, suffering, and the central place of the heart (figure 7).

Further, the mass-produced religious picture was not merely an illustration of socially prominent values; it was itself an object of marketing and ideology, as were the books that girls read. Images surrounded consumers in the early nineteenth century due to an eruption in the number and types of prints available for purchase, leading no less a figure than Baudelaire to call the cult of images the most important development of his era.[4] Developments in lithography, woodblock printing, and machine and paper technology had fueled an explosion in mass communication, one in which French publishers quickly took the lead from other nations, producing an astonishing more than 90 percent of the globe's printed religious imagery between 1840 and 1870.[5] In the technological changes of the nineteenth century, this proliferation of prints meant that individuals could exercise more choice over which images to purchase, to exchange, or to promote. Illustrations can be read together, not just as portraits to depict a moment, but also as sources, chosen by purchasers, that indicate the preoccupations and goals of an era.[6]

Despite the significance of these images and their important commercial function in France, scholars sometimes ignore or even deride nineteenth-century prints—now cheap, mass-produced, and transient—as kitsch or drivel.[7] This is especially true when the intended audience was relatively unimportant or powerless: semiliterate, impoverished, rural, female. Additionally religious images are frequently read with an assumption that they were produced in a context in which domesticity and political reaction loomed large, whether or not those frameworks drove consumers. Nineteenth-century expectations about the value of mass-produced images, as well as more recent assumptions about the relationship between religion, irrationality, and modernity, therefore often discourage historians from understanding the environment in which children received pictures.[8]

This chapter seeks to address those lacunae by inquiring more deeply into the context in which images were produced and experienced. In particular, revisiting the relationships between girls' authority, print culture, and religion reveals that images were embedded in the lives of the young French women who read the books of the preceding chapters as well as girls who came after them. It demonstrates the widespread significance of the sentimental tropes upon which the images relied as well as the fact that commercially successful religious images offered female believers a model for demanding emotional and spiritual authority over their own lives. Investigating the images and texts produced during the nineteenth-century revolution in printing offers entry into the *mentalité* of an age past, one in which religious belief and women's authority were not necessarily experienced as opposing forces. Both played important roles in nineteenth-century lives. This fact was especially true as the proliferation of illustrated print culture created a newly feminine sense of the sentimental and religious. Illustrations and engravings reaffirmed religious values and emphasized women's importance in both religious and nonreligious functions.

Both secular and religious mass-produced images developed out of a longer trajectory; the history of prints in France began well before the first half of the nineteenth century. The earliest prints and engravings, from the fourteenth century, were devotional in inspiration and nature.[9] During the Counter-Reformation, priests and religious were inspired by the possibilities inherent in pious images and promoted their use for general religious instruction. For example, while the expansion of printing technology after Gutenberg made it easy for Lutherans to produce illustrated pamphlets depicting the pope as an anti-Christ, Catholics also used devotional images to reinforce contested points of their own theology, including the communion of saints, Eucharistic veneration, and the special role of Mary.[10] In 1648 Jacques Marchant, pastor of Couvin, insisted on the important role of images in the religious and moral formation of a Christian. If a primary spiritual work of mercy was to instruct the ignorant, then those who offered images were providers of mercy: "Images are the doctors of the ignorant, who cannot read. What others learn in books, the simple ones learn by regarding the images: they read their duty there."[11] More famous pedagogical counterparts to Couvin, Theresa of Avila and Francis de Sales, also recommended the use of images for devotional practice. They believed that images honoring saints would inspire emulation and offer useful direction in meditation.[12]

As early printing technology expanded, religious images could be produced in greater numbers and distributed on a wide scale in formats ranging from small pamphlets with devotional text to variously sized prints that could be tacked up in the home or tucked into a prayer book.[13] The district around the Sorbonne came to be an early center for production of these pictures. This was so true of one particular Paris street, the Rue Saint-Jacques, that people around the world came to call religious prints "Saint-Jacques images."[14] The pictures were especially recognizable given that they were often reused. For example, the exact same image of St. Paul, holding a sword as the symbol of his martyrdom, might appear first in a book, then multiple prints, or a pamphlet. Similarly, a single printed symbol might be used to identify different saints. For instance, a generic set of papal arms, paired with a papal tiara, could be used to symbolize any pope. One image of the cross, lit by divine rays of light, could accompany both Stephen, the first martyr, and Helen, mother of Constantine and finder of the True Cross.[15] The malleability of the images meant that they could invoke various meanings made clear by context.

By the late eighteenth and early nineteenth centuries, more changes in technology meant that images of saints could also be produced in much larger formats for devotional use within the home. For example, the Pellerin images of saints, produced widely after 1800, could be nearly two feet tall.[16] Despite their size, these images and others like them were inexpensive and sold across a large swath of northwestern Europe by itinerant peddlers. Even when they imitated artwork by famous artists, the images were not of high quality, and the paper on which they were printed was rarely sturdy. Nevertheless, these prints had great emotional and spiritual influence within both wealthy and poor homes. For example, no less a figure than Chateaubriand wrote that his nurse's woodcut print of the Virgin Mary "inspired in me more devotion than a Raphael Madonna."[17]

Often, the large religious images were printed in a way that left room for the addition of prayers or other religious texts around the edges, a format that was also used for summaries of popular novels (figure 5).[18] The images were then framed by prayers or other devotional texts, all of which were as important as the picture itself. The words did not simply offer a physical border; they also offered a framework for interpretation or use. Sometimes the instructions were surprisingly direct. For example, in addition to two columns of prayers in a small type, Desfeuilles's 1824 *Bénédiction des maisons* (a crucifixion scene) had a stern injunction in large print at the bottom: "Prostrate yourself before the image of our Savior Jesus Christ."[19] An image of *Jesus Christ Nailed to the Cross* included the phrase "ungrateful sinners, I suffer for you."[20] Alternately, prayers might invoke a known patronal role. For example, Saint Sebastian could be appealed to against plague when cholera threatened. Other prayers might offer the opportunity for a miracle, as in the case of the various miracle-working statues of the Blessed Virgin.[21] Each of these was available in poster form, so that one could make a pilgrimage without leaving home. The interaction of text and image offered viewers a way to incorporate pictures into their own prayer lives.

Some of the most common types of devotional images were small and highly portable.[22] Holy cards are small (4–8 cm wide by 6–12 cm tall) prints made on light cardboard or paper. The front depicted a religious scene of some sort, and the back often contained a prayer or another text on which one could meditate.[23] If the card commemorated a special event—a baptism, an ordination, or a parish mission—there might be information about the event instead of (or in addition to) the religious text. Although they were preserved in missals or prayer books, the cards themselves are ephemeral. They were made in large numbers, but few last to the present day because they were cheaply made and inexpensive to acquire. Their transient nature should not be taken as an indicator of their impact, however; these were profoundly significant images for childhood.[24]

Holy cards appeared in three general categories, grouped by the subject they depicted. First, some holy cards emphasized Jesus Christ himself, perhaps in the form of an infant or a man or simply the presence of the Eucharist (depicted most often as a large round wafer). Christ might also be depicted by the Sacred Heart, a devotion that appeared in the early Church and had a resurgence in the seventeenth and nineteenth centuries.[25] Other cards depicted Jesus's mother, Mary, sometimes with her son, whether as an infant or in the form of a Pietà, but also on her own, representing purity and devotion to the will of God.[26] The final—and perhaps largest—category included depictions of saints, often with iconography chosen from the popular medieval hagiography the *Golden Legend*.

According to the Catholic Church, saints are persons who are presumed to be in heaven by virtue of a praiseworthy life on earth. The saints share in the glory of heaven and offer otherworldly spirituality and devotion to God. However, as Theresa of Avila and Frances de Sales understood, saints also have the benefit of a human (and sinful) earthly life that offered didactic opportunities to the card's beholder. A single saint might have different characteristics that allow for veneration in multiple ways. For example, Margaret Mary Alacoque was celebrated for her promulgation of dedication to the Sacred Heart. Images featuring St. Margaret Mary could thus emphasize her obedience to the revelation of God. Or they might emphasize her in the context of the Sacred Heart devotion, which included discussion about the special place of France in salvation history and the important role of the Sacred Heart of Jesus, itself representing Christ and emblematic in the seventeenth century of characteristics such as courage or fortitude.[27]

The text on the back of a holy card, similar to the framework of a larger print, might offer a citation from Scripture, a famous prayer, or an excerpt from another text with an imprimatur. For example, one common text was Thomas à Kempis's famous devotional work, so often recommended by spiritual directors, the *Imitation of Christ*.[28] These words were "safe" given their long history of use within the Church and the likelihood that they would not be misconstrued. Like the writing on the larger images, the text also served to contextualize and deepen one's understanding of the image; a picture in which the Sacred Heart was central might be accompanied by a novena to the Sacred Heart, while an image of a saint might include a reflection based on the saint's life or a prayer related to an established type of intercession. The cards, despite being less expensive than books and increasing in circulation from the sixteenth century on, were not insignificant.[29] Children and adults carefully preserved them in missals and other books, giving us a sense of cards' cultural value as well as the collectors' spiritual and temporal preoccupations.[30]

Though the images and texts on the cards offer clues about the concerns of the owner, the ideological transmission from them cannot be assumed to be clear and direct. First and foremost, the physical form of the printed image was often changed by those who received it, especially in the case of women. Many of the best-preserved examples of small devotional images from the period before mass production involve a combination of hand work and printed matter, carried out by nuns and women of leisure who decorated and altered images as a form of silent or quiet recreation.[31] In convents this was likely a practice that came from the habit of constant handiwork for nuns, so that Satan would always find them occupied.[32]

One of the most common types of these hand-decorated holy cards is the *canivet*. *Canivet* refers to the penknife, or *canif*, that was used for detail work on the cards.[33] Women took parchment or vellum paper and, by painstakingly making holes in the paper, produced a border that resembled fine Alençon or Venetian lace. The image—often, but not always, printed—would then be inserted within the decorative margins. The artist's contribution, especially in France, was often far more than a frame; the detail, imagery, and symbolism of the paper lace all demonstrated a conscious choice on the part of the artist about what to emphasize or reinforce in the image itself.[34] One might see lilies for purity, thorns and crosses for struggle and sacrifice, roses for virginity or the Passion. While some of the sixteenth- and seventeenth-century examples are relatively austere, by the eighteenth century, artists added color and bouquets of flowers, garlands, and roses, perhaps echoing the feminine study of botany in that era.[35] Additionally, the *canivet* often drew on other iconographic sources and codes, most notably, again, the hagiography of the *Golden Legend*.[36]

While the *canivet* was a recreational activity particularly appropriate to women in convents and other places where time-consuming, detailed art forms such as calligraphy and the art of miniatures also flourished, it was not without larger context at the time, which included a cultural mania for cutting and pasting from prints.[37] In fact, by the early eighteenth century, it had become so fashionable to cut from engravings that a 1727 issue of the *Mercure de France* offered its readers a letter about the obsession with snipping apart books. It claimed that this hobby was "almost the only occupation" of the women of Paris and of the Court, who would cut pieces from engravings, both for decorative accents and in order to make decorations for the chosen picture. The 1727 letter warned of the destruction and damage that this fad was wreaking. The author complained of a young woman who had taken a rare book on natural history from her uncle's library and then proceeded to make cuttings from it.[38]

This brief account of the *canivet* shows women personalizing religious images, not only by what they chose to cut, color, and paint, but also by the ways in which they highlighted virtues and characteristics in their own designs, which often drew on texts that had circulated for hundreds of years. This practice was also echoed in a larger cultural context. Thus, even as one might emphasize the religious contexts of personalization—idle hands are the devil's workshop; saints offer living models of holy behavior—one could equally follow the *Mercure de France* in seeing the decorative aspects as destructive rather than fruitful. Regardless, it is clear that even at the most fundamental physical level, religious images were not passed on without being processed, interpreted, and changed at the hands of the women who cut them.

Physical modifications to the images were only one part of transmission patterns. At first glance, the iconic images of holy cards or devotional images can appear regressive and unsophisticated, with an emphasis on acceptance of one's station and withdrawal from the world.[39] But a broader look at the range of images shows diversity in topics, including different Marian devotions, an emphasis on Jesus, especially the Sacred Heart, and numerous saints. The saints range from early Christian martyrs (including Barbara and Philomena) to Jesuits such as Ignatius Loyola, Aloysius Gonzaga, Stanislaus Kostka, and Francis Régis. Though all of the saints offered models of self-abnegation, notably few of them had withdrawn from the world. Unlike Jesus, who was often depicted only in the form of his Sacred Heart or in the Eucharistic host, all saints have bodies, sometimes with clear evidence of the physical sacrifices that they have endured for Christ.[40] The saints also reinforced the notion that the viewer was confronting a world in which she was incarnate, as were the saints who came before her.[41] The power of this text, then, was not that it offered a static model, but instead that it was "a living story, carried out of the text and into the [reader's] narrative, to be somehow carried on by [her] . . . as a living example, [because] the Saint is a mediator who helps in the imitation of Christ, is a human of flesh like us."[42] The images were not passive. They were designed to encourage both adoption and emulation, something that holy cards themselves reminded viewers of, telling them to "Take the saints for models."[43] Purchasers could choose particular saints to intercede for them as they faced a trial, they could choose models that they wished to appropriate, or they might see the values of their own epoch in a saint sometimes held as a model for an earlier moment. For example, the lionization of early Church martyrs, intended to represent struggle against worldly contamination, simultaneously advanced narratives of political resistance and female independence.

In fact, the saints could not be limited to fixed representations, communicated from the paper to the viewer, because images' significance relied on the fact that they reminded—or even offered—the viewer a piece of a real relationship with persons who had really existed on earth and continued to exist in heaven. In *Soldier and Peasant* David Hopkins reminds us how a "local legend tells of a peasant woman hanging round the imagery stall in Epinal market in order, she told the stall-holder, 'to see Saint Peter in order that he might know me when I arrive up above.'"[44] Anecdotes like this make it clear that in popular religious practice, images involved dialogue between officially sanctioned forms of holiness and one's own life of devotion.

Additionally, the texts that accompanied images also reminded the viewer of the narrative context in which each saint's story was told.[45] For example, Peter did not have to be depicted at the gates of heaven for a viewer to see him as the possessor of keys to heaven. Hagiographies—both visual and textual—provided the doctrine of the Church in the guise not only of "model of Christ [and] evangelical example" but also "a legendary hero or a romantic figure."[46] Once the model was provided, it could be adopted for whichever reasons struck a particular viewer's imagination. The saints thus offered not passive acceptance of a defined past or a current moral lesson, but engagement with a future of possibility.

Because the words presented in the context of the images were often both formal and historic, the text also linked the card's holder with a larger community of believers. Sometimes this link was explicit, as when the prayer was associated with induction into a confraternity or presented as a memoir of a public and communal event. Other times it was implicit: a reminder of the guidance of the Church as an institution, an indulgence that one would receive for a prayer, or an opportunity to reflect on the life of a holy person who had gone before. Each card thus served as a reminder not merely of one's individual devotional responsibility but also of how engaging the sacred meant being part of a community of believers. While one might be tempted to see increased devotion and the circulation of small prayer cards as confirming a dogmatic, sequestered, and insular faith—just another example of religion being moved from public spaces to the private spaces of the home—a closer look at the cards reveals something different. Instead of a limited and private faith, holy cards encouraged identification with an independent piety that was set in a context of both individual and communal authority.

The most significant problem, then, is not to determine what the printer or designer wanted to communicate, but to understand what the hagiographic models meant in the life of the viewer. While images themselves might have contributed to the veneration of particular saints or to the maintenance of certain beliefs, the subjects, styles, and visual preferences of the images offer us a glimpse into the moments in which young women were shaped and themselves made choices about their futures.[47]

The meaning of the prints is especially complicated in the nineteenth century, as commercial, technological, and cultural changes expanded the reach of devotional books, images, and objects to persons who might not have been targets before.[48] This was true even as women's busy hands were no longer as likely to adorn religious works. While more females than ever were choosing religious life, they tended to choose active orders (such as the Religious of the Sacred Heart) over contemplative orders (such as the Carmelites). As a result, acts of pious recreation in cloistered convents declined.[49] Despite that, after the Restoration of Bourbons to the throne, industry responded to a growing demand for devotional objects to replace those destroyed or left to decay during the French Revolution.[50] Mechanization increased the ease with which holy cards and religious images could be printed and soon included the printing of cards with elaborate imagery and intricate lacelike edging. This mechanization, combined with a more active approach to spirituality, all but put an end to the creation of *canivets*.[51] While "penknifings" continued to be made until the early nineteenth century, mechanization supplanted handcrafting of personal devotional images. *Canivets* were almost entirely supplanted by *dentelle mécaniques* after 1840; additionally both production and sales of devotional images generally moved from Rue Saint-Jacques to Rue Saint-Sulpice after 1832.[52] France quickly took the lion's share of this market, 92.7 percent of the globe's religious imagery between 1840 and 1870.[53]

While individual ornamentation in the style of the *canivet* decreased, consumers still had the opportunity to purchase elaborate machine-produced cards. Those who presented the holy card to someone else as a token of affection, a memento, or a devotional aid often chose to add text of their own, with dedications or messages on the back, alongside the accompanying text.[54] This pattern of personalization indicates that the message of individual images was still not received in a fixed form from the printer, straight to the viewer, who internalized what the designer of the card intended, and then preserved the card as a symbol of that transmission. Nor, as previously indicated, did the small size and the nature of the keepsake necessarily reinforce a perception that religious experience was private rather than communal.

The first third of the nineteenth century not only saw fewer hand-crafted religious images and more printed ones, but it also witnessed increased public exposure to images of all sorts as prices dropped and use exploded. Just as Baudelaire had indicated, the way that Europeans viewed the world changed as access to visual resources of all kinds expanded.[55] Increasingly, religious and historical topics—once the primary type of peddler's images—were found alongside political commentary or tales of fire, flood, or murder. In fact, Théodore Géricault, an artist who is best known for his painting *The Raft of the Medusa* (1818–1819), found designing for popular—secular—lithographic work to be more lucrative than academic painting. In 1821 Géricault wrote a letter justifying his abandonment of religious topics, saying, "I send to the devil all those Sacred Hearts of Jesus; it's a fool's game to die of hunger. I'm abandoning the tragedienne's stage and the Holy Scriptures to shut myself up in the stables, from which I'll emerge covered with gold."[56] While Géricault noted the traditional importance of religious topics in lithography, he believed that offering nonreligious engravings, suited to the tastes of the moment, would be the surest path to financial success.[57] Though he was writing from London, his experience was echoed even in the collections of prints designed for rural Continental audiences. For example, the designs coming out of Pellerin's press, in Epinal, hawked across France and Germany by peddlers, moved away from a primarily devotional and religious model to include substantial secular material (figure 5).[58] As Hopkin notes, "The memoirs of a whole parade of nineteenth-century French writers and artists from Lamartine to Romain Rolland, whose patriotic, religious, or aesthetic senses were awakened by images, testify to the power of these cheap prints."[59] Even in more expensive engravings, such as those by Dopter or Turgis, both religious and secular material was widely available, covered similar ground, and was increasingly influential in cultural formation.

The shift toward more widespread marketing of nonreligious content, which hastened after 1830, took place even as changes to wood engraving allowed both texts and images to be combined on the same page. Additionally about this same time mechanized steam-driven presses were first imported into France. Printing production went from roughly 150 sheets each hour to a thousand sheets per hour or more. While some printers celebrated this achievement, both for the success of their bottom line and for the potential education of the masses, others worried that the multiplication of images was unseemly. As L'Artiste noted in 1834, lithography had become increasingly popular. "It has lent that assistance and facility of its crayon to everything. Lithography has popularized itself to such an extent by prostituting itself in this way that it has ended by being disparaged and by provoking the scorn and disdain of serious artists who want to preserve the dignity of art."[60] Such fears about the debasement of art arose from the reach of printing as well as a shift in the themes of printed imagery. Not only could an inexpensive weekly production like Le Magasin Pittoresque reach fifty thousand readers with its images, but it also used an almanac-like style to engage questions of popular interest such as technology, exploration, and the natural world. In particular, children could now choose images that were designed with them in mind. Some, though certainly not all, were religious in nature. However, many of the largest printmakers invested in unsectarian works for children. Most of these prints were didactic with respect to education and morality.[61] In this context, artists understandably worried that the popularization of art meant that serious topics were being ignored.

The fear of "debasement" also speaks to the increasing reach and impact of images. For example, the increase in production by presses like Epinal and a decrease in consumer prices due to industrial advances meant an explosion in the number of inexpensive paper games. One type of game, the *Game of the Goose*, had a particularly long history, as it had been produced for nearly as long as religious images. The *Game of the Goose* was seen as a good influence despite the fact that it used two dice—a problematic component, having intimations of unseemly gambling—to determine players' moves.[62] This game was often portrayed as supporting religion and orthodoxy in addition to offering solid moral guidance, including its representation in one of Chardin's sentimental works, painted in 1745.[63] Given that Chardin is typically considered the "painter par excellence of the bourgeoisie in France," and that his art was often seen as prescriptive for the middle class, we can see the *Game of the Goose* as indicative of popular amusements in circles with leisure and money.[64]

The increasing volume and diversity of games offered a new opportunity for educators. Games moved away from classical mythological and historical themes toward topics that could be influenced by contemporary figures and pressing issues of the day, such as political events— the French Revolution—or the ideal relationship between love and marriage. Given the "varying degrees of economic advantage . . . [and] uneven educational levels" of the era, images and games now helped indoctrinate the "growing ranks of the semiliterate—poorly educated, but newly affluent subjects produced by the incipient rise of industrial capitalism."[65] These games served a didactic purpose for all of society, though children in families of leisure were the first and most obvious market. Many versions of the *Game of the Goose* continued to be popular, and paper lotteries joined them.

In the *Game of the Goose* players find that their path to the finish is sometimes circuitous, as they encounter both snares and rewards. While not every game conforms to the typical structure, there is a standard organization, composed of 63 boxes (figure 8). Within this structure certain boxes provided known pitfalls while others offered advancement. For example, box 6 gave an opportunity to double one's first turn(s), as landing on box 6 automatically sent the player to box 12. Advancement looked like a blessing, but landing on box 12 sometimes sent a player back to the beginning of the game or required the payment of a fee, sending a message that decisions made in haste were soon regretted. Box 19 was the "Hotel" or place of rest. Though the name sounded encouraging, players knew better; landing on 19 meant missing two turns. Box 58 was the most obvious problem for players. A child who was almost to the end of the game and then landed on box 58 would learn that almost being to the end could be dangerous. Box 58 contained the symbol of death or destruction and sent the player back to the starting gate.[66]

Games with a political message used these individual punishments to make moral and political lessons explicit. For example, a revolutionary game used box 19 to depict the café as a possible site of counter-Revolutionary activism and the box of death to offer a warning about destruction coming to enemies of the Revolution.[67] During the Third Republic the box of death brought a vision of Napoleon, which was enough to make the player recoil in terror . . . all the way back to the start of the game![68] Many games were entirely unsectarian. In the *Instructive Game of Flowers*, death was represented by a flowering belladonna plant, designed to bring paralysis or death to those who ingested it, though the game's actual end, sometimes referred to as Paradise, was represented by a lily.[69] The boxes that trapped or delayed players on their way to "Paradise" sent negative messages that players could internalize.

The moral and pedagogical context was certainly not accidental or lost on adults. For example, in 1865 Claude Bataillard gave a speech to the Imperial Academy of Sciences, Arts, and Literature in Caen, entitled, "The Goose Rehabilitated." In it, he made the point that box 19, representing the moral danger of the world, provided an important lesson for all citizens. He explained that this box in particular would serve as a notice to those who might otherwise have been tempted to waste their paychecks outside the home. "How many people make a habit of wasting their money and their time, especially in the evening, in opposition to the domestic comforts that await them at home?! And why? Because they did not, in childhood, appropriately internalize the profound moral sense of Number 19!"[70] The didacticism of children's games was obvious; the games offered concrete explanations of social behavior that were intended to help children adopt norms.

In the nineteenth century specialized children's games often emphasized marriage or family life. Board games offered young girls ways to internalize the rules of the world around them, whether it was in games designed for convent education, those that helped children memorize particular Scripture passages, or those that focused on lessons about the pitfalls of seduction. Thematic versions offered players biblical and spiritual emphasis, including the Stations of the Cross and recreation for young women living in convents, as well as games that emphasized manners, virtue, and love and marriage.[71]

So what types of relationship lessons did children see in boxes 19 and 58 of the *Game of the Goose*? If box 19 was a worldly trap that led away from the path to heaven—or at least the path to contentment on the earth—what was so beguiling and dangerous? We would, I expect, not be surprised if games intended for young women being educated in convents would warn of the entrapments of the world. Certainly two versions of *Spiritual Recreation*, intended for use in convents, led from an initial "Contempt of the World" to the final box, which was "Entry Into the Room of the Celestial Spouse." Along the way, players met various temptations, including giving in to vanity, neglecting one's obligations, and complaining about one's trials. Detachment from parents was the only mention of family life. The game instead emphasized the virtues and vices that would have been most important to a vocation in the religious life such as acceptance of one's state in life, remembering one's responsibilities, spiritual happiness, and diligence.

However, many of the explicitly religious games chose not to critique lukewarm devotion and instead emphasized doctrine and proper behavior. For example, the Ursulines had their own version of the *Game of the Goose,* but its pitfalls were marked only by boxes with wreaths.[72] All images and phrases were used to reinforce proper behavior, almost as if the mention of negative examples might encourage—rather than discourage—their emulation. In its place the girls were reminded to behave like the wise virgins and to strive to internalize holy ideals. A *Way of the Cross, or Spiritual Recreation* from 1830 told players who landed on box 19 that they found themselves in the Temple, subject to the loss of the next two turns.[73] Like Jesus, as a child visiting the Temple without his parents, they rested and did not continue on the path with their companions. Box 58 was less subtle: the large skull and crossbones clearly indicated death and sent the player back to the beginning, without other comment. These games emphasized Bible stories and moral virtues without using the punishments to make a larger moral point.

Overtly religious games, then, did not engage questions of marriage or family life in any significant way. What about players and games in other contexts? As the *Amusing and Instructional Game of Love* from 1809 noted, players would pass "fatal encounters in Love, before reaching the glory of the final box," including, in box 19, the quest for love as emblematized in the Voyage to Cythera.[74] This allegory to the island retreat of love was not, in this early nineteenth-century game, a positive sanctuary like that of Watteau's eighteenth-century painting, but a trap, where the player lost valuable time while others proceeded to the real goal, which was the Glory of the Arts and Sciences. This was certainly a more productive—if not markedly less abstract—goal than love until death (box 58) or hyperbolic idealized union (box 19). Emotional attachment and affection were distractions, not positive goals.

The *Game of Life Stages,* published in 1810, had a deeply negative perspective on love and marriage (figure 8).[75] This game portrayed an individual's movement through life and encounters with vice, virtue, and passion. While the Napoleonic Code of 1804 had substantially limited the scope of Revolutionary divorce laws, the game still demonstrates the unsettling impact of contemporary questions surrounding marriage and divorce. Players began on a square labeled "infidelity," which depicted an oblivious young woman reading a book while two lovers embraced in the background (figure 9, upper left). After this beginning, players would progress through infancy and a childhood of toys. Adult setbacks included "Bankruptcy" or the "Death of a Spouse" and "Lost Fortune," with the latter showing a man with a small child, perhaps hinting at the decrease in fortunes that might accompany fatherhood. Passionate moments were marked by ambivalence or negativity, as with the first box. Box 19, which represented a trap, was simply labeled "Love" (figure 9, lower right). Perhaps most telling of all, the "advance" from box 6 to box 12 was a direct path from "Marriage" to "Divorce" (figure 9, upper right and lower left). This hardly offered players a friendly and reassuring look at a life of companionate marriage.

Even games primarily intended to teach manners, such as the *Familiar Game of Civility*, found love to be secondary to more important matters. While many squares were devoted to advice such as "Don't stand with your arms akimbo" and "It is rude to cross your legs while seated," the ultimate treasures were the wisdom of God, a good education, and honesty in friendship.[76] One exception might be noted in the *Game of Fortune*, from 1819, which included some images of maternity and morals with discussion of family life, such as the reminder that "A good household is a reward for virtue."[77] However, the reliability of even that message was mitigated by the numerous other squares in the same game that offered visions of unfaithful lovers, love lost, and virtue standing against masculine importuning and threats.

Another common form of printed game, paper lotteries, pointed children in the same direction. In a lottery, children put money into a kitty and then drew individual squares out of a box. The illustrated papers were worth different amounts, ranging from winning or losing the entire kitty to greater or lesser values in between. For example, in the *Little Lottery of Strengths and Weaknesses*, from 1869, drawing "prayer" would win the player everything.[78] Charity was also highly positive, claiming 80 points. Dedication and self-sacrifice would win 40 points, and "humanity" and "love of nation" each commanded 10 points. On the side of faults to avoid, idleness would lose 80 points, while its counterpart, indolence, would lose 40 points. Keeping bad company and pessimism were each accompanied by losses of 10 points. In this lottery and others like it, the miniature scenes did not come from family life. While young girls could be found alongside other women ("gossip loses 2"), positive qualities that could have been depicted in the context of marriage or household were portrayed outside of domestic scenes. For example, "religious education (+8)," "respect (+5)," and "douceur (+6)" were depicted with a priest, a teacher, and a dog.[79]

The *Little Lottery* showed fewer ideas and more concrete examples, but the outcome was similar.[80] "Toilette" lost 3 points. Perhaps even more tellingly, a "serenade" and a profession of love were both worth nothing, as was an argument between women. However, St. Veronica won 3 points and the Greek philosopher and historian Xenophon won 8 points. In this game, drawing Napoleon allowed you to take the kitty, though royalist lotteries offered positive outcomes for drawing kings and ladies-in-waiting. The *Little Ladies Lottery* offered players rewards for drawing the Holy Virgin, Joan of Arc, baptism, communion, or the prize for wisdom at school.[81] Dancing and picnicking with a man all lost the player points.

The clearest lesson to be drawn from this disparate group of images (ranging from a carp or pansy to St. Thérèse, a gorilla, a turkey, or a Zouave) was that work was rewarded and saintly behavior was ever present. Neither politics nor relationships between men and women were stable markers. Marriage was not, even as late as 1870, emphasized or prioritized. Love did not lead directly to marriage, which was itself neither encouraged nor rewarded. Both love and marriage were the source of traps, a temptation rather than a path to success. Lesley Walker has argued that eighteenth-century fiction had an astounding "lack of confidence in the sustainability and hence desirability of the heterosexual love match as such."[82] Children's games reveal similar—and similarly surprising—moral lessons and values. These games also indicate that skepticism about both marriage and romantic love extended into the second half of the nineteenth century. Marriage might have loomed large in a girl's life, but it rarely came with honor or rewards, nor did it lead directly to virtuous behavior. While we can certainly note that the literature and philosophy of the nineteenth century had begun to valorize maternity, that valorization did not accompany an emphasis on domestic bliss. Fidelity and other virtues could be found, but they were more easily accomplished with a heavenly spouse than an earthly one.

Even as children saw more and more games and pictures targeted to them and peddler's packs included depictions of Napoleon alongside Saint Barbara, religious imagery retained great appeal and marketability, as well as frequently using similar forms. For example, yearly Catholic calendars were visually similar to both lotteries and board games; they relied on individual iconography, set into small boxes, to reinforce lessons about the world.[83] Perhaps Géricault was right to say that there was more money for him in a new and clever satire than in a reworking of the Sacred Heart, but that did not mean that the Sacred Heart or saints' lives stopped selling, especially as engravers placed them in newly appealing styles. Nor, equally importantly, did that indicate that the intellectual foundation of children's worlds abandoned religious forms.

In fact, Sacred Hearts of Jesus and their counterparts were produced in vast numbers. Ever more religious works were available for sale, and the new technique of lithography was adapted to the production of holy cards.[84] Pious objects in particular—holy cards, statues, crucifixes—were sold in such large numbers that by 1847, the *Almanach du commerce de Paris* began to list "seller of religious objects" as a profession. The 1847 *Almanach* listed only six merchants under this designation; by 1868, there were 141.[85] This division into a seller of religious images, as opposed to a seller of images of any kind, certainly implies that marketing religious objects on their own had its own commercial importance. Though the market for images was expanding and now included secular material, religious consumerism flourished at a scale that was orders of magnitude larger than it had been only a decade or two prior. There was plenty of room in the popular market, and nonreligious material complemented rather than replaced the rapidly growing market for religious material.[86] Thus, even as more secular material and themes were offered in printmaking, religion sold extremely well and exercised a powerful ideological pull.[87]

One manifestation of the primacy of religious imagery is the fact that religious images often served as the physical and philosophical models for secular imagery.[88] While readers and viewers found more ornamentation in their books and their lives, the images that were included in secular works were often those that came from religious works in the first place. For instance, images of the pansy were first used in religious works, where they were a reminder of death and judgment (*pensez-y-bien*), but the same vignettes also appeared in lotteries, ABC primers, and games.[89] Other primers, such as the *Nouvel alphabet de la vie des saints*, used the exact same illustrations as those in readers with a secular theme.[90] The shifts involved in a transition from the *canivet* to mechanically produced holy cards, colored woodcuts, and lithographic caricatures are not, therefore, likely to be in a world where the mental architecture of the past had been destroyed. Instead the world was unsectarian, with new imagery sitting on a foundation of religious texts and images that was already familiar to young readers.[91]

A reader who encountered common images in works that we identify as secular might imagine that all stories could be possible vehicles for the sacred, or at least that both secular and sacred images were part of the same cultural landscape. There is no reason to assume that viewers abandoned religion for the secular or even saw them as opposed; both kinds of images existed together. Pictures were malleable. Just as the cross could indicate either St. Stephen or St. Helen, so could a pansy, appearing on a game or a holy card, be religious or not, and viewers kept both meanings in their head.

In fact, in the post-Revolutionary moment, the multiplication of images also seemed useful for increasing the influence of Catholicism in society. "After the political upheavals, religion appeared as a sort of antidote to revolutionary abuses, and in daily life it manifested itself through the opportunities for personal meditation provided on the backs of holy cards."[92] Thus, even as secular images increased, so did a market for religious images. Some of these purchases were driven by priests, religious, and teachers, who bought holy cards to promote a particular cause or distributed cards as an incentive for work, a sort of "gold star."[93] Even archbishops sometimes passed out holy cards. For example, the biography of the archbishop of Malines notes that he would say his daily prayers in public, walking up and down the streets with his breviary, so that he might give out holy cards to children, who, upon seeing him, would run and ask him for the images they knew he carried.[94] The inexpensive images could be easily presented and exchanged, not only from a cleric to a child, but as small gifts from one believer to another.[95]

Of course, as the nineteenth century progressed, religious images and the texts that accompanied them were one significant part of consumer culture rather than a primary source of visual representation. While priests might offer a holy card as a sign of a job well done, so too might teachers give "bons points," or small nonreligious pictures that praised an excellent performance in school.[96] Small images, holy or not, circulated in a culture increasingly inundated with pictures of all kinds. Children's books had more and more images alongside the text, and prints also served to provide commentary on political, social, and cultural relationships.[97] Like political prints, religious images abounded, but viewers could see them as one more representation of the world that they knew.

The evolution of visual style and textual choices increasingly expressed the practical appeal of images that were commercially successful. This point is especially important with didactic and religious texts. Although one might be tempted to emphasize only the inflexibility and dogmatism of a religious text, images had to operate within the framework in which readers and viewers operated.[98] By the mid-nineteenth century, individuals could exercise more choice over which holy cards to purchase, to exchange, or to promote, which meant they could increasingly demonstrate their own values and priorities. Saints whose lives had an appealing character, texts that spoke to contemporary concerns, or styles that reinforced a vision of the world as consumers desired it to be—these were the foundation of the images that were purchased, produced, and reproduced. Especially in the world of mass production, the image of devotion was not merely Christian propaganda, an object that attempted to construct belief. Rather, the commercial success of particular ideas and styles sheds light on the power of specific images in the already-existing world of a believer.[99]

The meteoric fame of Saint Philomena is particularly useful for understanding the intersection of commercial popularity and viewers' frameworks because Philomena's cult was entirely a product of the nineteenth century, a moment when questions about religious authority and female independence were both visible and contested. Philomena's bones were discovered in 1802, and the growth of her appeal in France coincided with the first expansion of printing technology. Philomena had much in common with other popular saints. She was a martyr, and her claims to physical autonomy rested on her virginity.[100] However, the image of Philomena is particularly striking because her fame relied on a sense that contemporary politics—and perhaps even Catholic parents—did not understand the hearts of individual believers, and that a female saint could provide a model of autonomy and resistance for the sake of Christ.

The discovery of Philomena was not, by itself, particularly noteworthy. Numerous bones of martyrs had been discovered in tombs and distributed throughout Europe (and beyond).[101] In this case bones were discovered while workers were digging in the catacomb of Priscilla, outside of Rome. Accompanying the bones were a vial of blood—then taken to be a sign of martyrdom—and three tiles that, when rearranged, read, in Latin, "Peace be unto you, Philomena." The tiles also displayed emblems of a palm (another confirmation of martyrdom), a lily (an indication of virginity), an anchor, and arrows. The relics were eventually transported to Mugnano, a small town in Italy near Naples. Miraculous events seemed to accompany the bones, including much-longed-for rain and personal healings. The town constructed a shrine to Philomena, and the shrine became a site for more reported miracles. Villagers told stories, devotees saw visions that filled in details of a hagiographic narrative, and books, images, and pamphlets spread the story of Philomena's martyrdom.[102] However, Philomena's greatest popularity, including formal approval by the church's institutional hierarchy and mass production of images, came after 1834, when Pauline Jaricot, a prominent French Catholic suffering from life-threatening heart disease, experienced an inexplicable—believers called it miraculous—healing at the shrine.[103]

Soon images of Philomena were produced throughout France. Those offered for sale by Turgis in the 1830s depicted scenes from Philomena's life: *Saint Philomena Receiving the Palm of Martyrs, Saint Philomena Thrown into the Tiber,* or the *Miracle of Saint Philomena.*[104] Less expensively, one could purchase a holy card with the anchor, arrows, and palm all reminding the viewer of the story of her martyrdom, which had been fleshed out by three different visionaries. According to them, Philomena was a Greek princess whose family went to Rome. There the parents and child encountered the emperor Diocletian, who, struck by the young girl's beauty, wanted to marry her. Philomena's father immediately accepted the offer, which would have given him political security and honor. Philomena, on the other hand, refused to submit to the marriage. Her parents pleaded and threatened to no avail; she remained unyielding. The emperor attempted to kill her by scourging, drowning her by tying her to an anchor, and shooting her with arrows. When all those failed, he finally cut off her head; she died at the age of thirteen.

Once Pope Gregory XVI approved veneration of Philomena, she was included on the list of saints as a Christian virgin and martyr. The narratives indicated that as a young woman—a girl—she had dedicated herself to Christ and refused to be swayed in the face of enticements and threats. Caroline Ford claims that the "enthusiasm [for Philomena] had a great deal to do with the growing popularity of the female religious vocation" and suggests that resisting sexual defilement was a primary motivation.[105] Certainly sexual renunciation and chastity were central to the models of ideal feminine Christian behavior promoted by the Church and therefore, correspondingly, to martyrdom.[106] The significance and appeal of Philomena's defense of virginity and bodily integrity were important parts of the story of her martyrdom. In this, however, she hardly would have been different from Agnes, Cecilia, Barbara, or a host of other early Christian virgin martyrs, many of whom also embraced a language of sexual resistance and renunciation even as they faced execution.[107] However, Philomena's cult quickly supplanted veneration of other—formerly popular—saints, many of whom shared her status as a virgin and martyr. Images of Philomena became widely available for purchase. Some of these prints were high-quality (and higher-cost) engravings, though there were also inexpensive holy cards or small prints that used emblems such as the palm, lily, or arrow to remind the viewer of Philomena's martyrdom. The pictures were not only produced by Parisian engravers such as Basset, Turgis, or Charles Letaille but also were offered as large-format prints sold by peddlers, such as those from Epinal and Montbéliard.[108] There was a spectacular consumer demand for visual reminders of Philomena's sanctity. It is this consumer demand that should be understood, both in its links to the popularity of women's religious vocations and to her appeal writ large.

Unlike earlier virgin martyrs, all of whom had a long iconographic history, most going back to the medieval *Golden Legend*, Philomena was new to the canon of saints and therefore was depicted with new imagery. In this case her consumer success, the conscious choice of Philomena and not an already well-established virgin martyr, another similar saint, demonstrates that something about this icon was particularly meaningful for purchasers and therefore encouraged printmakers to respond to the demand for Philomena's image. While one might assume that novelty alone could help carve out a niche in a market, tradition was an important signifier for Catholics, especially in the post-Revolutionary era. Additionally, repetition in naming and saint choice also played an important role in family heritage and namesakes. In this context one might look back not only to the *Golden Legend* but also to an Aunt Cécile, or a Grandmother Agnès, if one's primary goal was choosing a virgin martyr for a model. Novelty would be more likely to prevent the choice of Philomena over older and more well-known saints. To become so popular, Philomena had to have been particularly meaningful in a nineteenth-century context.

As with the marketing of *Paul et Virginie* alongside devotional prints, so too did sellers link Philomena's commercial appeal to the popularity of sentimental novels. Like the fictional women found in sentimental novels, Philomena offered a story that reinforced the importance of women's demands for emotional and intellectual independence, even when it led to self-sacrifice. Unlike many of the virgin martyrs with whom she might be linked in a religious canon, Philomena's fame relied on a sense that the world could be interpreted through the lens of a family drama, one where parents, especially fathers, did not understand the hearts of their faithful daughters. Engravers reinforced this notion; they linked Philomena's commercial appeal to the popularity of sentimental novels. For example, in 1844 the engraving company Turgis offered a catalog of their available prints. Though "seller of religious objects" would soon be listed as its own profession, it had not yet been distinguished from a seller of any sort of engravings, and the Turgis catalog did not begin its list with an emphasis on religious images. Rather, the classifications began with "Historical Subjects," a literary and historical catchall. Philomena was the only nonbiblical religious figure listed in this opening section, and she was found alongside both *Atala* and *Paul and Virginie*.[109] In other words, Turgis marketed Philomena—but not Agnes or Cecilia or any other virgin martyr—in the front of their catalog, and they did so by placing Philomena next to famous sentimental heroines from novels.

Indeed, both Philomena's sentimental companions in sales and closer consideration of Philomena's story indicate that sentimental heroism was a central part of Philomena's appeal. The story of the discovery of the bones and the miracles attributed to them, as well as the martyrdom narrative provided by visionaries, were circulating across Europe in the 1830s. (Pauline Jaricot encountered it in one of the many editions by Barelle; this was what inspired her to travel to Mugnano with her resultant healing and the ensuing expansion of the cult of Philomena in France after 1835.)[110] A popular format of nine-day prayer, a novena, had also been printed and disseminated in multiple versions. Some of these works included a preface and images of Philomena; others contained only text. In these widely varied sources, what emerged was a narrative of Philomena's life that depicted her as a Greek princess who rejected the hand of Diocletian and that also told a story of her refusal to be corrupted by her family and their worldly considerations. For example, the narrative, sentimental in tone, often described a fraught conversation with her loving parents, who begged her to think of the havoc that the emperor would wreak on their small territory if she rebuffed him. Resisting the pleas of her loving—and Christian—parents, Philomena claimed that "my kingdom is Heaven" and remained steadfast to "God and Virginity before all, before you, before my country."[111] The key dramatic fact was that Philomena's father—himself a Christian—had accepted Diocletian's offer of marriage and that Philomena stood stronger than her father, resisting political enticements for the sake of the kingdom of heaven.

The theme of necessary resistance to one's own family was hardly accidental. An 1839 novena to Philomena included the following words, "*A little faith, as a mustard seed, can obtain the greatest graces. Ask and you shall receive; seek near to St. Philomena and you will find; knock with her on the door of the father of a family, it will be opened to you.*"[112] As the novena—just like sentimental novels—reminded the viewer, pure hearts resisted corruption, even when paternal authority might encourage compliance with other agendas, and it was always better to please God than to please men.[113]

The prints of Philomena—and their texts—demonstrate a more this-worldly resonance than those of Barbara, Agnes, or Cecilia. Certainly, in the older stories of Roman martyrs, both Agnes and Cecilia defended their virginity. Agnes is often depicted with a lamb, Cecilia with a harp. Philomena, too, was depicted with a lily for purity as well as the symbols of her suffering—arrows and anchor. But in addition to reminders of her martyrdom, Philomena stands in front of a tower or buildings—a symbol of the worldly kingdom that she was born into and rejected for Christ. She was accompanied by text that reinforced the ascetic conflict between heaven and earth and reminded viewers of suffering and sacrifice (figures 10, 11, and 12). Despite her resistance to things of this world, Philomena was not a domestic saint, with a private or individual spirituality. In both holy cards and larger icons, she was dressed as royalty, wearing ermine or a jeweled crown, reminders that Philomena had rejected compromise with her parents and Diocletian, despite a legitimate claim to an elevated place in society. Even when Philomena was the centerpiece of a large-format icon for the blessing of homes—a domestic context—her image continued to manifest these sartorial signs and appear in front of a city. The text also reminded readers of "the good use of her strength."[114] Despite her asceticism, Philomena was not a private saint, with an inward-facing spirituality. Pious images used iconographic resources, including buildings or secular crowns (even thrown upside-down on the ground!), to make her public significance clear.[115] Captions and texts reinforced this interpretation by referring to her power, courage, and the importance of her example of detachment from corrupting values.[116] All of this makes it clear why Turgis marketed her with the protagonists of novels in their catalog: she was a real-life example of sentimental heroism!

Philomena was an evocative martyr for the nineteenth century because her message of independence and sacrifice reverberated in the post-Revolutionary era. In the narratives constructed around her popular cult, Philomena was not simply a virgin: she was a heroine. She served as a reminder of the perceived conflict between the imperfect world as it existed and the world as it might be created. The forceful opposition of heaven and earth did not, however, mean that Philomena was private. On the contrary, it was a call to action. As another early novena explained, "God . . . wants to glorify His holy name in the midst of a depraved and perverted nation, and to console at the same time His Church, now plagued by so many desolations. Consequently, to demand graces in Philomena's name, is to enter into her views, and to give her an opportunity to manifest, for the confusion of the wicked, the power of her arm and the perpetuity of her love for her unique spouse and Beloved, the Holy Church of Jesus Christ."[117] Philomena's popularity cannot be removed from a sense that the Catholic Church was in danger of corruption. Catholic women who sought models for action might need strength to defend themselves, not only, or even explicitly, against ravishment, but from those who had failed to remember the true needs of the Church.

Given the political upheaval of the era, that message might not seem particularly surprising. However, it also included as a central part of its message the idea that women would need strength not for domesticity or marriage but for forceful action and even the rejection of masculine guidance. Philomena's popularity therefore also makes sense alongside the dramatic increase in female religious vocations. Rather than understanding virginity as marking the primary appeal of Philomena's message, the explosion in vocations to women's religious orders—no longer contemplative and cloistered—is centered in the same qualities reinforced in the narrative of Philomena: the ability to act for God, to be a force for change, and to do so independent of the direction of a father or husband.

Perhaps the force of Philomena has been overlooked because the most popular religious style of this period—Sulpician art—was sentimental and emotional. At first glance this style (figure 2) seems to make an unlikely pairing with Philomena's powerful rejection of corruption.[118] Despite—or perhaps because of—its popularity, Sulpician art was often referred to in derogatory terms. It was a "honeyed, sentimental, soft, sugary, and antimasculine" form of art, that sculpted Jesus as if "he has been crafted from gingerbread cake!"[119] Sulpician art not only was highly emotional in its composition of images but was also denigrated for the playfulness of its construction. Nineteenth-century catalogs of publishing houses offered descriptions of increasingly complex holy cards, with images that were not only edged with lace, but "spangled, berobed, decorated with rice paper" or had varied forms of pop-ups and cut-outs.[120] Today, these works are often referred to with adjectives like "kitsch," words that dismiss the art as tasteless, cheap, or vulgar—and consequently unimportant. Scholars admit that works in this style "were attractive to contemporaries" but do not see this point as admitting the style's significance.[121]

Indeed, despite its massive commercial popularity, many contemporaries also scorned Sulpician religious art. Over the course of the nineteenth century, numerous scholars and clerics saw these images, as well as the devotions that they accompanied, as the equivalent of religious pablum, while others were deeply threatened by them.[122] For example, the ecclesiastically moderate bishop Félix Dupanloup warned his clergy of the dangers of Sulpician art in a pastoral letter: "A certain religious image has freed itself from all control and sometimes reaches the limits of ridiculousness and insipidness. . . . Any entrepreneur . . . can throw as sustenance for the devotion of the faithful any food!"[123] The French novelist Joris-Karl Huysmans called Sulpician art the devil's revenge, and he was not alone in seeing this art as anti-intellectual, anti-masculine, and particularly dedicated to individual devotional practice rather than emphasizing clerical oversight and the Catholic Mass.[124] Nineteenth-century literary critic Léon Gautier claimed that what pious images had in common was their "sickly sentimentality," and he wondered if the printmakers were all female, given the feminizing tendencies of the art. He said, "What we lack most is virility. Truthfully, we have no more men. Therefore, stop making 'baby Jesuses' and show us the Word made man, in his virile splendor."[125] Denigration of this art—also symptomatic of the depiction of Thérèse of Lisieux discussed in this book's introduction—could be found from midcentury to the current day. For example, Michelet, unlike the convert Huysmans or legitimist Dupanloup, would not have wanted women to follow clerics, but he, too, argued that a piety that emphasized "the minute and humble . . . the lesser beings of the creation, such as little children, lambs, birds, and bees," was linked to feminine and emotional forms of religious practice, characterized by "meanness of style and littleness of heart."[126]

Sulpician artistic norms indicate that something had shifted in the dominant character of mass-produced spirituality. Religious expression had become more emotional and transformed in such a way that an increasing "emphasis on 'particular devotions' could only favor the multiplication of objects of piety," rather than primarily emphasizing participation in the Mass or the following of a clerical lead.[127] These objects were produced in a style that was "uncontrolled" and feminine. Many historians have taken this shift as prima facie evidence that religion had ceased to be a public concern and became soft, maudlin, and relegated to the home. However, a closer look at the qualities that male contemporaries denigrated in Sulpicianism—lack of control, emotionalism, and individual devotion—challenges that point of view. Instead, those qualities offer continuity with women's religious activism during the Revolution and Philomena's appeal. Additionally, though the Sulpician objects are sentimental, their larger context relied on a sense of crisis and battle, characteristics that were often coded as masculine and were certainly not private.

Holy cards that emphasized devotion to the Sacred Heart offer a particularly striking example of how Sulpicianism combined individual devotion, sentiment, and battle in order to authorize action on the part of the believer. The iconography for Sacred Heart of Jesus had developed a fairly standard form beginning in the seventeenth century: a flaming heart encircled by a crown of thorns, surmounted by a cross, pierced by a wound (figure 13).[128] Charles Letaille, Turgis, and Bouasse-Lebel were just three of the most prominent publishing houses that produced holy cards in the Sulpician style from the mid-nineteenth century forward. While Géricault had argued that Sacred Hearts were no longer profitable, each of these engravers offered dozens of images that featured Sacred Heart iconography in some way. All of the images might give a modern viewer the mistaken impression that the Sacred Heart was a wholly individual devotion. For example, a midcentury image from Letaille featured the traditional flaming heart hovering in midair, dripping blood on the landscape below, all beneath the watchful eye of God. The heart floated like a kite, tethered to the Eucharist at the base of the image. The accompanying message reminded the viewer: "There, in the heart of Jesus, called and alone, I lose myself!" (figure 14).[129] Turgis cards followed the same theme, showing a single pilgrim throwing himself on Jesus and his Sacred Heart, to have consolation in exile or refuge where she could hide.[130] As with Philomena, the texts promoted rejection of worldly values and were set alongside loving embraces, doves, and bleeding hearts, even as they highlighted the connection of one heart to another that was a centerpiece of sentimentality (figures 15 and 16). At once oddly saccharine and macabre, in their emphasis on solitary worship and individual connection to Jesus, they seem to reinforce the idea that devotion to the Sacred Heart is individual and private, set apart from the world.

However, just as with the devotion to St. Philomena, to read these images without reference to a larger cultural context would be a mistake. The most formulaic image of the Sacred Heart was based on the image drawn by Margaret Mary Alacoque in the last half of the seventeenth century. Alacoque's 1670s visions did have a deeply personal component, one that included an emphasis on the wounds of Christ. In this they echoed the emotional language of earlier saints, like Francis de Sales and Jeanne Chantal, who also saw the heart of Jesus as a refuge. However, these visions underscored far more than the individual safety found in Jesus. Not only did devotion to the Sacred Heart promise protection and grace to households that displayed it prominently, but Alacoque claimed that it could redeem France, too. If France were to dedicate itself whole-heartedly to the Sacred Heart, the nation would be protected by Jesus's Divine Heart and would be able to take its place as the leading nation of the world, carrying out God's mission.[131]

Additionally, in its seventeenth-century context Alacoque's vision was situated within a theological context where the heart was the center of willed action—*volonté*.[132] However, to understand the translation of the Sacred Heart into nineteenth-century sentimental ideals, it is important to understand that the heart "took on sentimental coloring after Jean-Jeacques Rousseau" and came to represent "*affectivité* rather than *volonté*, which was then understood restrictively as [only] the faculty of decision."[133] The theology of the Sacred Heart thus changed, becoming much more like how it is ordinarily received today, where the heart represents love and emotional connection as well as true judgment.

The Sacred Heart, tied to sentiment, continued to have political resonance after 1789, when leaders of the Catholic Church and the Revolution came to see themselves as inextricably opposed. The implications of the Sacred Heart in a counter-Revolutionary context were well understood: scapulars with the image of the Sacred Heart not only demanded divine protection but claimed authority for a vision of France that stood for armed resistance to the Republic.[134] In this context, tricolors with the Sacred Heart placed as a shield on the white field might be accompanied by language that demanded the same protection that an individual or a household would claim, stopping the scourge of secular revolution.[135] There was indeed isolation—the world was hostile to believers, and they stood alone and in need of protection—but the Sacred Heart offered a way to contest that isolation, both by identifying philosophical and spiritual allies and by claiming communal authority. Like Philomena's asceticism, the Sacred Heart was a malleable image, one that allowed the embattled believer to locate herself within a particular moment of crisis even as she affirmed her emotional authority and independence of action.

Before the Revolution, the Church had attempted to eradicate an undue emphasis on unsupervised religious practice such as pilgrimage and private devotion. Clerics often tried to redirect devout practitioners toward the Mass rather than practices that were, from the perspective of the Catholic hierarchy, illicit and uncontrolled, which included various forms of popular devotion.[136] However, as the Revolution progressed, opposition to state clergy became a moral obligation, and individual devotions became pious. Devout Catholics understood pilgrimages, Masses, and rosaries as acts that undermined the Revolutionary regime. For women, children's religious education was an important responsibility, because catechism, which had been conducted by the priest, after Mass, was no longer offered. Much devotional authority devolved from priests to mothers.[137]

The fact that religious practice increasingly relied on individual devotion did not mean that Catholic practice was a private act. Certainly, representatives from the Jacobins, sent to dechristianize and revolutionize France, downplayed women's activism and argued that they could ignore women chanting their beads as a matter of no political concern.[138] However, those statements alone should not convince the historian that rosaries and other devotions were merely personal, especially when the acts were set in a context of political opposition from a Catholic perspective, and popular piety, a "a commonly overlooked or merely ridiculed reality," became admirable in the eyes of religious officials rather than deprecated.[139]

Community renewal and emotional Catholicism became linked in a "Sacred Heart theology [that] emphasized a God who was more a forgiving redeemer than a stern Jehovah . . . After 1793, however, the Sacred Heart also served as an object of memory and a rich source of associations about France, its Christian mission, and the post-revolutionary task of renewal."[140] One's salvation hinged not only on being in the right relationship to God but also adopting the new Christian identity, which demanded both repentance and promotion of Catholic values in all of French life, at home and in the world.

Understanding the Sacred Heart as an emotional source of mercy, a symbol of unity with Jesus, and a call to action against a hostile world also helps interpret the varied prayers attached to Sacred Heart devotions. For example, the large Pellerin icon of the Sacred Heart from 1836 offered the following prayer: "O God, who has shut up all the treasures of your wisdom and knowledge in the most Holy Heart of your beloved Son, that through him we may have life, and have it more abundantly, hear the wishes of your people, and, opening this heavenly source of all gifts, make us worthy to receive from its fullness a superabundant grace. Amen."[141] This prayer differs from many earlier Sacred Heart prayers that focused on protection and love. Instead it highlighted wisdom, community, and grace. However, set in the context of a Sacred Heart that represented emotional connection, and a continued debate over the values of public life and the role of individual commitment to the "right" identity, this prayer's communal engagements become clearer. Loyalty to the Sacred Heart was responsiveness to true wisdom, which would make one worthy of receiving grace. The Sacred Heart therefore stood as a sign of a need for both emotional and social change within France.

Not surprisingly, then, a shift in image toward an emphasis on soft features and emotions like love and mercy did not make the Sacred Heart a more palatable symbol to opponents, who recognized that the devotion reminded readers that all their commitments, whether religious or political, were related. The realist author Stendhal understood the Sacred Heart—and the education provided by the Religious of the Sacred Heart—as representative of reaction.[142] Michelet, too, opposed the devotion, describing it as a carnal symbol that operated to seduce women.[143] He argued that Alacocque was a prime example of a celibate woman who sought to satisfy her sexual urges in unhealthy ways.[144] It was not only the sentimental and irrational tone of the Sacred Heart devotion that bothered Michelet, but the fact that it freed women from men's control. The image of the Sacred Heart was, of course, physical and sentimental. It was also communal and public. An individual believer who laid claim to Christ's love did so not only for herself but also on behalf of her nation.

The dual sense of crisis and liberation alongside the freeing and public nature of sentimental devotion was not limited to images of the Sacred Heart, either. Bouasse-Lebel is one of the publishing houses most closely identified with the development and commercial success of the sentimental Sulpician style. Its foundress, Eulalie Lebel, developed cards that hit exactly the right tone, and her business on the Rue St. Sulpice thrived because of the craze for pious objects, not only in France but globally. For example, in 1851 the bishop of Savannah went on a European tour. While in Paris, he followed a recommendation that he pay a visit to Bouasse-Lebel and the newly booming religious trade district around St. Sulpice. He "was so pleased with what [he] saw & with the prices, that [he] fell to work at once and commenced purchasing, & did not discontinue" until his bill totaled nearly 1,500 francs, or more than $10,000 in today's currency.[145] He also noted that the store was very busy selling images to other priests and religious as well as secular customers.

The cards produced by Madame Lebel echoed themes in previous chapters. They relied on an interplay between text and image that took for granted the threat posed by the world and the need for the believer to appeal to God for intercession and mercy. For example, one of the earliest cards (ca. 1845) depicted a bishop's miter, crosier, and stole (symbols of clerical authority), scattered across the ground. Above these objects, in the sky, there was a dove and shining rays of light, as well as a butterfly, the symbol of transformation. Below this image is the text: "The Holy Spirit has changed his weakness into strength, his impotence into power; his inconsequence into wisdom, so that he may be the support and example of his brothers."[146] This card clearly depicts the sense that the Church's hierarchical power had been decimated and must be replenished through prayer. The language also echoed that found in Margaret Mary Alacoque's autobiographical writings, where God promises her that He will be her strength if she agrees to do his will.[147] Another early card has a Marian monogram floating in the sky, hurling out bolts of lightning against a dragon—a sign of Satan and spiritual evil—across a blackened landscape. A dove flies nearby, and the text below reads "Most chaste Mother," reinforcing the sense that devotion to Mary will save the believer (figure 17, right).[148] Sometimes this deliverance was depicted physically, when Mary saved those who "abjured their errors" by intervening between them and a tempest (figure 18).[149] At other times, it came in the form of a good death or flowers from heaven.[150] In this larger context garden retreats, protecting angels, and spangled hearts were not as lovely, meek, or trifling as they might appear. The Good Shepherd might survey his flocks as the sheep slept peacefully or, alternately, he might take possession of his wounded and devastated flock.[151] While many cards relied only on sentimental and lovely images and words, the availability of other cards helps contextualize and interrogate the "simple" Sulpician card. For example, a recipient of a card with a calm sea, a boat, and a rising sun would encounter the following text: "Each morning, when I raise my heart to my creator, I will say to Him, 'My God, protect my mother, share with her the indulgences attached to my prayer.'"[152] While one could certainly read this as a devout respect for a biological mother, stormy seas were frequently depicted in pious images, serving to underline a sense of crisis that came through many of the cards. The context of the sea also reminded the viewer of how France as mother also needed the individual's prayer. Just as one would not look at the butterfly and flowers without understanding the transformation in the context of clerical crisis, so too, even momentary calm implied the possibility of a storm. Taken together, these images indicate that holy cards and pious images should be read in the context of a Christianity where remaking the world was a choice. Language that emphasized removal from the world was tied to suffering and rejection as a call to action.

Bouasse-Lebel soon produced numerous holy cards that featured the Sacred Heart. At first glance, the images sold under this label seem to have little in common other than the shared symbol of the Sacred Heart. One of their first Sacred Heart cards, produced around 1850, shows Jesus, holding his heart—in the form drawn by Alacoque and promoted by counterrevolutionaries—with the caption, "Jesus' love for us is equal to his power," surrounded by spangles and painted roses.[153] A later image, copied directly from Turgis's 1850 lithograph, depicts a very large Sacred Heart, surrounded by a wreath of grapes, vines, and wheat in addition to the usual attributes of flames and wound. The heart is dripping blood into a basin that resembles a holy water font. Multiple doves are bathing in that basin. The only text below the image is an inscription that reads, "Sacred Heart of Jesus." There are multiple allusions in this image to theological sources of grace and mercy: blood, Eucharist, baptism. Yet another card shows Jesus, with his Sacred Heart displayed prominently, turning to offer his cloak as shelter to a soul. The text reads: "Poor soul, frozen by the cold breath of the world. Come and warm up near the heart of Jesus."[154] Finally, a Bouasse-Lebel image from about 1860 shows young people kneeling at the feet of Christ, his Sacred Heart on display. The text below this image instructs the reader that the "perfect gifts of the heart of Jesus are faith which clarifies, hope that consoles, and charity that enlivens."[155] On face, these seem like dramatically different messages held together by a common publisher, symbol, and style.

It is true that Sulpician images shared a sentimental style that included things such as flowers, doves, or feminine-looking men with soft features. The cards and icons were certainly objects of private devotion. However, when understood in the context of the political and social engagements of the moment—and the particular resonance of a language of the heart, as well as the Sacred Heart—it is clear that religious cards relied on a powerful set of assumptions that were decidedly not removed from the world or merely individual. Instead the cards emphasized the relationship of believers to each other and the responsibility of the Christian to act to "inaugurate an alternative culture."[156] While the images did not emphasize a language of political opposition, they did take for granted a background of sacrifice and cultural resistance (figures 19 and 20).

Resistance to corruption did not imply retreat from society writ large. Instead the pious images were united in their conviction that the Christian was a member of a community, defined by faith and acts. Take, for example, the multiple doves bathing beneath the blood of the Sacred Heart. Not only were they receiving sacramental graces, but they were doing so together. Similarly, the children who knelt at the feet of Jesus represented a community of believers whose acts went beyond private devotion. One might be renewed for a time next to Jesus's heart, one card seems to say, but that is to prepare oneself to continue to suffer the disdain of the world in a process of conversion. Another reminded the viewer that a response to Jesus was individual, but could be accompanied by others who also responded to the call (figure 15). Like the initial holy cards that popularized the Bouasse-Lebel style, or the daughter bringing the mother her prizes from school, private devotion could not be separated from the believer's life writ large.

Ultimately, these images appeared sentimental and religious, but they built on an unsectarian framework that did not valorize traditional family structures. Instead, in their critique of the current world, they authorized the believer to value her own religious experience. Hostility to this Sulpician and midcentury spirituality makes the contemporary point explicit. For, just as Michelet argued that women should be removed from the power of the priest so that no one would usurp a man's power over his wife, so too, no male authority wanted to sanction women's independent thought and action.[157] We have already seen that Bishop Dupanloup criticized the Sulpician form for "freeing itself from all control." Across the political spectrum French men condemned the permissiveness that they saw as part and parcel of the Sulpician style. Even many of those who might have agreed with the Sacred Heart's language of political opposition argued that Sulpicianism offered too much leeway to believers. Its messages, which were simple and empowering, combined with the freedom offered by individual devotions, presented the possibility of dangerous assumptions of authority. For example, in 1866 a legitimist newspaper took the time to denounce a popular holy card by Letaille (figure 21) that had been circulating since the 1840s. The card depicted an "entry ticket for heaven, earned in the divine school of patience." The text says: "None will have the [heavenly] crown who has not legitimately fought."[158] The newspaper, on the other hand, insisted that it was "persuaded that among sincere Catholics, there will be only one voice in condemning a license as impious as it is irreverent."[159] Given that the holy card had been selling for decades—and that Sulpician images continued to sell in massive numbers—consumers had embraced the idea that battles of all sorts were fundamental to one's spiritual destiny. A "ticket to heaven" based on sacrifice and a battle against the world appeared neither impious nor irreverent to those purchasing the item.

In fact, Sulpician images that promoted suffering, exile, and martyrdom continued to experience stunning commercial success across the globe. Themes of suffering, exile, and martyrdom continued to appear in pious images throughout the century and were a sign of the sure path to God, an indication of how the world could be central to attaining heaven, even as it paled in importance next to the heavenly Jerusalem (figure 22). Resistance to corruption did not imply privacy or domestic retreat. Instead, as with Philomena's story, found in one of Eulalie Lebel's earliest holy cards, the images were united in their conviction that private devotion could not be separated from the believer's public witness (figures 10 and 11). In their critique of the current world, sentimental religious forms authorized the believer to free herself from the constraints of contemporary society to work for the creation of a better world. Through the language of sentiment, popular religious images valorized women's emotional authority. Although Michelet and legitimists alike would have had girls believe that a midcentury "ticket to heaven" was found in acceptance of the leadership of rational men, sentimental images did not reinforce this notion. Instead, consumers—and the women of the following chapters—demonstrated that tears, suffering, and independent-minded martyrdom were their preferred model.

< 4 >

Preferring Jesus Christ to Any Man

Chastity, Sacrifice, and the Religious of the Sacred Heart

But you realize, dear Sister, that my vocation is a consecration to sacrifice and to privation of natural joys. So I am now making the exchange of the sweet pleasure of embracing you for that of keeping my promises and proving to God that His Will is always lovable, for there is joy in making sacrifices for anyone we love.

—Philippine Duchesne to her sister, Mme Jouve (March 1805)

In the United States few would place Rose-Philippine Duchesne in a sentimental or French context. Rather, most Americans pair her with Catholic education on the nineteenth-century frontier, where Duchesne established the first overseas mission of the Religious of the Sacred Heart (RSCJ).[1] The order, founded by Madeleine Sophie Barat in France in 1800, certainly intended to educate young women as future mothers, winning parents and children in one fell swoop. This impulse came out of a desire to re-Christianize France after the destruction of the French Revolution. However, the RSCJ Constitutions foregrounded the women's mission in the context of ascetic self-abnegation and devotion to the Sacred Heart. The Constitutions asked the religious to reject the things of the world and "unite themselves with the inner sentiments of the Heart of the divine spouse, who is the master of every good on heaven and on earth."[2] When Duchesne begged to be sent from France to the United States, she wanted to fulfill the Sacred Heart mission in a heroic way, one situated in the sacrificial poverty and hardship of the Louisiana Territory.[3]

137

In reflecting on her life, Duchesne said that her inspiration for missionary ideals had begun long before the Revolution. When she was young, perhaps eight, the personal stories of a Jesuit missionary from Louisiana inspired her and reminded her of the stories of the martyrs that she was also reading.[4] Though the stories of the North American frontier reminded Duchesne of possible martyrdom—a prominent theme in late eighteenth- and early nineteenth-century Catholic literature—her ambition to travel the world for Christ remains remarkable. While Duchesne was hardly the only nineteenth-century woman to become a missionary, and she eventually carried out her plans under the auspices of an increasingly powerful and international order of nuns, her trajectory was far from what her wealthy bourgeois family would have imagined for her.[5] While Philippine's cousins were making marriage matches that enhanced the political and business prospects of the Duchesne and Perier families, Philippine rejected marriage to an earthly spouse and removed herself from temporal attachments. Later, instead of embodying the domestic model, she struck out on her own, with the support of a female superior. More than one of her nieces joined her in choosing religious life, also over the objections of family.

Why did parents object to their daughters pursuing a sacrificial life dedicated to Christ, and in the face of that disapproval, how did increasingly large numbers of young women insist on their right and even obligation to pursue life as consecrated religious? The sources of this chapter— family letters, journals, and spiritual autobiography—tell of Duchesne's desire to go to the farthest reaches of the earth and suffer privation in order to demonstrate her love. Like her famous Ursuline predecessor, Marie de l'Incarnation, Duchesne wanted to introduce the Gospel to groups that had no one to teach them about Jesus. Additionally, like a sentimental heroine, she imagined herself in a setting removed from everyday life and ripe for the creation of a new order, one where the love of the Sacred Heart of Jesus was made known to all.[6] She was joined in these ideals by thousands of young women, including several of her own relatives. Duchesne's story is thus one that tells us about the sentimental construction of an idealistic life even as it offers insight into the values that other women religious shared with her.

The sources of this chapter were not spontaneous productions of the heart, even when they used sentimental language. Numerous studies have examined the function of letters in maintaining kinship ties.[7] Philip Lejeune has explained the importance of journals in the construction of post-Revolutionary identity. He observes that nineteenth-century journals were carefully curated and came out of pedagogical impulses.[8] Though Duchesne's educational training was pre-Revolutionary, Duchesne's communications with her family, her Grenoble journal, and her early spiritual autobiography were intended to be shared with readers and were constructed to address that audience's expectations.[9]

This curating of ideas should not be seen as a negative or dishonest depiction of Duchesne's values but instead confirms that these works were also literary formulations produced in conversation with nineteenth-century cultural currents. For example, when Philippine Duchesne looked back on her first years, she asserted that she had, uncompromisingly, from the age of twelve, wanted to devote her life to Christ.[10] Her self-construction, as well as the image that emerged from hagiographic materials about her, emphasized Duchesne's single-minded devotion to Christ, her rejection of the world, and her willingness to sacrifice everything for God. While this vision of the world might not be surprising in religious material, the idealism it offered fit neatly with sentimental ideals writ large.

Duchesne had multiple vocational identities and recognized that she had other life alternatives. She was first a cloistered nun in Grenoble, then a single woman active in social work during the Revolution. After the Revolution, she was a religious sister in France, then a missionary on the American frontier. As a central figure in the expansion of the Religious of the Sacred Heart, Duchesne was certainly aware of the cultural freight of her choices, and she pursued and defended celibacy and religious activism with great eloquence. As a woman of high social standing, vision, and energy, she also represents one of the many "foundresses" of French women's congregations before 1850.[11] Understanding her choices and the ideals that she promoted, especially in their larger sentimental context, gives us a better sense of how women like her read the norms surrounding celibacy, marriage, and the call of their hearts.

Becoming a vowed religious was not a culturally popular choice at the turn of the nineteenth century. Literature's vision of the consecrated religious was replete with images of exploitation and manipulation.[12] Melodramatic theater and gothic stories were particularly prone to paint a picture of nuns locked away in convents where they could be abused with impunity. Popular plays such as Boutet de Monvel's *Cloistered Victims* or Olympe de Gouges's *Forced Vows* offered stories of bondage and liberation, with young women hidden away to serve their families' nefarious ends, all in cooperation with greedy or corrupt church officials who were willing to force girls to take vows for their own benefit.[13] Though the idea of the exploited nun was not new, this image operated as a potent social charge in the Revolutionary and post-Revolutionary era. The nun demonstrated how families might use corrupt institutional power for their own ends, destroying individual lives in the process.[14] Indeed, this location for the oppression of women and their loss of autonomy offered a powerful parallel to more explicit political critiques of absolute political and clerical power, making it unsurprising that plays with a claustral theme were performed hundreds of times in the years from 1790 to 1815.

However, even as the lack of freedom for women could be read as an indictment of an oppressive government, the stories that attacked the cloister demanded only a limited and domestic autonomy for women. Much of the power of these plays rested on the assumption, so eloquently promoted during the Enlightenment and beyond, that female celibacy was unnatural and that an autonomous woman, liberated from the confines of the convent, would naturally seek completion through marriage and biological motherhood. The argument against claustration was not that women had been deprived of their right to exist as public beings, but that they had been robbed of their freedom to get married and to have children. As a convent servant explained in *Forced Vows* (1790), "Undoubtedly God does not forbid living honestly and quietly in a convent; but I am of the opinion that he much prefers marriage, and

I assure you, Ladies and Gentlemen, that I am going to get married as soon as I am able."[15]

This distinction between a real concern with women's autonomy and a preference for the control of women within a family context became even more explicit when women religious, like Philippine Duchesne, no longer lived "honestly and quietly" in convents but continued to refuse to get married "as soon as they were able." After the Revolution, women's religious orders shifted their focus from contemplative lives to active public service. Women continued to join religious orders in large numbers—much larger than in the years before the Revolution, in fact—but they no longer remained behind the walls of a convent.[16] This rapid growth in numbers of noncloistered religious offers a look at a particularly thorny moment for the enunciation of female autonomy. Theoretically, claustral literature depicted only the convent as a place of oppression, but it also reinforced and valorized newer cultural norms that promoted the domestic home as the location for women's freedom. Women religious had community visibility and authority while they built schools, worked in hospitals, and administered institutions, which complicated the question of what female autonomy meant and reversed the narrative about women's claustration. The active and committed—but celibate—sister, who often chose religious life in opposition to her family's expectations and desires, gave the lie to the idea that all women naturally gravitated toward marriage or that marriage was the only site for women's freedom.

This new religious, who remained independent and publicly visible while rejecting biological motherhood and the control of husband and family, presented a powerful threat. As discussed, some authors directly confronted the question of celibacy, marriage, and women's vocation in their literary works. Others made passing references that demonstrated their uneasiness with the level of influence that such sisters had. For example, in the *Red and the Black*, both of Stendhal's female protagonists (Louise de Rênal and Mathilde de la Môle) were said to have been taught by Religious of the Sacred Heart. In his "Chronicle of 1830," Stendhal decried the convent education that wealthy girls like Louise and Mathilde received, which, he said, ruined their best and most natural characteristics. Instead of a real education, they were pampered and flattered, educated to value prestige and power and the appearance of prudent behavior.[17] Rather than being adequately trained, they were taught to think irrationally and to "hate the French as being enemies of the Jesuits."[18] These were both women of exceptional promise who were led astray by nuns who valued worldly influence. The Religious of the Sacred Heart could serve, at least in Stendhal's world, to provide reinforcement of what society already "knew," which was that the public nun was a corrupting force. These images also vividly came to life in Jules Michelet's anticlerical *Priests, Women, and Families* (1845), which claimed that maternity was a biological imperative. Consecrated religious life was, Michelet argued, an abnormal and lifeless state, given the ways in which it was removed from women's necessary family context; unsurprisingly, the convent, organized by unnatural women, worked to destroy the females within it.[19]

One might say that these images of the celibate sister—one exploited, the other exploiting—were two sides of the same coin.[20] Their force rested on the revulsion that a reader or theatergoer would have for celibacy and independent women. It was given further power by the irony that a woman who gave up everything for Christ, making vows of poverty, celibacy, and obedience, would become, in the end, unchaste, power-hungry, or controlling. Either way, as a stock cultural figure, the nun often represented something dangerous and demonstrated how women were "captives of their female embodiment," no matter how much they might wish to escape.[21] This is not to say that the services that nuns provided—education, health care, social work—were not appreciated, nor that sisters were generally unwelcome. These images, however, reinforce that women's usefulness was frequently situated in their position as bargaining chips, reproducing wombs, and emblems, rather than as independent thinkers and actors. Further, given that the cultural weight attached to female celibacy carried these meanings, it is surprising that the early nineteenth century would see an explosion in vocations to the celibate religious life.[22] This is especially true when the anticlerical

Michelet could agree with the Catholic reformer Louis-Aimé Martin that women's choice of celibacy was like a plague, threatening the future of the nation.[23]

For Philippine Duchesne, perhaps the choice to resist society's expectations was not particularly aberrational. Duchesne came from a family of forceful and determined people, and her personal tendencies to stubbornness and fiery temper were often depicted in a negative light and said to be an inheritance from the Duchesne side of the family.[24] Her father, Pierre-François, was a distinguished and culturally influential lawyer. He had founded the first public library in Grenoble and was also politically prominent in the city, notable in both the early and late phases of the Revolution.[25] Uncles and cousins also acquitted themselves well in terms of social influence. Like Pierre-François, Philippine's uncle, Claude Perier, was a member of the municipal council of Grenoble and an early leader of the French Revolution.[26] The men of her family generally made it through the Revolution unscathed, though Pierre-François and his son were forced to retire from political life after taking a principled stand against Napoleon in 1802, when Pierre-François was one of only one of two men in the legislative body to oppose Napoleon's design to declare himself Consul for Life.[27] Throughout the upheaval of the Revolutionary years, the men of her family moved in high political and social circles. Casimir Perier, Philippine's cousin, came to political prominence in the Revolution of 1830 as a staunch liberal opponent of Charles X. He had the confidence of Louis-Philippe and became president of the council and minister of the interior. Though his meteoric rise was cut short by his death from cholera in the epidemic of 1832, representatives of the family remained active in politics until the Second Empire.

The reality of Duchesne's life, however, was that unlike her brother or cousin, neither Napoleon nor disease stood in the way of any political plans. After all, though she was the first healthy child born to this wealthy and prominent bourgeois family in 1769 in Grenoble, France, she was female and therefore not heir to the opportunities of her brother and cousins. Though the men of her family were politically engaged and socially reformist, their women were supposed to be engaged in reproduction, not political activism. While women's domesticity did not pre-clude participation in culturally significant activities, as the eighteenth century progressed, these accomplishments increasingly centered on the home and child-rearing.[28] Additionally, Duchesne's religious devotion is unusual when compared with the religious practice of most of her male relatives; it was, however, typical when her gender is taken into consideration. While some of Philippine's male relatives continued to identify themselves as Catholics, most followed the trajectory that has been outlined in so many historical works, becoming free-thinkers. For example, Pierre-François was a Deist who supported the Revolutionary nationalization of Church property and only returned to Catholicism on his deathbed.

The women of her family, on the other hand, did not provide her with examples of political activism and fervor, but they certainly offered her illustrations of devoted religious adherence. Philippine had at least two aunts who were cloistered in a Visitation monastery, and her own mother, Rose-Euphrosine Duchesne (née Perier), was a devout Catholic. When Philippine turned twelve, she and her cousin Josephine Perier were sent to board at the Visitation monastery in Grenoble, Sainte Marie-d'en-Haut, in preparation for their First Communion. Duchesne's education at this monastery put her in a long line of young women in her family who had been educated in a cloister, according to the seventeenth-century precepts developed by Saint Francis de Sales and Saint Jane Frances Chantal.[29]

At a glance, then, neither Duchesne's energy nor her religious devotion seem particularly unusual given her gender and familial context. However, even in this economically privileged and politically engaged family, Duchesne's "unbending will" and other "virile qualities" often seemed like flaws that a young girl should root out of her soul.[30] Although the women of her social class were often notably more religious than the men to whom they were married, the Duchesne family did not intend for Duchesne to take the veil but planned for her to make a match that would increase the prosperity of the family. Her refusal to consider marriage demonstrated the strength of will upon which so many biographers commented. It also upset her family's plans for social advancement.

On the day of her First Holy Communion, when she was fourteen years old, Duchesne offered herself to God and planned to become a religious.[31] She began to imitate the Visitation nuns, rising early like they did so that she might make morning prayers with them. One of the girls who was at the monastery with her remembered her zeal, which sometimes meant that she would hurry to the chapel half-dressed rather than skip or cut short the devotion.[32] Her parents soon heard the rumor that Philippine might be feeling pulled toward a religious vocation, and not wishing to encourage her in this notion, they immediately withdrew her from Sainte Marie-d'en-Haut and brought her home, where they proceeded to train her in the arts that a marriageable young woman should learn. Though they could have expected a battle, it seems that Philippine left the convent without complaint.

On the Grande Rue, in the double home that the Perier and Duchesne families shared, Philippine's family trained her to be a young lady, with the habits that went along with her social class and an education to match. She studied languages and music; she learned to dance. She read, wrote, drew, and was encouraged to dress fashionably as she took part in Grenoble social life.[33] Even if she continued to pray as at Sainte Marie, she joined fully in family life, including rounds of concerts and dances. Her parents thus continued to believe that she would go along with their plans for her, that she was not particularly opposed to marriage. However, first Philippine's younger sister Amélie's marital contract was finalized, then that of her sister Euphrosine, who was even younger than Amélie. Both married well, and their weddings also made it clear that it was high time for Philippine to be wed. This became even more obvious when Philippine's dear cousin Josephine Perier, almost exactly the same age as she, married a prominent lawyer in the Grenoble *parlement*, Jacques Fortunat Savoye-Rollin.

Family plans became less suggestive and more forceful, offering direction to the seventeen-year-old Philippine. They proposed that she marry a specific young man of their circle. She refused and instead asked to be allowed to be a nun, as other Perier and Duchesne girls had done in the past.[34] These other girls, however, were not the oldest living children of

Pierre-François, nor were they in the current generation. Her family was strongly opposed to Philippine's disposition. Her father did not wish her to become a religious, and her mother, while less opposed to Philippine's becoming a nun, believed that she was still too young to make such a decision. Neither parent believed that she was too young to marry, however, and they pushed her toward this choice.

The battle lines were drawn, and Duchesne felt compelled to make it increasingly clear that she would have nothing to do with worldly things. She changed her manner of dress and her sociability; she began to pray more and attempted to follow the rule of life as if she were at Sainte Marie, avoiding dances and parties and dressing in sober colors and styles. No longer having her cousin Josephine to confide in, she begged her mother's sister to intercede on her behalf. At this point Duchesne had been away from Sainte Marie for many years, and the stalemate with her family had been ongoing for months, with Philippine behaving as if she would become a nun and her family insisting by turns that she was too young to make such a decision or that she ought to agree to marry.

Eventually, the eighteen-year-old Philippine decided that the time was right to push the issue further, and her Aunt Perier agreed to accompany her up the hill to the Visitation monastery so that she might speak with the superior of the convent regarding discernment of her vocation. Once in the convent at Sainte Marie, Duchesne let her aunt know that her resolve to stay could not be shaken. The woman returned home alone to break the news to Philippine's mother and father. A few days later, the Duchesnes went up the hill to Sainte Marie in an attempt to persuade Philippine to come home with them, but she had not changed her mind. Nothing would dissuade her; Philippine remained at the Visitation convent as a postulant, as she had wished from the time of her First Communion.[35]

The six years in which Philippine had been home were ones in which the young woman not only came closer to the age of majority but also, it seems, came to a deeper understanding of her own place in the world. She spent a great deal of her time caring for the younger Perier and Duchesne children and acted as an educator within her family home. As Duchesne explained, though the Visitation was of course familiar, it was not just the surroundings at Sainte Marie that called to her. Rather, "a desire to share in the apostolate made me choose the Visitation, where children were educated, in preference to Carmel, which I loved very much."[36] Although Duchesne did not wish to marry and felt actively called to religious life, she also cast her decision into a context where her religious life would have an active component. This course was one she would continue to follow through the rest of her life.

When she refused to come out of the convent, her parents were likely unsurprised that she was going against their expectations for her. However, she was not yet at the age of majority, so when she asked for permission to make her final vows, Pierre-François forbade it. He cited the instability of the political situation—this was September of 1789, and the confiscation of Church property had already begun—and asked her to promise that she would make no religious vows before the age of twenty-five.[37] Given the fact that the age of majority was twenty-five, this was not much of a promise. Instead, Pierre-François was essentially recognizing the stalemate that existed between him and his daughter on the question of religious vocation. He refused to offer his permission, and she would have to wait for his blessing until she was old enough to join the convent without his legal assent.

In the years that she was at Sainte Marie, both before and after her adolescence on the Grand Rue, Duchesne was deeply influenced not only by the seventeenth-century spirit of Chantal but also by written tales of missionaries.[38] Duchesne told fellow sisters about the lives of the Jesuits. Francis Xavier was one of her favorites, because of his desire to serve in the missions. She believed herself to be similarly called, and she communicated her desire to Xavier in prayer. "How often have I not said to him since then, in my impatience, 'Great Saint, why do you not call me? I would respond at once.' He is the saint of my heart."[39] Furthermore, Xavier and the Jesuits were not the only missionaries who animated Duchesne's thoughts at the convent. She also repeatedly read *The Life of the Venerable Mother Marie of the Incarnation* and reflected on Marie's work among the Native Americans. As an Ursuline and a missionary to New France, Marie's sacrifices and ambitions gave context to Duchesne's seemingly impossible desire to be a missionary and a cloistered religious; she could believe that her heart was not leading her astray.[40]

The French Revolution rendered the dispute between Philippine and her family moot and put an end to her reading in the convent library. Indeed, it seemed to put an end to all plans of a future as a consecrated religious, as the decree of February 1790 secularized monastic orders. Philippine's aunts, Visitandine nuns in Romans, were forced to leave their convent and come back to Grenoble in 1791, and in 1792 Duchesne herself left Saint Marie. While she wished to go into exile with the Visitation nuns in Italy, she instead returned to her family, as they requested. She went first to the Duchesne home on the Grande Rue and then with the family as they moved to their property at Grâne, a rural area between Lyon and Avignon. This was a safer choice than Grenoble or Lyon, both of which were in a state of upheaval. At Grâne, Duchesne returned to the life that she had set up for herself as an adolescent, helping with siblings and cousins while also trying to keep her life to a monastic pattern of prayer and fasting.

This did not mean that Duchesne had reconciled with life outside a religious community. Her spiritual autobiography demonstrated the importance of exile to her understanding of her calling.[41] In the *Story of Sainte Marie*, which offered a narrative of her path to the Religious of the Sacred Heart, Duchesne explained that though she was forced back into the world by Revolutionary decree, "I never attached my heart to [the world]. It was always for me a land of exile, a foreign land. Zion, my homeland, remained the object of my desires and of my most dear projects."[42] Additionally, though Philippine believed that she had a special destiny beyond worldly goals, the Duchesne family grumbled about Philippine's religiosity and distance from the world.[43] Duchesne's growing devotion to Francis Régis meant that she wanted to take frequent trips to visit his nearby tomb. This was not possible, so as her narrative explained, "my heart often brought me [to the tomb]."[44] In this way, she continued to see herself in exile from the world, connected to God by her heart's desires and inspired by a Jesuit missionary who had also wanted to travel the world but had instead ministered to the faithful in France.

As the Revolution progressed, letters from her cousin, Josephine Savoye-Rollin, soon made it clear to Philippine that people were suffering far more in Grenoble than in sheltered Grâne. Taking Josephine's usefulness as she aided the poor as a gentle rebuke, Philippine went back to Grenoble to engage in active charity.[45] For some of the most radical months of the Revolution, from 1793 until the fall of Robespierre in 1795, Duchesne lived and worked in Grenoble. While there she rented an apartment with a single female companion, rather than with relatives. This preserved her independence and limited her family's exposure as Duchesne aided nonjuring priests who were providing spiritual care for Catholics in the city, especially the imprisoned and the sick and dying throughout the city.

In addition to the possibility of incurring severe penalties for engaging in counter-Revolutionary action by bringing priests to the dying, Duchesne was engaging in physically risky work, including ministering to the sick throughout the typhoid epidemic of 1794 in Grenoble.[46] However, she continued to argue that worldly values were not her concern. For example, when she visited priests who had been sentenced to death, rather than fearing for her life, she regretted that she was not going to the scaffold alongside them. As she was said to have explained to one priest who tried to reassure her that he went willingly, for he believed that she was upset on his behalf, "It is only that I very much wish I could go with you and my sorrow is that I cannot die for the Lord."[47] Like Régis or the Jesuit martyrs, Duchesne intended to serve the poor and imprisoned face-to-face and directly, even if—or especially if—it might lead to martyrdom.

After the most radical phase of the Revolution had passed, Duchesne returned home. While there were still pressing social needs, her mother was nearing the end of her life, and Philippine cared for her in her final months. After Madame Duchesne died, Philippine acquiesced to her father's request and went to the family home at Romans to live with her paternal grandmother, well known for being difficult. This experiment was a disaster. Her grandmother, of a similar temperament to both Philippine and Pierre-François, seems to have felt little reason to concern herself with the feelings or needs of others. When Duchesne left Romans, thrown out by her grandmother, she felt liberated from family expectations and "able to ward off the reproaches Father might have made me for refusing to carry out his wishes."[48] Though she did continue to grieve her inability to please her father, Duchesne explained in her spiritual autobiography that prayer led her to believe that "God did not intend for me to remain in the world," and a "passage of the gospel that speaks about detachment from parents fell into my hands and revived my courage."[49] From her perspective, divine guidance had pushed her toward a life devoted to God and not biological family.

Self-assured about Jesus's call to her, Duchesne did not listen to her family's requests to return to the family home. Instead, she returned to Grenoble and devoted herself again to charitable work among the sick and poor, with an older woman who was "free like [her]."[50] Given the fact that she hoped for her family's financial assistance in renting an apartment, she did, however, need to deal with their feelings of betrayal and abandonment.

Her sister Amélie, for example, felt like Philippine had tricked the family into believing that she was not going to live on her own, when she intended to leave them all along. Philippine wrote a long letter to her sister in which she tried to soothe the hurt feelings, but ultimately she defended her right to dispose of her own life. Philippine said, "My father especially, having no religion to fall back on, will always be prejudiced against me, and I shall carry to my grave the sorrow of having caused him pain."[51] She did not dwell on her inability to please her father, however. She explained, "I have no power over the heart to bring him peace. In uniting myself to Him who directs all events and consoles all hearts, I can do more for my father than by seeking to please him by my attentions and constant companionship."[52]

She also asked her sister to avoid spreading gossip about her choices. She said, "We shall not undertake anything dangerous, but only some good works. We shall live in obscurity—this is our wish—so do not talk to anyone about me or what I am doing. Prudence requires this."[53] Indeed, given the resumption of various dechristianizing pushes, including the arrest of refractory priests in the fall of 1797, Philippine was reminding her sister of the political implications of her work and seeking her support in the form of silence, if nothing else. Duchesne's confidence in the love and comfort of Jesus's heart demanded that she move outside of her family, and she then asked her family to stand behind her, both financially and socially.

Duchesne justified her decision in practical and emotional terms. First, she explained that any role she might fill would be amply met by her sister, and her father would be well cared for. Her choice to leave the family would not result in any inconvenience to him. "Can Father complain as long as you remain with him? You are his daughter, you have almost taken our mother's place by managing the household; your children, whom he loves as his very own, increase the family circle and promise him years of happiness."[54] As much as Duchesne insisted on support for her choices, her letters also demonstrated engagement with the constructs that demanded respect and compassion for parents.[55] Duchesne thus had an ongoing need to reassure herself that she was not abandoning family obligations or failing to act lovingly. She saw a conflict between individual choice and the expected social good of filial obedience, but she believed that her devotion to Christ would "console all hearts," including her father's.

Thus, even as she worried about her refusal to meet family expectations, Duchesne used the language of sentiment in discussing her individual choices. Duchesne's time with her family at Grâne and Romans had confirmed for her that she did not wish to marry and that, indeed, she truly did wish to devote her life wholly to God, doing good works outside of her family context. Instead of pleasing her earthly father, she would follow God's calling for her life. At the same time, she recognized that her devotion to public good works would be something that her family and others would find hard to understand. She defended herself, explaining that it was not selfishness that compelled her to act; it was love for God. "But how could merely human sentiments have part in a resolution that forced me to lift myself above nature in order to correspond to a higher, stronger attraction? . . . Few people will understand my language, and few will refrain from blaming me."[56] Here Duchesne claimed that she was operating against her nature—which preferred the cloister—and for a higher purpose, that of undertaking a mission in the world. Her binary division between human desire and higher sentiment accepted emotion as a basis for decision-making, but she claimed that her vision was consonant with the highest form of sentiment. Just as the revolutionary Saint-Just had argued that "[w]e must not confuse the sentiments of the soul with the passions. The first are a gift of nature and the principle of social life. The others are the fruit of usurpation and the principles of savage life,"[57] so too, Duchesne argued that her desires could be divided into base desire and a higher desire. She resolved the conflict between individual choice and the public good by responding to Christ's love and desire rather than her own.

Some of this resolution came from her reading and prayer. Duchesne reflected on the lives of Jesuit saints, especially Francis Xavier and Francis Régis, as they offered her useful lessons about the vocational questions in the moment facing her. Before returning to Grenoble, she had spent long hours in prayer before the altar of Francis Xavier, so well-known for answering the call to the missions.[58] We already know that the story of Xavier's zeal and personal sacrifices resonated with Duchesne. Francis Xavier's missionary life spoke to her early and impetuous desires to give up everything and become a martyr for the faith, and his radical commitment to offering his life in the service of God, without consideration for the cost, offered Duchesne another way to characterize the risks she had run during the Revolution. In this same context of the Revolutionary experience and the current state of Catholicism in France, Francis Régis's example pointed her closer to home. After all, like Duchesne, Régis had wished to go to the foreign missions, but he had instead preached within France and focused on the education of the young and the poor to reconvert France.

Duchesne made a pilgrimage to the tomb of Régis, going to the nearly destroyed shrine at La Louvesc to seek guidance as to the direction of her life now that cloistered living was no longer possible. The tomb, which "reeked of the sadness and devastation" wrought by the Revolution, was not consoling. However, its very desolation inspired her to work for the restoration of the Church in France as Régis had done.[59] Duchesne left determined to model her life on that of the saintly Francis, to educate little boys and thereby work for their salvation.

In Grenoble, boys ran wild in the streets, and it was difficult for her to entice them to come to her for religious instruction, but with the promise of "[a] few meals and the assurance of some clothing, they were induced to come regularly at one o'clock every day," she said in a letter. She added, "They attracted in their turn many of their friends, and I soon had fourteen or fifteen children of good will, if of an untenable laziness and so loud that they would make everyone in the house exasperated with me."[60] She continued: "Their eagerness to greet me in the street is a torment to me. I now appear to know all the manure carriers. They introduce me to their parents, who resent me because I forbid them to work on Sundays. If the love of St. Francis Régis did not support me, I would have several times left my apostolate. But I have some consolation: these children, who knew no name of any of the divine persons, learn their catechism, prayers and hymns. They all confess and many of them will make their first communion."[61] This catalog of what the boys would learn demonstrates Duchesne's commitment to the boys' own welfare as Duchesne understood it. This was not an undertaking like those proposed by wealthy financiers such as her uncle Claude, which intended to get boys off the street and teach them to be useful, making textiles in a factory. Duchesne's primary concern was not with productive work, but with the young boys' spiritual health. While we may think that Duchesne's goal of teaching them catechism and prayers was not ambitious, it was indeed personal and vocational. Duchesne's reliance on the "love of St. Francis Régis" indicated how other heroic models for action also served to provide a framework for her activity as well as emotional support.[62] Additionally, while teaching the boys may have been a trial and a public embarrassment, it gave Duchesne a sense of the significance and public nature of her mission. She saw that her dedication made a spiritual difference for some of the youth and perhaps even their parents. Even hardships confirmed her vocation, insofar as they looked like those endured by the saints: hostility from non-Christians, misunderstandings, and trials. Creating a new world did not exempt her from trials in this world; rather, the trouble that she encountered along the way demonstrated the need for her work.

After Napoleon's rise to power, many church buildings that had been nationalized became available for religious purposes. In that context Duchesne soon came to believe that her mission in the world not only required her to live on her own but even to reconstitute religious life. She decided to reclaim the Visitation convent at Sainte Marie-d'en-Haut and reconvert it into a religious institution with a boarding school. Though the religious superiors around her generally supported the idea, they were not in favor of purchasing the monastery, so she sought out her family's approval and financial assistance. In the end Madame Rollin— her cousin, Josephine Perier—persuaded her well-connected husband to petition the prefect on Duchesne's behalf, and Philippine used personal funds from the Duchesne family to pay rent on the building. Sainte Marie was to be hers in December 1801, and she planned to move back to the convent that had been so important to her religious formation.

Duchesne invited the former sisters of the Visitation convent to return with her, but they were unwilling to move because the disrepair of the building and the lack of funds on which to live. She, however, did not let that dissuade her. She said, "I was not going to delay for a single hour my return to that holy asylum, for which I had longed so much. It was time to show that the world had lied in daring to say that we were forced victims [in the convent] and that we were happy to be back with Him."[63] Duchesne linked her vocation as religious educator with her physical return to the cloister. The language that she used explicitly recognized that the rhetoric of the Revolution had claimed that nuns were useless and unnatural and depicted them as the prey of clergy and victims in a system that had locked them away. Duchesne rushed back to her convent to demonstrate that she embraced—longed for—religious life and rejected individual secular life, to show that her embracing of a religious mission was a decision freely made.

However, further trials on this score awaited Duchesne, as taking up the mantle of free choice hardly relieved her from scrutiny but instead placed her more firmly into the sphere of public criticism. Duchene's recounting of the *Story of Sainte Marie*, which echoed the form of sentimental novels, had as a central plot component the strength of opposition to Duchesne's plans. Duchesne described how, as she moved into Sainte Marie and invited former Visitation nuns to join her, she began to experience comments that disapproved of her leadership and public mission.[64] There was much be suspicious of and to criticize. The monastery itself was no longer a particularly hospitable location for the Visitation nuns. The convent had fallen into disrepair during the Revolution, when it had been used as a prison, and many of the former nuns were reluctant to return. Once some did come back, the community was divided by different priorities and expectations, including disagreements about the role of cloister and the place of a public mission. Duchesne found herself as the center of gossip about her role in the upheaval, especially as former community members deserted Sainte Marie. Now, instead of being a dupe of external forces, she began to hear, both within the convent and in Grenoble, that she was headstrong and selfish, that her mission was an attempt to impose her will on the world and not born out of a desire to do good.[65] Duchesne took this hostility to heart. She wrote, "I was desolated; I was a subject of scandal. People said loudly that I had driven away the religious, that I would not yield in anything, that no one could possibly live with me, that Fathers Brochier and Rivet with their exalted ideas were the only ones who took my part."[66] Duchesne was accused, in the fashion of Saint-Just, of acting not in response to love but out of a desire to impose her will on others.

Amid these charges Duchesne's heart was indeed consoled by Father Rivet, who appreciated—at least to some degree—her strength and faithfulness, which he saw as a sign of growth for the future. When former Visitandines abandoned the convent, the women who remained chose to call the community by a new name: Ladies of the Propagation of the Faith, a name that was linked to missionary outreach and the Sacred Heart (figure 22).[67] Rivet soon spoke to Duchesne about joining these women to a new congregation, one whose mission was centered in devotion to the Sacred Heart and was also influenced by the Society of Jesus.[68] Given that devotion to the Sacred Heart was linked to Visitation spirituality and also mediated through Jesuit devotion, this combination was ideal to Duchesne and the women who joined. It was also in keeping with Michelet's description of the tenor of nineteenth-century religion and fears about Jesuit influence leading women astray.[69]

Though Duchesne could not know it at the time, the forceful advocacy for her ideals that had made her such a target also marked her, to some, as a woman of exceptional promise. Father Varin, the priest who was working most closely with Sophie Barat in establishing the congregation that Duchesne would later join, heartily approved of Duchesne's vigor and told Barat that she could rest easy, knowing that Philippine Duchesne was nearby.[70] Even if she had known about Father Varin's deep faith in her, this affirmation might not have provided a great deal of consolation in Grenoble. Duchesne agreed to unify her community with Barat's, but delays in communication meant that her letters went unanswered, even as legal concerns about the ownership of Sainte Marie also mounted. Duchesne worried that she had offended Sophie Barat and that the delay would destroy her community. Father Varin reassured her that Barat would soon arrive, and that both groups were fully united in spirit and in heart; there was no difference between them.[71] However, Duchesne's community continued to undergo serous trials, as the local community in Grenoble gossiped about the developments at Sainte Marie. In particular Duchesne's attempt to lead the community toward religious life in a vocation of which she had taken ownership clearly struck a chord with the community at large. When Madeleine Sophie Barat came to be the superior in 1804 and to absorb the community at Sainte Marie into the Religious of the Sacred Heart, the pace of rumors only quickened.

Conscious of community disapproval of consecrated religious life and of the anti-Revolutionary implications of the use of the term "Sacred Heart," the sisters tried to clothe themselves respectably, both in name and demeanor. Their public name was not "Religious of the Sacred Heart," but "Daughters of Faith," and they adopted clothing that was essentially secular in inspiration. Instead of habits, they wore plain black dresses with white fichus and triangular shawls. On their heads, they wore a white cap or bonnet, much like other women of the day would have chosen.[72]

Dressing respectably and carefully was not enough. Some people in Grenoble claimed that the women who were joining the Religious of the Sacred Heart were doing so to expiate a life of sin or wished to hide from their past. Duchesne worried in her journal: "People just cannot remain silent about our house. . . . They are so tasteless as to call the girls 'penitents,' to question their faith. We live the mystery of a path entirely hidden in God with Jesus Christ; they therefore conclude that we hide because we should be ashamed. . . . Others question the teaching ability of the religious, making fun of their youth, especially that of the superior. . . . As if the gifts of God were limited to a certain age, as if the Holy Spirit relied on our human nature."[73] Young women who insisted on living outside of a family context were all potentially "public women," expiating their life of sin, and if not that, too immature to know what was best. These criticisms demonstrate the ways in which any woman who pursued an active life could have her virtue called into question. Some criticized the convent for abandoning strict cloister to carry out its public mission of service. Others attacked the women's ability to carry out their stated goals, claiming that success at their public mission was impossible and following their chosen leader a fool's errand. They were too young, too inexperienced, and too female to succeed in independently educating young women. They should return to a less public, more moderate lifestyle.

The women's spiritual directors urged them to ignore the publicity. Of course, the very fact that the rumors about the women's motives became fodder for spiritual growth and content for the priests' homilies demonstrates the fact that the women knew that they were the source of public discussion and that their lifestyle was causing scandal. As Duchesne's journal recounted, a priest offering Mass "congratulated us on being fools in the eyes of the world, as he himself was a fool. He explained the divine folly, the folly of the cross which makes us pleasing to Jesus Christ but contemptible in the eyes of the world."[74] The content of the homily offers a glimpse at the accusations surrounding the women who joined the community and the ways in which the women were being attacked from both sides. The homily also echoed the sense of estrangement that was both highlighted and valued in the literature that surrounded these women. The daily trials and the hostility of the world were not signs that they were wrong, but rather that they were doing God's work. Their souls had rejected the world but were united with Christ, pleasing in sacrifice and love of charity.

Duchesne also had the great reassurance of knowing that her own family at least no longer disapproved of her choices. In 1804 one of Philippine's sisters, Madame Jouve (née Charlotte-Euphrosine Duchesne), sent her daughter, Euphrosine, to Sainte Marie to be educated by the Religious of the Sacred Heart. Philippine sent letters to her sister with news about Euphrosine's adjustment to life with the religious, telling her, for example, that the eight-year-old's "studies go well, in spite of her great exuberance, which makes study time seem very long to her. I can recognize her by her animation of her little body."[75] Duchesne also noted that Euphrosine was healthy, despite a bit of a cold. The aunt took care to send updates in her letters, along with samples of the girl's work. It was clear that she understood looking after her niece to be an important trust and was letting her sister know that the niece was being well cared for. Indeed, she closed this same letter by saying, "Adieu dear Sister. How happy I am to have here at Sainte Marie a proof of your affection for me in which I can find you again."[76]

Mme Jouve soon sent Euphrosine's younger sister, Amélie, to be educated at Sainte Marie as well. Duchesne sent letters to her sister offering thoughts on their spiritual development, their personalities, and their character flaws. Through her work, Duchesne found a new connection to her sister.

Despite this sympathy, storm clouds disturbed the concord between Madame Jouve and Duchesne after the oldest daughter, Euphrosine, finished her formal schooling at Sainte Marie. Shortly after Euphrosine made her First Communion, her parents brought her home. Like Philippine's parents, they introduced her to young men in anticipation that she would make a good match, and given Euphrosine's good looks, there was no shortage of prospects. The family hoped that she would agree to marry a banker's son.[77] However, Euphrosine soon fell seriously ill. When she heard the news, Duchesne wrote to Jouve and suggested that perhaps the loving mother ought to offer her child as a permanent sacrifice, "since human means were powerless to save her." She continued, "Euphrosine has never given me her secret confidences, but I have reason to suspect that she has some idea of the cloister. One day when they were speaking of chastity, she let fall this remark: *That is the virtue I love above all others*."[78] Jouve not only rejected the idea but was deeply wounded by her sister's suggestion; the frequent exchanges diminished.

In addition to quiet games and family reading of tragedies and comedies, Euphrosine read stories of the saints as she convalesced, especially those of Aloysius Gonzaga (who fought his noble family and gave up his aristocratic title to become a Jesuit) and Francis Régis, who had been so important to Duchesne.[79] Euphrosine helped her mother with the housework and the education of her sisters.[80] Duchesne and Jouve's relationship became even more strained as Euphrosine's piety increased, especially once it became clear that she did indeed wish to become a religious of the Sacred Heart and join her aunt at Sainte Marie. Duchesne wrote to Madame Jouve in 1813 to explain that the niece had finally confided to her that she wished to be a nun.

> I have suspected the secret yearnings of your eldest daughter for a long time, though she tried to keep them well hidden from me. And this was the subject of a thought I offered to you when she was so ill—a thought which, I was told, caused you much pain. Yet what I merely suspected then is now a reality. Euphrosine wishes to leave you, not for a human husband, not for an earthly home, but to give herself to God, who has given her everything she has. . . . I have promised to [speak to you] for her, knowing, of course, that I speak to a loving mother, but still more to a Christian mother who is accustomed to the most heroic acts of resignation.[81]

The mother, despite being offered the opportunity to engage in heroic and Christian acts, was not ready to yield. Angry and frustrated, she refused to send her third daughter, Constance, who had been planning to join her sister in boarding and even threatened to withdraw Amélie from Sainte Marie.[82] Duchesne's letter in response betrays her irritation with her sister's priorities, as in it she admitted, "I am really vexed that you refused to send us Constance," and went on to detail Amélie's character flaws by way of insisting that she would do better in the convent than at home.[83]

To understand Jouve's resistance, one might note that she eventually gave birth to fifteen children, many of whom died young. Both Euphrosine and Duchesne recognized that Jouve wanted to keep her oldest child close and to have her assistance with the other children. For example, Duchesne wrote, "through natural sentiments, I place myself in your position, and I realize what a weight of sorrow this project must cause you, especially in the case of one of your children from whom you expected so much help."[84] Duchesne also referred more than once to the hardships of maternity. Upon hearing of a new pregnancy from other family members, she wrote to her sister, saying "I have learned . . . that you are much thinner and seem to be pregnant again, and I realize that this condition is a new cross for you. For no matter how much one loves the children God sends, there is still fear at their coming, a certain right and natural dread of suffering and of the burden which a large family entails."[85] Duchesne hoped that educating her nieces would lighten her sister's load, but she did not ignore the difficulty of her sister's position and her desire to have her oldest living daughter nearby, even as she placed them into the context of worldly concerns, natural and not higher sentiments. The exchanges also remind us that the sentimental appeal of domesticity was tempered by the danger of pregnancy and childbirth and the work involved in parenting, especially with a husband who was often away in Paris.

We do not have letters that detail Duchesne's struggle between her family's wishes for her and her own wishes to enter the cloister. However, the letters between Jouve and Duchesne are significant for understanding celibacy, sentiment, and vocation because they offer insight not only into what Euphrosine herself saw as a vocation and calling but also how

Duchesne understood religious life in the context of a family that was hostile to that choice. Duchesne's words also show us the emotional and practical reasons behind Jouve's opposition. Duchesne acknowledged that Madame Jouve worried about Euphrosine's health as well as the loss of her assistance. But close on the heels of that admission, Duchesne defended Euphrosine's right to make a choice about the disposition of her own soul and justified her preference for a higher calling, most specifically in joining the Sacred Heart sisters.

> You may be sure that this blow comes from God Himself. Euphrosine is not the kind of person to be influenced—she decides for herself . . . I knew that if she put no obstacles to the inspiration of grace, all this would lead her to choose the cloister, with freedom from a husband and the mission to save souls. Do you think she has made a poor choice in preferring Jesus Christ to any man? The riches of heaven to those of earth? Occupations that draw us upward to those that fasten us to earth? . . . There is nothing low or human in Euphrosine's views, and there is no outside pressure urging her on. Her desires come from God who governs hearts as He wills.[86]

These words defended Duchesne as much as her niece, for they absolved her of interference and hearkened back to the choice that Duchesne had also made—more than once—to live a life attached only to God and not to a human father or husband, with her human heart responding to God's desire.

For that reason, when Duchesne wrote as a loving sister and aunt, she could plausibly say "I share your suffering" even as she immediately went on to say "while at the same time I rejoice in a vocation whose value I realize."[87] She reminded her sister of their mutual Christian faith and called Jouve to embody her belief in the value of Christian sacrifice for her daughter. "If a loving mother was offered the most attractive prince in the world as a fiancé for her daughter, but one who would take her far away, the mother would forget the pain of separation and think only of the illustrious alliance and speak of it with joy. Why is Jesus Christ the only one to whom it is so terrible to give oneself? Where is our faith?"[88] Thus, even as these letters ostensibly speak of Euphrosine's vocation, they also serve as a poignant reminder of Philippine Duchesne's years of struggle and her insistence on her freedom of choice for the sake of love. They remind the reader of her sense of the value of her apostolate, including devotion to the Sacred Heart as well as martyrdom in the service of God.

As a woman enmeshed in family relationships, Duchesne also knew that rebuffing family plans for marriage and alliances and striking out on one's own could be a rejection of the family itself. She had addressed her own sisters' concerns when she returned to Grenoble from Grâne and now Duchesne reminded Madame Jouve that her daughter loved her deeply and felt pain at leaving her family. She did this in multiple letters. When Duchesne first intervened on Euphrosine's behalf, she explained that she was serving as an intermediary because her niece could not bring herself to speak of her vocation, knowing how it would upset her mother. She explained that Euphrosine's early illness should be interpreted as "the effect of too much sentiment," as her love for family was warring with "her desires that came from God, who governs hearts as he wishes."[89] Later, after Madame Jouve had finally given her permission for Euphrosine to explore life as a religious, Philippine reassured Jouve, "As to her love for you [*sensibilité*], never doubt it . . . the tears that she spills when she receives your letters . . . demonstrate the deep love in her soul for her good mother."[90] Jouve might have doubted her daughter's love for her, because Euphrosine had hidden her vocation from her parents. She refused to agree to family plans for marriage and insisted on finding her own path. Her aunt explained all this as the result of excessive, not insufficient, sentiment.

> She has such great strength of character, which she needed in order to leave such loving parents. She had no attraction for married life. Several times she said, "the virtue I love most of all to hear about is virginity." She aspired, in the times where she was teaching the poor, to suffer martyrdom. . . . If you never heard her speak of her vocation, do not be surprised. When the desires of one's heart call

for separation from a dearly loved family, it is not easy to speak of them. The heart suffers, knowing that it must cause suffering.[91]

The desires of the heart were united with Christian sacrifice, but in her context of sentimental affection and domesticity, Euphrosine asked her aunt to mediate, to reassure her family that a wish to leave them was not because they or she were lacking in love.

Once her desires were known, Euphrosine could address her mother herself. She used the language of Christian devotion both to speak to her mother's heart as well as to remind Mme Jouve that God was the rightful director of lives, and He wanted Euphrosine to be a religious. Her letters home tried to break down her mother's resistance. She said, "I do not doubt that at birth you offered me to God, as is the duty of a Christian mother. Well! He accepted the offer. No doubt, since he calls me to religious life, I would have lost myself in the world."[92] Here, Euphrosine tried to recast her mother's wishes for her toward salvation, explaining that if she were to marry, it would be a vocation for which she was unfit, and would likely put her soul in danger. She also defended her desire, explaining that she sought "the happiness of being freed from the continual anxieties with which one is tested in the world."[93]

Euphrosine employed several other strategies, all of which recognized the emotional impact of her departure. She was sure to tell her mother that she was touched by her concern, and that Euphrosine recognized that her mother's resistance to her vocation was a sign of affection. She wrote, "I cannot help but see that you are guided in your refusal by a tenderness that makes you try to prevent hardship for your children."[94] She also acknowledged that her mother's love for her made it difficult to let her daughter go, and said that she ought to, as a Christian mother, "show ... gratitude to God with a sacrifice that is hard on your heart, but which will make your daughter happy. It is not to a man that you give her, it is to God. How can we call lost what is always found in him, when He will repay you with accrued interest?"[95] Like Duchesne, the daughter used sacrificial language not only for herself but to convince her mother to let her go. In practical terms Euphrosine wrote frequently, in part to make certain that her mother did not "accuse [Euphrosine's] heart of forgetfulness and indifference."[96] She also looked to fill the void in her mother's heart by finding her a friend and suggested that the mother of a fellow novice might be well suited to her temperament.

Eventually Euphrosine believed that her mother had been convinced of her position, and as the time for final vows approached, she told her mother that the idea of professing final vows was "very sweet balm for her heart," and asked that her mother would not only agree but also obtain the consent of her father.[97] Her father did acquiesce and even had a gift—a goblet engraved with an image of the Sacred Heart—made for the occasion. After the fact, Euphrosine reported that her mother made the sacrifice of final vows with "a good heart."[98] When she made her final vows, Euphrosine took the name Aloysia, in honor of Aloysius Gonzaga, the young Jesuit who went against family expectations that he, as the oldest of seven children, would be a political heir. Euphrosine's younger sister Amélie told her that the name was novelistic and did not fit her, but the emotional connotations of the name, as well as the history of the patron saint to whom it referred, were surely part of the appeal.[99]

This sacrifice was played out again: both Amélie and Constance also decided to become consecrated religious. Aloysia followed her aunt's example and intervened on behalf of at least one sister. Like Philippine, Aloysia shared that she understood her mother's pain, "You would have the right to accuse my heart if I did not come to testify to you that I share with you in the various sentiments which Amélie's resolution will cause you."[100] She went on to say that she wrote well in advance in order to prepare her mother for the blow, knowing that "your tenderness would make you resent a separation for which you have not been prepared."[101] Aloysia reassured her mother that her daughters still loved her, even though their decisions would separate them from their families and wound their mother's heart.

Families grieved when their daughters declared that they wished to become consecrated religious. This suffering was not limited to the moment of declaration or of final vows but continued as the needs of the order reminded them of their sisters' and daughters' separations from biological family. News about the outcome of difficult illnesses had to be sought by letter, visits were hoped for but canceled when the order's needs changed, and in Duchesne's case, thousands of miles and an ocean eventually separated her from her entire family in France, a distance that meant she would likely never see her biological family again. Not surprisingly the young women who chose, against their families' inclinations, to pursue a celibate religious life hardly had to look to literature or society to experience disapproval. Family responses made it clear that everyone suffered because of the destruction of traditional hopes and expectations. The women who became consecrated religious understood that and worried about it in nineteenth-century language of sentiment, emotion, and the heart; words that echoed rather than rejected their feminine obligations to love and nurture within their homes. However, they also used that language to underline the depths of the sacrifice that they were making and to demonstrate the significance of their calling as ordained by a higher power. Family sacrifice could serve as further confirmation of the value of the vocation itself.

At the beginning of the nineteenth century there were hardly more than ten thousand nuns in France. Eighty years later, there were ten times as many. There had not been a similar increase in male religious vocations; instead of being outnumbered by male clerics, sisters now substantially outnumbered priests and brothers.[102] Claude Langlois notes that most congregations created in the first part of the nineteenth century were founded by women of the elite. He attributes this to several causes, including the fact that clerics were too busy reconstructing parish life to be concerned with founding orders. Women, he argues, were more available for the task, and women of privilege had the resources to devote to the work. Additionally their charity was more likely to fly under the radar during the Terror and even be encouraged after the Concordat.[103] While these statements are true, they are incomplete. Philippine Duchesne and Euphrosine Jouve's own words demonstrate that the women of these congregations were not unaware of the controversial nature of their mission and that they often forged their path forward in opposition to social and familial norms, convinced that they had a higher calling of service to the world. Rather than merely taking the place of men who were too busy to handle this work, they saw their calling as sacrificial and uniquely authorized by God.

An examination of these decisions and letters indicates that martyrdom and sacrifice, far from serving as detractions, were central to the appeal of religious life in the first half of the nineteenth century. It was a powerful vocational choice to serve God outside of one's own family context, to join this cadre of sisters across France and, indeed, across the globe. While families often sat in opposition, their daughters and sisters consciously preferred celibacy over marriage and individual vocational ideals over the plans of their families, even as sentimental language allowed them to communicate the power of their vocational obligations. An emphasis on the heart as a seat of emotion and honest judgment gave women space for independent action and even criticism of the world as it existed. Although William M. Reddy argues in his *Navigation of Feelings* that there was a move away from sentiment because it was overly idealistic and "lowered expectations . . . were more in tune with the reality of human emotional experience," the evidence of this chapter indicates that some women searched for a way to reconcile sentimental high expectations—and the belief that their desires could not be met within marriage—with everyday life.[104] Sentimentalism may have looked like a "private code" to nineteenth-century men, who intended to limit emotions to the private sphere, but for women, sentimentality and idealism could not be so easily segregated.

Fifty years after Duchesne first entered the convent against her parents' will, a philosophical emphasis on biological determinism had advanced in such a way that some authors argued a woman's life without maternity was meaningless, and that the emotional language that supported the sacrificial vision of the world was dangerous when uncontrolled. For example, Jules Michelet lauded the power of women, but only in the context of their biological abilities: "We all are, and ever shall be, the debtors of women. They are mothers; this says everything."[105] He went on to explain that the best portion of women's life was "her family and her domestic hearth." When she left this, she bartered away what mattered most.[106] Michelet also argued that women were distracted by piety derived from seventeenth-century forms—like that of the Visitation and the Sacred Heart—which spoke a language of love. Instead of giving life through their domesticity, they chose to spend their love outside the home. "[B]y mingling the language of love with that of devotion," they could satisfy both carnal pleasure and the desire for penitence. Michelet even claimed, "If, without being seen, you could listen to the conversation in a coquettish neighborhood, you would not always be able to say whether it is the lover or the spiritual director who is speaking."[107] Michelet's claim, like his language about the carnal nature of devotion to the Sacred Heart, was located within fears that priests controlled young girls through religious ideas, especially manifested in the practices of confession and spiritual direction. He wrote, "We can only get authority over ideas by the will itself . . . a particular and personal will, which attaches itself perseveringly to a female and truly dominates her because it makes her in its own image. To truly reign is to rule over a soul. . . . The end thus settled, the priest has a great advantage which no one else possesses. His business is with a soul which gives itself up of its own accord."[108] Michelet demonstrated his belief that women would be always, necessarily, subordinate to men; the question was who would have control over women's individual judgment, priests or husbands. Philippine Duchesne and Euphrosine Jouve, however, argued that no mortal had control of their hearts. Once they dedicated their lives to Christ, no one—male or female—could dissuade them from their choice.

< 5 >

Changing the World

*Pauline Jaricot, Social Reform, and
the Power of the Heart*

> I was around seventeen years old when my poor heart, tired of its fruitless
> pursuit of happiness in a corrupt and perishable world, finally resolved to
> fix its inconstancy in God's love.... I could no longer remain in sentimen-
> tal inaction, and I eagerly sought something that could fill the immensity
> of my heart.
>
> —Pauline Jaricot, *Story of My Life* (ca. 1822)

Pauline Jaricot was born on July 22, 1799, in Lyon, France. Like Euphrosine
Jouve, born three years earlier, Jaricot was a child of the Revolutionary
era, steeped in a sentimental understanding of the world that valorized
heroism and martyrdom. Both women grew up in wealthy and influential
families where Catholic teaching shaped their characters. The birth—and
death—of children figured prominently in their homes and extended
families. Dechristianization marked their communities, and their early
years were also directly touched by the upheaval surrounding Napoleon's
rule, including the warfare that reached the southeast of France.

Even though she dedicated her life to Christ and vowed to remain unmarried, Jaricot never entered a convent; she argued that life as a consecrated
religious was not her destiny. Rather than joining a religious order, where
she would have had the immediate support of other women religious, Jaricot stayed in the world to work for change. She spent time with workers and
used her financial resources and business contacts to alleviate the misery of
their existence. Jaricot focused on what she could organize as a layperson,
and she grounded her work in a desire to ease the difficulty of carrying on

the faith in a modern, industrializing world. Pauline Jaricot thus sought to facilitate global missionary work, but she also acted in the vein of lay activism and social Catholicism, long before Pope Leo XIII's publication of *Rerum Novarum* (1891) addressed the rights and duties of capital and labor.[1]

From the moment that she dedicated her heart to God at the age of seventeen, Pauline Jaricot said that she worked for the spiritual and material redemption of the world.[2] She spent her life in hard work, prayer, and sacrifice, as she had envisioned at a young age and again in her teens. She corresponded with priests and religious; she worked with the poor of her community and appealed to her wealthy contacts for assistance. The narrative of her life was similar to that of Philippine Duchesne; she was devoted to missionary work and to the belief that the world she lived in needed to be improved. She used language emphasizing sacrifice, the rejection of a flawed world, and emotional unity with God.

As with Duchesne, the sources that tells us about Jaricot's life are hagiographical and often curated.[3] Jaricot's spiritual autobiography, written in her late teens and early twenties, was produced at the direction of her spiritual director. It shares much in common with other nineteenth-century autobiographical writing.[4] It emphasizes her call from God as the necessary response by the heart of a discerning individual. *Infinite Love*, Jaricot's widely circulated theological treatise, reinforces sentimental constructs as well. These texts, as well as the hagiographic literature that collated material corresponding to her life, cast Jaricot's life in the context of a spiritual battle and foregrounded martyrdom, heroism, and the power of a loving heart. Although the texts were produced in the context of nineteenth-century Catholic devotion, the larger cultural setting echoes through their paragraphs. Jaricot's biography, when read in conjunction with her early writings and her milieu, conveys her powerful debt to sentimental language. It also demonstrates the authority that these ideas offered to devout women.

Unlike Duchesne or Jouve, Jaricot did not describe herself as always having been in exile from the world. Though the beginning of her life was centered in religious devotion, her early adolescence was not. She had been raised in a devout and charitable family; her father's work on behalf of the Church was recognized by Pius VII, who personally blessed the Jar-icot family when he spent time in Lyon.[5] Pauline and her brother Philéas fantasized about missionary work as young children, though Philéas insisted that girls could not go to the missions, because they didn't know Latin and couldn't ride camels, tigers, or crocodiles. Pauline eventually accepted his statement that, as a girl, the safest role for her would be to raise money for the missions rather than participate directly.[6] However, Jaricot's early dream of supporting missionary work was quickly subsumed by other interests. As a young girl, she was socially ambitious. She was the youngest daughter of a prominent Lyon family, the only unmarried girl. Well dressed, attractive, and an excellent singer, she set the fashions for her circle. Social life was no chore; she described herself as "boy crazy" from an early age.[7] Jaricot certainly did not replicate Jouve's early passion for the virtue of chastity, though she shared the same desire for heroic action. Instead, in her spiritual autobiography, Jaricot emphasized that she had enjoyed dressing to advantage, reading novels, dancing, and singing love songs. She even contracted a secret engagement to a family friend.[8]

Her life changed when, in 1814, she fell off a high stool. The fall precip-itated a medical crisis that removed her from the whirl of social activity. Her movements became uncontrolled, and she suffered from convul-sions.[9] While ill, she spent time in contemplation and read religious material. After a long period of convalescence, Jaricot recovered. Pleased to be well—though her heart continued to give her trouble for the rest of her life—in 1816 she again took up her place as the arbiter of fash-ion in her group of friends. Soon, however, this ended. Jaricot heard a fiery Lenten homily about the perils of vanity by the Abbé Jean Wendel Würtz.[10] She was deeply affected by the message and approached Würtz after Mass. After posing some questions to him about the application of his sermon, she asked him to hear her confession. She cast aside the fashionable clothes that she'd long fancied and instead purposely wore ill-fitting and unfashionable purple clothing as a way of keeping herself from vanity.[11] She stopped reading novels and quit attending balls. Like Philippine Duchesne, Jaricot went on a pilgrimage to the tomb of St. Fran-cis Régis. By Christmas of 1816 she made a personal vow to never marry.[12]

Following these changes, in one of Jaricot's earliest public actions, in 1819, at only twenty years old, she created an organization to support Christian conversion both at home and abroad by collecting "pennies and prayers" from workers for the support of missionary priests. The women who joined, called "Reparatices of the Heart of Jesus," not only promised to donate a sou (five centimes) from their salaries each week but also met to pray together and read aloud missionary letters.[13] The association combined sacrifice, religious instruction for the poor, and prayer for the conversion of non-Christians, along with reinforcement of the need for spiritual perseverance by the faithful.

Jaricot explained that her design grew out of a vision of two lamps, one overflowing with oil and the other empty but being filled from that which was full. The empty one represented France as a place where the faith was dying out, having been decimated under the Revolution. The abundant lamp, on the other hand, represented the faith of missions, which would be strong enough to renew the faith of Europe.[14] In this way the group was rooted in a sense that the French must atone for their rejection of Christianity and commission of sins against religious belief, as the name "Reparatices of the Heart of Jesus" indicates.[15] Additionally, the intersection of reparation, the Sacred Heart, and Alacocque's vision for the Christian destiny of France resonated with the experience of turmoil in the Revolutionary era.

The organization grew rapidly from Saint-Vallier (where Jaricot's brother-in-law ran a silk mill), to Lyon, Paris, and beyond. Jaricot's bourgeois family and friends joined the workers in donating money; the Reparatrices collected significant contributions. Jaricot felt called to turn the mission of the Reparatrices into a source of consistent financial assistance for missionaries, one that was systematic and could be counted on. To accomplish this, she decided on a plan for expansion, which also included more regular record keeping and methods of collection. Jaricot organized the contributors into groups. One person would collect the donations of ten members, another would collect the donations of those tens as part of supervision of one hundred, and so on; each member was encouraged to recruit others to be part of a group of ten.

She called the organization by a new name: The Society for the Propagation of the Faith. This name, with its suggestion of global missionary work and martyrdom, was also linked to the Sacred Heart. As one pious image explained, missionaries were a sign of God's power in the middle of the fallen world (figure 22). By naming her society in this way, Jaricot demonstrated her adherence to a reparational and ascetic perspective where the heavenly Jerusalem was uncorrupted by and loftier than the world. However, subscribing to this point of view did not alleviate responsibility; if anything, it made it more pressing. Jaricot's society allowed the faithful, organized within communities, to participate in mission work and view their lives in relationship to a global faith that needed recuperation at home as well as abroad.

The success of the young woman's efforts—more than 1,500 francs sent to missionaries in the first year, more than double the previous year's collections for the Paris Mission Society—did not escape notice.[16] Local priests demanded that she stop her collections because they claimed that her group caused division and confusion for other missionary agencies.[17] Her spiritual director reassured her that she could continue to collect, saying that she was too stupid to have come up with this idea on her own, so it must have been God's plan.[18] He explained that he would personally intervene on her behalf. When this did not stop the attacks, Jaricot herself wrote to the episcopal vicar, asking if she had done something wrong in forming this group without his permission. She offered to disband. He wrote back and gave her permission to continue but said that she should refrain from trying to increase the reach of the organization.[19] Encouraged, Jaricot continued to direct the society.

Nevertheless, the amount of money coming in at her behest, now totaling over seven thousand francs, led priests to take over the society's direction in 1822. It seemed obvious to them that a young woman could not possibly administer a worldwide organization of increasing financial power. Jaricot was "allowed" to continue to collect from the group of one hundred that she headed but otherwise was eliminated from the planning and running of the society. By 1826 the society was bringing in such large amounts of money for the missions that it drew the attention of newspapers; both *Le Journal des débats* and the *Gazette universelle de Lyon* commented on it.[20] The former was suspicious, while the latter defended its organization, calling attention to the prominence of the men running it. Pope Pius VII sent approval, accompanied by a personal benediction for Jaricot and her initial work.[21] However, he was one of the few who remembered her founding role. Most, like the newspapers, saw the society as a product of men's organizing. To any casual observer, Jaricot's role had been effaced. The society continued, under the supervision of clerics and influential laymen.[22]

Both working hard for the society and being pushed out took a toll on Jaricot's health. In the main she accepted the transfer of control to men, saying that she had "too worldly a soul" to run a spiritual work of this nature.[23] However, Jaricot felt the loss deeply. When she sought the advice of her spiritual director, he counseled her to spend more time in prayer and contemplation, rather than wearing herself out in public service to the poor and sick, as she had been doing.[24] He asked her to refrain from all physical works of charity for three years, to focus on her spiritual life and allow her body to heal.[25] This was a real deprivation; Jaricot felt that people needed her outside her home and chapel. However, she trusted Würtz. In coming to terms with his advice, she compared her condition to that of a silkworm, deprived of leaves, which occupied itself in making a cocoon among twigs.[26] The worm's end would seem disastrous but would effect glorious results.

Jaricot thus followed her confessor's advice, but her private reflections soon bore a public component. Jaricot saw the possibilities of using the modern power of the press, demonstrated to advantage during the Revolution, to defend, rather than attack, Catholic faith. In 1820 she had written a pamphlet on the love of Christ and the meaning of the Sacred Heart. After she was removed from the Society for the Propagation of the Faith, she revised her treatise, had it printed, and offered it for sale. The title of the work was *Infinite Love in the Divine Eucharist, or the Heart of Jesus, Health of the Church and of Society*.[27] In an excellent demonstration of both the importance and the flexibility of sentimental idioms, *Infinite Love* mixed catechetical, hagiographic, and sentimental forms. It underlined Jaricot's early sense of herself as a public actor, responding to and promulgating the call of God's mercy and love. Like Duchene and Jouve, Jaricot wrote in ways that demonstrated a concern with her obligations to others, engagement with the conflict between social expectations and individual desires, and the importance of sacrifice. Even more than Philippine and Euphrosine, Jaricot's writing emphasized the heart's role in knowing truth and directing her toward public action.

An introduction, written by Würtz, authorized the young woman's writing and centered her theological reflections in a context of French political and religious conflict.[28] Würtz emphasized humanity's trespasses against divine love, including the destruction of the Catholic Church in France. For ultramontanists, Gallicanism stood as an example of undue compromise and disobedience to the head of the Catholic Church. This critique condemned both past and present—Constitutional clergy, Napoleonic bishops, and the acceptance of restrictions on papal authority. The preface, however, went beyond political commentary to insist on an emotional response from readers. If Jesus's heart was the center of spiritual life, just as human hearts were the center of temporal lives, society needed to accept God's mercy and return to true Catholic religious practice, including daily prayer and obedience to the pope.[29]

This work, written by Jaricot in her early twenties, thus intended to convince a reading public of the need for religious change and reparation in France as well as the path to mercy shown by Jesus's Sacred Heart. As early as 1823 Jaricot's treatise used modern forms of communication in ways that would be echoed by later devotions, including the promulgation of devotion to the Miraculous Medal (after 1830) and veneration of Our Lady of Lourdes (after 1858). *Infinite Love* directly addressed Jaricot's desire to engage the broader world; the work began with an appeal that placed itself in the context of a public mission. Jaricot wrote that she dared to hope that God inspired her work as "the fire of my expressions, the intelligence of my mind, the love of my heart, the support of my weakness," such that she could "faithfully accomplish [God's] designs."[30] In this case those plans included using the press to defend and promote the faith. Jaricot's reflection on the obligation of all Christian hearts to respond to God's call first went on sale in Lyon. Within a year publishers in Paris also printed editions of the work and included a new introduction dedicated to the memory of Pius VII.

In this treatise Jaricot denounced an intellectual approach to the faith that might allow political concession but prioritize worldly values over obedience to Christ. The annihilation of the Church—continued by those who were charged with assisting it—demanded an emotional response. Jaricot wrote: "Ah! I feel [the pain you experience]; it comes from your ministers, a thousand times more dear to your heart than even the most beloved wife is to her husband. . . . Nothing consoles a wounded love."[31] The thought that Jesus would continue to look after His Church, despite its deplorable state, "should move the heart of every adorer, and inspire them to the most tender sentiments and generous devotion."[32] The condition of the Church required that the heart respond to the wounds that humanity had caused; the "bright contrast of good and evil" that it depicted fit perfectly with the language of sentiment and the problems of the era.[33]

Indeed, Jaricot's treatise, over a hundred pages of exalted language extolling the need to respond to Christ with one's heart, may strike modern readers as both mawkish and narrow-minded. However, as William Reddy has demonstrated, understood in the setting of post-Revolutionary politics, intransigent sentimentality staked a political and public claim; it revealed rational concessions, centered in sense experience, as artificial and untrue, even a form of slavery.[34] In that context the following passage should be read not as a private thought but as a public reflection on the role of belief in the modern world: "Jesus Christ entered the outer vestibule of the senses, where the carnal man resides. From there, his touching voice penetrated the inner apartment of the soul, where the spiritual man resides. However, He found the doors closed, because sinners have been trained [to respond] not to the true regret of their hearts, but only the actions ingrained in their senses. In a word, the heart has not triumphed over the senses, but the senses have conquered the heart."[35] Sensory experience and rational reasoning were not the deepest source of truth; truth came from hearts speaking directly to each other. Through devotion to the Sacred Heart, individuals would reach true spiritual wisdom. "It is, therefore, principally to help our hearts to triumph over the senses, and to break the shameful chains which restrain it in so fatal a slavery, that devotion to the Sacred Heart of Jesus is established."[36] Commitment to the Sacred Heart, with its political weight of counter-Revolutionary activism, transcended the merely personal. It was a response made with the understanding that one was responsible for one's individual salvation as well as actions that would save the whole nation of France (figure 15).

Jaricot expected sensitive Christian readers to respond to the invocation of these powerful ideas. The work assumed that the human heart, with its emotional response to the heart of Christ, would be the center of true repentance and spiritual reform. "Your Heart becomes the center of our spiritual life," she reasoned, "just as the body's own heart is the principle of temporal life."[37] Operating on the sentimental assumption that hearts in union could speak to each other, Jaricot reminded readers that Jesus would speak directly to their hearts. Those unable to devote themselves wholeheartedly to Christ lacked passion for Him or "neglected to speak to him, heart to heart."[38] This idea was both theological and sentimental; the contemporary understanding of the Sacred Heart relied on the idea that an individual human would only see Christ in his wholeness when their hearts connected. Sensory experience offered only external truth, without deep connection. As Jaricot explained, "Water reflects the face, but the hearts mirror one another."[39] Penetrating hearts were those who let themselves be transformed by the heart and wisdom of Christ, rather than the wisdom of the world.[40]

Jaricot thus undermined rational assumptions about religious belief, contemporary living, and even political compromise. She went further, however. By using a language of opposition, she foregrounded the claim that true and lasting spiritual health would necessarily involve rejection of wisdom of the "the savants of the age," which focused on logic and brilliance.[41] Philosophers used reason, rather than the "science of salvation," centered in the heart.[42] Where some hearts might respond only to the earthly desires for wealth, prestige, and authority, rejection of these marked true wisdom.[43] *Infinite Love* thus offered a vision of the world in which the principled rejection of contemporary values and a dedication to the Sacred Heart—both demonstrated by public action—were the only possible paths forward.

The sentimental importance of the heart as well as the social and political implications of Jaricot's writings were not lost on religious contemporaries, either, who understood connection with the Sacred Heart as a central way to call for religious activism.[44] By the later nineteenth century, in a revolt against the Heart and its "science of salvation," one preacher argued "devotion to the Sacred Heart and devotion to the Eucharist should not be confused."[45] More significantly, he continued: "But why, one might ask, does one go to the Heart of Jesus to remind us of His love for us? It is not his heart that loved men, it's his soul, because his corporeal heart, being nothing more than a part of organized matter, was as incapable of producing the sentiment of love as it is of producing thought."[46] Here, the decoupling of the heart from both the production of knowledge and the love of Christ demonstrates a desire to discredit an "irrational" and sentimental belief that the heart was the source of wisdom. It also implicitly admits that this "feminine" devotion and threatening forms of public action were linked.

Infinite Love was not Jaricot's only writing to draw a connection between sentimentality, devotion, and action. In her spiritual autobiography, *The Story of My Life*, sentimental language figured prominently to emphasize the power of a loving heart, united to Christ. This work, an introspective look at Jaricot's position with respect to God and the world, was written in Jaricot's late teens and early twenties, at the behest of her spiritual director. In this work she outlined how she arrived at the sense that she was called to do great things for Jesus and why she committed to a dramatically new life. The narrative offers the reader several important themes: the central role of the heart in understanding and responding to God's call, a forceful and ascetic rejection of the world as it existed, and the importance of the Sacred Heart for conversion and reparation.

These ideas resonated with Jaricot as well as with her confessor and spiritual director. In 1817 Jean Würtz had written a long polemic against the rationality of the Enlightenment and the philosophes.[47] Given its aggressive tone and exegetical orientation, it offended both religious and secular authorities in France. Würtz was therefore removed from his priestly functions and sent away from his diocese in Lyon. Both he and Jaricot saw the hand of God in this exile. She attempted to console him by reminding him of Jesus's suffering in the garden of Gethsemane; she told him that "the Heart of Jesus Christ watches with he who suffers."[48] Jaricot had chosen a confessor whose intellectual leanings reinforced her own sense that the world could not be experienced primarily through reason, and that sacrifice was evidence of a holy life.

Despite the context of exile, *The Story of My Life* should not be read as a public statement, like *Infinite Love*. Rather, it is a private reflection written by Jaricot with the encouragement of the ultramontane Würtz. It examined her "interior universe," or her foundation and motivations as she reoriented her life away from worldly concerns such as fashion and romance, or even love for family. The work demonstrates Jaricot's tendency to see religious commitment as the truest form of passion and places it in a context Würtz and Jaricot would both have welcomed: the necessity of listening to one's heart.[49] Like Jaricot, Würtz relied on the power of sentiment. He was known as a man of emotion, who would respond to the suffering of others with a flood of tears.[50]

Jaricot's narrative, following in the same vein as her treatise on the Eucharist and Sacred Heart, used language about proper feeling and the place of the heart to explain how God's will conformed to a higher call than individual preference. This distinction between the world's wisdom and the knowledge found in the heart also lay behind her rejection of marriage and her commitment to radical public action. Reading *Infinite Love* and *The Story of My Life* together thus offers a more complete explanation of how sentimental assumptions shaped Jaricot's understanding of the world.[51]

In *The Story of My Life* Jaricot demonstrated the importance of the sentimental idiom. First, Jaricot railed against her own literary and social formation; she spoke of rejecting sentimental novels as poor influences that had led her astray.[52] However, Jaricot's emphasis on her history as a reader does not demonstrate a rejection of sentimentality writ large.

Even though she committed to no longer reading novels soon after her conversion, the spiritual autobiography was itself indebted to the sentimental forms that had been central to Jaricot's early life as a reader. The autobiography repeatedly appealed to the heart as a source for knowledge and demanded emotional responsiveness to the world. Its structure, which emphasized the tension between Jaricot's natural desires for human love and her ability to overcome worldly desires for a higher purpose, also owed much to novelistic conventions.[53] Although the work moves in a narrative form from her childhood through her "fall" and eventual conversion, knowledge of her ultimate destination runs underneath the entire narrative. Like *Paul and Virginie*'s hermit pointing to island ruins or Chateaubriand's Chactas telling a dead Atala's story, Jaricot imagined her life as necessarily leading to an end that removed her from her ties to worldly desires.

Indeed, given Jaricot's widespread use of sentimental language in both *Infinite Love* and *The Story of My Life*, it is clear that her rejection of novels and other worldly pleasures, as well as her sense of herself as uniquely chosen to serve God, were forms of intensity deeply conditioned by sentimental norms. William Reddy has argued that for a woman of the early nineteenth century, sentimental passion and emotional force were centrally important and could even serve to exonerate aberrational behavior.[54] Similarly the power of emotional intensity and its role in women's experience of the world contextualize the language found within Jaricot's early writings. As Jaricot explained in her spiritual autobiography, "I always had a secret presentiment that told me: 'God wants you to serve for His glory! You have been chosen to fulfill hidden plans.'"[55] Just as with Philippine Duchesne and Euphrosine Jouve, an emphasis on "passion" contrasted base—untrue or shallow—desires with truly holy ones. The dramatic choices that these women made as they embarked on a religious mission consequently offered further evidence of the truth of their vocations.

The idea that French Christianity was embattled also offers important context to Jaricot's vision of the world. An awareness that martyrs gave their lives for the Church during the Revolution was omnipresent during the nineteenth century. Many devout Catholics had relatives or friends who had been victims of the Terror or dechristianizing pushes.[56] References to Christ's crucifixion and to ancient Roman martyrs appeared not only in reviews of sentimental literature but also in theological treatises that encouraged the true Christian to willingly suffer mortification and death, like Christ, if necessary.[57] The mission literature that Jaricot read as a child and eventually shared with communities of believers as an adult played into the same tensions, insofar as it contrasted the sacred and profane and valorized total commitment, even martyrdom.[58] If even Jerusalem had been destroyed for her sins, what personal sacrifices might be required for reparation in France?[59] Jaricot's vision of the two lamps made these conflicts and assumptions visually resonant. Faith at home had been devastated by revolution and post-Revolutionary compromise. The French abandoned both belief and true practice. However, missionary sacrifice and a commitment to the expansion of belief could reignite France's flame.

Accordingly, while many of Jaricot's more modern biographers note with surprise the difficulty of the choices that she made as she turned her life toward strict religious adherence, the sweeping changes in her behavior underlined the power of her decision in the face of threats from the contemporary world. Jaricot herself emphasized that radical transformation was the only path open to her. She explained that remaining in the world, socializing as usual and continuing to wear stylish clothes, would have destroyed her will to live her newly religious life. However, if she turned her life inside out, wholeheartedly dedicating herself to a new path, she could find refuge in the all-encompassing nature of her choice. Reddy might call this dramatic passion; it certainly echoed the quasi-theatrical nature of the climactic choices in sentimental fiction. Jaricot saw it as the total commitment demanded by God, one which allowed her to feel "alive in her proper life."[60]

Growing out of all these contexts, the story of Jaricot's life offered a narrative of her heart's conversion. Though we know that Jaricot wanted to serve God as a missionary when she was young, she began her spiritual autobiography with an indictment of her pride, jealousy, and vanity.

She says that she was not good with her hands or at feminine tasks such as housekeeping.[61] She noted, however, that she possessed a heart that was naturally pious and oriented toward God, and given her passionate nature, that meant that she should have been wholeheartedly attached to God from the beginning. She was not "born to love the world and worldly things." Rather, as with the decision to wrench herself completely from her former social life, she believed that her "soul was too fervent and too indivisible in its affections to be attached, as it was, to things that would perish."[62] Instead of allowing her heart to speak directly to God's heart, however, she fell in love with the world. She fantasized with a close friend about conquering the hearts of young men, she sang love songs, and one only had to speak to her about a possible family alliance with a young man for her to begin to dream of him as a lover and husband.[63] At the Jaricots' home in the country, with the approval of her parents, Jaricot spent much time socializing with other well-to-do young people, often through playing games and dancing.[64] She read novels and purchased objects to adorn herself: flowers, ribbons, even pleated handkerchiefs.[65] Jaricot described these years, whiled away on romance and conspicuous consumption, as a misguided search for a "dignified object on which to fix her heart."[66] Since her heart "could not serve two masters at one time," when it "beat for the world, it ceased to beat for the Lord . . . Poor heart! If you had only adored God, you would not have spent the best years of your life far from his Heart."[67] Jaricot was in danger of being lost to her best self because of a misguided attachment to consumer items, vanity, and adornment.

Jaricot believed that God did not want her to be lost to worldly desires, however. In vivid language, reminiscent of the images found on holy cards, Jaricot proclaimed, "Yes, it was on this stormy sea that Jesus flew to the assistance of the boat of my heart, in order to preserve it from the unhappiest sinking."[68] Her fall, injury, and subsequent ill health pushed her toward contemplation. Even so, she resisted. Because the music of the Mass touched her heart, leaving her in tears, she sought out other musical experiences, including attending the theater.[69] While the only true solution was for her to exist in union with Jesus, she "searched outside his Heart, for remedies that [she] could never find."[70] The Comédie Française did more than leave her unmoved; it began to convince her that secular life only offered "abominable recreations."[71]

She reported that only when she finally followed the urgings of her truest self did her heart experience its own revolutionary change. Her heart, "formerly so immense that creatures and the whole world could not fill it," overflowed. In language like that employed by sentimental novels such as *Paul et Virginie* or *Claire d'Albe*, Jaricot rhapsodized about nature. She described being so overcome by the Creator's goodness in nature—the flowers, the trees, the stars, and the moon—that she kissed the leaves of the trees.[72] As part of this extraordinary response to religious sensation, she gave away her clothing and sold her jewelry to donate the money to charity.[73]

How did Jaricot interpret the path to opening her heart in such a dramatic way? After her negative experience at the Comédie Française, Jaricot said that she turned more and more toward God. She read religious works and reflected on Jesus's sacrifice and the mercy of God.[74] Sickness continued to haunt her, a fact that she later interpreted as God's plan to remove her from worldly desires so that she would devote all her love to Him.[75] However, despite her unhappiness and deep sense that life in the world was meaningless, she continued to struggle with sacrificing everything for God. As she described it, "A heart that has only loved and known God alone would be incapable of understanding the power of the illusions of the world."[76] She believed that she would have to change her entire way of life, moving from coquetry to modesty, to "the simplicity of the saints, away from the search for all the alterations of vanity"—in short, from "earth to heaven"—because only the "law of God could make me truly happy. The world, its pleasures and passions, were only fit to dry out, exhaust, and tire my poor heart."[77] The profane world could not hold her affection; all of her heart would have to commit.

When she heard the Lenten sermon of Abbé Würtz, Jaricot believed that she heard the voice of God calling her to a full conversion. In her spiritual autobiography Jaricot referred to Würtz as "Ananias," or the disciple of Jesus who restored the sight of Saul, as he had caused her eyes to be opened.[78] Recognizing Würtz as Ananias also meant that Pauline placed herself in the position of her saintly namesake, Paul, "a chosen vessel unto God" who would carry Christ's name "before the Gentiles, and kings, and the children of Israel."[79] Jaricot's autobiography offered Würtz in an important role even as it let Jaricot act as the protagonist of her own narrative, holding fast to an intellectual and spiritual framework in which she heard God's voice telling her that she had been uniquely chosen to fulfill an important destiny.[80]

Jaricot then outlined how she changed her entire way of life to remove all idols from her heart. She burned her novels and love songs, because "profane love had left [her] heart in order to give way to Jesus Christ, who alone was worthy of reigning over it."[81] She dropped all concern for fashionable dress and walked, purposely, with a heavy gait rather than a light step.[82] She informed the young people with whom she socialized that her "soul was resolved to serve the Lord and to forget the world" and that she could not be friends with them unless they "resolved to renounce the truths of the world."[83] She stopped going to dances and socializing as she had earlier in her life.[84] These changes shocked her friends and relatives, and her family attempted to mitigate the radicalism. They forbade her from giving away her clothing and asked her to spend less time helping the poor and sick.[85] Jaricot, however, underlined the ways that Christ demanded an ascetic rejection of the world. She argued against the half measures proposed by others, saying that "the thorns that fill the road of salvation cause pains only to divided hearts, which still mourn the poisoned flowers, the fleeting joys that the world seductively offered them."[86]

Jaricot used similar language to explain her total devotion to Christ. She described one instance in which notions of marriage crept back into her head. After she changed her way of life and pledged to associate only with young people who shared her precepts, one young man in her circle converted to her point of view. He engaged her in discussions of faith and became a regular visitor at her family's home.[87] Jaricot herself began to think that perhaps she could marry him, until she realized that marriage would mean sharing her soul with a husband, rather than God alone. She could not do that, as she had promised to live her life entirely dedicated to God, who was a jealous lover, not wishing to share Jaricot with another.[88] Jaricot's sacrifice of worldly life was now complete. Indeed, her spiritual autobiography ended by praising God for her narrow escape from the "hidden abyss that the Enemy had prepared for her, with respect to her fidelity to Jesus Christ."[89] Jaricot's direct confrontation between Christian marriage and vowed celibacy offers an important contrast between human passion—read as carnal—and the complete devotion to God that she saw as her vocation to the world.

In terms of public mission, if Paul was apostle to the Gentiles, Pauline was an apostle to France, leading hearts back to God. In *Infinite Love*, Jaricot connected the Sacred Heart directly to the Eucharist and emphasized how irreligion and sin required Christ's sacrifice. Certainly, it was not new to understand the Eucharist in the context of the Sacred Heart or the Sacred Heart as linked to reparation for offenses against God.[90] However, Jaricot explicitly related the Eucharist and the Sacred Heart in her treatise, making an individual heart's response to Christ's heart the foundation for individual and social change. As she explained in a direct address to God: "Man's pride is so disproportionate and outrageous with respect to the Divinity, that . . . You were forced to annihilate Yourself to the depths of human nature, hiding Yourself under the appearance of bread and wine to become our own food."[91] Despite this, Jaricot lamented that the modern world offered "nothing for Jesus Christ, nothing for the glory of His temple and His altars," even as people spent "excessive amounts to decorate their own homes" and their bodies.[92] She was horrified by what she saw in the world around her. She saw people, as she had once been, prostituting "themselves to idols of flesh, to gold and silver, to the phantoms of pleasure, ambition, pride, and licentiousness."[93] Putting herself in the position of the apostles who woke Jesus during a storm, she exclaimed, "Drivers of the boat! Allow me to tell you what the Apostles said to Jesus Christ: wake up! We are dying!"[94] Pride, consumption, and politics were leading individuals astray. The only solution was for individuals to change their hearts and make sacrifices for God, even as they became more attached to Jesus in the Eucharist and the Sacred Heart.

The logic of divine sacrifice demanded a sacrificial response from humans, who should "repent of knowing Him so late and offer [themselves] in expiation to His justice."[95] The linking of individual human hearts to God's Heart was a necessary foundation for the conversion of others. Indeed, Jaricot offered herself as an example. "I have nothing but my will, and I felt how you had made your own captive in the Eucharist, to bring all mortal wills to your law, by their free and determined choice. Alas! could the sacrifice of my poor heart be a compensation for so many ungrateful hearts who refuse to love you and give themselves to you?"[96] Pauline thus served as an example of how devotion to the Sacred Heart would allow "this clay, watered with your precious blood [to] become an instrument in your hands."[97] The blood of Christ, in the Eucharist, would free believers from their passions and make them worthy to work for God. Similarly devotion to the Sacred Heart would "help our hearts to triumph over the senses" and the impiety and worldliness of the current moment.[98] Jaricot was a symbol of how each person could respond to God's love and be saved. She said, "Let us hasten to finally recognize that the divine Heart of Jesus, adored on our altars, is the only sign of salvation. Let us address him with tender confidence, and by the ardor of our good wishes and our honorable amends . . . obtain the miracle of deliverance."[99] Jaricot made it clear that attachment to Christ's Sacred Heart, with its promises of liberation from punishment, was most easily accomplished by reception of the Eucharist.

The Story of My Life offered a narrative of a life lost to worldly passion and deaf to the true needs of the heart. The "boat" of her soul was, like the sinners she had directly addressed in *Infinite Love*, in danger of sinking, and only by letting her heart's truest sentiments have free reign was she saved. Early in the autobiography Jaricot explained that her heart, which was in fact naturally pious, became susceptible to sin and distance from God because she had not taken refuge in the Eucharist. When she did not receive the "sacrament of love," she did not stay attached to Christ's desires for her.[100] Jaricot used herself as living proof that a heart, left to its own devices, was fragile, because her distance from the sacraments was directly related to the fact that her heart became colder to God and warmer to vanity and the world.[101] After her conversion, however, Jaricot received the Eucharist, and Christ's presence in her heart strengthened her.[102] "Revived by the warmth of God's Heart," she could sacrifice the objects that she had previously prized: bracelets, necklaces, and beautiful dresses.[103] The more she sacrificed, the closer she became to Christ.

Jaricot then experienced Christ's love as "immense desire" and a "devouring thirst."[104] She claimed, "By the flames with which he burned my heart, his Heart appeared to seek my heart."[105] For someone else, this passionate rhetoric might have meant a choice to join a religious order, but not Jaricot. Even as she struggled with how a woman, in poor health, could aspire to be an instrument of God, she knew that religious life held no appeal.[106] With the approval of her spiritual director, Jaricot made a personal vow of perpetual virginity and devoted her life to God.[107] In this new life she described her relationship with God in deeply personal terms. She "dared to take tender familiarities with Him that spouses would entrust to one another."[108] She experienced "sweet inebriation" and "pure delight." She received "the favor of caresses from my God."[109] She said that if someone had witnessed her in these moments, they would surely think that something extraordinary had come over her. They would know that "God speaks to me since here I am, entirely penetrated."[110] The heart that burned in Jaricot, as well as the underlying ecstatic nature of her vision, offered an elision between suffering and pleasure.[111] While Jaricot's narrative seemed singularly personal, her work as a whole promised that everyone could experience this intimacy with Christ, if only they would pray, receive the Eucharist, and change their lives.

Jaricot's mystical union with Jesus inspired her to found other public works by which people might engage in an active life of prayer and devotion, union with God. In 1826, using her family contacts and previous experience, Jaricot—not yet thirty—created yet another organization. It again relied on the power of individual recruitment and communication from small groups to larger ones. This society, the Association of the Living Rosary, encouraged small communities, both silk workers and bourgeois women, to band together in daily prayer and reparational sacrifice.[112] Through their prayers and good deeds, they would ease the pain of the Heart of God and offer reparation to respond to the hard hearts of the age.[113] This time, however, Jaricot sought official approval in advance, making sure that she would not run afoul of the local hierarchy or the Dominicans (patrons of the rosary).[114]

The money collected by the association funded the distribution of holy cards, medals, and appropriate reading material, devotional objects that were being produced in ever-greater numbers. These items, Jaricot believed, were particularly important for counteracting the corrupting ideas prevalent in society.[115] More editions of Jaricot's *Infinite Love* were also published across France; modern methods of communication functioned to share and spread her important ideas. Here Jaricot found herself in the company of groups such as the Society for Good Books and other publishers who offered particularly Catholic reading, though she also continued to engage in active works of charity, including volunteering at the Hotel-Dieu in Lyon.

Jaricot made a wide name for herself with her works. Madeleine Sophie Barat, founder of the Religious of the Sacred Heart, Jean Vianney, known as the "Curé d'Ars," and more than one pope corresponded with Jaricot. They praised her devotion, her good work, and her willingness to sacrifice for others. However, despite her strong spirit, her activity was often limited by her weak heart and opposed by those who—not incorrectly— saw her designs as politically and socially threatening because of their ultramontane tones.

By 1834 heart disease, exacerbated by tireless work, threatened to end Jaricot's life, and this led to yet another turning point in her activism. She decided that God willed her to make a pilgrimage to Italy, to the shrine of Philomena, where she might be healed. It is little wonder that Philomena appealed to Jaricot's sensibilities. Her story shared with Jaricot's writings a novelistic denunciation of half measures as well as a demand to prioritize complete obedience to Christ over worldly values. Though a trip over the Alps seemed like the last thing that Jaricot should be doing—Jaricot's doctor contended that it was likely to kill her—she insisted. After communicating with Sophie Barat, she received permission to stay in the Sacred Heart convent in Rome. She also wrote to Pope Gregory XVI and asked to meet him.

Before she set out on her journey, Jaricot received last rites. She made her first stop at Paray-le-Monial, the convent where Margaret Mary Alacoque had experienced her famous visions. There, she asked for the intercession of the saint of the Sacred Heart before continuing her journey.[116] As the journey proceeded, the doctor's dire predictions seemed probable. By the time Pauline arrived in Rome in 1835, her illness kept her entirely bedridden. Because she was too sick to visit the pope, he came to the convent to visit with her himself. Contemporary accounts said that Pope Gregory saw a woman near death, unable even to rise from her bed; he asked her to pray for him when she reached heaven.[117] She agreed but also told him that she planned to make a pilgrimage to the shrine of Philomena, in Naples. Jaricot asked, if she were healed there, would Gregory promise to advance the cause of Philomena's canonization? Gregory agreed.

Jaricot left for Naples. Once there, she had to be carried on a chair to the shrine. At the site of Philomena's bones, Jaricot's health took an unbelievable turn for the better. She began to walk on her own and abandoned her chair. When Jaricot returned to Rome, this miraculous improvement shocked Pope Gregory. He asked her to remain in Rome to be certain that the healing was permanent. Jaricot remained healthy and in Rome for months, at which point Gregory did indeed advance Philomena's cause.[118]

Pope Gregory's acceptance of the cult surrounding Philomena allowed Jaricot to promote unimpeded veneration of the saint when she returned home to France. After her 1835 pilgrimage, Jaricot carried relics of Philomena back to France, and from there she promoted Philomena as an excellent intercessor, in large part due to the healing of her own heart.[119] Jaricot's celebrity and her saintly reputation served to advance Philomena's fame. Images of and prayers to Philomena became increasingly popular owing to Jaricot's efforts and the related efforts of her friend Jean Vianney, the Curé d'Ars.[120]

Jaricot's devotion to Philomena reinforces the context of sentimental heroism. The story of Philomena—marketed alongside Atala and Virginie—was that of a woman who rejected marriage because she believed that she belonged to God, one who obdurately opposed political and personal concessions. In her story, as in Jaricot's understanding of the world, compromise and acceptance of worldly goals over heavenly ones was both cause and effect. It pulled one away from union with Christ's heart but also served as evidence of an already-present distance from Him. Veneration of Philomena reinforced the idea that devotion to Jesus implied engaging in all-encompassing battle on His behalf. It promised suffering united with Christ, as well as a path to salvation (figures 10, 11, and 12).

Given an emphasis on suffering and sacrifice, perhaps it seems paradoxical that the prayers offered to Philomena also assumed that she was a healer of bodies and souls.[121] Many who sought Philomena's intercession were married women who wished to become pregnant. Numerous children were named after Philomena, too.[122] It was therefore not only women who had renounced marriage who venerated Philomena; wives and mothers also saw her as inspirational and asked her to offer relief from their suffering, which Philomena shared.

Many who purchased holy cards, prayed novenas, and venerated the relics believed that Jaricot's ailing heart was healed when she sat next to Philomena's bones. From their perspective, once made whole, Jaricot then came back to France and continued to work for the poor and disenfranchised, trying to assuage physical misery even as she encouraged people to devote their lives to Christ. In this broader context appeals to Philomena were calls to solidarity in suffering with Christ, in a world that needed salvation. Perhaps Pauline Jaricot, the "servant of workers and missionaries," was healed because of her suffering on behalf of others.[123] Certainly, to Jaricot and the women who prayed for her intercession, "to demand graces in Philomena's name [was] to enter into her views," to accept that God's desires were opposed to one's experience of the contemporary world.[124] Especially for women, both Jaricot and Philomena served as reminders of the conflict between women's needs and society's expectations, even as they offered miraculous hope for change.

Once returned to health, Jaricot had intensified her commitment to the combined physical and spiritual health of workers. She was a wealthy young woman, having inherited a house from her brother in 1830 and nearly a million francs upon her father's death in 1834. For years she had invited poor women interested in prayer and contemplation to share her home at Fourvière in Lyon.[125] She also spent her money trying to alleviate the suffering of workers. However, Jaricot increasingly felt compelled to find a more comprehensive solution to the terrible living and working conditions of the workers. Silk workers threatened urban violence, but despite that, many employers resisted making changes. Jaricot worried, "The question of a just wage is hardly considered."[126]

In order to resolve this problem, Jaricot dreamed of establishing a Catholic workers' commune, based on devotion to God, care for others, and self-sustaining work. In the mid-1840s she purchased a blast furnace using her money and funds from well-off people in her circles. Fifteen industrialists invested a hundred thousand francs each. As the project looked to provide a strong return, smaller stakeholders also joined in.[127] Unfortunately the managers Jaricot chose were dishonest. The project not only failed to get off the ground, but the investors lost all their capital.[128]

Jaricot was determined that others should not suffer because of her mistakes. She had lost her own fortune in her attempt to create this ideal society, but she remained determined to pay back all the investments, especially those from people of modest means. Even living frugally, she did not have enough to make reparations. She asked for assistance from Rome, hoping to draw on some of the funds that she had raised for the missions. Pope Pius IX wrote a letter on her behalf, noting her great works on behalf of the Church and asking the Council for the Society of the Propagation of the Faith to pay her debts. That society refused to recognize her as its foundress—only men's names were on the original constitution, written after they took control from Jaricot—and said that it had no money to spare.[129] Jaricot had dressed like a worker since her conversion, wearing rough clothing and wooden shoes. She now also lived like the most impoverished and sent all her money to pay off debts. Before her death in 1862, she was so poor that the city of Lyon gave her an attestation of poverty that authorized her to beg on the streets.

The two extremes on which Jaricot reflected in her spiritual autobiography, sweetness and suffering, were significant to sentimental experiences of the era; they were also frequently tied to the Sacred Heart.[130] Jaricot's deep experience of God was, like the physical connection to the Eucharist, not an end in itself but something that inspired her to suffer on behalf of the one she loved.[131] Just as the ticket to heaven discussed in chapter 3 claimed, so too Jaricot accepted: "None will merit being crowned if he has not fought with courage."[132] In her spiritual autobiography she had promised that the sacrifice of everything that she possessed—a reality at the end of her life—would matter nothing to her, if that was what Christ asked.[133] Dedication to God and an intimate relationship with him were the foundation for her continued expiatory work on His behalf.

All of this demonstrates that the world that Pauline Jaricot inhabited was deeply physical and communal, embedded not only in human suffering but also in the corporeal body of Christ. While believers like her rejected the flawed world that surrounded them, they did not remove themselves from society or abandon community. Indeed seeing themselves as united with God offered them authority to demand change. Even though men had attempted to efface Jaricot's role—and refused to come to her aid when she needed it—Jaricot continued to act, believing that she had been divinely called to engage her society, to win souls and contribute to God's glory.[134]

It is easy to see how Jaricot's worldview, seen through the lens of men such as Michelet, offered evidence of the ways in which religion corrupted women's hearts and supplanted men's "natural" authority over women. It is no stretch to imagine Jaricot's language of love for Christ as whispered words to a lover. Jaricot also worked from a conviction that her heart spoke truly when it told her to spurn profane love. She emphasized the need for a physical connection to the Sacred Heart, through the Eucharist, and a desire to wage battle against the corruption of this world. She saw herself as a public actor, and her suffering confirmed divine approval of her path. None of these characteristics were ready-made to produce a domestic "companion, a friend, a partner, an alter-ego."[135] Jaricot's sentimentalism and love for Christ combined to offer her freedom from this world to act for the creation of a new world.

< 6 >

Becoming a Saint

Zélie Martin, Suffering, and Heroism in a Consumer Society

Madame Tifenne appears to be much happier than you. She lives only for luxury and pleasure. She gives balls in mid-Lent. And yet would you believe that I would rather see you with your trials rather than believe that you, like her, are forgetting Heaven for the passing joys of the world?

—Zélie Martin to her sister-in-law, Céline Guerin, 1873

The apostle Paul recommended that Christians not marry. In a letter to the Corinthians, he said that unmarried people focused on the Lord's work, while married people worried about mundane matters, including pleasing their husbands and wives.[1] The novels, hagiographies, and visual culture described in the first three chapters affirm Paul's assumptions about the Christian's relationship to the world, with celibacy and widowhood acting as sites for agency and independence, rather than being sterile or unfree. Women's writings from the previous two chapters also reinforce the sense that child-rearing and domestic responsibility were not a likely path to heroic action. Philippine Duchesne and Pauline Jaricot rejected marriage to devote their lives to public service. They traveled the globe, established foundations, and corresponded with popes, bishops, and diplomats. Ironically, given the nineteenth-century depictions of sentimentality, privacy, and religion as linked, an emotional and feminine language offered women authority to transcend the preoccupations of family life. Women's legal and economic disenfranchisement also limited the mark of wives and mothers in historical sources. In the end, religious women's actions had a tremendous social and historical impact, far beyond that of most married women.[2]

While Philomena and women religious could serve as objects for veneration, loving mothers were common enough to be stereotypical. They might exist as a generic image or trope, but producers of material culture did not individually name or recognize them. This invisibility is a theological as well as a social and cultural truism. While women religious who had the approval of a bishop or superior might write extensively or offer spiritual leadership to the women they led, there was little room for married women to do so. After all, the Pauline epistle to Timothy had warned against permitting women to "teach or exercise authority over a man," given Adam's preeminent position over Eve.[3] Numerous nineteenth-century bishops reinforced this teaching.[4] Any nineteenth-century woman who rose to significance in the historical record was exceptional, but a devout married woman with many children would have been doubly extraordinary, and if her visibility was the result of religious teaching, it might have even been dangerously unorthodox.

Marie-Azélie (Zélie) Guérin Martin (1831–1877) was just such a typical wife and mother of the nineteenth century. Shaped by Pauline assumptions and the historical context of the nineteenth century, the letters Martin left behind bear little obvious political or theological significance. They emphasize domesticity, reproduction, and consumerism.[5] As she admits, the everyday occupations of a wife and mother, including sickness, death, and the needs of her children, frequently distracted her, even from devotion and prayer.[6] When she died of breast cancer in 1877, it was primarily a matter of concern to her husband and daughters.

While we know a great deal about the youthful years of Duchesne and Jaricot, at least as seen through the lens of autobiographical and hagiographical recollections, Guérin's childhood remains opaque. What we do know about Martin comes primarily from the recollections of her daughters, the material culture that surrounded her, and the letters that Martin wrote as a married woman.[7] Additionally, although there are more than two hundred extant letters written by Zélie Martin, these letters from adulthood were preserved and published not because she was an award-winning lacemaker or a savvy businesswoman (though both were true).[8] Rather, they were saved—and have been published—primarily because Martin was the mother of Thérèse of Lisieux, a defining symbol of modern Catholicism in France.[9]

This chapter does not examine the now-famous daughter in any great detail. Instead, it seeks to explain what Zélie Martin's life and writings demonstrate about her contemporary understanding of sentiment and religious belief and of a married woman's role in the world. On the one hand Martin comes to us as a nineteenth-century Catholic everywoman, a mother who taught her daughters to love God and accept suffering as necessary and even productive. On the other hand, as one half of the first couple to be canonized together, a parent whose every living child became a professed religious, and a mother to one of the most famous saints of the modern era, she was exceptional in her own right. This juxtaposition between the everyday and the exceptional strikes at the heart of the problem of sentiment.

Martin's letters also demonstrate how a religiously fervent wife and mother was likely to live a life with little room for public service not only because of the assumptions of the men surrounding her but also because of the varied demands placed on her by domestic responsibilities, which divided her attention, fragmented her life, and chopped up her days. It was sometimes difficult for her to communicate a single idea, let along enunciate an intellectually and spiritually uniform worldview.[10] Like most married French women, Martin didn't present herself as an intellectual or a religious theorist; her responsibilities gave her more than one kind of invisibility. This did not mean, however, that Zélie Guérin Martin abandoned the sentimental ideals that made celibacy, suffering, and religious practice comprehensible together. Like Duchesne and Jaricot, Martin subscribed to a worldview in which it was possible to be religiously heroic, a saint, even though she was domestic and fully immersed in contemporary culture.

Like the other women of this book, Martin's life was shaped by her family's experience of the Revolution, desire for advancement, and emphasis on a sentimental and theological understanding of the world. She brought those themes into her life as a wife and mother. However, unlike both Jaricot and Duchesne, Martin was born well into the nine-teenth century and was deeply immersed in a world of consumerism, both religious and secular. To understand her properly, we must situate her not only in her post-Revolutionary French context but also as a mar-ried bourgeois Catholic woman who lived at midcentury. Her livelihood depended on others' taste for her expensive lace. She did not live in a cloister or reject finery; her position in society was on display through her purchases and her public demonstration of her image, as well as the images of her children. For Martin, the choice to be a saint was not to be found in a rejection of marriage or of material goods, but in everyday choices that prioritized God's will over her own.

Martin's letters demonstrate how ideas about marriage, religion, and family life worked together in midcentury France. Martin was aware of her responsibilities within her family and society in addition to those she owed to the Christian community and to God. She saw God at work in life and believed that her prayers were answered in tangible ways; she also emphasized the ways in which wives and mothers had a responsibil-ity to pass on the faith and to refashion the world as necessary. Many of the same elements that allowed celibate women to think of themselves as heroic individuals who were authorized to act in the world appear in Martin's work. Her letters demonstrated the influence of sentimental ideas and emphasized the role of spiritual reading, devotional practices, and the contrast between the world as it ought to be and as it was.

Like many of the young women of the preceding chapters, Martin initially wished to live life as a celibate, seeing it as the highest possible calling. When she agreed to get married, she dedicated the remainder of her life to her spouse and, eventually, to her children. Religious forma-tion would have taught her that her new role as wife demanded "purity of morals, mutual and inviolable fidelity, and if the covenant bore fruit, virtuous Christian education of children by example and instruction."[11] She and her husband believed that the sacrament of marriage was not a worldly alliance but a union designed to sanctify husband, wife, and children and prepare them for heaven. In this context Martin found much consolation in the doctrine of expiatory suffering, especially as the nearly twenty years of her married life saw her give birth to nine children, four of whom died. Sickness, death, and hard work defined her life.[12]

Martin was not unique in being shaped by her theological understanding of the world. Her letters, like the religious stories of chapter 1, demonstrate that a married woman's writing and vocational identity existed in a different framework than those of celibate or widowed women. Martin also recognized that she was responsible to society for her choices as a wife and mother, and that all of her decisions, be they related to work, prayer, or even decoration of the home, had spiritual implications. Martin also acknowledged that in the modern world in which she lived, she was surrounded by people of different beliefs, including ones who were living nonreligious lives. These people made other decisions, ones that ignored or even rejected the assumptions on which she based her life. Her letters confirm that she was deeply imbedded in the possibilities inherent in nineteenth-century culture, even as she wanted to "become a saint."[13] An examination of her life therefore offers insight into the ways in which the marketing of devotional objects for a faith community— even an embattled one—relied on the transformation of sentiment into modern unsectarian consumer culture.

Zélie Guérin's life began in Normandy in 1831. Her parents were devout Catholics whose childhoods had been experienced through the upheavals of the Revolutionary era; they passed down family stories of locks on the church, hidden clerics, and secret Masses.[14] Adding to the drama was the knowledge that one of the priests in hiding was her own great-uncle Guillaume, a nonjuring cleric concealed by the family. Louis Martin's father, Isidore, born in 1789, played a central role in one of the tales. The family recalled how, as soldiers came into the home, looking for the priest, the boy had spread his toys across a board, covering the kneading trough in which the man was hiding. When the searchers came into the room and saw the young Isidore sitting there, calmly playing with his things, they went into other locations in the house to look for the priest.[15] Though a few years later the uncle was caught, imprisoned, and deported, the concordat saw this uncle's release and return to the Orne as a parish priest, a vindication of his perseverance in counter-Revolutionary agitation.

Martin's father also left home in the turmoil of the Revolutionary era, as he was conscripted into the Imperial Army just before he turned twenty. Isidore was decorated as a Napoleonic soldier and chose to continue in the military. He acted as a constable throughout the Restoration and only retired at the end of a long career. He remained a practicing Catholic throughout his life. He married Zélie's mother, Louise-Jeanne, in 1828.[16] Martin's parents thus served both the Napoleonic regime and the ones that followed. Though they left few traces of their ideological commitments, the nineteenth century saw the family fortunes improve, as the father of Louis Martin worked as a day laborer before advancing through the military ranks.[17] Consequently they were not yet firmly in the economic and social class that Pierre Serna refers to as weathervanes, or *girouettes*, ones who were loyal to France and their own patrimony before all else.[18] Additionally, unlike the Duchesne or Jaricot families, their ascension into the bourgeoisie was made possible by an increased openness in post-Revolutionary society, along with their exercise of family strategies that prioritized the consolidation of capital and the acquisition of education and career training. They ascended because of society's changes, even as they sometimes saw themselves as embattled and living in opposition to those same changes.

Zélie was born in 1831, shortly after the July Revolution brought Louis-Philippe to the throne. She described her childhood as difficult, one in which her "heart suffered deeply."[19] This was not a reference to physical suffering, though she was subject to frequent headaches, which continued through her entire life. Rather, in a letter to her brother she drew a distinction between his treatment and how she experienced her own childhood. Though her little brother, ten years younger and named after their father, was spoiled and pampered, she recalled her youth as "sad as a winding-sheet" due to the severity of their mother.[20] The family saved money for education, training, and the favored son. Neither money for recreation nor much in the way of emotional energy seems to have been "wasted" on the girls.[21] Zélie never even had a doll.[22] She read books and had a solid religious upbringing, but when she was young, neither she nor her family were avid consumers of the new products marketed for children, a situation that changed dramatically when it came to Martin's own offspring.

Her parents did, however, invest in her schooling. Indeed, some of her mother's discipline and demands seem to have been related to an insistence that Zélie and her sister Marie-Louise (Elise) take full advantage of their education.[23] As the time for her father's retirement from the army approached, the family moved to Alençon, where they could find better opportunities for schooling their daughters. They enrolled both Zélie and Marie-Louise as day students with the Religious of the Sacred Hearts of Jesus and Mary (the Picpus).[24]

The Picpus's founding impulses, shaped in the turmoil and religious persecution of the French Revolution, meshed with the Guérins' own social and theological view of the world.[25] The order's founders, Pierre Coudrin and Henriette Aymer, had worked to shelter nonjuring clerics in the area around Poitiers. They formed an Association of the Sacred Heart—with its counter-Revolutionary implications—and gathered other people around them who also wished to rebuild the Church. Like Jaricot and so many others of the era, Coudrin and Aymer's political experience of the world was closely related to their belief that society was suffering because it ignored the love incarnate in the Heart of Christ. God, exemplified by His Sacred Heart, was rich in mercy that needed to be advertised to others and sought out individually. The order that they founded emphasized education and promoted perpetual Eucharistic adoration in its schools, seeing these efforts as educational enterprises that were central to the formation of an evangelized Christian world.[26] They also attempted to convert at home and abroad, sending priests on parish missions in France and, eventually, missionaries to Asia.[27]

Zélie learned her lessons well at the Picpus school in Alençon. She was a particularly good writer; as a day student she won the top prize in her class for French composition nearly every year.[28] Given the format and content of the most popular prize books, Zélie's time at the school would have not only reinforced her early religious training but also offered the intelligent girl more material by which she could see the world through the lens of heroism and sacrifice.[29] Her experiences and vision of life as a celibate inspired still more expressions of devotion; she began to think of dedicating her life to Jesus as a vowed religious.

The Sisters of St. Vincent de Paul, an order that served the poor and sick in the world, appealed to Martin's sense of the world as a place in need of sacrificial acts. If she joined their order, she could devote herself to sacrifice for the social and spiritual improvement of society. This choice had practical financial implications as well. Even as she began to think about her future, Zélie knew that she could count on little in the way of a dowry from her parents, because her family's savings were earmarked for young Isidore's education.[30] Joining the Sisters of St. Vincent de Paul, who would demand no dowry, fit with her sense of service as well as her financial limitations.

Martin sought to be admitted to their ranks after she was finished with school. However, she was dissuaded from joining them, perhaps because they saw her lifelong headaches as an impediment to her ability to serve.[31] Although she could have attempted to join a different order—her sister Marie-Louise eventually became a Visitation nun, despite concerns over her health—Zélie seems to have seen the rejection as a message that she should get married. So, she changed her plans.

If she could not serve God as a consecrated religious, then Zélie would serve Him as a wife and mother, one who bore many children and raised them to be holy. She prayed, "Lord, since unlike my sister, I am not worthy to be your bride, I will enter the married state in order to fulfill Your Holy Will. I beg of You to give me many children and to let them all be consecrated to you."[32] Thus, despite her initial desire to become a religious, Zélie began to prepare for a life of marriage.

To this point, then, Zélie's life had demonstrated characteristics common to nineteenth-century French Catholic women. She understood celibacy as the highest state, a singular gift from God. Her religious and devotional life was centered in a belief that life on earth was both sacrificial and penitential. Even as she saw life as necessarily entailing suffering, Guérin's sense of service was grounded in an understanding of God's love and mercy, exemplified by his Sacred Heart, as being available to those who asked for it. Her maternal responsibility was to raise her children to prepare them for heaven. As with Carron's books, Fleury's *Catechism*, or *Morality in Action*, self-abnegation and heroic sacrifice were the means for guiding future generations.

The fact that Martin recalled her prayer as being immediately turned toward marriage provides no sense that a celibate single life, like that of Pauline Jaricot, was ever an emotional or intellectual possibility.[33] Rather, once religious life was clearly not an option, Guérin sought to conform herself to the purpose of marriage—to have many children and to get them all to heaven.[34] This required that she find a way to make herself marriageable. The problem of the dowry remained, so Zélie prayed to the Virgin Mary for a way to earn enough money that she might marry. On December 8, 1851, she believed that the Virgin Mary spoke to her and told her that the answer lay in training to make the famous Alençon lace.[35]

The lace, which was a luxury item made in that region, was extremely labor intensive, taking roughly seven hours for each square centimeter.[36] Even as factory-made lace began to spread, Alençon continued to be in high demand. Napoleon had favored it for the Imperial entourage when he was emperor, and it continued to be sought after during the Second Empire.[37] In fact, the *canivet* popularized by Bouasse-Lebel and other houses relied on a paper imitation of lace that was indebted to the sense that lace borders were an indication of expensive and time-consuming design.

For her part Guérin showed great promise in the art of lacemaking. Within two years of her initial decision to become trained in lacemaking, she had set herself up as an independent "Maker of Point d'Alençon." This meant that she had mastered all ten steps of lacemaking and could over-see workers, a process that usually took at least twice as long.[38] Martin was to engage in this business enterprise successfully for her entire life.

As an independent proprietor, Guérin took orders and directed and coordinated other lacemakers in their crafting of individual pieces, which she would then join and deliver to customers. Her shop was not primarily a workplace—except insofar as Martin herself was constantly at work and engaged in the most complicated joining of individual pieces.[39] Rather, it was more like an office, where potential customers could see sam-ples of her work and where the lace workers that she hired would come each Thursday to meet with her so that she could collect their finished pieces, pay them, and assign them new tasks.[40] Despite the difficulty of the work—and her frequent complaints about the business and the frantic pace that too many orders required—Martin found happiness in this work and could lose herself in the meticulous nature of it. She wrote, "I am never happier than when sitting at my window assembling my Point d'Alençon lace."[41] Her attention to detail showed, as her lace was known for its exceptional quality. In 1858 she won a silver medal at the Alençon lace exhibition.[42]

The year 1858 was significant in other ways as well. In April Zélie's sister, Marie-Louise, finally joined the convent of the Visitation. This was a blow for the younger sister, who enjoyed Elise's company and often sought out her sister rather than be by herself. While she did not begrudge her sister happiness as a nun, losing the sister to whom she was so close was extremely difficult. For her part Marie-Louise worried about Zélie and asked, "What will you do when I am no longer here?" Zélie, who had accepted that she was not meant to be a nun, replied that she would also go away, though not by the same path.[43]

The path that she foresaw, and the one for which she was earning a dowry, was marriage. The same month that her sister entered the Visitation, Zélie met her future husband. Upon seeing Louis Martin on a bridge in Alençon in April 1858, she believed that she heard an interior voice speaking to her, telling her that Louis was the man whom she was to marry.[44] She was soon introduced to him. Family stories detail Zélie's familiarity with her future mother-in-law, Fanie, through lace instruction. They indicate that Fanie was actively in favor of the match. Despite the fact that both of Zélie's parents were still alive and Zélie's mother had accompanied each of her daughters to the convents that they hoped to join, her parents' direct role in her marriage choice is less clear-cut.[45] A distant relative had already offered to bring the young lacemaker to Paris and introduce her to eligible young men, an offer that Zélie had refused, at least in part because of concerns about the immorality and worldliness of the capital.[46] There is no record of her parents' intervention on her behalf or their opinions about potential suitors. While Zélie, like Elise, went straight from the parental home to her new life, the dowry that she brought with her had been earned in large part by her own work. While she certainly would not have married against their will, family stories cast the decision as one made by Zélie and by God; an "interior voice" told her that Louis was her intended. Perhaps Zélie's financial success had also led to a measure of independence on her part, but in any case her vision of the decision to marry was individual and subject primarily to divine inspiration.[47] In this way Martin's story resembles Duchesne's and Jaricot's, rather than being like the engagement stories of many other young girls of the bourgeoisie, who were not cast as independent decision-makers.[48] She knew her own mind and was in charge of her destiny.

Both the choice and the engagement were quick. Louis and Zélie first encountered each other in April; their church wedding took place at midnight on July 13.[49] Because of her extraordinary lacemaking, Zélie offered a dowry of five thousand francs for herself, and she brought another seven thousand francs in savings to the marriage.[50] Louis, a watchmaker and jeweler, gave Zélie a wedding gift of a silver medallion, depicting Tobias and Sarah, the biblical story of sacrificial marriage.[51]

Zélie's prayers of discernment and Louis's medallion speak to the Martins' understanding of marriage, one that resonated with nineteenth-century catechetical teaching. The *Dogmatic and Moral Catechism* shared the Martins' understanding of marriage as primarily designed for rais-ing holy children who would be destined for heaven.[52] This catechism had also used the story of Tobias and Sarah, depicted in the wedding medallion, to demonstrate the proper attitude toward marriage and one's spouse. Its author emphasized how the book of Tobit offered an emphatic lesson against lust in marriage and instead demonstrated that the marital relationship was an important site for self-giving. Similarly the father of Louis Martin, Pierre-François, had outlined the purpose of marriage in an 1828 letter to a newly married relative, asking "that our divine Master may deign to bless your union with my beloved niece, and that you may be as happy as one can be in this world, and that when you draw your last breath God may receive you into His mercy and place you among the number of the blessed, there to live forever."[53] The purpose of marriage was not, first and foremost, for happiness in this world, but to achieve eternal happiness with God, and ideally to do so with the blessing of children, whom one would also help on the path toward heaven.

However, like young women of her generation, Zélie was raised as an innocent, in near total ignorance of the reproductive realities of life.[54] The disclosure of what it took to conceive children shocked her. Indeed, the couple had married at midnight so that they might travel to visit Zélie's sister at the Visitation convent in Le Mans, and Zélie spent much of that wedding day in tears. "I cried as I had never cried in my life and as I was never to cry again," she recalled.[55] The sobbing upon visiting her sister was not because she was sad to see Elise as a nun, but rather, because she lamented what her future life held, compared to the "calm and tranquil life" of a nun.[56] She was "so unhappy at being in the middle of the world" and "yearned to hide [herself] and share [Sr. Dosithée's] life."[57]

Martin's rejection of a fashionable marriage match from Paris, her emphasis on the seclusion of lacemaking, and her desire to be unmarried because the life of a nun was peaceful and celibate, unlike the life of a married woman, which was lived "in the middle of the world," all indicate that she saw the same set of antagonisms as many other religious women of her day. She thought that God's world was the natural setting for wholehearted devotion, and Martin could not imagine how she could have a life dedicated to God when it was also subject to the cares of the world.

Zélie was not alone in her desire for the life of a vowed religious. Louis had spent a great deal of time in prayer and contemplation of his religious vocation. His inability to learn Latin meant that he could not become a priest or monk. However, his contemplation of the ideal of marriage led him to think that a celibate marriage could be a perfect union, being similar to the marriage of Mary and Joseph and representing the service of Jesus Christ to His Church.[58] Zélie's shock at finding out the facts of life, as well as her latent desire to be a nun, inclined her to agree with Louis. They decided to live as brother and sister. For ten months their marriage remained unconsummated, though they did take a young boy who was motherless into their home, by way of being fruitful, as demanded by the Bible.

Zélie and Louis's initial commitment to a Josephite marriage indicates how important celibacy was for dividing the world into heavenly and worldly camps. The Pauline injunction to place God above worldly things was certainly part of this, but so too was a nineteenth-century vision of sexuality in which virginity and innocence played central roles. However, the fact that the couple, in conjunction with their spiritual director, soon decided to abandon the plan of celibacy, is equally telling, as it indicates that celibacy was not the only path to heaven. Before the first year of marriage was out, Martin redirected her spiritual goals, embracing the idea that she would live fully in the world even as she would raise children in order to help them attain heaven.[59] The Martins had nine children in thirteen years; the last, Marie-Françoise-Thérèse, was only four years old when Zélie Martin died of breast cancer.

The marriage was deeply affectionate. Louis was known throughout his life as a sentimental man, one who loved nature and lavished attention on his daughters.[60] He called each of them a pet nickname, many of them based on the precious stones that he worked with as a jeweler and watchmaker.[61] He was equally effusive with his wife, and there was a shared vocabulary of affectionate language in the household. For example, on an early trip to Paris to negotiate lace orders on Zélie's behalf, Louis wrote: "I cannot arrive in Alençon before Tuesday [five days hence]; the time seems long to me; I cannot wait to be close to you." He signed the letter, "Your husband and true friend, who loves you for life."[62]

The same language was echoed by Zélie in letters to her husband. For example, just after she arrived in Lisieux for a visit with her brother and sister-in-law, she wrote to her husband, "I look forward to being with you. My dear Louis. I love you with all my heart, and I feel my own affection for you doubled when I am deprived of your presence. It seems to me as if it would be impossible to live apart from you."[63] On another occasion Louis traveled to Paris to conduct business for her lacework. She wrote a newsy letter to him, which closed with the following words: "I kiss you with all my heart, I am so happy today at the thought of seeing you again that I cannot work. Your wife, who loves you more than her life."[64] Louis surely read this as a powerful affirmation of her connection to him, as Zélie was almost always occupied with work and described herself as "bad at relaxation . . . like a fish out of water."[65] Being forced to be inactive was a nightmare for her.[66] For her to say that the idea of her husband's return distracted her from making lace was itself a potent statement of love and of her unity with him.

Near the end of her life, just after she was diagnosed with breast cancer, Zélie went to Lisieux for a second opinion, at the insistence of Louis. He was "inconsolable . . . as if he is shattered."[67] She wrote home with the news that the tumor was inoperable but added that her greatest pleasure would be returning home, because she "could only be happy" when she was with him.[68] Their letters communicate not only their love but also the deep connection that they shared, one that enabled each of them to see the other as a necessary part of life.

The sentimental language of the Martin family was not limited to spouses but was shared with other relatives as well. Both joys and sorrows evoked forceful emotion. When Isidore wrote with news that he had passed his pharmacy exam, his sister wrote back with a letter that gushed with happiness, telling him about their father's joy in his son's success. She said that "when my husband gave him your letter to read, he cried. We pretended not to notice, so as not to irritate him, but finally we all joined in the enthusiasm, our heart [sic] overflowing with affection for each other."[69] Martin also made certain that her brother knew that it was extremely important to her that he remain in close contact even when he settled in another city, so that they could share their lives together.[70] Once Isidore married, Zélie's sister-in-law Céline was also part of this circle of affection and meeting of hearts. After spending time with Isidore and Céline in Lisieux, Zélie wrote to her biological sister, now Sr. Dosithée. Zélie enthused about her sister-in-law, saying, "I was enchanted with our trip to Lisieux. I have a sister-in-law who is of an incomparable goodness and kindness." She elaborated, describing the love that her sister-in-law had for her and her daughters, caring for them as if they were her own relations. "I assure you that I love her as a sister, she appears to feel the same, and she shows my children an almost maternal affection. . . . If I seemed worried, she looked at me with sympathy; this seemed to pain her."[71] They were not merely united by their love for Isidore; their hearts were unified in their response to the world.

For her part Martin also felt her brother and sister-in-law's sorrows. When she heard that Isidore and Céline's second child, a son, was stillborn, she told him, "I'm desolate, I have a heart that is as broken as when I lost my own children. I see you in tears, next to this dear small being, dead under such troubling conditions."[72] On another occasion, reflecting on her relationship with Isidore, she wrote, "I believe that I wish for the well-being of my brother more than mine. I have an ardent desire to see him happy, him and his wife, and I would be ready to make every sacrifice for their happiness."[73]

A desire to seek the good of others and to be united with them emotionally was, in Martin's view, an important part of an ideal life. For example, in a letter to her brother about his business, she applauded his attachment to his wife's extended family. She said, "This is such a good family, so united to you, that your interests are theirs. You cannot be happy, one without the other. It is truly beautiful to live in accord like this."[74] The sentimental ideal of hearts living in connection with each other influenced how she interpreted family life. This was true even when the sense that she should live in harmony with others conflicted with Martin's natural tendencies. For example, she worried that, given the severity of her upbringing, she did not always respond affectionately enough to those she loved and would therefore wound them.[75] However, even though she criticized herself for being insufficiently effusive, her letters demonstrate that she loved her relatives and recognized the uniting of one's heart and sacrifices as a central part of human experience.

Martin's sentimentalism expressed itself as effusive desire for unity in affective relationships. It also made itself known by the sense of embattled heroism, victimization, and suffering common to many post-Revolutionary Catholic circles.[76] For example, while she claimed that she tried to remain aloof to prophecies, Martin was surrounded by people who discussed the role of the beleaguered Church in the modern world.[77] During and after the Franco-Prussian War she worried about future revolutions and heard predictions about the restoration of the papacy to temporal power. In the wake of the Commune, Louis went on a pilgrimage to Chartres.[78] He and approximately twenty thousand people gathered to pray for peace and to seek intercession from Mary. They believed that bloodshed, especially an attack on clerics and the Church, was imminent and sought grace because of past sins.[79] Their world often emphasized a contrast between belief and unbelief and placed that conflict in a political context.[80] Martin's world thus shared much in common with Sulpician images, with storms, attacks on the clerical hierarchy, a wounded flock, and dragons to fight. In this context, questions of salvation and expiatory suffering continued to have great resonance, and everyday suffering carried greater weight than usual. For example, in the middle of the Franco-Prussian War Martin wrote to her sister-in-law, "We're not on this earth to have great pleasure, those who wait for pleasure are truly wrong and completely deceived in their hopes. We see this every day and sometimes, in a truly striking way."[81] Suffering was both punishment and purification.

While the Franco-Prussian War may have served as a powerful confirmation of trials on earth, throughout her life Martin accepted suffering as a part of Christian experience. She reminded herself and her family, over and over again, that life in this world was not intended to be enjoyable. She wrote often of death, illness, and business troubles, and she repeatedly said things like, "One cannot be happy on the earth."[82] In a letter to her second oldest daughter, she offered further specifics on her worldview, saying: "As you see, Pauline, 'On earth, it's not all roses, neither happiness nor sweet hope! In the morning, the flower blooms, but often withers by evening.'"[83] Suffering was a central part of the Christian's life.

This view, however, did not mean that Martin felt persecuted by God or fatalistic about her life. Instead she saw suffering as something that was meant to bring the penitent closer to Jesus. She explained, "One way or another, each person must carry his cross. One may say to the good Lord, "I don't want that one." Often that prayer is granted, but it's to our misfortune. It is better to patiently take that which comes to us;

there is always joy alongside the pain."[84] Trials, with their suffering and potential for refinement, were necessary. When her brother and sister-in-law wondered if their pharmacy would be profitable enough, she encouraged them to see their adversities as temporary but essential. "If the trial lasts a little longer, you must take courage. Those who hope in God will never be mistaken."[85] When the pharmacy caught on fire, she commiserated with their economic distress and reminded them that accepting hardship and adversity with patience was an important part of a path toward eternal life with God. She said to them, "It is true that everyone has a cross to bear, but there are some that are heavier. . . . The good Lord allows this so that we will be more detached from this earth and turn our thoughts toward heaven."[86]

In this worldview suffering could be more than something to be passively endured. It was also something to seek out, by way of becoming more united with Jesus and atoning for other's sins. For this reason, all her life Martin had offered daily sacrifices and penitential acts for her salvation and that of her family.[87] She noted that her intentions to suffer joyfully for others succeeded less than she would have hoped. In a letter to her brother she poked fun at herself: "However, I am so bored with suffering! I don't have courage worth a dime. I am impatient with the whole world, and there go the beautiful sacrifices for my dear [departed] father!"[88] On another occasion she reflected on her oldest daughter's desire to be a nun and how Marie wanted to become a saint. "I too would like to be a saint," Martin said, "but I don't know where to start; there is so much to do that I stop at the wanting. I often say during the day: 'My God, how I would like to be a saint!' Then, I don't do any of the work!"[89] Shortly before her cancer diagnosis, she wrote to her sister-in-law, "If I had the choice, I would prefer to die of a slow illness. But not great suffering, no, I don't have enough virtue to want that, I dread it."[90] Martin joined confraternities, prayed novenas, and read devotional material, but she saw suffering as particularly central to her salvation, even when she recognized that her ability to suffer failed to match her aspirations for sanctity.

Martin's letters remind readers that she was consumed with the question of salvation. She was envious of what she saw as the singlemindedness of the life of a consecrated religious, and she regretted the busy pace of her life, with its constant work and distractions. She said that she often felt "the need to recollect a little to think about my salvation, something that the cares of the world have made me forget."[91] For that reason moral and religious literature and imagery constituted an important part of the Martin household. Martin read devotional literature nearly every evening and believed that reading was part of spiritual reflection.[92] She also sent didactic stories as gifts to her nieces and requested popular Catholic books for her daughters in return.[93] Her daughters were surrounded by religious imagery in the home, and Sulpician constructs influenced them as they thought about ideal visions of sanctity.[94]

When communicating with her family, Martin asked that any books given as gifts be inexpensive because of the hard use to which they were put. In one case, she explained, "Léonie goes through a *Catechism* each month, and still knows nothing at the end!"[95] While her daughter Léonie was a special case—she struggled her whole life to learn and retain information—all the books were likely put to good use and even consumed entirely. When the children were studying in Le Mans at the Visitation convent, Martin wrote letters that indicated her deep familiarity with the reading material in the household, as well as her belief that the girls would remember specific lessons from the authors.[96] She included discussion of the books she was reading for her spiritual improvement. She was particularly enamored of the biographies of Jane Frances Chantal and Frances of Rome, both of whom were married women who, once widowed, lived as religious, devoted to the poor.[97] In addition to Marian feast days, she also took time in the family to celebrate the feast day of St. Catherine, patron saint of lacemakers, and St. Anne, Mary's mother.[98] Over and over again she reminded her daughters of holy women who had lived long before her, and she made these women's heroic Christian examples relevant to the contemporary moment.

While Martin might not have believed that she was able to suffer well and thus become a great saint, her letters and reading reveal how contemporary ideas about sentiment, heroism, suffering, and religious devotion played a prominent role in her life. She read books that she believed offered her glimpses at sanctity or Christian heroism. She also reinforced these ideas in her construction of family life, even though the pace of her work and the difficulties of everyday life sometimes meant she failed to keep saintly practices in the forefront of her mind.[99]

Martin therefore chose to offer up everyday sacrifices and problems, which she thought of as a small form of suffering that she could tie to her own salvation and that of others. She taught her daughters the same method, encouraging them to count "practices" when they offered a prayer, sacrificed something they wanted, or otherwise engaged in self-abnegation. Her letters frequently discussed how many "practices" the children did for the benefit of others and how they understood the process of making sacrifices and tying them to prayer intentions, including ones centered on otherworldly suffering.[100] She recognized that sometimes her children forgot or offered up very little, but despite that, she could see them as good children with "angelic nature[s]."[101] The "practices" that they offered were a way to remind themselves of heaven and the important role of suffering in the life of a believer, despite the distractions that surrounded them.

Though emotion and sacrifice were often discussed in a family context, Christian experience was not limited to the home, nor was the life of a married Christian lived in a disembodied, otherworldly way. Zélie and Louis both saw being actively involved in charitable giving as a central part of their lives; their home was known as a place where hungry people could get alms or a meal.[102] The couple also interceded on behalf of the poor and exploited. When they encountered an elderly man suffering from frostbite and hunger, they worked to get him admitted into the hospice in Alençon.[103] Similarly when Martin became aware of a young girl being exploited by two elderly women who claimed to be nuns, she went to extraordinary lengths to get the girl freed from their control.[104]

The desire to be continuously attuned to doing good for others, however, was only part of what it meant to live in the world. Despite the heroic and often otherworldly narrative of sentimentalism, the Martins were steeped in the economic and social changes of the nineteenth century. Martin's letters detailed the numerous objects that were important to life as a member of the bourgeoisie in Alençon. She delighted in dressing her children well, so much that Louis sometimes teased her.[105] She sought out matching clothing and described how she chose coats, hats, and dresses for her daughters, even to the point of employing up to three dressmakers at once.[106] She wrote letters in which she claimed, "I have too many preoccupations to be completely at peace; the worries surrounding dress never end! . . . I do nothing but shop every day; Your father jokes that it's a passion for me!"[107] Martin was immersed in the materiality of life.

Not surprisingly, her daughters understood clothing as a public marker of status and respectability, even availability for marriage. The oldest daughter, who had decided that she did not wish to get married, worried that Louis and Zélie dressed her well to find her a husband. To make this point Martin wrote a letter to her sister-in-law that told how Marie, dressed in new finery, ran and cried in the garden. Marie sobbed that her family "dressed her like a young girl that one wants to marry off at any price, and that certainly we would be the reason that her hand would be asked for!" Martin continued, "Even the thought of this drives her out of her mind, because right now, she would rather have her throat cut!"[108] On another occasion Martin lamented the difficulty in getting Marie to dress appropriately. She was uninterested in social life, and "[w]e had to get angry to make her get [properly] dressed. All of her hats displease her; she has a very pretty toque, but she won't even look at it. . . . [She] only wants her everyday hat because it has a wide brim that hides her well."[109] Though of course the family spurned immoral entertainments, Marie rejected even innocent recreation and socializing, preferring to stay hidden.[110]

Despite this, Marie did not reject all fashion, in the vein of Pauline Jaricot. Rather, she remained concerned about what being unfashionable would indicate, and before a trip to visit her aunt and uncle she made sure that she and her sisters would be well turned out. She did not care for herself, especially, but she wanted to be beautiful to make her aunt and uncle look good. She also wanted her sisters to be better dressed than anyone else, so that they would shine at home and away.[111]

Clothing was not the only symbol of both status and affection that the Martins purchased. The girls had ribbons, dolls and doll carriages, jewelry boxes, paint boxes, sewing kits, travel bags, and copper foot warmers.[112] Their mother was familiar with games ranging from lotto to badminton and spoke of new toys in shops; her letters were filled with the objects that were available for purchase.[113] When Pauline could not come home for Easter because of illness in the house, Martin sent a box with paints, lacemaking tools, and drinking chocolate to distract her from the fact that she was missing home.[114] Before Isidore and Céline came to Alençon to visit, Marie wanted to make sure that the house would gleam like new. She wanted her mother to "wallpaper, polish [silver], buy new curtains for all the beds, and put trellises all over the garden."[115] For her part Martin was not opposed to making the house over to guarantee that it would be particularly inviting for her brother and sister-in-law. She reported, "Some of this [work] is done; there is also a swing for the little cousins from Lisieux to amuse themselves and a small garden for Jeanne."[116]

Pauline Jaricot may have seen fancy dress and nice things as a distraction from God, but in Zélie Martin's world, consumer objects were part of how one showed affection and approval. In fact, rather than expecting her daughters to forsake material objects, Martin rewarded them with purchases. When Pauline—always a good student—became ill from studying too much, Martin asked her to prioritize her health and work less. "I want you to renounce your prizes for this year," she directed. "I will buy you beautiful books that you have already earned, because you have worked too hard."[117] Martin wanted Pauline to know that she did not have to earn prizes to get the accompanying books; she already approved of her daughter and would buy her gifts to demonstrate that fact.

That is not to say that honors were irrelevant. Martin took great pride not only in her daughters' dress and demeanor but also in their scholastic achievements. Many of her letters encouraged them to continue to work hard so that they would make the honor roll. Others spoke of her or her daughters' pride at being on the list of prize students.[118] The sisters at the Visitation school named Marie a "Child of Mary" in 1874. Entry into this confraternity recognized both behavior and academic achievement, and it was only offered when there was a young woman who seemed worthy. When Marie received it, very few other boarders had been thus named; Martin saw it as a special mark of favor for her daughter.[119] Prizes were rightly a cause for the joy that flooded a mother's heart, as the Bouasse-Lebel card with the mother and daughter embracing had demonstrated.[120]

There was a fine line to be drawn, however, between enjoying accolades and material objects and becoming overwhelmed by pride or consumerism, and Martin often contemplated where that distinction lay and what the temptations of the world were. For instance, in December 1876 she wrote to her daughter about the man for whom she and Louis had sought entry into the hospice, explaining how happy they were to see him "crying with joy to find himself so completely happy; despite his weak spirit, he tried hard to thank [Louis] in order to prove his gratitude."[121] She immediately contrasted this with the sad story of a well-known merchant who was handsome and strong and "thought more of himself than God."[122] He had recently died unexpectedly, without recourse to either a priest or a doctor. She observed, "It's so sad to die like that, especially when one no longer practices one's religion."[123]

Being successful was no guarantee of being saved, and in fact, it was likely to lead one away from God. Martin explained her understanding of the relationship between suffering and pride to her brother, by way of warning. "I often remark how those who have made their fortune are, for the most part, given to an insufferable smugness . . . constant prosperity takes one away from God. Never has he brought his chosen along that path, they have, on the other hand, passed through the crucible of suffering, in order to be purified."[124] Material objects and the experience of daily life could serve as a distraction to Christian holiness, inspiring people to trust in themselves rather than God.

In Martin's vision of the world, being a success was often tied to un-Christian behavior. She saw people who destroyed their personal relationships to have financial and social triumphs. They would pretend to like others, whom they could not stand, because of their class and position. She was determined to avoid such behavior. "All of this detaches me more and more from the falseness of the world; I do not want to attach myself to anyone except the good Lord and my family."[125] She therefore tried to prioritize God's will and the ultimate goal of life on earth: reaching heaven. On a trip to visit Thérèse at the wet nurse when the baby was very sick, Martin observed that the magnificent homes and vistas were worth "nothing; we will only be happy when we, us and our children, are reunited on high, and I offered my child up to God as a sacrifice."[126] The key to not being overcome by everyday things was to make a constant choice for holiness, even if it meant the loss of social connections or the sacrifice of loved ones.

Martin's vision of conflict between heaven and the world did not involve rejecting secular culture but instead emphasizing the active choice to be religious. This meant that vocational identity, as a representation of the choice to follow God's call, was a frequent topic of discussion for Martin in her letters to and about her daughters. Time and again she said that she wanted them to be saints.[127] Like their mother, they saw sanctity as being most easily accomplished in a celibate life.[128] Léonie, for example, insisted that she would be a Visitation nun. Neither Marie nor Pauline were attracted to married life either. Marie loved her sisters, but seeing the work of marriage and children, she believed that it would be easier to be unmarried.[129] Eventually she actively repudiated the idea that her future would hold marriage. Both Pauline and Marie made it clear that they intended to be nuns even before they finished their schooling.[130]

Martin was deeply devout and still had much sympathy for life in a cloister, in large part because it allowed more uninterrupted time to focus on God, time that was not consumed by work and family.[131] "It seems to me," she reasoned, "that one is not sad like this when one is a religious; above all, one has fewer cares, and me, I have them hanging over my head."[132] Even so, she was apprehensive about the possibility of her daughters becoming nuns. She admitted, "Notwithstanding my strong desire to give them to the Good Lord, if He asked me right now for these two sacrifices [Pauline and Marie], while I would endeavor to do my best, it would not be without difficulty."[133] Martin could wish for the cloister because of what it represented, but even as she wanted to follow God's will for herself and her children, she recognized that the choice to be a saint was complicated. Like Philippine Duchesne's sister, Martin had looked forward to the assistance that her daughters could provide to a busy mother as well as their companionship. Outside of the cloister one could not escape the world; it remained a constant distraction.

In this way the question of vocation or identity with respect to God was different for Martin than either Duchesne or Jaricot. Unlike either of these women, Martin understood the world as a place in which it was entirely possible to be surrounded by distractions and leave God behind. After all, she frequently encountered people who did not make religious practice an important part of their life. In addition to the handsome haberdasher who died without a priest, Martin observed that the former mayor was an unbeliever and that a young lady of Alençon did not have faith in in miracles.[134] Another woman, one who had assembled lace for Martin for years, died unexpectedly, and Martin lamented the fact that she had rarely gone to Mass.[135]

Martin's observation about the lack of religious observance by those around her, a fact of life in the second half of the nineteenth century, underscores Martin's own understanding of her place in the world. First, they demonstrate that Martin believed that heroic virtue, "to be a saint," required the constant action of properly orienting oneself toward heaven. Second, they reveal that Martin also recognized that it was entirely possible to make a choice to direct one's life in such a way as to ignore religion and questions about salvation. Like her neighbors Martin cared, perhaps too much, about questions of status. Work distracted her. She was enmeshed in a culture of material objects. For her, the difference between being a saint and being damned was a refusal to turn oneself toward God, to be so distracted by the world that one no longer prioritized heaven.

The images, words, and practices with which she surrounded herself were part of becoming holier, remaining attuned to God even as one was within the world. When a neighbor was dying, Martin went to help the family. She wrote to Pauline, "My God, how sad is a house without religion! How terrible death appears there! In the sickroom, we saw no pious image, wherever we looked. There were plenty of pictures, but relating to every subject except religion!"[136] Martin saw no evidence that this woman had attempted to shape herself spiritually. Her lack of religious images, so unlike the Martin household, symbolized the woman's inattention to heaven. Martin's immersion in material culture was thus directly related to her desire to become a saint. Only by using the things of the world appropriately could she, who lived in the world, properly position herself.[137]

Martin was less visible than Duchesne or Jaricot, but she was no less concerned than they were with the question of heroic virtue or the sentimental ideal. Her "practices," her prayers, and her objects of belief all offered her points of entry by which she could both live within the world and live to become a saint. Like them, Martin saw the world as a trap, a distraction from true holiness, even as she used mass culture and a sentimental language of suffering, sacrifice, and choice to demonstrate how she could work for God's kingdom and, at the same time, live in the modern world.

Conclusion

Roses, Elevators, and Modern Heroism

I want to both suffer and rejoice for love. . . . I will sing, even when I have
to pick my flowers among the thorns and my song will be all the more
melodious when the thorns are long and spiked.

—Marie-Françoise-Thérèse Martin (1896)

The women of this book lived in a world where religious belief demanded
a fully conscious choice. Like sentimental heroines, each affirmed her right
to act for her—and the world's—own well-being, even if everyone were
to stand against her. None ignored the world even when she adhered to
Catholic ritual and surrounded herself with objects of devotion. On the
contrary each used progressively more modern methods of engagement
to promulgate her vision. Rose Philippine Duchesne ran risks during the
Revolution, purchased property to start a school, and eventually traveled
to the frontiers of America. Pauline Jaricot ran organizations, wrote treatises, and attempted to improve the conditions of industrial work. Zélie
Martin promoted her business, educated her children, and enveloped
herself in consumer culture. These women were not insulated from the
rapidly and dramatically changing outside world, and they understood
their choices in that world as significant and potentially heroic. Those
who promoted the women as possible saints also emphasized characteristics that were consonant with nineteenth-century sentimentalism. An
emphasis on the women's independent judgment, heroism, and public
vision reaffirmed the women's sentimental authority in a philosophically
modern sense that relied on critical spheres of communication.

The writings of the women examined here affirm they did not see a language of rationality as the only—or even the most important—authoritative position. From their perspective, as devout and sentimental women, they were not cut off from the world but were occupied with important communal struggles that demanded their active participation. To be sure, ascetic and sentimental language was conducive to the argument that modern society was in desperate need of reform and restoration. However, to believe that one was surrounded by sin and corruption was different from a belief that one could turn back time or live outside of the social, cultural, and technological changes of the nineteenth century. Instead, immersion in a language of sentiment and piety authorized women to envision important roles for themselves in the shaping of a modern world, something that often threatened nineteenth-century masculine authority.

As evidence of the widespread impact of sentimental ideals in action, as well as their influence within a modern and self-determining context, one need look no further than Zélie Martin's youngest daughter. Thérèse was devout and deeply sentimental. As a cloistered Carmelite nun who died before reaching her twenty-fifth birthday, she seemed an unlikely candidate to replace popular and venerated women—including Philomena—to become "Saint Thérèse, the Little Flower," one of the most widely known French women of the modern era.[1] However, Thérèse's sentimental spiritual autobiography, *Story of a Soul*, was printed for the first time in 1898, a year after her death, and rapidly eclipsed all other devotional works in France in popularity.[2] Thérèse became a legendary model for devotional life.[3] Pictures of her were in such high demand that more than thirty million photographs of Thérèse were produced globally between 1898 and 1925, making her image the most reproduced subject of the early twentieth century.[4] Her image was not only offered on paper but also on cards, plates, and other items for purchase; she was a cult object of modern consumption. Here Thérèse continued a trend that had begun much earlier in the century with plaster statues and Sulpician holy cards as well as religious souvenirs, including, for example, images of Bernadette and the grotto at Lourdes.[5]

Historians disagree about the reasons for the massive popularity of the cult of Thérèse. Caroline Ford claims that Thérèse was more obviously "real" than Philomena, whose historical status was increasingly contested in the later nineteenth century. Ford adds that Thérèse also likely had greater appeal than Philomena because her values were more applicable to a modernizing world. Furthermore, the type of suffering that she represented, more psychological than physical, was easier to relate to than the tortures suffered by martyrs.[6] This explanation sounds like Michelet and theorists of secularization understood it best: even the women buying holy cards and images of saints increasingly preferred to be led by ideas that were acceptable to the modern imagination, less bloody and more bourgeois.[7]

Given the widespread appeal of Thérèse's autobiography, even in households that were not particularly devout, Ford's account has obvious merit. However, this explanation exists in conflict with the idea that Thérèse's popularity was due to her usefulness as a symbol for reparationists who held the line against modern society and predicted an imminent triumph of the Church over secularism.[8] If Thérèse spoke to increasingly secular sensibilities, how could she also be the banner bearer of anti-*laïcité*, or antisecularism? Resolving the tension between these two poles requires an understanding of sentimentalism as an intellectual foundation for heroic and authoritative behavior that was not tethered to a particular political foundation.

The devotional model of Theresian spirituality offered individual believers a paradigm in which everyday experiences of suffering and sanctity were prominent even as the individual believer attached them to love. As one theologian argues, the life and canonization of Thérèse demonstrated "that sanctity consists essentially in union with God and in the love with which we perform ordinary actions."[9] The role of love, suffering, and desire were made particularly evident in Thérèse's autobiographical writing, the central means by which she intended to communicate her ideas, including the sense that true desires came from God and could be realized by attentiveness to one's soul.[10]

The response to Thérèse's written language and, indeed, the image of the young woman herself demonstrated that suffering through love had immense cultural resonance. Through Thérèse's appropriation of sentiment, any "state" in life could be at once supernatural and natural. The reverberation of Thérèse's sentimental and theological language across political and religious divides thus indicates how the heroic call of a believer was translated into modern practice. In this way, Philomena—or Virginie—could be surpassed not because the underlying values had changed so substantially, but because their rejection of the world had been translated in a way that was applicable to more consumers than ever. The massive popularity of Thérèse's sentimental image, disseminated in large part by means of modern mechanical reproduction, thus serves as the crowning example of the cultural success of heroic sentimental ideals, not the eclipsing of them.

As further evidence, one should note that both Thérèse's devotional style and her public image were deeply shaped by Sulpician sentimentality.[11] In her cell at the Carmelite convent she kept images of the Sacred Heart, of Jesus knocking to be received into a soul, and of guardian angels battling serpents, complete with a quotation from the book of Tobit.[12] An engraved image of Theresa of Avila, an important predecessor in the Carmelites, reminded her to emphasize "God alone, and nothing more, only love and sacrifice." In style, the holy cards and many of her favorite images emphasized a sugary Jesus, replete with flowers and the other symbols common in Sulpician images. The images are often as "treacly" as some find the breathless and exclamatory prose of Thérèse herself.[13] Nevertheless they connected to darker Sulpician themes by emphasizing a battle against the world and the need to sacrifice for God. The images that surrounded Thérèse were not only indicative of the beliefs that shaped her but also demonstrated the "'protocol' that led the believer beyond [herself] and through ritualized interaction [that] helped one master the dramas of life."[14] For Thérèse and those like her, the Sacred Hearts, guardian angels, and flowery sentiment were inviting and approachable even as they harnessed immense power for battles facing the believer.

Thérèse's own words offer some of the best evidence for the metaphysical authority of this worldview. Her self-construction—hagiographical, autobiographical, and sentimental—depicted sacrifice as something intensely personal, not subject to outside critique or evaluation. For example, Thérèse defined the central experience of her conversion as occurring at Christmas in 1886, when she overheard her father complaining about the fact that Thérèse had not yet outgrown childish things. Instead of complaining or bursting into tears as she would normally have done, she swallowed her tears and resolved to do better. As Claude Langlois notes, Thérèse did not view the death of her mother or her entry into Carmel, milestone experiences that were shared with others and could therefore be commented on from the outside, as her most singular moments.[15] Rather, this experience, like her language of emotion, was deeply self-reflexive; only Thérèse knew how her heart had been changed in that experience. Similarly, in her writings she used a language of self that enabled her followers to see their own individual sacrifices as authorized by God and as part of significant, even heroic, changes.[16]

Like her mother, aunt, and many other French women, Thérèse aspired to become a saint, a Christian hero. Thérèse did more than just reach for heaven or authorize her desire; she claimed the right to distinction. She believed her glory consisted in "becoming a great Saint!!!"[17] "Despite my smallness," she claimed, "I would like to enlighten souls like the Prophets or the Doctors [of the Church]; I have the vocation to be an Apostle."[18] Even sympathetic readers have criticized her for this "conscious auto-canonization," whereby she single-mindedly claimed for herself the idea of exemplary holiness.[19] And yet, like her mother, Thérèse also admitted the gap between the reality of her life and her yearning for heroic sanctity. She said, "Unfortunately, when I have compared myself with the saints, I have always found that there is the same difference between the saints and me as there is between a mountain whose summit is lost in the clouds and a humble grain of sand trodden underfoot by passers-by."[20] However, she did not allow those thoughts to prevent her from striving for—and claiming—exemplary holiness. "I told myself: God would not make me wish for something impossible and so, in spite of my littleness, I can aim at being a saint. It is impossible for me to grow bigger, so I put up with myself as I am, with all my countless faults. But I will look for some means of going to heaven by a little way which is very short and very straight, a little way that is quite new."[21]

This new way, she argued, was modern in inspiration. She explained, "We live in an age of inventions; now it is now longer necessary to laboriously climb up flights of stairs. In the buildings of the wealthy, elevators have replaced them. And I was determined to find an elevator to carry me to Jesus, because I was too small to climb the difficult stairs of perfection."[22] Thérèse's route to sanctity was modern and accessible by the powerless. Thérèse looked to the Bible to find affirmation and found it in the passages that said that the little children should come to Jesus. She said that if God called the little children, they would not have to work to get to Him. Rather, He would find a way for them to come, lifting them up, placing them on his knees, and hugging them to his chest. His arms would be the elevator to heaven.[23] Her spiritual secret, based on this passage, was offering her entire heart to Jesus, with childlike openness. If she remained entirely open and loving, like a child, she could be brought directly to Christ. The shortcut to reaching God was thus "nothing less than plenary love of God and total surrender to him down to the least thoughts and actions."[24] Thérèse could thus say "my vocation is love" and argue that the significance of her understanding of love was missionary and apostolic.[25]

Thérèse believed that her understanding of union with Jesus and his Sacred Heart was different than what was commonly understood, less about reparation and more about adoration.[26] She argued against seeing sacrifices as works that would earn Jesus's mercy. "He does not need our works, but only our love. . . . Alas! Few hearts give themselves to him without reserve, understand all the tenderness of His infinite love."[27] There may have been some truth to her sense that she stood alone, especially in the circles that surrounded her in the period after the Franco-Prussian War, all of which emphasized France's need to atone. However, an emphasis on becoming one with God had a long history in keeping with the Sacred Heart devotion both as promoted by Margaret Mary Alacocque and as experienced within the larger sentimental history of the nineteenth century.[28] The vision of the Sacred Heart, like Thérèse's image of devotion, "affirmed one persistent objective: establishing and nourishing a direct relationship between individuals and God."[29] Hearts that were unified spoke directly to one another, holding nothing back.

This did not mean that suffering ceased to become important. Instead, it was omnipresent, such that every choice became an invitation for unity with a suffering Jesus and a suffering world. Thérèse explained to God, "I have no other way to prove to you my love, than to throw flowers, that is to say, not to let any small sacrifice escape."[30] Suffering and love were united in this vision, because they unified the lover and the beloved. Thérèse explained, "I want to both suffer and rejoice for love . . . I will sing, even when I have to pick my flowers among the thorns and my song will be all the more melodious when the thorns are long and spiked."[31] Thérèse would be an example to the world by making multitudes of small sacrifices for Jesus. In this way her spirituality, which was deeply personal, was also public. One could emulate her in any state or at any time of life. The "little way" could provide the foundation to a radical change to one's way of living without changing one's state of life.

Coming full circle and returning to the holy card image of Thérèse demonstrates the sentimental appeal of Theresian spirituality. The image crafted for the public after Thérèse's death was bourgeois and Sulpician in inspiration, much like Thérèse's personal collection of images and holy cards (figure 1).[32] It emphasized the "little way," or childlike simplicity in suffering. The roses, which symbolized trials that were borne for the love of Christ, offered a shorthand for Theresian spirituality: every sacrifice on behalf of the believer, no matter how small, was united to the cross. The roses were thus not only Thérèse's roses but also a sign of how any believer could offer flowers of sacrifice to God. When suffering could be heroic even as it was part of an everyday context, expiation became available to everyone.[33]

Thérèse's family, including the most capable and self-conscious promoters of her image, were politically conservative and deeply embattled in the wake of the Franco-Prussian War and under the anticlerical Third Republic.[34] For them and others of their circles, Thérèse's devotional emphasis on suffering could easily be reconciled with a sense that afflictions were necessary to atone for France's sins against the Church, to inaugurate a new political order that was opposed to the current one. However, Thérèse also enunciated a spirituality that offered all believers the opportunity to become saints, without the violent sacrifice that had been foregrounded earlier in the century. In her emphasis on love and childlike devotion, the "little way" offered ordinary individuals direct access to Jesus's heart and the authority of belief.[35]

Thérèse enunciated her missionary vision as a theology of love that should be brought to every continent. Given the foundation of sentiment, heroism, and consumer culture, this devotional language opened up the possibility of being heroic in any context, including, as Ford has seen, the modern and public world. One did not have to choose between the sacred and the profane; one could act both significantly and devoutly without being celibate or without rejecting the world.

In the end this was a path by which anyone could become a hero, even in situations that might be hostile to such a choice. This is how we can understand Thérèse's popularity with both reactionaries and secularists: Thérèse not only highlighted sacrifice and authorized individual responses to the world but also transformed the individual faith of the cloister into a public example, bridging the gap between the consecrated celibate and lay believer.

Sentimental devotion was often mawkish. It was frequently opposed to rationalism, and its emphasis on individual emotion offered a counterweight to the "ordered drive of modernity."[36] Perhaps most significantly for the course of the nineteenth century, in its claims about heroism and individual action, it offered liberatory potential and heroic significance to those who employed it, a sanction that eventually encompassed not only celibates who devoted their lives to Christ, but all people who were willing to offer their hearts in sacrifice for the salvation of the world.

Women such as Duchesne, Jaricot, and Martin were shaped by, shaped, and embraced a new, thoroughly modern discourse of popular, pervasive, sentiment-based cultural activism. Thérèse's spirituality, the construction of her image, and her immense popularity all demonstrate how devotion and sentiment offered women the responsibility and power to act in a world that needed their assistance. Appeals to the heart, in conjunction with sentimental piety, authorized women to be empowered modern actors for heroic projects of cultural change.

Notes

PREFACE

1. Ulrich, "Vertuous Women Found," 20.
2. Fouilloux, "Femmes et catholicisme"; Carroll, "Give Me That Ol' Time Hormonal Religion"; B. G. Smith, *Ladies of the Leisure Class*; Ford, *Divided Houses*; Mills, "'Saintes Soeurs' and 'Femmes Fortes'"; Curtis, *Civilizing Habits*; Harrison, *Romantic Catholics*. Of course there are exceptions, especially excellent studies of particular women religious and the histories of female orders. However, those studies, which often investigate the agency of a foundress or particular sisters, do not engage the cultural dynamic of religious belief but too often remain as apologetic texts or separated out as if their history is identity politics. While Fouilloux—and Curtis and Harrison—confirms the overall historiographical trend, Curtis's and Harrison's work demonstrates an increasing interest in the question about the intersection of religion, gender, and the public construction of identity. Mills's essay is excellent and often cited, but its insights that nineteenth-century French feminine Catholicism was political are otherwise ignored. Smart, *Citoyennes*, thinks through the problem of French women's domestic and civic identity in useful ways.
3. Vinken, "Wounds of Love."
4. J. W. Scott, *Sex and Secularism*.
5. Harrison, *Romantic Catholics*, 19.
6. C. Taylor, *Secular Age*, 2.
7. Kaufmann, "Religious, the Secular, and Literary Studies."
8. Kaufmann, "Religious, the Secular, and Literary Studies."

INTRODUCTION

1. Soeur Geneviève (Céline Martin), "Recueil des travaux artistiques de Soeur Geneviève," Archives de Carmel de Lisieux (ACL) 44; this holy card image of Thérèse is derived from a 1912 charcoal drawing by her sister Céline (Soeur Geneviève); the original can be found at the Archives de Carmel de Lisieux.

2. Deboick, "Image, Authenticity," 91–93.

3. Deboick, "Image, Authenticity."

4. Critics such as Joris-Karl Huysmans and Léon Bloy saw Sulpician objects as kitschy, in poor taste, and made with little virtuosity or talent. Given Huysmans and Bloy's complicated relationship to both masculinity and the Church, their distaste for Sulpician art also affirms that this was perceived as a "girly" form of religious art.

5. Reddy, *Invisible Code*; Andress, "Living the Revolutionary Melodrama"; Denby, *Sentimental Narrative*.

6. To contextualize the importance of these images, see Kselman, *Miracles & Prophecies*; T. Taylor, "Images of Sanctity," 270; McCartin, "Sacred Heart of Jesus," 54–55; Pirotte, "Les Images de dévotion."

7. Gaucher, *Story of a Life*, 212–13.

8. Bryden, "Saints and Stereotypes," 8.

9. Ghéon, *Sainte Thérèse de Lisieux*, 18.

10. Sackville-West, *Eagle and the Dove*, 156.

11. Merton, *Seven Storey Mountain*, 353.

12. Merton, *Seven Storey Mountain*, 388.

13. Neal, "Beautiful Death of Thérèse of Lisieux," 218; Furlong, *Therese of Lisieux*.

14. Richards, *Practical Criticism*, 255.

15. Merton, *Seven Storey Mountain*, 353.

16. Merton can only go so far as to say that this art is indifferent to sanctity; Merton, *Seven Storey Mountain*, 389.

17. Gorres, *Hidden Face*; Robo, *Two Portraits*; by contrast, Lavabre, "Sainte comme une image," like Deboick, contextualizes Thérèse's cult as an historical creation.

18. Bryden, "Saints and Stereotypes."

19. "Divini Amoris Scientia."

20. Reddy, *Invisible Code*.

21. This observation might be expanded to other locations beyond the scope of this project. For example, Thérèse was deeply popular in the United States, for many of the same reasons. American culture also had currents that emphasized emotion and sentiment in the context of women's activism. For example, see Engbers, "With Great Sympathy"; Stevenson-Moessner, "Elizabeth Cady Stanton"; Wolff, "Emily Dickinson."

22. An overview of the historical interpretations can be found in Tine Van Osselaer, "Images of the Catholic Male in the Sacred Heart Devotion," in Pasture, Art, and Buerman, *Gender and Christianity*, 121–35.

23. The language of sentiment did not only appeal to women. However, this book investigates women's relationships to religion and sentiment.

24. Popiel, *Rousseau's Daughters*.

25. S. Samuels, *Culture of Sentiment*, 4. Chapter 2 provides further evidence of this in the French context.

26. Reddy, *Invisible Code*, 6.

27. Andress, "Jacobinism as Heroic Narrative"; Reddy, *Navigation of Feeling*.

28. Gutermann-Jacquet, *Les équivoques du genre*; Davidson, "Making Society 'Legible.'"

29. Harrison, *Romantic Catholics*. This is not a claim that this "feminine" spirituality actually excluded men.

30. Savart, "A la recherche de l'"art'"; R. D. E. Burton, *Holy Tears*; Cova and Dumons, *Femmes, genre et catholicisme*; Lerch, "Le sentiment religieux"; Reddy, *Invisible Code*.

31. Cholvy, *Histoire religieuse de la France*; Gibson, *Social History of French Catholicism*; Delumeau, *La religion de ma mère*.

32. Arnold, *Le corps et l'âme*.

33. Turin, *Femmes et religieuses*.

34. Langlois, "Les effectifs des congrégations féminines."

35. Michelet, *Du prêtre* (Hachette, 1845), 2.

36. Seeley, "O Sainte Mère"; Outram, "Le Langage mâle"; B. G. Smith, *Ladies of the Leisure Class*.

37. Art, "Cult of the Virgin Mary," has noted that if men were in charge of the hierarchy, one still ought to explain why their discourse emphasized femininity.

38. J. W. Scott, *Sex and Secularism*.

39. Mahmood, *Politics of Piety*.

40. Mahmood, *Politics of Piety*, xxiii, x.

41. Harrison, *Romantic Catholics*, is an important corrective to the sense that a "feminized" Church meant one that only appealed to women. My argument about feminization is not that men did not or could not find themselves in this type of piety but that it was indeed an institution and a cultural form associated with women and one that women used to shape the world around them.

42. Curtis, *Civilizing Habits*, 9.

43. Bracke, "Conjugating the Modern/ Religious," 52. These questions are relevant in other patriarchal contexts as well. See Wilkinson, *Women and Modesty*.

44. Mack, "Religion, Feminism," 150–51.

45. Mack, *Heart Religion*, 10.

46. J. W. Scott, *Sex and Secularism*, 97.

47. Harris, *Lourdes*, 361.

48. Mack, "Religion, Feminism," is an excellent essay on devout belief, agency, and public action; Curtis, *Civilizing Habits*; and Smart, *Citoyennes*, think through the problem of French women's domestic and civic identity in useful ways. In general, however, Curtis's observations about the apparent contradiction are prescient; devout action, under the impulses of doing God's will, is "antimodern."

49. Bracke, "Conjugating the Modern/ Religious," 52–53, claims that the presumption of oppression within women's experience of patriarchal religion is itself an outgrowth of an epistemology that is based on European feminist thought that forces religious belief into a dichotomous position. See also Offen, *European Feminisms*; Moses, *French Feminism*; Margadant, *New Biography*; Fuchs and Thompson, *Women in Nineteenth-Century Europe*. A notable exception that calls attention to the historiographical problem is Curtis, *Civilizing Habits*. Similarly, Mack, "Religion, Feminism," begins by juxtaposing religious obedience to the statement "A feminist is a woman who does not allow anyone to think in her place" to problematize the question of agency.

50. Fouilloux, "Femmes et catholicisme"; Carroll, "Give Me That Ol' Time Hormonal Religion"; B. G. Smith, *Ladies of the Leisure Class*; Ford, *Divided Houses*, 2005; Mills, "'Saintes Soeurs' and 'Femmes Fortes'"; Curtis, *Civilizing Habits*; Harrison, *Romantic Catholics*. Of course there are exceptions, not only in the Ancient or Early Modern eras. Often, however, these studies investigate the agency of a foundress or particular sisters and do not engage the cultural dynamic of religious belief but remain as apologetic texts or separated out as if their history is merely (religious) identity politics. While Fouilloux—and Curtis and Harrison—confirm the overall historiographical trend, Curtis's and Harrison's work demonstrates an increasing interest in the question about the intersection of religion, gender, and identity construction. Mills's essay is excellent and frequently cited, but its insights that nineteenth-century French Catholicism was political and even feminist are otherwise ignored.

51. Adams, *Poverty, Charity, and Motherhood*.

52. Bracke, "Conjugating the Modern/ Religious," 59.

53. Bracke, "Conjugating the Modern/ Religious"; Habermas, *Awareness of What Is Missing*; Asad, *Formations of the Secular*; Kyrlezhev, "Postsecular Age"; King, *Postsecularism*.

54. Coleman, *Virtues of Abandon*. Coleman's current work, on a Catholic ethic of capitalism, continues this trend.
55. Mahmood, *Politics of Piety*; Nongbri, *Before Religion*.
56. Harrison, *Romantic Catholics*; Izzo, *Liberal Christianity*.
57. Jonas, *France and the Cult*; Kselman, *Conscience and Conversion*.
58. C. Taylor, *Secular Age*, 2; Casanova, *Public Religions*; Ward, "How Literature Resists Secularity," 73–74.
59. Heuer, *Family and the Nation*, observes that civic identity is far more than political rights; Ford, *Divided Houses*, 2005, 171, says, "We still await a study that will do justice to the complex and ambiguous process of female acculturation that produced, in turn, the legions of women who entered religious communities and who attended mass and Easter services without their spouses."
60. This work uses the word "unsectarian" to indicate cultural content that has not been divided by a binary opposition, especially but not limited to "religious" versus "secular." Some excellent works that think through similar problems are Coleman, *Virtues of Abandon*; Pasture, Art, and Buerman, *Gender and Christianity*; Harrison, *Romantic Catholics*; Carroll, "Give Me That Ol' Time Hormonal Religion."
61. Habermas, *Structural Transformation*; Calhoun, *Habermas and the Public Sphere*. One important work founded on these distinctions is Landes, *Women and the Public Sphere*; Fraser, *Unruly Practices*, contests the traditional reading.
62. Calhoun, "Afterword."
63. Reder and Schmidt in Habermas, *Awareness of What Is Missing*, 6; Ricken in Habermas, 55–56.
64. Peperzak in Bloechl, *Christianity and Secular Reason*, 17–32.
65. While this work generally acts to accentuate the positive ways in which nonrational experiences expand human experience, that should not be taken to imply that nonrational—religious, spiritual, ecstatic, hysterical, etc.— experiences cannot act in ways that have a negative impact.
66. Peperzak in Habermas, *Awareness of What Is Missing*, 21.
67. Peperzak in Habermas, *Awareness of What Is Missing*, 22.
68. Beauvoir, *Second Sex*.
69. Denby, *Sentimental Narrative*; Cohen, *Sentimental Education of the Novel*; Reddy, *Invisible Code*; Reddy, *Navigation of Feeling*; Andress, "Jacobinism as Heroic Narrative."
70. Ogden, *Credulity*, 2–5, helpfully recaps recent work on mesmerism and enchantment.

71. Habermas, *Structural Transformation*, 168–70.

72. Habermas, *Structural Transformation*, 171.

73. Habermas, *Structural Transformation*, 171.

74. Careel and Osiek, *Philippine Duchesne*, 15.

75. Some of the works that I have found most useful for understanding autobiography and its liberating potential are Goldsmith, *Publishing Women's Life Stories*; Baggerman, Dekker, and Mascuch, *Controlling Time and Shaping the Self*; Treadwell, *Autobiographical Writing and British Literature*.

76. Goujon, *Prendre part à l'intransmissible*; see also Verjus and Davidson, *Le roman conjugal*; Hennequin-Lecomte, *Le patriciat strasbourgeois*; Boureau et al., *La correspondance*.

77. Langlois, *L'autobiographie de Thérèse de Lisieux*, 49, thinks about letters and religious formation as both creating spaces for an "écriture de soi," or self-writing.

78. Bloechl, *Christianity and Secular Reason*, 5.

79. Mack, *Heart Religion*, 10.

80. Latour, *Inquiry into Modes of Existence*, 20; Asad, *Formations of the Secular*, 70.

81. See, for example, Kselman, *Conscience and Conversion*.

82. Glotin, *La Bible du Cœur de Jésus*; Walch, *La spiritualité conjugale*; Maryks, *Companion to Jesuit Mysticism*.

83. Habermas, *Structural Transformation*, 156. In his early work on the public sphere, Habermas argues that the conjugal family and its practices are an interior domain.

84. Popiel, *Rousseau's Daughters*; Walker, *Mother's Love*.

85. Harrison, *Romantic Catholics*, 277. Socially or politically dangerous implies a level of engagement with "the public" that cannot be ignored; it is not irrelevant or removed from public constructs.

86. J. W. Scott, *Sex and Secularism*, introduction and chap. 1.

87. Jonas, *France and the Cult*.

88. Taylor, *Secular Age*, 4.

89. I am influenced here by the theoretical apparatus of Blanca Santonja, "Mary Berry and Her Religious Sensibilities."

90. Bruyn, review of *Pure Language*, 18.

91. Vincent-Buffault, *History of Tears*, viii.

92. Reddy, *Invisible Code*, 3.

93. Lysaught, "Witnessing Christ in Their Bodies."

94. Coakley, *New Asceticism*; Valantasis, *Making of the Self*.

95. Walch, *La spiritualité conjugale,* chap. 1. However, as Walch notes in the introduction, emphasis on conjugal spirituality does not imply that teaching was "unequivocal and frozen" (14).

96. Hufton, "Reconstruction of a Church"; Davis, "City Women and Religious Change"; see Bilinkoff, *Avila of Saint Teresa,* for a description of one particular way in which changes in religiosity and emotion could be construed as a threat.

97. Aston, *Religion and Revolution in France,* 42.

98. Walch, *La spiritualité conjugale,* 198.

99. Mitchell, "Resistance to the Revolution," 123.

100. McManners, *Church and Society;* Muchembled, *Culture populaire;* Le Goff, Rémond, and Joutard, *Histoire de la France religieuse,* 3.

101. Aston, *Religion and Revolution in France,* chap. 9.

102. Not all constitutional priests agreed with this turn; the Abbé Grégoire continued to wear clerical robes and argue against this religious policy. See Sepinwall, *Abbé Grégoire.*

103. Van Kley, "Christianity as Casualty and Chrysalis," 1083.

104. Hufton, "Reconstruction of a Church."

105. Mills, "'Saintes Soeurs' and 'Femmes Fortes,'" 140–41; Desan, "Role of Women," 455; see also chap. 4.

106. Jonas, *France and the Cult;* R. D. E. Burton, *Holy Tears.*

107. Hufton, "Reconstruction of a Church," 30.

108. Desan, "Role of Women," 460.

109. This narrative is opposed to one that argues that women were religious because it was the only sphere that was left to them. To some degree, this is a question of optics; I agree with Hufton, Desan, and other Revolutionary historians that women were both activist and engaged in questions about religious prerogatives. Many nineteenth-century historians begin with the fact that women were excluded from roles that they might have earlier played. While this is true, it need not define their motives for action. Outram, "Le langage mâle"; B. G. Smith, *Ladies of the Leisure Class.*

110. Aston, *Religion and Revolution in France,* 285.

111. Aston, *Religion and Revolution in France,* 320–22.

112. Aston, *Religion and Revolution in France,* 287.

113. Cage, *Unnatural Frenchmen;* Woshinsky, *Imagining Women's Conventual Spaces;* Ford, *Divided Houses,* 2005.

114. Langlois, *Le catholicisme au féminin.*

115. L.-A. Martin, *Education des mères de famille.*

116. Smart, *Citoyennes*; Popiel, *Rousseau's Daughters*; Walker, *Mother's Love*.

117. Surkis, *Sexing the Citizen*, 1.

118. Michelet, *Du prêtre* (Comptoir, 1845).

119. J. W. Scott, *Sex and Secularism*, 37.

120. Some historians seem to accept the nineteenth-century argument that vigorous and active women were emasculating or virile. For example, R. D. E. Burton, *Holy Tears*, 23, dealing with Zélie and Thérèse Martin. Additionally, bestselling and feted works such as Pinker, *Enlightenment Now*, demonstrate another way in which these claims continue to exert force.

121. Michelet, *Du prêtre* (Comptoir, 1845); Michelet, *Woman*; Michelet, *Love*.

122. Michelet and Quinet, *Des Jésuites*, 13n.

123. Michelet, *Du prêtre* (Comptoir, 1845), 206.

124. Michelet, *Priests, Women, and Families* (1846), xxii.

125. Michelet, *Du prêtre* (Comptoir, 1845), 13.

126. Michelet, *Du prêtre* (Comptoir, 1845), 71–72, 172–74; Jonas, *France and the Cult*, 21.

127. Verhoeven, "'Perfect Jesuit in Petticoats,'" 627–28.

128. Harrison, *Romantic Catholics*, 16.

129. Ogden, *Credulity*. Ogden's argument that skeptics redeployed religious power to manage behavior—and indeed, that this discourse was a prescriptive one—has relevance here.

130. Asad, "What Might an Anthropology?"

131. An exception to this statement is Machen, *Women of Faith and Religious Identity*.

132. Aston, *Religion and Revolution in France*.

133. Cole, *Power of Large Numbers*; Van de Walle, *Female Population of France*. The numbers of never-married women who did not join orders increased, but not dramatically. This is a logical outcome in a society where most women did not have the financial means to live on their own.

134. Michelet, *La femme*, in Vinken, "Wounds of Love."

135. Michelet, *Le prêtre, la femme*, 216. "Le mari trouve la maison plus grande et plus vide. Sa femme est devenue tout autre. . . . Tout est changé dans leurs habitudes intimes, toujours par bonne raison: 'Aujourd'hui, c'est jeûne.'—Et demain?—'C'est fête.'—Le mari respecte cette austérité; il se ferait un scrupule de troubler une si haute dévotion, il se résigne tristement: Cela devient embarrassant, dit-il, je ne l'avais pas prévu; ma femme devient une sainte."

136. One sees this particularly with Jaricot and Thérèse Martin. Langlois, *L'Autobiographie de Thérèse de Lisieux*, 14, observes quite specifically, refer-

ring to Thérèse, that her most important work is at once hagiographic and autobiographical.

137. Hagiographic constructions demonstrate that frequently the sources were collected and culled shortly after the women's deaths; the choices and statements about their personalities and vision thus valorize the women in nineteenth-century terms. See, for example, Careel and Osiek, *Philippine Duchesne*, 1; Quantin and Quantin, *Zélie et Louis Martin*; Jaricot, *Jésus*, and Brac de la Perrière, *Écrits de jeunesse*.

138. Andress, "Jacobinism as Heroic Narrative," 7. Andress finds these characteristics in Jacobin ideals; that similarity alone should help us rethink the meaning of this rhetoric, even if it was deployed by post-Revolutionary women.

139. For example, B. G. Smith, *Ladies of the Leisure Class*; Taylor and Knott, *Women, Gender and Enlightenment*; P. D. Johnson, *Equal in Monastic Profession*; Machen, *Women of Faith and Religious Identity*.

1. SHAPING THE SENTIMENTAL ORDER

1. Michelet, *Du prêtre* (Comptoir, 1845). For example, historian Edgar Quinet and feminist and dramatist Ernst Legouve both agreed with Michelet. Not all men were of this philosophical bent; notably, in Lyon, many prominent businessmen and academics continued to practice devoutly.

2. Michelet, *Priests, Women, and Families* (1845), 241.

3. Michelet, *Priests, Women, and Families* (1845), 230.

4. Seeley, "O Sainte Mère," 889.

5. Marcoin and Chelebourg, *La litterature de jeunesse*; Williams, *Social Life of Books*.

6. For example, the missionary tales of Le Gobien, first published at the turn of the eighteenth century, were reprinted multiple times and added to in the early nineteenth century. See Le Gobien, *Lettres édifiantes et curieuses*.

7. Lyons, *Readers and Society*, 11.

8. Boone, *Les mauvais livres*; Boone, *Catalogue d'une bibliothèque choisie*; Dupanloup, *Avertissement à la jeunesse*.

9. Lyons, *Readers and Society*, 11.

10. Lyons, *Readers and Society*, 16.

11. Smart, *Citoyennes*; Cott, *Bonds of Womanhood*; Heuer, *Family and the Nation*; Popiel, *Rousseau's Daughters*; Broers, *Europe under Napoleon*.

12. Walker, *Mother's Love*; Popiel, *Rousseau's Daughters*.

13. Rogers, *From the Salon*.

14. Certeau, *Practice of Everyday Life*.

15. I return to other constructions of femininity in later chapters.

16. See, for example, McMahon, *Enemies of the Enlightenment*.

17. Tackett, *Coming of the Terror*; Aston, *Religion and Revolution in France*; Sepinwall, *Abbé Grégoire*; Desan, *Reclaiming the Sacred*.

18. AN F/19/5435 contains correspondence between the Society of Good Books and the state, outlining their goals and process and seeking official protection and patronage. They note that the wide distribution of inexpensive or even free books was central to their design.

19. Fleury, *Catéchisme historique* (1814); Lamennais, *Bibliothèque des dames chrétiennes*.

20. Because the form of the catechism itself was so ubiquitous, it was deployed not only for buttressing but also, sometimes, for undermining religious dogmatism. See, for example, *Catéchisme sur l'Eglise*; *Catéchisme d'un curé intrus*; Maréchal, *Catéchisme du curé Meslier*; Froberville, *Catéchisme des trois ordres*; Lyon, *Catéchisme historique de la papauté*.

21. *Catéchisme du diocèse de Saint-Claude*, 5–6. Mme de Sévigné was the daughter of Celse Bénigne de Rabutin, baron of Chantal, making her the granddaughter of Jeanne Chantal.

22. Carter, *Creating Catholics*; *Catéchisme du diocèse de Saint-Claude*, 4–5.

23. AN F/19/5439.

24. Napoleon's *Imperial Catechism* is often dated to 1806, though many areas would not have received a printed version until 1810 or later, making it a recent addition even during the Restoration. See *Catéchisme à l'usage de toutes les eglises de l'Empire français*.

25. AN F/19/5439.

26. *Catéchisme du diocèse d'Orléans*; *Catéchisme du diocèse de Poitiers*; additionally, the letters of complaint to the government found in AN F/19/5446 indicate that instructors were often required to lead schoolchildren preparing for their First Communion from school to their catechism classes and back.

27. Fleury, *Catéchisme historique* (1815); Couturier, *Catéchisme dogmatique et moral*.

28. *Catéchisme du diocèse de Saint-Dié*; *Catéchisme du diocèse de Lyon*; *Catéchisme du diocèse de Poitiers*; *Catéchisme du diocèse d'Amiens*; *Catéchisme de Versailles*; *Catéchisme à l'usage du diocèse de Beauvais*.

29. Olier, *Catéchisme chrétien pour la vie intérieure*; Olier, *Catéchisme de la vie intérieure*.

30. A few of the editions are Fleury, *Catéchisme historique* (1833); Fleury, *Catéchisme historique* (1854); Fleury, *Catéchisme historique* (1816); Fleury, *Catéchisme historique* (1821); Fleury, *Catéchisme historique* (1834); Fleury,

Catéchisme historique (1831); Fleury, *Catechisme historique* (1810); Fleury, *Catéchisme historique* (1814); Fleury, *Catéchisme historique* (1852); Fleury, *Catéchisme historique* (1814); Fleury, *Catéchisme historique* (1805).

31. Bérenger and Guibaud, *La morale en action* (1813); Berruyer, *Histoires saintes*; Bérardier de Bataut and Le Tellier, *Précis de l'histoire universelle*; Cassé de Saint-Prosper et al., *Le Monde*.

32. Fleury, *Catechisme historique* (1810), 1.

33. Fleury, *Catéchisme historique* (1814), 5.

34. Carter, *Creating Catholics*, 4–5, notes that the early modern era downplayed doctrine to focus on public practice. Fleury's catechism critiqued that approach; it emphasized doctrine and correct belief.

35. For example, Fleury, *Catéchisme historique* (1814).

36. Fleury, *Catéchisme historique* (1814), 13.

37. Fleury, *Catéchisme historique* (1814), 19.

38. Fleury, *Catéchisme historique* (1814), 20.

39. Fleury, *Catéchisme historique* (1814), 24.

40. Fleury, *Catéchisme historique* (1814), 41.

41. Fleury, *Catéchisme historique* (1814), 42.

42. Fleury, *Catéchisme historique* (1814), 41.

43. Fleury, *Catéchisme historique* (1814), 49–50.

44. This was not always true, as it was sometimes referred to as "Adam's sin" and emphasized the fall from grace as a fall made more significant by Adam's moral authority over creation.

45. Fleury, *Catéchisme historique* (1814), 67–68.

46. Fleury, *Catéchisme historique* (1814), 99.

47. Fleury, *Catéchisme historique* (1814), 76.

48. Fleury, *Catéchisme historique* (1814), 138.

49. Fleury, *Catéchisme historique* (1814), 152–53.

50. Fleury, *Catéchisme historique* (1814), 153.

51. Fleury, *Catéchisme historique* (1814), 153.

52. This is consistent with the fact that seventeenth- and eighteenth-century catechetical teaching had de-emphasized human aspects such as love and the physical body. Walch, *La spiritualité conjugale*, 67–71.

53. Walch, *La spiritualité conjugale*, 74.

54. Walch, *La spiritualité conjugale*, 358–59.

55. *Catéchisme du diocèse de Saint-Claude*, 70–83.

56. *Catéchisme du diocèse de Poitiers*, 111.

57. 1 Corinthians 7:32–36.

58. Couturier, *Catéchisme dogmatique et moral*, 369.

59. Walch also notes that Jean Girad de Villethierry uses the same example while François de Sales makes a similar argument using the example of Isaac and Rebecca. Walch, *La spiritualité conjugale*, 167.
60. Tobit 8:7.
61. Louis had medals made to commemorate his marriage to Zélie; the image on the front was from the book of Tobit.
62. Olier, *Catéchisme chrétien pour la vie intérieure*, 15.
63. Couturier, *Catéchisme dogmatique et moral*, 375.
64. Couturier, *Catéchisme dogmatique et moral*, 430.
65. Walch, *La spiritualité conjugale*, chaps. 3, 7.
66. For example, both of these works figured prominently in the prospectus for Lammenais's *Bibliothèque des dames chrétiennes* (BNF D2 6008 [1–4]).
67. See, for example, the frontispiece of Carron, *La vertu parée de tous ses charmes*.
68. Lyons, *Readers and Society*, 41.
69. The jump backward in time had a significant tension inherent within it. The domestic, nurturing mother was a product of the eighteenth century, but devotional works emphasized the woman of the seventeenth century, one for whom personally nurturing and educating children was substantially less important. This meant that there was often an unrecognized difference between ideal models of the past and those of the present, especially in terms of what women were expected to do and how they organized their lives.
70. Michelet, *Priests, Women, and Families* (1845), 18, 23.
71. Michelet, *Priests, Women, and Families* (1845), 18, 23.
72. Michelet, *Priests, Women, and Families* (1845), 179.
73. Ernst Renan saw the same opening and offered a novelistic exploration of the life of Jesus that engaged the feminine taste for sentimentality. Priest, "Reading, Writing, and Religion," 260–61.
74. Marcoin, *Librairie de jeunesse et littérature*.
75. Google Ngram Viewer.
76. Carron, *Vies des justes dans l'état du mariage* (1816); Carron, *Vies des justes dans les conditions ordinaires* (1825). The word "état" has the implication of a way of life or a status.
77. Carron, *Les trois héroïnes chrétiennes*.
78. Chateaubriand, *Memoirs of François René*, 102–3; Pérennès, *Dictionnaire de biographie chrétienne*, 263.
79. Rousseau addresses "a good mother, who knows how to think" in his preface to Rousseau, *Emile; or, On Education*.
80. Carron, *Les trois héroïnes chrétiennes* (1810), iii.

81. Carron, *Les trois héroïnes chrétiennes* (1810), iii.

82. Carron, *Les trois héroïnes chrétiennes* (1810), iv.

83. Année littéraire, 1785, in Carron, *Les trois héroïnes chrétiennes* (1810), viii.

84. Carron, *Les nouvelles héroïnes chrétiennes* (1815), 1:8.

85. Carron, *Les nouvelles héroïnes chrétiennes* (1815), 1:11.

86. Carron, *Les nouvelles héroïnes chrétiennes* (1815), 1:11–12.

87. De Sacy in Spencer, *Politics of Belief*, 53.

88. Carron, *Les nouvelle héroïnes chrétiennes* (1825); Carron, *Vies des justes dans l'état du mariage* (1825); Carron, *Vies des justes parmi les filles chrétiennes* (1824). The term "fille chrétienne" is clearly understood in its meaning of consecrated sister, not just a virgin or unmarried Christian female, though virginity was also important, as evidenced by some of the stories offered in the *Lives of the Just in Ordinary Conditions*.

89. Even a quick glance at seventeenth-century hagiographies makes it clear that seventeenth-century devotion had a set of conflicts between spiritual independence and patriarchal authority that grew out of Church-State conflicts and the post-Tridentine religious experience, in ways that were similar to the post-Revolutionary moment. See Lane, "Vocational Freedom"; Diefendorf, "Give Us Back Our Children"; Hanley, "Engendering the State."

90. Carron, *Vies des justes dans l'état du mariage* (1825), 1:xiii.

91. Ford, *Divided Houses*, 14.

92. Carron, *Vies des justes dans l'état du mariage* (1825), 1:viii.

93. Carron, *Vies des justes dans l'état du mariage* (1825), 1:viii.

94. Carron, *Vies des justes dans l'état du mariage* (1825), 1:x.

95. Carron, *Vies des justes dans l'état du mariage* (1825), 1:ix.

96. See, for example, the stories referenced in Lane, "Vocational Freedom"; Diefendorf, "Give Us Back Our Children"; Hanley, "Engendering the State."

97. Carron, *Vies des justes dans l'état du mariage* (1825), 1:89, 221.

98. Carron, *Vies des justes dans l'état du mariage* (1816), 65–66.

99. Carron, *Vies des justes dans l'état du mariage* (1816), 66–67.

100. Carron, *Vies des justes dans l'état du mariage* (1825), 1:37–38.

101. Carron, *Vies des justes dans l'état du mariage* (1825), 1:169. Frémiot is also known as Jeanne François Chantal.

102. Carron, *Vies des justes dans l'état du mariage* (1825), 1:423–24.

103. Carron, *Vies des justes dans l'état du mariage* (1816), 103.

104. Carron, *Vies des justes dans l'état du mariage* (1816), 1–3.

105. Carron, *Vies des justes dans l'état du mariage* (1816), 3.

106. Carron, *Vies des justes dans l'état du mariage* (1816), 435–44.

107. Carron, *Vies des justes dans l'état du mariage* (1816), 183.

108. Carron, *Vies des justes dans l'état du mariage* (1816), 184.

109. Zélie and Louis Martin took a similar vow in the nineteenth century; see chap. 6.

110. Carron, *Vies des justes dans l'état du mariage* (1816), 142.

111. Carron, *Vies des justes dans l'état du mariage* (1825), 1:401.

112. Carron, *Vies des justes dans l'état du mariage* (1825), 1:343–45. Marie Guyard/Guyard/Guyart is also known as Marie de l'Incarnation.

113. Carron, *Vies des justes dans l'état du mariage* (1816), 227.

114. This is a very different image of Chantal's life than the one found in Michelet!

115. Many of these stories are exactly the narrative conflicts explored in Diefendorf, "Give Us Back Our Children"; the same saints also appear in other sources explored by Lane, "Vocational Freedom."

116. Michelet, *Priests, Women, and Families* (1845), chap. 2.

117. Carron, *Vies des justes dans l'état du mariage* (1825), 1:95.

118. Carron, *Vies des justes dans l'état du mariage* (1825), 1:136.

119. Carron, *Vies des justes dans l'état du mariage* (1825), 1:15.

120. Carron, *Vies des justes dans l'état du mariage* (1825), 1:224.

121. *Catholic Encyclopedia*, 8:283.

122. See, for example, the reflections made by Carron, *Vies des justes dans l'état du mariage* (1816), 375.

123. Carron, *Vies des justes parmi les filles chrétiennes* (1824), iii.

124. Carron, *Les nouvelles héroïnes chrétiennes* (1815), 1:34.

125. Carron, *Les nouvelles héroïnes chrétiennes* (1815), 1:99.

126. Carron, *Les nouvelles héroïnes chrétiennes* (1825), 2:159.

127. Carron, *Les nouvelles héroïnes chrétiennes* (1815), 1:165.

128. Carron, *Les nouvelles héroïnes chrétiennes* (1815), 1:176.

129. Carron, *Les nouvelles héroïnes chrétiennes* (1825), 2:140.

130. Carron, *Les nouvelles héroïnes chrétiennes* (1825), 2:90.

131. Carron, *Les nouvelles héroïnes chrétiennes* (1825), 2:frontispice.

132. Carron, *Les nouvelles héroïnes chrétiennes* (1815), 1:58.

133. Carron, *Les nouvelles héroïnes chrétiennes* (1815), 1:47.

134. Carron, *Les nouvelles héroïnes chrétiennes* (1825), 2:225.

135. Carron, *Vies des justes dans l'état du mariage* (1825), 1:213.

136. Carron, *Les nouvelles héroïnes chrétiennes* (1825), 2:217.

137. Carron, *Les nouvelles héroïnes chrétiennes* (1825), 2:234. This story sounds similar to that of Philippine Duchesne (chap. 4).

138. Carron, *Les nouvelles héroïnes chrétiennes* (1825), 2:248.

139. Carron, *Les nouvelles héroïnes chrétiennes* (1815), 1:25.

140. Carron, *Les nouvelles héroïnes chrétiennes* (1815), 1:29.

141. Carron, *Les nouvelles héroïnes chrétiennes* (1815), 1:31.

142. Carron, *Les nouvelles héroïnes chrétiennes* (1815), 1:32.

143. Carron, *Vies des justes dans l'état du mariage* (1816), 431.

144. Carron, *Vies des justes dans l'état du mariage* (1816), 432.

145. Greer, "Colonial Saints." While Greer's conclusions are not the same as mine—perhaps a difference between books produced in the seventeenth century and those produced in the nineteenth—his observation about hagiographic significance resonates here.

146. Michelet, *Priests, Women, and Families* (1845), 193.

2. CONTESTING OPPRESSION

1. Denby, *Sentimental Narrative*; Cohen, *Sentimental Education of the Novel*; Brissenden, *Virtue in Distress*.

2. Heller, "Tragedy, Sisterhood, and Revenge," 213.

3. Pérez, "Against 'Écriture Féminine'"; Paskow, "Rethinking Madame Bovary's Motives"; Cohen, *Sentimental Education of the Novel*.

4. Cohen, *Sentimental Education of the Novel*, 123.

5. Stewart, *Gynographs*, 7.

6. Lyon-Caen, *La lecture et la vie*, investigates readers' responses to novels at midcentury but is relatively unconcerned with earlier readers, those from the first third of the century, and emphasizes readers of Balzac and Sue, exactly the kind of readers who had made a move away from the material that this book considers more fully.

7. Denby, *Sentimental Narrative*; Waller, *Male Malady*.

8. Aliaga-Buchenau, *Dangerous Potential of Reading*, 4; Lyon-Caen, *La lecture et la vie*, 93; Armstrong, *Desire and Domestic Fiction*, 10.

9. Hunt, *Inventing Human Rights*, chap. 1.

10. Darnton, *Great Cat Massacre*, chap. 6.

11. Cohen, *Sentimental Education of the Novel*, 33.

12. Cohen, *Sentimental Education of the Novel*, 9.

13. Coulet, "Révolution et roman," 651.

14. Staël, *Des circonstances actuelles*, 284.

15. Worley, "Gentle Art of Persuasion," 178.

16. Marso, "Defying Fraternity," 650.

17. Reddy, *Navigation of Feeling*, 240.

18. "Essai sur les fictions," in Staël, *Oeuvres complètes*, 69. "Les romans peuvent peindre les caractères et les sentiments avec tant de force et de détails, qu'il

n'est point de lecture qui doive produire une impression aussi profonde de haine pour le vice, et d'amour pour la vertu . . . la vérité des tableaux."

19. Allen, *Popular French Romanticism*, 9.

20. Williams, *Social Life of Books*.

21. Cohen, *Sentimental Education of the Novel*, chap. 1; Williams, *Social Life of Books*.

22. Margaret Waller, "Being René, Buying Atala," discusses the popularity of Chateaubriand's characters, but similar trends have also been noted for *Paul et Virginie*, the Duchesse de Vallières, and others.

23. Cohen, *Sentimental Education of the Novel*.

24. Flaubert, *Madame Bovary*, 94.

25. Flaubert, *Madame Bovary*, 95. "Comme elle écouta, les premières fois, la lamentation sonore des mélancolies romantiques se répétant à tous les échoes de la terre et de l'éternité!"

26. Cohen, "Flaubert Lectrice"; Cohen, *Sentimental Education of the Novel*; Hurlburt, "Educating Emma."

27. Flaubert, *Madame Bovary*, 149.

28. Cohen, *Sentimental Education of the Novel*, 12; Allen, *Popular French Romanticism*.

29. Flaubert, *Complete Works of Gustave Flaubert*, 2:113.

30. Gans, *Madame Bovary*.

31. Pérez, "Against 'Écriture Féminine'"; Cohen, *Sentimental Education of the Novel*.

32. Flaubert, *Madame Bovary*, 49; Paskow, "Rethinking Madame Bovary's Motives," 328.

33. M. Scott, *Struggle for the Soul*, 4. While Scott is referring to Romanticism, the traits to which he refers are equally present in Sentimentalism, with the added fact that it was a "woman's" genre and therefore even more suspect.

34. Diaconoff, *Through the Reading Glass*, 49; Goldsmith and Goodman, *Going Public*, 2.

35. Appleyard, *Becoming a Reader*, 182. Even though female literacy grew more quickly, men's literacy remained higher overall.

36. Chartier and Martin, *Histoire de l'édition française*; Aliaga-Buchenau, *Dangerous Potential of Reading*, 4–5; Darnton, *Great Cat Massacre*.

37. Williams, *Social Life of Books*.

38. Diaconoff, *Through the Reading Glass*, 50.

39. Rogers, *From the Salon*, 6.

40. Parent-Lardeur, *Les cabinets de lecture*; Parent-Lardeur, *Lire à Paris*; Cohen, *Sentimental Education of the Novel*, chap. 1.

41. Denby, *Sentimental Narrative*; Hunt, *Inventing Human Rights*, 50.

42. Hurlburt, "Educating Emma."

43. Diaconoff, *Through the Reading Glass*; Montfort-Howard, *Literate Women and the French Revolution*; Trouille, *Sexual Politics in the Enlightenment*.

44. Diaconoff, *Through the Reading Glass*.

45. Diaconoff, *Through the Reading Glass*, 7.

46. Diaconoff, *Through the Reading Glass*, chap. 3.

47. Williams, *Social Life of Books*, chap. 2.

48. Popiel, *Rousseau's Daughters*, chap. 4.

49. Popiel, *Rousseau's Daughters*, 112–13.

50. Hurlburt, "Educating Emma," 88.

51. Genlis, *Les veillées du chateau*, 1:xv.

52. Genlis, *Les veillées du chateau*, 1:xiii.

53. Berquin, *L'ami de l'adolescence*, 13–15.

54. Berquin, *L'ami de l'adolescence*, 15.

55. *Correspondance de deux petites filles*, i–ii.

56. Mallès de Beaulieu, *Contes d'une mère à sa fille*, 1:xiii–xiv.

57. Bérenger, *La morale en action* (1823), 8. In Latin: "Adolescent juxtà viam suam, etiam cùm senuerit, nen recedetat eû."

58. See, for example, Bazot, *Historiettes et contes*; Bernard, *Contes et conseils à la jeunesse*; Mallès de Beaulieu, *Contes d'une mère à sa fille*; Coeurderoy, *Dialogues d'une mère avec sa fille*; Wandelaincourt, *L'ami des moeurs*.

59. Lyons, *Readers and Society*, 418–22. Bérenger's work was second only to Fleury's catechism as a preferred prize book for excellent students.

60. Williams, *Social Life of Books*, 27.

61. Bérenger, *La morale en action* (1804).

62. Bérenger, *La morale en action* (1823), 8.

63. Genlis, *Les veillées du chateau*, 1:ix.

64. Mallès de Beaulieu, *Contes d'une mère à sa fille*, 1:xiii.

65. Brown, *Critical History of French Children's Literature*; Marcoin, *Librairie de jeunesse et littérature*; Marcoin and Chelebourg, *La litterature de jeunesse*.

66. Glénisson and Le Men, *Le livre d'enfance*; Clark, review of *Le livre d'enfance*.

67. See, for example, Muller, *La morale en action par l'histoire*; Delessert and Gérando, *Les bons exemples*; Bérenger and Guibaud, *La morale en action* (1813); Bédollière, *La morale en action illustrée*.

68. Bérenger and Guibaud, *La morale en action* (1813), 177, 313, 335–36.

69. See, for example, in Bérenger and Guibaud, *La morale en action* (1813): Basil and Gregory of Nanzien (46–50), Athanasius (290–91), desert fathers (297), Louis IX (324), Irenaeus of Lyon (344), Roman martyrs (349–52).

70. Bérenger and Guibaud, *La morale en action* (1813), 17–18.

71. Bérenger and Guibaud, *La morale en action* (1813), 23.

72. Bérenger and Guibaud, *La morale en action* (1813), 280–82.

73. This fits with the discoveries of Gutermann-Jacquet, *Les équivoques du genre*.

74. Bérenger and Guibaud, *La morale en action* (1813), 300, 127, 183.

75. Bérenger, *La morale en action* (1804).

76. Bérenger and Guibaud, *La morale en action* (1813), 7, 57–59.

77. Allen, "Toward a Social History," 32.

78. Bérenger and Guibaud, *La morale en action* (1813), v. "Nous ne sommes pas au monde pour amasser des richesses, pour mener une vie de plaisir; nous n'y sommes pas aussi pour remplir notre esprit de sciences curieuses, pour faire des vers, pour tracer des lignes, etc. Notre principale vocation est de travailler à nous rendre dignes de l'héritage céleste par une vie vraiment chrétienne."

79. This is indicated by the many editions and translations, the books' presence in libraries, their popularity for lending, and their impact on cultural artifacts such as engravings, china, and home décor.

80. Alexandre de Saillet (1846), in Marcoin, *Librairie de jeunesse et littérature*, 12.

81. Pucci, "Snapshots of Family Intimacy," 94; Spaas, "*Paul et Virginie*," 316–17; Lyon-Caen, *La lecture et la vie*, 97.

82. Race and exoticism are problematized in recent critical literature about the novel, though these were not the concerns of contemporaries. While these issues are not the concern of this chapter, it is clear that *Paul et Virginie* is not opposed to slavery, only "cruelty" in the ownership of human persons.

83. Saint-Pierre, *Oeuvres complètes*, 123–25.

84. Saint-Pierre, *Oeuvres complètes*, 179.

85. Cohen, "Flaubert Lectrice," 750–56.

86. Denby, *Sentimental Narrative*, 179.

87. Emma Bovary proceeds to read *Paul et Virginie* after her first exposure to didactic literature.

88. Saint-Pierre, *Oeuvres complètes*, 75, "croyez-que l'homme même le plus dépravé par les préjugés du monde, aime à entendre parler du bonheur que donnent la nature et la vertu." Margrave, *Writing the Landscape*, argues that the emphasis on nature is not casual; here we see one use that follows her interpretation.

89. Wiedemeier, *La religion*; Cook, "Harmony and Discord"; Cook, "*Paul et Virginie*."

90. Garfitt, "What Happened to the Catholic Novel?," 222–23.

91. Cohen, "Flaubert Lectrice," 756. Cohen claims that substituting compromise for tragedy, limiting the force of idealism, is part of the intent and power of realist literature.
92. Cook, "Harmony and Discord," 207.
93. Hurlburt, "Educating Emma," 90.
94. Hurlburt, "Educating Emma," 83.
95. Chateaubriand and White, *Genius of Christianity*, 290.
96. Spaas, "*Paul et Virginie*," 324.
97. Schor, "Triste Amérique," 158.
98. Robinson, "Virginie's Fatal Modesty," 35. Robinson is not unsympathetic, but he also provides a list of hostile scholars, including Vivienne Mylne, Roseanne Rune, and Pierre Trahard.
99. Vallois, "Exotic Femininity."
100. Waller, "Being René, Buying Atala," 160.
101. Cook, "Harmony and Discord," 208.
102. Cook, "Paul et Virginie," 249.
103. Outram, "Le langage mâle."
104. Diaconoff, *Through the Reading Glass*, 51.
105. Diaconoff, *Through the Reading Glass*, 12.
106. Saint-Pierre, *Oeuvres complètes*, 157.
107. Saint-Pierre, *Oeuvres complètes*, 171.
108. Cohen, *Sentimental Education of the Novel*, 34.
109. Spininger, "Paradise Setting of Chateaubriand's *Atala*," 530.
110. Waller, "Being René, Buying Atala," 159. Emma Bovary contemplates naming her daughter "Atala."
111. Despland, "To Interpose a Little Ease," 27.
112. Hamelin and Gayot, *Une ancienne muscadine, Fortunée Hamelin*, 292.
113. Vallois, "Exotic Femininity."
114. Despland, "To Interpose a Little Ease," 28–29.
115. Flaubert, *Madame Bovary*, 153.
116. Irlam, "Gerrymandered Geographies," 902.
117. Schor, "Triste Amérique," 142.
118. Schor, "Triste Amérique," 146. *Jouissance* means enjoyment, but it really means orgasm or sexual pleasure to final culmination in this context.
119. Schor, "Triste Amérique," 145.
120. Vallois, "Exotic Femininity," 189–91.
121. Vallois, "Exotic Femininity," 182.
122. Schor, "Triste Amérique," 149.
123. Schor, "Triste Amérique," 149.

124. Waller, "Being René, Buying Atala," 164; Lyon-Caen, *La lecture et la vie*, 101–2.

125. Diaconoff, *Through the Reading Glass*, 202.

126. Lyon-Caen, *La lecture et la vie*, 104–5.

127. Waller, "Being René, Buying Atala," 159.

128. Hollier, "Incognito," 27.

129. Outram, "Le langage mâle," 129.

130. Diaconoff, *Through the Reading Glass*, 9.

131. Chateaubriand, *Atala and René*, 92. "Atala étoit aux pieds du religieux: 'Chef de la prière, lui disoit-elle, je suis chrétienne. C'est le ciel qui t'envoie pour me sauver.'"

132. Chateaubriand, *Atala and René*, 95. "[L]es feux de l'incendie allumé dans les forêts par la foudre brilloient encore dans le lointain; au pied de la montagne, un bois de pins tout entier étoit renversé dans la vase, et le fleuve rouloit pêle-mêle les argiles détrempées, les troncs des arbres, les corps des animaux et les poissons morts, dont on voyoit le ventre argenté flotter à la surface des eaux."

133. Wang, "Writing, Self, and the Other," 143.

134. Chateaubriand, *Atala and René*, 115–17. "Connoissez-vous le cœur de l'homme, et pourriez-vous compter les inconstances de son désir? . . . Eve avoit été créée pour Adam, et Adam pour Eve. S'ils n'ont pu toutefois se maintenir dans cet état de bonheur, quels couples le pourront après eux? . . . Mais l'âme de l'homme se fatigue, et jamais elle n'aime longtemps le même objet avec plénitude. Il y a toujours quelques points par où deux cœurs ne se touchent pas, et ces points suffisent à la longue pour rendre la vie insupportable."

135. Wang, "Writing, Self, and the Other," 142.

136. Chateaubriand, *Atala and René*, 115.

137. Wang, "Writing, Self, and the Other," 147. "[Q]ui a fait une vertu de l'espérance."

138. Despland, "To Interpose a Little Ease," 36.

139. Bouvier, "How Not to Speak of Incest," 228.

140. Landes, *Women and the Public Sphere*, 13; Popiel, *Rousseau's Daughters*.

141. Nodier, *Œuvres de Charles Nodier*, 405–6. "[L]es affections naturelles les sentiments tendres les pensées morales et pieuses . . . tant le besoin de satisfaire aux goûts d'un grand nombre . . . une action essentielle du principe moral qui régit toutes les sociétés c'est la marque du retour de l'opinion vers les idées saines et les principes conservateurs. Il faut savoir gré aux romanciers d'avoir donné un asile à la vérité quand la fausse politique et la fausse philosophie l'ont proscrite."

142. Cohen, *Sentimental Education of the Novel*, 71.

143. Cohen, *Sentimental Education of the Novel*, 36.

144. Hunt, *Inventing Human Rights*; chapter 1 deals with Rousseau's novel in great detail.

145. Cottin and Cohen, *Claire d'Albe*, 7.

146. For example, Cottin, *Claire d'Albe*, Letters I, V, XII, and XVIII,

147. Cottin, *Claire d'Albe*, Letter III.

148. Cottin, *Claire d'Albe*, Letters VII and XXXIV.

149. Cottin, *Claire d'Albe*, Letter XIII.

150. Cottin, *Claire d'Albe*, Letter XXXII.

151. Cottin, *Claire d'Albe*, Letters XXXIX–XLIII.

152. Cottin, *Claire d'Albe*, 187; Call, "Measuring Up," 199–200.

153. Genlis, *De l'influence des femmes*, 345–46.

154. Genlis, *De l'influence des femmes*, 345–46.

155. Genlis, *De l'influence des femmes*, 346. "[M]ais comme il a eu le triste honneur de former une nouvelle école de romanciers, qu'il est le premier où l'on ait représenté l'amour délirant, furieux et féroce, et une héroïne vertueuse, religieuse, angélique, et se livrant sans mesure et sans pudeur à tous les emportemens d'un amour effréné et criminel."

156. Cottin, *Claire d'Albe*, Letter III.

157. Cottin, *Claire d'Albe*, 196.

158. Cottin, *Claire d'Albe*, Letter II.

159. Cottin, *Claire d'Albe*, Letter XXI.

160. Cottin, *Claire d'Albe*, Letter XXVII.

161. *La Minerve francaise par Aignan*, 14. "Ainsi, quand le despotisme sanglant du prétoire opprimait l'univers, l'amour ardent, et l'ardent christianism qui, bien compris, est l'amour même, consolaient de leurs calamités es générations naissantes, et les fervens néophytes des deux sexes s'encouragaient ensemble à cueillir les palmes du martyre."

162. Cohen, *Sentimental Education of the Novel*, 70–71, 91.

163. Jones, "Madame de Staël and Scotland," 245, makes the conflict between law and art explicit. For the widespread influence of the novel, see Staël, *Corinne or Italy*; Moers, *Literary Women*, 173–210.

164. Fraisse, *Reason's Muse*, 103.

165. Coulet, "Révolution et roman," 658.

166. Works that are frustrated by the antifeminism of Staël include Peel, "Contradictions of Form and Feminism," 281–98; Marso, "Defying Fraternity," 645–74; Heller, "Tragedy, Sisterhood, and Revenge"; Moers, *Literary Women*.

167. Marso, "Defying Fraternity," 656.

168. Staël, *De l'Allemagne*, 478 "'Il n'est rien de plus insensé que de se mêler dans des circonstances tout à fait indépendantes de la volonté individuelle,' écrivait-elle en 1794 ou 1795; en 1799: 'il faut exister seul' et 'c'est un grand bien, je le crois, pour la majorité des hommes, que cette possibilité d'exister isolément des affaires publiques'; et en 1808 ou 1809: 'Les législateurs anciens faisaient un devoir aux citoyens de se mêler des intérêts politiques. La religion chrétienne doit inspirer une disposition d'une tout autre nature, celle d'obéir à l'autorité, mais de se tenir éloigné des affaires de l'État, quand elles peuvent compromettre la conscience.'"

169. Coulet, "Révolution et roman," 642.

170. Bérenger and Guibaud, *La morale en action* (1813), v. "Nous ne sommes pas au monde pour amasser des richesses, pour mener une vie de plaisir ; nous n'y sommes pas aussi pour remplir notre esprit de sciences curieuses, pour faire des vers, pour tracer des lignes, etc. Notre principale vocation est de travailler à nous rendre dignes de l'héritage céleste par une vie vraiment chrétienne."

171. Staël, *Corinne; ou, l'Italie*, book 15, chap. 1, 380.

172. Staël, *Corinne; ou, l'Italie*, book 4, chap. 1, 63.

173. Staël, *Corinne; ou, l'Italie*, book 14.

174. Staël, *Corinne; ou, l'Italie*, book 16.

175. Coulet, "Révolution et roman," 657. "Oswald, le seul homme capable de la comprendre, elle le reconnaît, est justement aussi celui qui détruit sa vocation, parce que, anglais, il est incapable de voir en une femme qui serait son épouse autre chose que la fidèle et discrète gardienne du foyer familial."

176. Heller, "Tragedy, Sisterhood, and Revenge," 214.

177. Staël, *Corinne; ou, l'Italie*, book 6, chap. 3.

178. Heller, "Tragedy, Sisterhood, and Revenge," 222.

179. Birkett, "Speech in Action," 399. "Je souffre, je jouis, je sens à ma manière, et ce serait moi seule qu'il faudrait observer, si l'on voulait influer sur mon bonheur" (1:265).

180. Marso, "Defying Fraternity," 645, book 14, chap 3.

181. Batsaki, "Exile as the Inaudible Accent," 36.

182. Staël, *Corinne; ou, l'Italie*, book 1, chap. 3.

183. Coulet, "Révolution et roman," 657.

184. Vallois and Wing, "Voice as Fossil," 52.

185. Staël, *Corinne; ou, l'Italie*, book 16, chap. 1.

186. Peel, "Contradictions of Form and Feminism," 289.

187. Staël, *Corinne; ou, l'Italie*, book 4, chap. 3. "[L]a pensée est détournée de la contemplation d'un cercueil par les chefs-d'œuvre du génie. Ils rappellent

l'immortalité sur l'autel même de la mort; et l'imagination, animée par l'admiration qu'ils inspirent, ne sent pas, comme dans le Nord, le silence et le froid, immuables gardiens des sépulcres."

188. Staël, *Corinne; ou, l'Italie*, book 10, chap. 4.

189. Staël, *Corinne; ou, l'Italie*, book 10, chap. 4. "Il lui semblait que c'était dans un tel moment d'exaltation qu'on aimerait à mourir, si la séparation de l'âme d'avec le corps ne s'accomplissait point par la douleur, si tout à coup un ange venait enlever sur ses ailes le sentiment et pensée, étincelles divines qui retourneraient vers leur source. La mor ne serait, pour ainsi dire, alors qu'un acte spontané du coeur, qu'un prière plus ardente et mieux exaucée."

190. Staël, *Corinne; ou, l'Italie*, book 14, chap. 1. "J'avais été dans les couvents d'Italie; ils me paraissaient pleins de vie à côté de ce cercle."

191. Marso, "Defying Fraternity," 649.

192. Staël, *Corinne; ou, l'Italie*, book 20, chap. 5. "Vous ne rejetez point, o mon Dieu le tribut des talens. L'hommage de la poésie est religieux, et les ailes de la pensée servent à se rapprocher de vous. Il n'y a rien détroit, rien d'asservi, rien de limité dans la religion. Elle est l'immense, l'infini, l'éternel; et loin que le génie puisse détourner d'elle, l'imagination dès son premier élan dépasse les bornes de la vie, et le sublime en tout genre est un reflet de la divinité. Ah! si je n'avais aimé qu'elle, si j'avais placé ma tête dans le ciel à l'abri des affections orageuses, je ne serais pas brisée avant le temps."

193. Staël, *Corinne; ou, l'Italie*, book 20.

194. Heller, "Tragedy, Sisterhood, and Revenge," 218.

195. Marso, "Defying Fraternity," 648.

196. Peel, "Contradictions of Form and Feminism," 286.

197. Staël, *Corinne; ou, l'Italie*, book 20, chap. 2. "Non je ne l'oublie pas . . . je ne me pardonnerai jamais."

198. Gray, *Madame de Staël*, 167.

199. Balayé, "Corinne et les amis"; Waller, *Male Malady*, 58; Caramaschi, "Le point de vue féministe."

200. Balayé, "Corinne et les amis."

3. SEEING THE PATH TO HEAVEN

1. Pirotte, "L'Imagerie de dévotion." While this chapter considers the particular impact of this rhetoric on girls, it was a genre that had implications for both boys and girls.

2. Image from 1848; Cammarano and Florian, *Santini e storia*, 48.

3. See, for example, Turgis's *Le Première Pensée* or Bouasse-Lebel's *Marie a prêché d'exemple* (1866).

4. Farwell, *Cult of Images*.
5. Pirotte, "L'Imagerie de dévotion," 234.
6. The following are some useful works on reception theory and the finding of meanings of texts that account for an array of cultural experiences. I have found them useful for thinking about the reception of visual images: Hall, *Cultural Studies 1983*; Jauss, *Toward an Aesthetic of Reception*; Eco, "Towards a Semiotic Inquiry," 103–21.
7. Schwartz and Przyblyski, *Nineteenth-Century Visual Culture Reader*; Mainardi, *Another World*. See, for example, Savart, "A la recherche de l'"art'"; Albaric, "Le commerce des objets religieux"; Waddy, *Images of Faith*.
8. Harrison, *Romantic Catholics*, makes a similar critique. Harrison's recent article on Alphonse Ratisbonne and the La Ferronnays family ("Conversion in the Age of Mechanical Reproduction") makes an excellent case for the difference between mass religious culture and a more elitist domestic religiosity.
9. Rosenbaum-Dondaine, *L'image de piété en France*, 4.
10. Racaut, *Hatred in Print*. "Mary continued to have an important role for believers. Given the constraints of this book, Marian devotion will not be a central concern, but it too offered feminine authority and emphasized suffering, sacrifice, and the central role of the heart."
11. Pirotte, "Images de dévotion," 11.
12. Rosenbaum-Dondaine, *L'image de piété en France*, 4.
13. Day, "Napoleonic Art," 3, confirms this point; Pettegree and Hall, "Reformation and the Book," 785–808, argues against the evangelical use of images in France and point to their continued relative high cost.
14. Duchartre and Saunier, *L'imagerie parisienne*; Taveneaux, *La piété en dentelles*.
15. Monaque, "L'illustration dans les abécédaires," 160.
16. Images by Desfeuilles (Nancy) and Deckherr (Montbeliard) were of similar size. See, for example, BnF Estampes FOL-LI-11.
17. Chateaubriand in Hopkin, *Soldier and Peasant*, 42.
18. The similarity in style and approach further demonstrates that religious and secular images should be cross-read rather than separated out by content.
19. "Prosternez-vous devant l'image de N-S Jésus Christ," BnF Estampes FOL-LI-11. In case the message was lost on the illiterate, this page also had a small image of a person making the sign of the cross and venerating a cross.
20. "Pécheurs ingrats, c'est pour vous que je souffre," BnF Estampes FOL-LI-11.
21. See, for example, BnF Estampes FOL-LI-11 for Deckherr and Desfeuilles, and FOL-LI-59 (1) and (2) for images d'Epinal.

22. Fuhring et al., *Kingdom of Images*, 206.
23. Devotional text on the back became extremely common after the middle of the nineteenth century, as printing technology made the process easier.
24. Pirotte, "L'Imagerie de dévotion," 233.
25. William O'Brian, S. J., notes that the devotion was only approved for the universal church in 1856 by Pius IX. Maryks, *Companion to Jesuit Mysticism*, 78:168n9.
26. There was also a depiction, increasingly popular through the nineteenth century, of Mary's Sacred Heart, which had different emblems than the Sacred Heart of Jesus and was not as clearly tied to counterrevolution.
27. Vircondelet, *Le monde merveilleux*, 63; Glotin, *La Bible du Cœur de Jésus*, 139, notes that in the nineteenth century the Sacred Heart went from being associated with will ("volonté") to emotion ("affectivité").
28. B. G. Smith, *Ladies of the Leisure Class*, 170; Jaricot also read this common work.
29. Magnien, *Canivets de la collection Gabriel Magnien*, 13.
30. Pirotte, "Images de dévotion," 5.
31. Abbaye de Landévennec and Parc naturel régional d'Armorique, *Dévotes dentelles*, 105.
32. Pellegrin, "Les vertus de 'l'ouvrage,'" 755.
33. In this sense, the object that produces the image gives it a name, in the same way that artworks like a painting or a lithograph take their name from that which produces the image. The most literal translation, then, would be "a penknifing."
34. Doussin, *Petite histoire des images pieuses*, notes that German canivets were more likely to be ornamental or based on patterns.
35. Magnien, *Canivets de la collection Gabriel Magnien*, 14.
36. Abbaye de Landévennec and Parc naturel régional d'Armorique, *Dévotes dentelles*, 35–36.
37. Magnien, *Canivets de la collection Gabriel Magnien*, 10.
38. Abbaye de Landévennec and Parc naturel régional d'Armorique, *Dévotes dentelles*, 20.
39. Mandrou, *De la culture populaire*; Greer and Bilinkoff, *Colonial Saints*.
40. For example, St. Denis—who was beheaded—sometimes is depicted as carrying his head under his arm. The story of St. Lucy's martyrdom includes the plucking out of her eyes. Lucy can be distinguished from other female Roman martyrs—who also wear tunics and carry a palm symbolizing martyrdom—by the fact that she carries a set of eyes on a plate. Due to her association with eyes, she is invoked as a patroness for those who suffer from blindness or vision problems.

41. Bollème, "L'enjeu du corps."

42. Bollème, "Religion du texte," 67–68. "La force du texte hagiographique . . . consiste justement en cette manière qu'il a d'être comme déporte hors du texte vers le récit, d'être en quelque sorte entraine par lui, et cela parce que la vie de Saint a un caractère tout particulier . . . exemple vivant, le Saint est médiateur aide à l'imitation du Christ, il est 'un homme de chair comme nous', l'histoire de sa vie est comme une image regardée."

43. "Prenez les Saints pour modèles," holy card by Ch. Letaille, 1840.

44. Hopkin, *Soldier and Peasant*, 42.

45. Bollème, "Religion du texte," 68.

46. Schmitt, *Les saints et les stars*, 66.

47. Pirotte, "Images de dévotion du XV siècle," 11.

48. Lerch, "Le sentiment religieux," 11.

49. Arnold, *Le corps et l'âme*; Langlois, *Le Catholicisme au féminin*.

50. Albaric, "Le commerce des objets religieux," 132.

51. Magnien, *Canivets de la collection Gabriel Magnien*, 10.

52. Savart, "A la recherche de l'''art,'" 268; Taveneaux, *La piété en dentelles*, 14; Abbaye de Landévennec and Parc naturel régional d'Armorique, *Dévotes dentelles*, 7.

53. Pirotte, "L'imagerie de dévotion," 234.

54. Despite the diversity of possible images, the majority of used nineteenth-century cards that are in collections today are thus marked in some way. See, for example, the scrapbooks in the BNF such as Estampes LZ 289 or the collections held by Jean-Pierre Doussin.

55. Bann, *Distinguished Images*, 13.

56. Letter found in Mainardi, *Another World*, 24–25. I am relying on Mainardi's translation.

57. Certainly, given the reuse of images, Gériculat was not exactly incorrect to say that there was no dramatic need for new religious images, but that did not seem to have a substantial impact on the consumer market, especially as the Sulpician style rose to popularity.

58. Day, "Napoleonic Art." This change is evident in collections such as the BNF Estampes FOL-Li-59.

59. Hopkin, *Soldier and Peasant*, 52.

60. *L'Artiste* (1834) in Mainardi, *Another World*, 69.

61. Dominique Lerch, "Diffusion en Belgique des lithographies et imageries de la France de l'Est. Quelques réflexions," in Pirotte, "Images de dévotion du XV siècle," 94.

62. Girard and Quétel, *L'histoire de France*.

63. Chardin, *Le Jeu de l'oye*, 1745.

64. Bellhouse, "Visual Myths of Female Identity," 127.

65. M. Samuels, "Illustrated Historiography," 266.

66. See, for example, *Fables de LaFontaine* (ca. 1780), BnF Estampes M306694, and *Jeu des Ages* (c. 1810), BnF Estampes M306719.

67. *Jeu de La Révolution Française* (ca. 1790), BnF Estampes M306703.

68. *Jeu du Troisième République* (after 1871), BnF Estampes M306726.

69. *Jeu instructif des fleurs* (ca. 1825), BnF Estampes M306742.

70. Bataillard in Girard and Quétel, *L'histoire de France*, 24.

71. *Chemin de la Croix* (Turgis, 1836), BnF Estampes M306753; *Recréation spirituelle* (1839, 1830), BnF Estampes M306761 and 6746; *Jeu du Nouveau Testament* (1820), BnF Estampes M306740; *Jeu familier de la civilité* (ca. 1825), BnF Estampes M306739; *Jeu moral et instructif* (ca. 1880), BnF Estampes M306825; *Nouveau jeu de l'Himen* (ca. 1750), BnF Estampes M306678; and *Jeu de l'Amour & de l'Hyménée* (1863), BnF Estampes M306808.

72. *Le Divertissement studieux des Religieuses Ursulines* (ca. 1789), BnF Estampes M306677.

73. *Chemin de la Croix ou Récreation spirituelle* (1830), BnF Estampes M306753.

74. *Jeu agréable et récréatif des amours* (ca. 1809), BnF Estampes M306700.

75. *Jeu des Ages.*

76. *Jeu familier de la civilité* (ca. 1825), BnF Estampes M306739.

77. *Jeu de la fortune* (1818), BnF Estampes M306733.

78. *Petite loterie des qualités et défauts* (ca. 1869), BnF Estampes M306892.

79. *Petite loterie des qualités et défauts.*

80. *Petite loterie* (ca. 1850), BnF Estampes M306868.

81. *Loterie des demoiselles* (ca. 1865), BnF Estampes M306866.

82. Walker, *Mother's Love*, 35.

83. For example, Bouasse-Lebel, *Calendrier Catholique* (1865).

84. Rosenbaum-Dondaine, *L'image de piété en France*, 7.

85. Albaric, "Le commerce des objets religieux," 132–33. This division into a seller of religious images (as opposed to a seller of images of any kind) certainly implies that marketing religious objects on their own was valuable. Rather than seeing it as proof of the separation of religious ideas from a time of universal impact, it is a sign of the ways in which religious consumerism was flourishing.

86. Lerch, Dominique, "En quoi l'imagerie populaire," 324.

87. Sellers of religious objects also published catalogs of their work, which showed the influence of both religious and secular topics. Turgis, *Catalogue des estampes et lithographies* (1844); Turgis, *Catalogue des estampes et lithog-*

raphies (1851). BNF Estampes Yd31 also contains catalogs of Bouasse Lebel and Bouasse Jeune.

88. Hopkin, *Soldier and Peasant*, 45.

89. Rosenbaum-Dondaine, *L'image de piété en France*, 21.

90. *Nouvel alphabet de la vie des saints*, 12; *Alphabet d'histoire naturelle*, 12.

91. As the catechisms in chapter 1 demonstrate, books continued to be read and used well after their initial publication date.

92. Taveneaux, *La piété en dentelles*, 18.

93. Pirotte, "Images de dévotion du XV siècle," 71.

94. Simon, *Le Cardinal Sterckx et son temps*, 419.

95. Pirotte, "Images de dévotion du XV siècle," 71.

96. One can see a clear similarity to holy cards in "bons points," which were also offered by the same publishers that produced holy cards. See, for example, BNF Estampes SNR-3 Bouasse (Lebel) 7/219 and SNR-3 Bouasse (Lebel) 1/214.

97. Monaque, "L'illustration dans les abécédaires," 162.

98. Bollème, "Religion du texte," 67.

99. Douyère, "L'image de piéte chrétienne," 41.

100. Ford, *Divided Houses*, 94–115.

101. Boutry, "Les saints des catacombes," 885.

102. Pellerin produced an image of Philomena as early as 1826, which can be found in BNF Estampes, *Images d'Epinal*, Li 59, vol. 1. However, the greatest detail about Philomena's life came from the 1833 visions of Mother Maria Luisa di Geus, foundress of the Oblates of Our Lady of Sorrows.

103. For more on Jaricot, see chapter 5.

104. *Bibliographie de la France ou Journal général*, 587.

105. Ford, *Divided Houses*, 107.

106. Ford, *Divided Houses*, 106.

107. Boutry, "Les saints des catacombes"; Ford, *Divided Houses*.

108. Basset, Turgis, and Pellerin were all producers of games, too.

109. Turgis, *Catalogue des estampes et lithographies* (1844), 1–2.

110. Yver, *Marie-Pauline de Jésus Christ*, chap. 9.

111. Barrelle, *La thaumaturge du XIXe siècle*, 38.

112. *Notice sur Sainte Philomène*, 14. "[S]i on a un peu de foi, comme le grain de sénevé, peu lui obtenir les plus grandes grâces. Demandez, et vous recevrez; cherchez auprès de Ste. Philomène, et vous trouverez; frappez par elle à la porte du Père de famille, et l'on vous ouvrira."

113. *Notice sur Sainte Philomène*, 11.

114. *St. Philomena* (Pellerin, 1836).

115. Greer, "Colonial Saints," 328–29.

116. See, for example, Letaille (1852), Bouasse-Lebel (1849, 1850, 1886).

117. *Notice sur Sainte Philomène*, 6–7. "Que Dieu, en répandant sur la terre, par les mains de Ste. Philomène, une si grande abundance de faveurs extraordinaires, veut glorifier son saint nom au milieu d'une nation dépravée et pervertie, et à consoler en même tempts son Eglise, aujourd'hui en proie à tant de desolations. Lui demander par consequent des graces, au nom de cette Sainte, c'est entrer dans ses vues, et lui donner occasion de manifester, pour la confusion des impies, la puissance de son bras et la perpétuité de son amour envers son épouse unique et bien aimée, la Ste Eglise de J. C."

118. Like the images of the Rue Saint-Jacques, Sulpician art is also named after the district of Paris in which it was produced, where commerce centered on merchants in the Rue Saint-Sulpice.

119. Albaric, "Le commerce des objets religieux," 134; Taveneaux, *La piété en dentelles*, 18.

120. Taveneaux, *La piété en dentelles*, 18.

121. Leonar Norman Primiano, "Kitsch," in Lyden and Mazur, *Routledge Companion to Religion*, 292–93; Fallon, *Messiaen Perspectives 1*, 274; Schloesser, *Jazz Age Catholicism*, 196; T. Smith, *Impossible Presence*, 189; Marion, *Crossing of the Visible*, 64.

122. One suspects that these were not the same clerics known for handing out holy cards on the street!

123. Taveneaux, *La piété en dentelles*, 18.

124. Art, "Cult of the Virgin Mary," 75, quotes a letter from the head of the Belgian Redemptorists to the papal nuncio in 1869 that says, "[T]rue and solid piety is being harmed by all the new romantically named devotions springing up on Belgian and French soil, and which instead of the serious and profound devotion of our ancestors, are elevating a certain vague, hazy, sentimental, effeminate religiosity." See also Schloesser, *Jazz Age Catholicism*, 196; Lyden and Mazur, *Routledge Companion to Religion*, 292.

125. Léon Gautier in Art, "Cult of the Virgin Mary," 76.

126. Michelet, *Du prêtre* (Comptoir, 1845), 71–72.

127. Savart, "A la recherche de l'art,'" 271.

128. "Quant au calice saint mon cœur se désaltère" (Bouasse Lebel, 1854).

129. "Là, recueille et solitaire, dans le sein de Jésus, je me perds!" (Letaille, 1842).

130. Turgis, mid-nineteenth century: "La vision bienheureuse. O Cœur de Jésus, vous êtes le paradis de délices de l'âme exilée sur la terre." Turgis, second half of the century: "Le refuge de la colombe"; and "Je veux te cacher dans mon Cœur, âme fidèle, ma bien-aimée."

131. Vircondelet, *Le monde merveilleux*, 65–67.

132. Glotin, *La Bible du Cœur de Jésus*, 136.

133. Glotin, *La Bible du Cœur de Jésus*, 136.

134. Jonas, *France and the Cult*, 57.

135. Vircondelet, *Le monde merveilleux*, 66. "Arrêtez! The Cœur de Jésus est là!" (beginning of the eighteenth century).

136. Jonas, *France and the Cul*, 80.

137. Hufton, "Reconstruction of a Church," 30.

138. Hufton, "Reconstruction of a Church," 32.

139. This was also true in early nineteenth-century intellectual shifts; for example, Chateaubriand's writing. Despland, "To Interpose a Little Ease," 22.

140. Jonas, *France and the Cult*, 133.

141. Pellerin, Galerie religieuse Sacré de Jesus, 1836. "O Dieu, qui avez renfermé tous les trésors de votre sagesse de votre science dans les très-saint Cœur de votre Fils bien-aimé, afin que par lui nous ayons la vie, et que nous l'ayons plus abondamment, exaucez les vœux de votre people, et, ouvrant cette celeste source de tous dons, rendez-nous dignes de recevoir de sa plenitude une grâce surabondante. Ainsi soit-il."

142. Stendhal, *Red and the Black*, 315.

143. Michelet, *Du prêtre* (Comptoir, 1845), 172–74.

144. Michelet, *Du prêtre* (Comptoir, 1845), 175–77.

145. *Records of the American Catholic Historical Society of Philadelphia*, 13:478. Bishop Gartland intended not only to give away the images but also to provide some of them to other establishments across the East Coast to sell in their institutions.

146. Madame Bouasse (1845); Cammarano and Florian, *Santini e storia*, 24.

147. Alacoque, *Vie et oeuvres*, 368–69.

148. Madame Bouasse (1846).

149. Madame Bouasse (1849); the image of the stormy sea breaking against a ship found in the bottom half of this image was also the image on early Bouasse-Lebel business cards.

150. Cammarano and Florian, *Santini e storia*, 48, 46.

151. Cammaranno and Florian, *Santini e storia*, 50.

152. "Chaque matin, en élevant mon cœur vers mon créateur je lui dirai 'Mon Dieu, protégez ma mère, qu'elle partage les indulgences attachées à ma prière.'"

153. Bouasse-Lebel 1036, "L'amour de Jésus, pour nous égale sa puissance."

154. Bouasse-Lebel 3020, mid-nineteenth century. "Pauvre Ame Glacée pour la froide halein du monde. Viens et réchauffer près du cœur de Jésus."

155. Bouasse-Lebel 3005, mid-nineteenth century.

156. Valantasis, *Making of the Self*, 8.

157. Preface to Michelet, *Du prêtre* (Comptoir, 1845).

158. Letaille, plate 274 (ca. 1845).

159. *La Phare de la Loire*, April 29, 1866, AN Pierrefitte F/19/5434.

4. PREFERRING JESUS CHRIST

1. Duchesne and Paisant, *Philippine Duchesne et ses compagnes*.

2. Introduction, Careel and Osiek, *Philippine Duchesne*, 21.

3. Paisant, *Litanie pour une nonne défunte*, 150–51. Aloysia, her niece and fellow RSCJ, wrote about Philippine's trip and its danger as a sacrifice that Philippine made joyfully, because it had been a long-standing desire.

4. Callan, *Philippine Duchesne, Frontier Missionary*, 23. Even if Duchesne's memory of this is faulty or shaped by later constructs, her letters and activity from the Revolution forward indicate a clear sense that missionary work was both heroic and an ideal to strive for.

5. See, for example, Curtis, *Civilizing Habits*; and Davidson, *France after Revolution*. Verjus and Davidson, *Le roman conjugal*, also investigates the family life and strategies of this family and social class and indicates how important marriage was.

6. Introduction, Careel and Osiek, *Philippine Duchesne*, 9. As Careel and Osiak explain, reading the correspondence of Philippine Duchesne allows the reader "to discover her invincible desire to be sent to the frontier and to make known there the love of the Heart of Jesus." They also explain that her call to be a missionary was "comparable to the intrigue of a novel" (18).

7. C. H. Johnson, *Becoming Bourgeois*; Verjus and Davidson, *Le roman conjugal*; Hennequin-Lecomte, *Le patriciat strasbourgeois*.

8. Lejeune, *Le moi des demoiselles*.

9. Lejeune, *Le moi des demoiselles*, 16, claims that the genre's success was delayed by Revolutionary upheaval. Duchesne's journal, kept after the "age of St. Catherine," does not contest Lejeune's argument about adolescent journals. However, the fact that Duchesne kept a journal for practical administrative reasons as well as personal ones reminds us of the importance of journalistic writing.

10. RSCJ, Duchesne, "Histoire de Sainte-Marie," para. 73.

11. Langlois, *Le Catholicisme au féminin*, 264. Langlois might not classify Duchesne as a foundress—that title would go to Sophie Barat—but Americans certainly did, and the Religious of the Sacred Heart often mark her as one of their most prominent members and a foundress of the global mission.

12. Choudhury, *Convents and Nuns*, chap. 4.

13. Ford, *Divided Houses*, 81.
14. F. E. Dolan, "Why Are Nuns Funny?," 526–29; Ford, *Divided Houses*, 80–82.
15. Gouges, *Le Couvent, ou Les Voeux forcés*, 83.
16. Arnold, *Le corps et l'âme*; Langlois, "Les effectifs des congrégations féminines."
17. Stendhal, *Red and the Black*, 315.
18. Stendhal, *Red and the Black*, 37.
19. Michelet, *Du prêtre* (Comptoir, 1845), xxv, 239.
20. The eighteenth-century versions of each of these constructs are demonstrated to great effect in chapters 3 and 4 of Choudhury, *Convents and Nuns*.
21. F. E. Dolan, "Why Are Nuns Funny?," 529n62.
22. Arnold, *Le corps et l'âme*; Langlois, *Le Catholicisme au féminin*.
23. Michelet, *Du prêtre* (Comptoir, 1845), 8; L.-A. Martin, *Education des mères*.
24. *Grain of Wheat*, 9.
25. Introduction, Careel and Osiek, *Philippine Duchesne*, 43n3.
26. In fact, Uncle Claude was particularly well known, as he was a wealthy industrialist and tax-farmer who had offered his chateau at Vizille for a pre-Revolutionary meeting of the Estates General of Dauphiny, the first to accord the right of voting by head and not by order.
27. Callan, *Philippine Duchesne, Frontier Missionary*, 71. (The other was Lazare Carnot.)
28. B. G. Smith, *Ladies of the Leisure Class*, 7–9.
29. Francis de Sales remained an important figure for Duchesne. She celebrated his feast day and sought consolation in his vision of the world.
30. *Grain of Wheat*, 9.
31. RSCJ, Duchesne, "Histoire de Sainte-Marie."
32. Madame de Coriolis, *Histoire de la Société du Sacré Coeur*, in Callan, *Philippine Duchesne, Frontier Missionary*, 24.
33. During the Restoration, Duchesne's niece, Euphrosine, relied on her family to purchase books they needed, commenting on the fact that her father was a known bibliophile; the girls were well educated, and the family engaged with reading and literature. Paisant, *Litanie pour une nonne défunte*, 163.
34. Introduction, Careel and Osiek, *Philippine Duchesne*, 44; Callan, *Philippine Duchesne, Frontier Missionary*, 29.
35. Callan, *Philippine Duchesne, Frontier Missionary*, 29.
36. Mooney, *Philippine Duchesne*, 43.
37. Introduction, Careel and Osiek, *Philippine Duchesne*, 45.
38. Some of the texts that she read and reread in the convent were likely Le Gobien, *Lettres édifiantes et curieuses*; and Charlevoix, *Vie de la mère*.

39. Introduction, Careel and Osiek, *Philippine Duchesne*, 25.

40. Mooney, *Philippine Duchesne*, 45.

41. Lejeune, *Le moi des demoiselles*, explains the force behind autobiographical writing, especially after 1830.

42. RSCJ, Duchesne, "Histoire de Sainte-Marie," para. 2. Though the events that Duchesne described often took place in the Revolutionary era, she recollected them as she began her mission in North America in 1818–19.

43. RSCJ, Duchesne, Histoire de Sainte-Marie, paras. 1–4.

44. RSCJ, Duchesne, Histoire de Sainte-Marie, para. 3.

45. Introduction, Careel and Osiek, *Philippine Duchesne*, 45, explains that she and Josephine both worked with the Dames de la Miséricorde to visit the imprisoned.

46. Baunard, *Histoire de Mme Duchesne*, 40.

47. Leflaive, *Philippine Duchesne*, 27–28.

48. RSCJ, Mauduit, Letter 2 (end 1797–beginning 1798).

49. RSCJ, Duchesne, "Histoire de Sainte-Marie," para. 4.

50. RSCJ, Mauduit, Letter 2 (end 1797–beginning 1798).

51. RSCJ, Mauduit, Letter 2 (end 1797–beginning 1798).

52. RSCJ, Mauduit, Letter 2 (end 1797–beginning 1798).

53. RSCJ, Mauduit, Letter 2 (end 1797–beginning 1798).

54. RSCJ, Mauduit, Letter 2 (end 1797–beginning 1798).

55. Vincent-Buffault, *History of Tears*, 23.

56. RSCJ, Mauduit, Letter 2 (end 1797–beginning 1798).

57. Saint-Just in Reddy, *Navigation of Feeling*, 177.

58. Leflaive, *Philippine Duchesne*, 23.

59. RSCJ, Duchesne, "Histoire de Sainte-Marie," para. 6.

60. Leflaive, *Philippine Duchesne*, 31–32.

61. RSCJ, Duchesne, "Histoire de Sainte-Marie," para. 7. "Leur empressement à me saluer dans la rue m'est un supplice. J'ai l'ai de connaitre tous les porteurs de fumier. Ils me montrent à leurs parents qui m'en veulent parce que je leur défends de travailler le dimanche. Si l'amour de saint François Régis ne me soutenait, j'aurais plusieurs fois quitté mon apostolat. J'ai pourtant quelques consolations: ces enfants, qui ignoraient le nom de toutes personnes divines, apprennent le catéchisme, leurs prières et des cantiques. Ils se confessent tous et plusieurs d'entre eux feront leur première communion."

62. RSCJ, Duchesne, "Histoire de Sainte-Marie," paras. 6–9. Duchesne recounts the vow she made to Régis; one of its important components was instructing poor children in religious precepts.

63. Duchesne clearly recognized the trope of the forced victim of the cloister; RSCJ Duchesne, "Histoire de Sainte-Marie," para. 21.

64. RSCJ, Duchesne, "Histoire de Sainte-Marie," para. 19; "Journal de Grenoble," 13 Décembre 1804.

65. RSCJ, Duchesne, "Histoire de Sainte-Marie," para. 19.

66. RSCJ, Duchesne, "Histoire de Sainte-Marie," para. 26.

67. RSCJ, Duchesne, "Histoire de Sainte-Marie," para. 45. Chapter 5 considers Pauline Jaricot's work for the Society for the Propagation of the Faith in more detail. As the image in chapter 3 also demonstrates, this name had a strong connotation of missionary work and martyrdom.

68. Code, *Great American Foundresses*, 210–11. The Jesuits had not yet been universally reestablished, but Varin was closely associated with men who were Jesuits or deeply indebted to Jesuit formation.

69. Verhoeven, "'Perfect Jesuit in Petticoats.'"

70. Cahier, *Vie de la venerable Mere Barat*, 88.

71. RSCJ, Duchesne, "Histoire de Sainte-Marie," para. 50.

72. Callan, *Philippine Duchesne, Frontier Missionary*, 122.

73. RSCJ, 20 February 1805, Duchesne, "Journal de Grenoble." "On n'avait encore pu se taire sur cette maison. . . . On eut l'indignité de les nommer des filles pénitentes, de rendre leur foi suspecte; on vit du mystère dans une conduite toute cachée en Dieu avec Jésus-Christ; on en conclut qu'elle était blâmable. . . . Enfin on nia leurs talents, on rit de leur jeunesse et surtout de celle de notre Mère, comme si les dons de Dieu ne se répandaient qu'à un âge et que son esprit dépendit de notre humanité." The implication that these women must be social undesirables would have been an even more logical comparison in a time when social undesirables including the poor and prostitutes were locked away.

74. RSCJ, May 1805, Duchesne, "Journal de Grenoble."

75. RSCJ, Letter 2, November 1804, "Jouve France."

76. RSCJ, Letter 2, November 1804, "Jouve France."

77. Paisant, *Litanie pour une nonne défunte*, 45.

78. RSCJ, Letter 26, 22 May 1811, "Jouve France."

79. Paisant, *Litanie pour une nonne défunte*, 51, 169. Euphrosine's father, Jean-Joseph Jouve, was known as a lover of books and had acquired quite a library; this was not out of character for the family, given P.-F. Duchesne's founding of the public library and the family's interest in literature and philosophy.

80. Paisant, *Litanie pour une nonne défunte*, 58.

81. RSCJ, Letter 29, 24 Novembre 1813, "Jouve France." "Je me doutais depuis longtemps des goûts secrets de ta fille aînée, quoiqu'elle me les eût toujours cachés. Et ce fut l'objet d'une réflexion que je te fis dans le temps de sa grande maladie, dont je te fis part et qui, [d'après] ce qu'on m'a dit, te fit beaucoup de peine. Cependant ce que je ne faisais qu'entrevoir est réel aujourd'hui. Euphrosine voudrait te quitter, non pour un époux mortel, non pour un établissement humain, mais pour se donner à Dieu à qui elle se doit avant tout. Il y a peu de temps qu'elle m'a fait connaître son attrait. . . . Je me charge de le faire la première, sachant que je parle à une mère tendre, mais encore plus chrétienne et accoutumée aux actes de la résignation la plus héroïque."
82. Both Amélie and Constance also eventually joined religious orders.
83. RSCJ, Letter 33, 1814. "Jouve France."
84. RSCJ, Letter 30, 2 Janvier 1814, "Jouve France."
85. RSCJ, Letter 27, 1813, "Jouve France."
86. RSCJ, Letter 33, 2 Janvier 1814, "Jouve France." "Tu peux être sûre néanmoins que ce coup part de Dieu seul. Euphrosine n'a pas une trempe d'âme à se laisser prévenir; elle le juge par elle-même. Dieu lui-même a fait sa vocation, elle l'a tenue secrète. Et si je l'ai pressenti, c'est l'effet de mes observations sur la nature de son caractère, par quelques goûts que j'apercevais en elle qui, si elle ne mettait pas obstacle aux desseins de la grâce, devaient la conduire à l'état de retraite, d'indépendance d'un mari, et de missions autour des âmes. Trouves-tu qu'elle fasse un mauvais choix de préférer Jésus-Christ à un homme? La fortune du Ciel à celle de la terre? Les occupations qui nous en rapprochent, de celles qui fixent à la terre? Il n'y a rien d'humain, rien de bas dans les vues d'Euphrosine. Il n'y a eu aucune impulsion étrangère; ses désirs sont venus de Dieu qui fait sentir qu'il gouverne les cœurs comme il veut."
87. RSCJ, Letter 33, 2 Janvier 1814, "Jouve France."
88. RSCJ, Letter 33, 2 Janvier 1814, "Jouve France." "S'il offrait à une tendre mère le prince le plus aimable pour l'époux de sa fille, mais qui devrait l'éloigner d'elle, oubliant la peine de sa séparation, elle ne songerait qu'à l'illustre alliance et en parlerait avec joie. Pourquoi Jésus-Christ est-il le seul à qui il soit affreux de se donner; où est donc notre foi? Où est donc le fruit de notre expérience?"
89. Paisant, *Litanie pour une nonne défunte*, 69–70.
90. RSCJ, Letter 36, 25 Novembre 1814, "Jouve France."
91. RSCJ, Letter 36, 25 Novembre 1814, "Jouve France." "Elle avait une grande force; il en faut pour quitter de bons Parents. Elle n'aimait point tout ce qui a rapport au mariage. Elle a dit plusieurs fois: 'La vertu dont j'aime le plus

à entendre parler, c'est la virginité.' Elle aspirait, dans les moments où elle se livrait à instruire les pauvres, à souffrir le martyre . . . Si tu ne lui as pas entendu parler sur ce ton, il ne faut pas t'en étonner; quand on porte dans le cœur des vues qui vont à se séparer d'une famille, cela n'est pas aisé à dire: le cœur en souffre et sait qu'il fera souffrir."

92. Paisant, *Litanie pour une nonne défunte*, 73.

93. Paisant, *Litanie pour une nonne défunte*, 90.

94. Paisant, *Litanie pour une nonne défunte*, 82.

95. RSCJ Letter 37, Decembre 1814; Paisant, *Litanie pour une nonne défunte*, 90.

96. Paisant, *Litanie pour une nonne défunte*, 111.

97. Paisant, *Litanie pour une nonne défunte*, 109.

98. Paisant, *Litanie pour une nonne défunte*, 133.

99. Paisant, *Litanie pour une nonne défunte*, 105.

100. Paisant, *Litanie pour une nonne défunte*, 186.

101. Paisant, *Litanie pour une nonne défunte*, 186.

102. Curtis, *Civilizing Habits*, 2010, 6–7.

103. Langlois, *Le Catholicisme au féminin*, 264–66, 272.

104. Reddy, *Navigation of Feeling*, 260.

105. Michelet, *Priests, Women, and Families* (1846), xxvii.

106. Michelet, *Du prêtre* (Comptoir, 1845), 66.

107. Michelet, *Du prêtre* (Comptoir, 1845), 61.

108. Michelet, *Du prêtre* (Comptoir, 1845), 256. "On ne s'empare de celles-ci que par la volonté même . . . spéciale, personnelle, qui s'attache avec persévérance à une personne et la domine vraiment, parce qu'elle la fait à son image. Régner, c'est régner sur une âme. . . . Le but ainsi posé, le prêtre a un grand avantage, que personne n'a comme lui. Il a affaire à un sujet qui se livre lui-même."

5. CHANGING THE WORLD

1. Jaricot is virtually unknown today, despite her ground-breaking importance in the nineteenth century.

2. Mgr. Giuseppe Andreozzi, "Presentation," in Giacovelli, *Pauline Jaricot*.

3. For Jaricot, the situation is further exacerbated by the fact that she had most of her correspondence burned before her death.

4. Unlike Duchesne's reflections, which came from an adult past the age of majority, the bulk of Jaricot's written legacy exists from her late adolescence. Though these are not journals per se, their emphasis on the believer's authority complicates the idea that autobiographical adolescent writing was

primarily a product of the second half of the century. Lejeune, *Le moi des demoiselles*, 16–26.

5. Giacovelli, *Pauline Jaricot*, 33; K. Burton, *Difficult Star*, 11–12; Lathoud, *La secret des origines*, 40–41.

6. Naïdenoff, *Pauline Jaricot*, 12; Giacovelli, *Pauline Jaricot*, 29–30.

7. Cahier 1, Jaricot, HMV.

8. Cahier 1, Jaricot, HMV; Maurin, *Vie nouvelle de Pauline-Marie Jaricot*, 154–56; Yver, *Marie-Pauline de Jésus Christ*, 36–38.

9. Cahier 1, Jaricot, HMV; Lathoud, *La secret des origines*, 52.

10. Cahier 2, Jaricot, HMV; Cristiani, *Marie-Pauline Jaricot*, 11.

11. Giacovelli, *Pauline Jaricot*, 66. Purple was her least favorite color.

12. Giacovelli, *Pauline Jaricot*, 66.

13. Lathoud, *La secret des origines*, 91. Most of these women were poor; a sou, similar to a nickel, was not a great amount to many people but was still a sacrifice to each of them.

14. Dollen, *Charity without Frontiers*, 16–17.

15. Giacovelli, *Pauline Jaricot*, 67; Dollen, *Charity without Frontiers*, 22.

16. Giacovelli, *Pauline Jaricot*, 92.

17. Lathoud, *La secret des origines*, 163.

18. Giacovelli, *Pauline Jaricot*, 83.

19. Lathoud, *La secret des origines*, 134–35.

20. *Article extrait de la Gazette Universelle de Lyon*.

21. Giacovelli, *Pauline Jaricot*, 92.

22. The fact that the division chiefs were well-known laymen was significant in the context of clerical politics and changes to modern church organization. Though the organization turned to men, they were laymen, professionals outside the clerical hierarchy. In this way they also broadened the base of Church activity in the world.

23. Lathoud, *La secret des origines*, 151–52.

24. Naïdenoff, *Pauline Jaricot*, 36.

25. K. Burton, *Difficult Star*, 78.

26. Naïdenoff, *Pauline Jaricot*, 36.

27. Jaricot, *L'amour infini* (1822). Here, Jaricot linked the Sacred Heart directly with the Eucharist, claiming that Jesus's body was best understood as his heart.

28. Épitre à Pie VII, pour servir d'introduction à un petit Ouvrage, in Jaricot, *L'amour infini* (1823), 8, 19. It is also relevant that her spiritual director's introduction served to "authorize" Jaricot's writing, making it clear that she had not overstepped her bounds by publishing a theological tract as a young woman.

29. Jaricot, *L'amour infini* (1823), 5.

30. Jaricot, *L'amour infini* (1823), 1.

31. Jaricot, *L'amour infini* (1823), 96.

32. Jaricot, *L'amour infini* (1823), 55.

33. Reddy, *Navigation of Feeling*, 166.

34. Reddy, *Navigation of Feeling*, 180.

35. Jaricot, *L'amour infini* (1823), 72. "Jésus-Christ est entré dans le vestibule extérieur des sens, où réside l'homme charnel; de là, sa voix touchante a pénétré dans l'appartement intérieur de l'âme, où réside l'homme spirituel: mais lui-même en a trouvé les portes fermées; parce que l'entraînement des pécheurs ne provenoit que du mouvement imprimé dans leurs sens, et non de la véritable componction de leur cœur. En deux mots, ce n'est pas le cœur qui a triomphé des sens, ce sont les sens qui ont subjugué le cœur."

36. Jaricot, *L'amour infini* (1823), 83.

37. Jaricot, *L'amour infini* (1823), 5.

38. Jaricot, *L'amour infini* (1823), 21, 26.

39. Glotin, *La Bible du Cœur de Jésus*, 139.

40. Jaricot, *L'amour infini* (1823), 60–62. See also 1 Corinthians 1:17–25.

41. Jaricot, *L'amour infini* (1823), 71, 36.

42. Jaricot, *L'amour infini* (1823), 36.

43. Jaricot, *L'amour infini* (1823), 77.

44. Lambert, *Le bienheureux Pierre-Julien Eymard*.

45. *Encyclopédie de la prédication contemporaine*, 706.

46. *Encyclopédie de la prédication contemporaine*, 707. "Mais pourquoi, me direz-vous peut-être, nous présenter le Cœur de Jésus pour nous faire souvenir de son amour pour les hommes; ce n'est pas son cœur qui a aimé les hommes, c'est son âme, puisque son cœur matériel, n'étant après tout qu'une partie de matière organisée, était aussi incapable de produire le sentiment de l'amour que de produire la pensée."

47. Würtz, *Superstitions et prestiges des philosophes*.

48. Maurin, *Vie nouvelle de Pauline-Marie Jaricot*, 152–53.

49. The work was never intended for publication, unlike her treatise on the Sacred Heart. Jaricot, HMV, 7.

50. Giacovelli, *Pauline Jaricot*, 60–61; Vincent-Buffault, *History of Tears*, examines the importance of tears as an expression of sentimental virtue.

51. Here, one might also think of the distinction that Rousseau made in the Social Contract between the will of individuals—what do I want or what will serve me well—versus the good of all. Jaricot does not often use political language, but she understands a similar distinction between the highest

sentiments, those which privilege God's will (seen by her as the good of all), and feelings that stem from lower impulses.

52. Jaricot, *HMV*, 40.
53. This is not dissimilar to the tropes found in Duchesne, "Histoire de Sainte-Marie."
54. Reddy, *Navigation of Feeling*, 289.
55. Jaricot, *HMV*, 15.
56. Jean-Marie Jouham, ed., in Jaricot, *HMV*, 12.
57. Paulmier, *Le chrétien de l'évangile*; Munkácsy, *Christ before Pilate*.
58. Dollen, *Charity without Frontiers*, 20, 29.
59. Jaricot, *HMV*, 70.
60. Naïdenoff, *Pauline Jaricot*, 9.
61. Jaricot, *HMV*, 19.
62. Jaricot, *HMV*, 19.
63. Jaricot, *HMV*, 20–29.
64. Jaricot, *HMV*, 28.
65. Jaricot, *HMV*, 32–33.
66. Jaricot, *HMV*, 29.
67. Jaricot, *HMV*, 19.
68. Jaricot, *HMV*, 34.
69. Jaricot, *HMV*, 42. Pauline's use of tears as an indicator of true feeling is another sentimental trope; see Vincent-Buffault, *History of Tears*.
70. Jaricot, *HMV*, 43.
71. Jaricot, *HMV*, 43.
72. Jaricot, *HMV*, 67.
73. Cristiani, *Marie-Pauline Jaricot*, 22.
74. Jaricot, *HMV*, 44.
75. Jaricot, *HMV*, 49.
76. Jaricot, *HMV*, 51.
77. Jaricot, *HMV*, 51–52.
78. Jaricot, *HMV*, 55.
79. Acts 9:15.
80. Jaricot, *HMV*, 15.
81. Jaricot, *HMV*, 62.
82. Jaricot, *HMV*, 56.
83. Jaricot, *HMV*, 57.
84. Jaricot, *HMV*, 59.
85. Jaricot, *HMV*, 59, 74.
86. Jaricot, *HMV*, 60.

87. Jaricot, *HMV*, 82.

88. Jaricot, *HMV*, 83.

89. Jaricot, *HMV*, 84.

90. See chapter 3. Also, Tesnière, *Somme de la prédication eucharistique,* offers a history of preaching related to this topic and affirms the general linkage of Communion and Sacred Heart.

91. Jaricot, *L'amour infini* (1823), 4.

92. Jaricot, *L'amour infini* (1823), 56.

93. Jaricot, *L'amour infini* (1823), 91–92.

94. Jaricot, *L'amour infini* (1823), 91–92.

95. Jaricot, *L'amour infini* (1823), 22.

96. Jaricot, *L'amour infini* (1823), 41–42.

97. Jaricot, *L'amour infini* (1823), 41–42.

98. Jaricot, *L'amour infini* (1823), 83.

99. Jaricot, *L'amour infini* (1823), 83–84.

100. Jaricot, *HMV*, 23.

101. Jaricot, *HMV*, 25, 41.

102. Jaricot, *HMV*, 58.

103. Jaricot, *HMV*, 59.

104. Jaricot, *HMV*, 68.

105. Jaricot, *HMV*, 63.

106. Jaricot, *HMV*, 68–69.

107. Jaricot, *HMV*, 69.

108. Jaricot, *HMV*, 70.

109. Jaricot, *HMV*, 70.

110. Jaricot, *HMV*, 71.

111. Bowman, "La circulation du sang religieux," 22.

112. Hours, "Autour de la fondation," 170.

113. Jaricot, *A mes bien-aimées soeurs,* 6.

114. Gorrée, *Pauline Jaricot,* 47.

115. Leo XIII, *Exultabat spiritus noster in Deo salutari nostro . . .*

116. K. Burton, *Difficult Star,* 108.

117. Cited in Maurin, *Vie nouvelle de Pauline-Marie Jaricot.*

118. Guiley, *Encyclopedia of Saints,* 284; Mohr, *St. Philomena,* chap. 7.

119. Poupelier, *Abrégé de la vie*; Darche, *Vie très complète.*

120. R. D. E. Burton, *Holy Tears,* xxiii–xxiv.

121. R. D. E. Burton, *Holy Tears,* xxiii–xxiv.

122. Ford, *Divided Houses,* 106–8.

123. Archevêché de Lyon, *Semaine religieuse du Diocèse de Lyon,* 11:259–60.

124. *Notice Sur Sainte Philomène,* 6–7.
125. The first woman came from a group of sisters who had nursed patients of the Hotel-Dieu in Lyon and knew Pauline's brother, Philéas. K. Burton, *Difficult Star,* 90–91.
126. Neill, *They Lived the Faith,* 137.
127. K. Burton, *Difficult Star,* 135.
128. Lathoud, *Victime pour la France,* 243.
129. Gorrée, *Pauline Jaricot,* 96–98.
130. *Notice sur Sainte Philomène,* 6–7; Archevêché de Lyon, *Semaine religieuse du Diocèse,* 11:259–60; Ford, *Divided Houses,* 106–8; R. D. E. Burton, *Holy Tears,* xxiii–xxiv; Jaricot, *L'amour infini* (1823), 102–3; Bowman, "La circulation du sang religieux," 27–28.
131. Jaricot, HMV, 72.
132. Jaricot, HMV, 73. "Et nul ne méritera d'être couronné s'il n'a combattu avec courage."
133. Jaricot, *L'amour infini* (1823), 102–3.
134. Lathoud, *La secret des origines,* 65.
135. Michelet, *Du prêtre* (Comptoir, 1845), 291.

6. BECOMING A SAINT

1. 1 Corinthians 7:32–34.
2. This is not to imply that letters written by women were insignificant for families and businesses or for understanding history, but to acknowledge that the significance of women's letters can be easily overlooked. On letter writing and letters, see Boureau et al., *La Correspondance;* for an example of the ways in which these sources can be fruitfully mined for important cultural insights, see Verjus and Davidson, *Le roman conjugal.*
3. 1 Tim 2:12–13.
4. Aston, *Religion and Revolution in France,* 287.
5. B. G. Smith, *Ladies of the Leisure Class,* 2.
6. Martin and Martin, *Call to a Deeper Love,* (letters 157, 172, 175).
7. For this chapter's use of family letters, I am indebted to the examples provided by Verjus and Davidson, *Le roman conjugal;* C. H. Johnson, *Becoming Bourgeois;* Hennequin-Lecomte, *Le patriciat strasbourgeois.*
8. Martin and Martin, *Call to a Deeper Love.*
9. Mayeur et al., *Histoire du christianisme,* 12:198.
10. Martin and Martin, *Call to a Deeper Love,* 266–67, 326–27, etc. (letters 171, 198).
11. Hénault-Morel, *Louis et Zélie Martin,* 81.
12. R. D. E. Burton, *Holy Tears,* 24–25.

13. Martin and Martin, *Call to a Deeper Love*, 234 (letter 154, February 26, 1876).
14. Piat, *Story of a Family*, 16.
15. Mongin, *Louis et Zélie Martin*, 16.
16. Piat, *Story of a Family*, 18.
17. Hénault-Morel, *Louis et Zélie Martin*, 25.
18. Serna, *La République des girouettes*.
19. Martin and Martin, *Call to a Deeper Love*, 37 (letter 15, November 7, 1865).
20. Martin and Martin, *Call to a Deeper Love*, 37 (letter 15, November 7, 1865).
21. B. G. Smith, *Ladies of the Leisure Class*, deals with this distinction for other families.
22. Thérèse, *La mère de Sainte Thérèse*, 15–16.
23. Hénault-Morel, *Louis et Zélie Martin*, 27.
24. The Picpus or Religious of the Sacred Hearts of Jesus and Mary are a different order than the Religious of the Sacred Heart of Jesus.
25. The Picpus were not as severe or as Jansenist in impulse as Zélie's mother was. Zélie herself generally rejected her mother's theological understanding of the world.
26. "Congrégation Des Sacrés-Coeurs de Jésus et de Marie-Province de France-Picpus."
27. Jedin and Dolan, *History of the Church*, 191–92.
28. Martin and Martin, *Call to a Deeper Love*, 23 (letter 3, November 12, 1863).
29. Lyons, *Readers and Society*, 418–22. This work was second only to Fleury's catechism as a preferred prize book for excellent students. Gréard, *Éducation et instruction*. "Site des Archives du Carmel de Lisieux" has a large bibliography of the Martin family library; see http://www.archives-carmel-lisieux.fr /carmel/index.php/.
30. Zélie does not seem to have harbored any grudge against her brother for this favoritism; her letters to him were deeply affectionate, and the two of them had a good relationship throughout her life. In letter 31, however, she spoke about her commitment to her own work as part of saving for her daughters' dowries, so that they would be provided for as they reached adulthood.
31. C. Martin, *Mother of the Little Flower*, 2.
32. Piat, *Story of a Family*, 33.
33. There were local women of independent means who used their unattached status to accomplish a great deal. Félicité Beaudouin and Pauline Romet, for example, were both known for their charity and zeal for public works. However, when Zélie discussed her own daughters and noted that Marie wished neither to marry nor to become a nun, she added, "I don't know how she'll manage that!" (Martin and Martin, *Call to a Deeper Love*, letter 111). Single

life was not an obvious destination for an unmarried woman, even if her family had become relatively wealthy.

34. For reflections on vocation and marriage see Martin and Martin, *Call to a Deeper Love* (letters 1, 10, 65, 72, 116, 145).

35. Martin and Martin, *Call to a Deeper Love* (letters 1, 16, 30, 117, 147).

36. "Craftsmanship of Alençon Needle Lace-Making-Intangible Heritage-Culture Sector-UNESCO." Alençon lace derives from Venetian lace; in the seventeenth century Colbert paid thirty women from Venice to come to France and pass along the craft.

37. Jackson, *History of Hand-Made Lace*, 48.

38. Piat, *Story of a Family*, 35.

39. See, for example, Martin and Martin, *Call to a Deeper Love* (letters 15, 20, 22, 41, 59, 66, 74).

40. Martin and Martin, *Call to a Deeper Love* (letters 15, 20, 22, 41, 59, 66, 74, 91, 119).

41. Martin and Martin, *Call to a Deeper Love*, 118 (letter 83, September 29, 1872).

42. Hénault-Morel, *Louis et Zélie Martin*, 69, argues that she received silver rather than gold because her work was attached to a Parisian distributer (Pigache), and it would have been impolitic to give first prize to a business that was outside of Alençon. See also "Zélie Une Femme Moderne," Sanctu-aire Louis et Zélie d'Alençon, https://louisetzelie.com/famille-martin/zelie -martin/.

43. Martin and Martin, *Call to a Deeper Love*, 310 (letter 192, March 4, 1877).

44. Hénault-Morel, *Louis et Zélie Martin*, 15, 73.

45. Lettre de Soeur Marie-Dosithée to M. and Mme. Guérin, May 10, 1874, in *Vie Thérésienne* 45 (1972): 68–69, indicates that Elise was expected to help Zélie establish her lace business; Elise and Isidore went to Paris to negoti-ate early lace contracts on Zélie's behalf; there is no remaining evidence of a corresponding effort to assist her in getting married.

46. Piat, *Story of a Family*, 40.

47. Quantin and Quantin, *Zélie et Louis Martin*; Tricot and Zambelli, *Le mariage*.

48. See, for example, Verjus and Davidson, *Le roman conjugal*, 173.

49. Flaubert's Emma Bovary sentimentally wishes for a midnight wedding, with torches. Flaubert, *Madame Bovary*, 85.

50. Hénault-Morel, *Louis et Zélie Martin*, 75.

51. Hénault-Morel, *Louis et Zélie Martin*, 82–83; Andrieu and Mazerolle, *Recherches sur Bertrand Andrieu*, 192.

52. Couturier, *Catéchisme dogmatique et moral*.

53. Piat, *Story of a Family*, 10; Hénault-Morel, *Louis et Zélie Martin*, 23. "[P]résentement je désire de tout coeur que notre Divin Maitre daigne bénir votre union avec ma bien-aimée nièce et que vous soyez heureux autant qu'on peut l'être en ce monde et qu'à votre dernier soupir, Dieu vous reçoive en sa miséricorde et vous place au nombre des immortels Bienheureux."

54. B. G. Smith, *Ladies of the Leisure Class*, chap. 7.

55. Martin and Martin, *Call to a Deeper Love*, 310 (letter 192, March 4, 1877).

56. Martin and Martin, *Call to a Deeper Love*, 44 (letter 20, December 23, 1866).

57. Martin and Martin, *Call to a Deeper Love*, 310 (letter 192, March 4, 1877).

58. There is a Catholic term for this type of marriage; it is called a "Josephite marriage" because of the theological assumption that the marriage between Mary and Joseph was not consummated.

59. Hénault-Morel, *Louis et Zélie Martin*, 81.

60. Louis's deep engagement with sentimental language and forms further demonstrates that this language had widespread appeal. Although Louis is not the focus of this chapter, one could inquire into the way that sentimental ideas also shaped men's visions of the world and their households.

61. Martin and Martin, *Call to a Deeper Love*, 388. See also letters 225, 228, and 230.

62. Louis and Zélie both use the familiar form (*tu*) in their letters to each other. Martin and Martin, *Call to a Deeper Love*, 22 (letter 2b, October 8, 1863).

63. Martin and Martin, *Call to a Deeper Love*, 150–51 (letter 108, August 31, 1873).

64. Martin and Martin, *Call to a Deeper Love*, 70 (letter 46, April 1869).

65. Martin and Martin, *Call to a Deeper Love*, 150 (letter 108, August 31, 1873).

66. Martin and Martin, *Call to a Deeper Love*, 103–4 (letter 70, October 1, 1871).

67. Martin and Martin, *Call to a Deeper Love*, 283 (letter 177, December 17, 1876).

68. Martin and Martin, *Call to a Deeper Love*, 287 (letter 179, December 24, 1876).

69. Martin and Martin, *Call to a Deeper Love*, 39 (letter 17, December 10, 1865).

70. Martin and Martin, *Call to a Deeper Love*, 64 (letter 41, October 1868).

71. Martin and Martin, *Call to a Deeper Love*, 204 (letter 138, August 31, 1875).

72. Martin and Martin, *Call to a Deeper Love*, 105 (letter 71, October 17, 1871).

73. Martin and Martin, *Call to a Deeper Love*, 204 (letter 138, August 31, 1875).

74. Martin and Martin, *Call to a Deeper Love*, 116 (letter 81, July 1872).

75. Martin and Martin, *Call to a Deeper Love*, 204–5 (letter 138, August 31, 1875).

76. This is not only a Catholic sentiment, as one can see in Andress, "Jacobinism as Heroic Narrative"; Andress, "Living the Revolutionary Melodrama"; Reddy, *Invisible Code*. However, all of these works argue that sentimentalism and its heroism give way to other forms of emotional expression in the mid-nineteenth century. This was not always true.

77. For example, Martin and Martin, *Call to a Deeper Love* (letters 69, 80, 111).

78. Martin and Martin, *Call to a Deeper Love*, 113–14 (letter 79, May 1872).
79. Martin and Martin, *Call to a Deeper Love*, 144 (letter 102, May 1873).
80. See especially Martin and Martin, *Call to a Deeper Love* (letters 107, 109, 110, 111).
81. Martin and Martin, *Call to a Deeper Love*, 99 (letter 65, May 5, 1871).
82. Martin and Martin, *Call to a Deeper Love*, 271 (letter 172, November 3, 1876).
83. Martin and Martin, *Call to a Deeper Love*, 217 (letter 145, November 7, 1875).
84. Martin and Martin, *Call to a Deeper Love*, 104 (letter 70, October 1, 1871).
85. Martin and Martin, *Call to a Deeper Love*, 180 (letter 127, January 13, 1875).
86. Martin and Martin, *Call to a Deeper Love*, 243 (letter 157, March 26, 1876).
87. Martin and Martin, *Call to a Deeper Love*, 63–64 (letter 41, October 1868).
88. Martin and Martin, *Call to a Deeper Love*, 63 (letter 41, October 1868).
89. Martin and Martin, *Call to a Deeper Love*, 234 (letter 154, February 26, 1876).
90. Martin and Martin, *Call to a Deeper Love*, 273 (letter 173, November 12, 1876).
91. Martin and Martin, *Call to a Deeper Love*, 268 (letter 172, November 3, 1876).
92. Martin and Martin, *Call to a Deeper Love* (letter 151, January 1876; letter 154, February 26, 1876).
93. Martin and Martin, *Call to a Deeper Love*, 160 (letter 113, December 13, 1873).
94. Deboick, "Image, Authenticity"; Deboick, "Céline Martin's Images."
95. Martin and Martin, *Call to a Deeper Love*, 160 (letter 113, December 13, 1873).
96. Martin and Martin, *Call to a Deeper Love*, 212–13, 268 (letters 143, 172).
97. Martin and Martin, *Call to a Deeper Love*, 220–22, 235 (letters 146, 154).
98. For example, Martin and Martin, *Call to a Deeper Love* (letters 146, 147, and 166).
99. Martin and Martin, *Call to a Deeper Love*, 206–8 (letter 140, September 29, 1875).
100. For example, Martin and Martin, *Call to a Deeper Love* (letters 169, 170, 172, 185).
101. Martin and Martin, *Call to a Deeper Love*, 263 (letter 169, October 22, 1876).
102. Martin and Martin, *Call to a Deeper Love* (letters 105, 134, 146, 159); C. Martin, *Mother of the Little Flower*, 68–69.
103. Martin and Martin, *Call to a Deeper Love*, 279 (letter 175, December 3, 1876).
104. Martin and Martin, *Call to a Deeper Love* (letters 127, 128, 129).
105. Martin and Martin, *Call to a Deeper Love*, 46 (letter 21, January 13, 1867).
106. Martin and Martin, *Call to a Deeper Love*, 215–22 (letters 145, 146).
107. Martin and Martin, *Call to a Deeper Love*, 213 (letter 143, October 1875).
108. Martin and Martin, *Call to a Deeper Love*, 251 (letter 161, June 4, 1876).
109. Martin and Martin, *Call to a Deeper Love*, 255–56 (letter 163, July 9, 1876).
110. It was not only Marie who saw the world as a threat. A letter in Martin and Martin, *Call to a Deeper Love*, 233–34 (letter 154, February 26, 1876), talked about a play at the Catholic Circle without mentioning it by name, in order to scandalize Pauline, who might think the family was going to the theater.
111. Martin and Martin, *Call to a Deeper Love*, 273 (letter 173, November 12, 1876).

112. Martin and Martin, *Call to a Deeper Love* (for example, letters 92, 113, 127, 149, 176, 210).

113. For example, Martin and Martin, *Call to a Deeper Love* (letters 26, 150, 176, 210).

114. Martin and Martin, *Call to a Deeper Love*, 131–33 (letter 92, April 11, 1873).

115. Martin and Martin, *Call to a Deeper Love*, 252 (letter 161, June 4, 1876).

116. Martin and Martin, *Call to a Deeper Love*, 252 (letter 161, June 4, 1876).

117. Martin and Martin, *Call to a Deeper Love*, 252 (letter 162, June 1876).

118. For admonishments to work hard or reports about prizes see Martin and Martin, *Call to a Deeper Love* (letters 44, 47, 50, 99, 101, 120, 121, 135, 144, 145, 146, 150, 151, 156, 162, 163).

119. Martin and Martin, *Call to a Deeper Love*, 166–67 (letters 118, 119, June 1874).

120. Image from 1848; Cammarano and Florian, *Santini e storia*, 48.

121. Martin and Martin, *Call to a Deeper Love*, 279 (letter 175, December 3, 1876).

122. Martin and Martin, *Call to a Deeper Love*, 280 (letter 175, December 3, 1876).

123. Martin and Martin, *Call to a Deeper Love*, 280 (letter 175, December 3, 1876).

124. Martin and Martin, *Call to a Deeper Love*, 117 (letter 81, July 1872).

125. Martin and Martin, *Call to a Deeper Love*, 116 (letter 80, July 21, 1872).

126. Martin used language that is reminiscent of Duchesne's explanation of the value of God's desires more than personal ones. Martin and Martin, *Call to a Deeper Love*, 128 (letter 90, March 30, 1873).

127. Martin and Martin, *Call to a Deeper Love* (letters 147, 154).

128. For example, Martin and Martin, *Call to a Deeper Love* (letters 111, 121, 161).

129. Martin and Martin, *Call to a Deeper Love*, 173 (letter 121, August 9, 1874).

130. Martin and Martin, *Call to a Deeper Love*, 253–54 (letter 163, July 9, 1876).

131. Martin and Martin, *Call to a Deeper Love*, 228 (letter 150, January 16, 1876).

132. Martin and Martin, *Call to a Deeper Love*, 257 (letter 164, July 16, 1876).

133. Martin and Martin, *Call to a Deeper Love*, 237 (letter 163, July 9, 1876). If Zélie Martin, who herself had wanted to be a nun, felt this way, one can imagine how much less sympathy for the religious life other parents might have.

134. Martin and Martin, *Call to a Deeper Love* (letters 131, 142, 145, 175, 210).

135. Martin and Martin, *Call to a Deeper Love*, 236 (letter 154, February 26, 1876).

136. Martin and Martin, *Call to a Deeper Love*, 216 (letter 145, November 7, 1875).

137. In this, Martin was not alone. Chinnici, "Deciphering Religious Practice," 7, demonstrates how important images were to engaging theological and social problems.

CONCLUSION

1. McCartin, "Sacred Heart of Jesus," 63; R. D. E. Burton, *Holy Tears*, 55; Ford, *Divided Houses*, 113.

2. R. D. E. Burton, *Holy Tears*, 55.

3. McCartin, "Sacred Heart of Jesus," 63.

4. McCartin, "Sacred Heart of Jesus," 63; R. D. E. Burton, *Holy Tears*, 55; Ford, *Divided Houses*, 114.

5. Deboick, "Image, Authenticity"; Harris, *Lourdes*.

6. Ford, *Divided Houses*, 115.

7. This explanation also assumes that engaging in modern methods of communication meant that devout women had capitulated, at least to some degree, to a process of "secularization."

8. R. D. E. Burton, *Holy Tears*, chap. 2; McCartin, "Sacred Heart of Jesus," 63.

9. Petitot, *Sainte Thérèse de Lisieux*, 85.

10. Langlois, *L'autobiographie de Thérèse de Lisieux*, 9.

11. Descouvemont and Loose, *Sainte Thérèse de Lisieux*.

12. Images of Jesus knocking on the door, the Sacred Heart, and guardian angel from "Site des archives du Carmel de Lisieux."

13. Sackville-West, *Eagle and the Dove*, 146.

14. Chinnici, "Deciphering Religious Practice," 7.

15. Langlois, *L'autobiographie de Thérèse de Lisieux*, 85.

16. Langlois, *L'autobiographie de Thérèse de Lisieux*, 159.

17. Manuscrit A, 32r, "Site des archives du Carmel de Lisieux."

18. Manuscrit B, 03r, "Site des archives du Carmel de Lisieux." "Doctor of the Church" is a title that applies to Christian theologians whose teaching is regarded as particularly formational. Some Doctors of the Church are St. Thomas Aquinas and St. Augustine of Hippo; Thérèse received this title in 1997 from Pope John Paul II, one of only four women to be so named, all after 1970. In other words, Thérèse aspired to a role that only men had filled up to that point.

19. Balthasar, *Thérèse de Lisieux*, 40.

20. Manuscrit C, 2v, "Site des archives du Carmel de Lisieux."

21. Manuscrit C, 2v, "Site des archives du Carmel de Lisieux."

22. Manuscrit C, 2v-2r, "Site des archives du Carmel de Lisieux."

23. Manuscrit C, 2r, "Site des archives du Carmel de Lisieux" (Thérèse is referring to Matthew 19:14).

24. A. H. Dolan, *Roses Fall Where Rivers Meet*, 59; Gheon, *Secret of the Little Flower*, 234.

25. Manuscrit B, 03v, and manuscrit B, 03r, "Site des archives du Carmel de Lisieux."

26. Lisieux, *Correspondance générale*, 2:620–21; R. D. E. Burton, *Holy Tears*, 38.

27. Manuscrit B, 1v, "Site des archives du Carmel de Lisieux."

28. Barat, *Dévotion pratique au Sacré Cœur de Jésus*; Saint-Jérôme, *Mois du Sacré-Coeur de Jésus*, 13; Guillemon, *De l'intelligence et la foi*; Bowman, "La circulation du sang religieux"; Aston, *Religion and Revolution in France*, 42.

29. McCartin, "Sacred Heart of Jesus," 59.

30. Manuscrit B, 4r, "Site des archives du Carmel de Lisieux."

31. Manuscrit B, 4v, "Site des archives du Carmel de Lisieux", ellipsis in original.

32. Sophia Deboick has explored in detail how representations of Thérèse owed a great deal to Sulpician imagery, with sentimental tones and similarities to depictions of ideal femininity. Deboick, "Image, Authenticity," chap. 2.

33. Indeed, the almost universal recognizability of Thérèse's face, made possible with the advent of photography and the use of new reproduction techniques, actually made the face of the saint—soft, sweet, and crafted as a Sulpician image—so well known that it came to exist independently from other aspects of her iconography, demonstrating how her popular appeal and her sanctity were difficult to separate from one another.

34. Martin and Martin, *Call to a Deeper Love*, especially letter 110; Deboick, "Image, Authenticity," 20.

35. McCartin, "Sacred Heart of Jesus," 61, discusses this in the context of the Sacred Heart; I would argue it is also important for understanding the exercise of feminine authority writ large. Kselman, "Claude Langlois's Vision," also demonstrates how the broader context of practice is relevant to belief, orthodox or not.

36. McCartin, "Sacred Heart of Jesus," 56.

Bibliography

ARCHIVES/MANUSCRIPT MATERIALS

ACL. Archives du Carmel de Lisieux
AML. Archives Municipales de Lyon
AN. Archives Nationales de France
BNF. Bibliotheque Nationale de France
DOUSSIN. Collections of the Doussin Family (Basse-Goulaine, France)
JARC. Jesuit Archives and Research Center (St. Louis)
OPM. Service d'archives, Oeuvres Pontificales Missionare (Lyon)
RSCJ. Archives of the United States–Canada Province of the Society of the
Sacred Heart (St. Louis)
UDHCC. University of Dayton Holy Card Collection

PUBLISHED WORKS

Abbaye de Landévennec and Parc naturel régional d'Armorique (France).
*Dévotes dentelles: Canivets des XVIIe et XVIIIe siècles: Legs de Morant: Expo-
sition, 15 juin–4 novembre 1990*. Le Faou, France: Parc Naturel Régional d'Armorique, 1990.

Adams, Christine. *Poverty, Charity, and Motherhood: Maternal Societies in
Nineteenth-Century France*. Urbana: University of Illinois Press, 2010.

Alacoque, Marguerite-Marie. *Vie et œuvres de la Bienheureuse Marguerite-Marie
Alacoque*. Vol. 2, *Ses lettres, sa vie écrite par elle-même, ses avis aux novices, ses
prières et ses cantiques*. Paris: Poussielgue, 1876.

Albaric, Michel. "Le commerce des objets religieux dans le quartier Saint-
Sulpice." In *De pierre et de cœur: L'église Saint-Sulpice, 350 ans d'histoire*. Paris:
Cerf, 1996.

Aliaga-Buchenau, Ana-Isabel. *The Dangerous Potential of Reading: Readers & the
Negotiation of Power in Selected Nineteenth-Century Narratives*. New York:
Routledge, 2004.

Allen, James Smith. *Popular French Romanticism: Authors, Readers, and Books in
the 19th Century*. Syracuse NY: Syracuse University Press, 1981.

———. "Toward a Social History of French Romanticism: Authors, Readers, and the Book Trade in Paris, 1820–1840." *Journal of Social History* 13, no. 2 (December 1, 1979): 253–76.

Alphabet d'histoire naturelle, orné de jolies vignettes en taille douce. Montbéliard: Deckherr frères, 1848.

Andress, David. "Jacobinism as Heroic Narrative: Understanding the Terror as the Experience of Melodrama." *French History and Civilization* 5 (2014), 6–23. H-France, https://h-france.net/rude/vol5/andress5/.

———. "Living the Revolutionary Melodrama: Robespierre's Sensibility and the Construction of Political Commitment in the French Revolution." *Representations* 114, no. 1 (2011): 103–28. https://doi.org/10.1525/rep.2011.114 .1.103.

Andrieu, Bertrand, and Fernand Mazerolle. *Recherches sur Bertrand Andrieu de Bordeaux, graveur en médailles (1761–1822): Sa vie, son oeuvre.* Paris: Evrard Fayolle, 1902.

Appleyard, J. A. *Becoming a Reader: The Experience of Fiction from Childhood to Adulthood.* New York: Cambridge University Press, 1991.

Archevêché de Lyon. *Semaine religieuse du Diocèse de Lyon sous le haut patronage de son Eminence le Cardinal Archevêque.* Vol. 11. Lyon: Impr. Emmanuel Vitte, 1898.

Armstrong, Nancy. *Desire and Domestic Fiction: A Political History of the Novel.* New York: Oxford University Press, 1990.

Arnold, Odile. *Le corps et l'âme: La vie des religieuses au XIXe siècle.* Paris: Seuil, 1984.

Art, Jan. "The Cult of the Virgin Mary, or the Feminization of the Male Element in the Roman Catholic Church? A Psycho-Historical Hypothesis." In *Gender and Christianity in Modern Europe: Beyond the Feminization Thesis*, edited by Jan de Maeyer, Leen Van Molle, Tine Van Osselaer, and Vincent Viane, 73–83. Leuven: Leuven University Press, 2012.

Artiaga, Loïc. *Des torrents de papier: Catholicisme et lectures populaires au xixe siècle.* Limoges: Presses Universitaires de Limoges, 2007.

Article extrait de la Gazette Universelle de Lyon où on réfute toutes les allégations mensongères contenues dans le "Journal des débats" du 1er mai 1826, sur le mode, les moyens et le but de l'association de la propagation de la foi. Paris: Impr. de Beaucé-Rusand, 1826.

Asad, Talal. *Formations of the Secular: Christianity, Islam, Modernity.* Palo Alto: Stanford University Press, 2003.

———. "What Might an Anthropology of Secularism Look Like?" In *Formations of the Secular: Christianity, Islam, Modernity*, 21–66. Palo Alto: Stanford University Press, 2003.

Aston, Nigel. *Religion and Revolution in France, 1780–1804*. Washington DC: Catholic University of America Press, 2000.

Avishai, Orit. "'Doing Religon' in a Secular World: Women in Conservative Religions and the Question of Agency." *Gender and Society* 22, no. 4 (2008): 409–33.

Baggerman, Arianne, Rudolf Dekker, and Michael Mascuch, eds. *Controlling Time and Shaping the Self: Developments in Autobiographical Writing since the Sixteenth Century*. Leiden: Brill, 2011.

Balayé, Simone. "Corinne et les amis de Madame de Staël." *Revue d'histoire littéraire de La France* 66, no. 1 (1966): 139–49.

Balthasar, Hans Urs von. *Thérèse de Lisieux: Histoire d'une mission*. Paris: Médiaspaul, 1996.

Bann, Stephen. *Distinguished Images: Prints and the Visual Economy in Nineteenth-Century France*. New Haven CT: Yale University Press, 2013.

Barat, Louis. *Dévotion pratique au Sacré Cœur de Jésus et au très-saint Cœur de Marie; par la médiation de saint Joseph, en union avec tous les anges et tous les saints*. Paris: Imprimerie ecclésiastique de Béthune, 1828.

Barrelle, Joseph-François. *La thaumaturge du XIXe siècle, ou Sainte Philomène, vierge et martyre*. Lausanne: Delisle, 1834.

Batsaki, Yota. "Exile as the Inaudible Accent in Germaine de Staël's *Corinne, Ou l'Italie*." *Comparative Literature* 61, no. 1 (Winter 2009): 26–42.

Baunard, Louis. *Histoire de Mme Duchesne religieuse de la Société du Sacré-Coeur de Jésus et fondatrice des premières maisons de cette société en Amérique*. Paris: Poussielgue, 1878. http://www.canadiana.org/ECO/mtq?doc=04308&language=fr.

Bazot, Etienne-François. *Historiettes et contes à ma petite fille et à mon petit garçon*. Paris: Chez Delarue, 1825.

Beauvoir, Simone de. *The Second Sex*. Translated by Constance Borde and Sheila Malovany-Chevallier. New York: Knopf, 2010.

Bédollière, Emile de La. *La morale en action illustrée: ou Recueil d'anecdotes, propres a former le coeur et l'esprit des jeunes gens . . .* Paris: A. Henriot, 1837.

Bellhouse, Mary L. "Visual Myths of Female Identity in Eighteenth-Century France." *International Political Science Review / Revue Internationale de Science Politique* 12, no. 2 (April 1, 1991): 117–35.

Bérardier de Bataut, François-Joseph, and Charles-Constant Le Tellier. *Précis de l'histoire universelle, avec des réflexions*. Paris: Chez C. Le Tellier, 1823.

Bérault-Bercastel, Antoine-Henri de. *Histoire générale de l'Église depuis la prédication des apôtres jusqu'au pontificat de Grégoire XVI . . . , 11*. Paris: Gaume frères, 1840.

Bérenger, Laurent Pierre. *La morale en action et exemples, ou élite d'anecdotes anci- ennes et modernes, de préceptes, de discours et de prières.* Paris: Leroy, 1804.

———. *La morale en action, ou Élite de faits mémorables et d'anecdotes instructives, propres à faire aimer la sagesse . . .* Paris: L. Tenré, 1823.

Bérenger, Laurent Pierre, and Eustache Guibaud. *La morale en action, ou, Élite de faits mémorables et d'anecdotes instructives.* Paris: Briand fils, 1813.

Bernard, Laure. *Contes et conseils à la jeunesse: Dédiés à mademoiselle Fénimore Cooper.* Paris: P. Maumus, 1833.

Berquin, Arnaud. *L'ami de l'adolescence.* Paris: Chez F. Dufart, 1786.

Berruyer, Isaac-Joseph. *Histoires saintes, les plus remarquables et les plus intéres- santes de l'Ancien Testament, propres à commencer l'instruction de la jeunesse, extraites du P. Berruyer . . .* 2nd ed. Paris: Belin-Mandar, 1823.

Bibliographie de la France ou Journal général de l'imprimerie et de la librairie et des cartes géographiques, gravures, lithographies et oeuvres de musique. Paris: Pillet aîné, 1839.

Bilinkoff, Jodi. *The Avila of Saint Teresa: Religious Reform in a Sixteenth-Century City.* Ithaca NY: Cornell University Press, 2015.

Birkett, Jennifer. "Speech in Action: Language, Society, and Subject in Germaine de Staël's Corinne." *Eighteenth-Century Fiction* 7, no. 4 (1995): 393–408.

Bloechl, Jeffrey. *Christianity and Secular Reason: Classical Themes and Modern Developments.* South Bend IN: University of Notre Dame Press, 2012.

Bollème, Geneviève. "L'enjeu du corps et la 'Bibliothèque Bleue.'" *Ethnologie française* 6, no. 3/4 (1976): 285–92.

———. "Religion du texte et texte religieux: Une vie de saint dans la Biblio- thèque Bleue." In *Les saints et les stars: Le texte hagiographique dans la culture populaire,* edited by Jean-Claude Schmitt, 65–74. Paris: Bibliothèque Beauch- esne, 1982.

Boone, Jean Baptiste. *Catalogue d'une bibliothèque choisie: Pour faire suite à l'ouvrage intitulé les mauvais livres, les mauvais journaux, et les romans.* Bruxelles, 1843.

———. *Les mauvais livres, les mauvais journaux et les romans.* 3rd ed., augmented with a triple catalog. Bruxelles, 1842.

Boureau, Alain, Cécile Dauphin, Pierrette Lebrun-Pezerat, Danièle Poublan, Michel Demonet, Jean Hébrard, and Anne Martin-Fugier. *La correspondance: Les usages de la lettre au XIXe siècle.* Paris: Fayard, 1991.

Boutry, Philippe. "Les saints des catacombes: Itinéraires français d'une piété ultramontaine (1800–1881)." *Mélanges de l'école française de Rome* 91, no. 2 (1979): 875–930.

Bouvier, Luke. "How Not to Speak of Incest: Atala and the Secrets of Speech." *Nineteenth-Century French Studies* 30, no. 3 (April 1, 2002): 228–42.

Bowman, Frank Paul. "La circulation du sang religieux à l'époque romantique." *Romantisme* 11, no. 31 (1981): 17–36.

Bracke, Sarah. "Conjugating the Modern/ Religious, Conceptualizing Female Religious Agency: Contours of a 'Post-Secular' Conjuncture." *Theory, Culture, and Society* 25, no. 6 (2008): 51–67.

Brejon de Lavergnée, Matthieu. *Le temps des cornettes: Histoire des Filles de la Charité, XIXe–XXe siècle*. Paris: Fayard, 2018.

Brissenden, R. F. *Virtue in Distress: Studies in the Novel of Sentiment from Richardson to Sade*. New York: Barnes and Noble, 1974.

Broers, Michael. *Europe under Napoleon, 1799–1815*. London: Hodder Arnold, 1996.

Brown, Penny E. *A Critical History of French Children's Literature*. 2 vols. New York: Routledge, 2008.

Bruyn, Frans de. Review of *The Pure Language of the Heart: Sentimentalism in the Netherlands, 1775–1800*, by Annemieke Meijer. *Eighteenth-Century Fiction* 11, no. 4 (1999): 509–11. https://doi.org/10.1353/ecf.1999.0046.

Bryden, Mary. "Saints and Stereotypes: The Case of Thérèse of Lisieux." *Literature and Theology* 13, no. 1 (1999): 1–16.

Burton, Katherine. *Difficult Star: The Life of Pauline Jaricot*. New York: Longmans, Green, 1947.

Burton, Richard D. E. *Holy Tears, Holy Blood: Women, Catholicism, and the Culture of Suffering in France, 1840–1970*. Ithaca NY: Cornell University Press, 2004.

Butler, Judith, Jurgen Habermas, Charles Taylor, and Cornel West. *The Power of Religion in the Public Sphere*. Edited by Eduardo Mendieta and Jonathan VanAntwerpen. New York: Columbia University Press, 2011.

Butler, Judith, and Elizabeth Weed. *The Question of Gender: Joan W. Scott's Critical Feminism*. Bloomington: Indiana University Press, 2011.

Cage, E. Claire. *Unnatural Frenchmen: The Politics of Priestly Celibacy and Marriage, 1720–1815*. Charlottesville: University of Virginia Press, 2015.

Cahier, Adèle. *Vie de la venerable Mere Barat fondatrice et premiere superieure generale de la Societe du Sacre-coeur de Jesus*. Paris: E. de Soye et Fils, 1884.

Calhoun, Craig. "Afterword: Religion's Many Powers." In *The Power of Religion in the Public Sphere*, by Judith Butler, Jurgen Habermas, Charles Taylor, and Cornel West, 118–34. Edited by Eduardo Mendieta and Jonathan VanAntwerpen. New York: Columbia University Press, 2011.

———, ed. *Habermas and the Public Sphere*. Cambridge MA: MIT Press, 1993.

Call, Michael J. "Measuring Up: Infertility and 'Plénitude' in Sophie Cottin's *Claire d'Albe*." *Eighteenth-Century Fiction* 7, no. 2 (1995): 185–202.

Callan, Louise. *Philippine Duchesne, Frontier Missionary of the Sacred Heart, 1769–1852*. Westminster MD: Newman Press, 1957.

Cammarano, Flavio, and Aldo Florian. *Santini e storia di un editori Parigino: Maison Bouasse-Lebel*. Marene: Litostampa Mario Astegiano, 2009.

Caramaschi, Enzo. "Le point de vue féministe dans la pensée de Mme de Staël." In *Voltaire, Madame de Staël, Balzac*, 137–98. Padua: Liviana Editrice, 1977.

Careel, Marie-France, and Carolyn Osiek. *Philippine Duchesne, pionnière à la frontière américaine (1769–1852): Œuvres complètes*. Vol. 1, *1769–1828*. Turnhout: Brepols, 2017.

Carroll, Michael P. "Give Me That Ol' Time Hormonal Religion." *Journal for the Scientific Study of Religion* 43 (May 7, 2004): 275–78. https://doi.org/10.1111/j.1468-5906.2004.00232.x.

Carron, Guy-Toussaint-Julien. *La vertu parée de tous ses charmes ou traité sur la douceur*. Nicolle, 1817.

——. *Les nouvelles héroïnes chrétiennes, ou vies édifiantes de seize jeunes personnes*. 7th ed. Vol. 1. Paris: H. Nicolle, 1815.

——. *Les nouvelles héroïnes chrétiennes, ou vies édifiantes de 17 jeunes personnes*. 10th ed. Vol. 2. Paris: Gosselin, 1825.

——. *Les trois héroïnes chrétiennes, ou vies édifiantes de trois jeunes demoiselles*. Paris: B. Morin, 1782.

——. *Les trois héroïnes chrétiennes, ou vies édifiantes de trois jeunes demoiselles*. 4th ed. Lille: L. Lefort, 1810.

——. *Vies des justes dans les conditions ordinaires de la société*. Rusand, 1825.

——. *Vies des justes dans l'état du mariage*. Le Clère, 1816.

——. *Vies des justes dans l'état du mariage*. Rusand, 1825.

——. *Vies des justes parmi les filles chrétiennes*. Rusand, 1824.

Carter, Karen E. *Creating Catholics: Catechism and Primary Education in Early Modern France*. Notre Dame IN: University of Notre Dame Press, 2011.

Casanova, José. *Public Religions in the Modern World*. Chicago: University of Chicago Press, 1994.

Cassé de Saint-Prosper, Antoine-Jean, Augustin-Amédée Duponchel, Modest Andréevitch Korf, Hippolyte Belloc, and De Saurigny. *Le Monde, histoire de tous les peuples*. N.p., 1844.

Catéchisme à l'usage de toutes les eglises de France. F.-G. Levrault, 1815.

Catéchisme à l'usage de toutes les eglises de l'Empire français. Veuve Nyon, 1806.

Catéchisme à l'usage du diocèse de Beauvais. Desjardins, 1827.

Catéchisme de Versailles. Angé, 1832.

Catéchisme du diocèse d'Amiens. Ledien-Canda, 1823.

Catéchisme du diocèse de Lyon. P. Valfray, 1715.

Catéchisme du diocèse de Poitiers. F.-A. Barbier, 1817.

Catéchisme du diocèse de Saint-Claude. C. Delhorme, 1804.

Catéchisme du diocèse de Saint-Dié. Pellerin et Cie, 1824.

Catéchisme du diocèse d'Orléans: Mandement de Mgr L-S. De Jarente de La Bruyère, 1762.

Catéchisme d' un curé intrus. De Guerbart, 1791.

Catéchisme sur l'Eglise. A Lekirch, de l'impr. de Jacob, 1795.

Catholic Encyclopedia. Vol. 8. New York: Appleton, 1910.

Certeau, Michel de. *The Practice of Everyday Life.* Translated by Steven Rendall. Berkeley: University of California Press, 2011.

Chappel, James. *Catholic Modern: The Challenge of Totalitarianism and the Remaking of the Church.* Cambridge MA: Harvard University Press, 2018.

Charlevoix, Pierre-François-Xavier de. *Vie de la mère Marie de l'incarnation: Institutrice des Ursulines de la Nouvelle France.* Briasson, 1724.

Chartier, Roger, Alain Boureau, and Cécile Dauphin. *Correspondence: Models of Letter-Writing from the Middle Ages to the Nineteenth Century.* Translated by Christopher Woodall. Princeton NJ: Princeton University Press, 1997.

Chartier, Roger, and Henri-Jean Martin. *Histoire de l'édition française.* Vol. 2, *Le Livre triomphant.* Paris: Fayard-Cercle de la Librairie, 1990.

Chateaubriand, François-René, vicomte de. *Atala and René.* Chicago: Scott, Foresman, 1901.

———. *The Memoirs of François René, Vicomte de Chateaubriand.* Translated by Alexander de Teixeira. New York: Putnams, 1902.

Chateaubriand, François-René, vicomte de, and Charles Ignatius White. *The Genius of Christianity: or, The Spirit and Beauty of the Christian Religion.* Baltimore: J. Murphy, 1870.

Chinnici, Joseph P. "Deciphering Religious Practice: Material Culture as Social Code in the Nineteenth Century." *U.S. Catholic Historian* 19, no. 3 (2001): 1–19.

Cholvy, Gérard. *Histoire religieuse de la France: Hommes et communautés.* Toulouse: Privat, 2000.

Choudhury, Mita. *Convents and Nuns in Eighteenth-Century French Politics and Culture.* Ithaca NY: Cornell University Press, 2004.

Clark, Linda L. Review of *Le livre d'enfance et de jeunesse en France,* by Jean Glénisson and Ségolène Le Men. *History of Education Quarterly* 36, no. 1 (1996): 80–83.

"Claude Langlois's Vision of France: Regional Identity, Royal Imaginary, and Holy Women." Special issue, *Historical Refections/Réflexions Historiques* 39, no. 1 (2013). https://doi.org/10.3167/hrrh.2013.390101.

Coakley, Sarah. *The New Asceticism.* London: Bloomsbury, 2016.

Code, Joseph Bernard. *Great American Foundresses.* New York: Macmillan, 1929.

Coeurderoy, Claudine. *Dialogues d'une mère avec sa fille.* Auxerre: impr. de L. Fournier, 1802.

Cohen, Margaret. "Flaubert Lectrice: Flaubert Lady Reader." *Modern Language Notes (MLN)* 122, no. 4 (2007): 746–58.

———. *The Sentimental Education of the Novel.* Princeton NJ: Princeton University Press, 2002.

Cole, Joshua. *The Power of Large Numbers: Population, Politics, and Gender in Nineteenth-Century France.* Ithaca NY: Cornell University Press, 2000.

Coleman, Charly. "Vagaries of Disenchantment: God, Matter, and Mammon in the Eighteenth Century." *Modern Intellectual History* 14, no. 3 (November 2017): 869–81. https://doi.org/10.1017/S1479244316000159.

———. *The Virtues of Abandon: An Anti-Individualist History of the French Enlightenment.* Palo Alto: Stanford University Press, 2017.

Cook, Malcolm C. "Harmony and Discord in *Paul et Virginie.*" *Eighteenth-Century Fiction* 3, no. 3 (1991): 205–16.

———. "*Paul et Virginie*: A Roman Poetique." *Australian Journal of French Studies* 24 (1999): 242–52.

Correspondance de deux petites filles: Ouvrage propre à former de bonne heure les enfans au style épistolaire. Paris: Belin, 1811.

Cott, Nancy F. *The Bonds of Womanhood: "Woman's Sphere" in New England, 1780–1835.* New Haven CT: Yale University Press, 1997.

Cottin, Sophie. *Claire d'Albe: The Original French Text.* Edited by Margaret Cohen. New York: Modern Language Association of America, 2002.

Cottin, Sophie, and Margaret Cohen. *Claire d'Albe: An English Translation.* Translated by Margaret Cohen. New York: Modern Language Association of America, 2002.

Coulet, Henri. "Révolution et roman selon Mme de Staël." *Revue d'histoire littéraire de la France* 87, no. 4 (1987): 638–60.

Couturier, Jean. *Catéchisme dogmatique et moral.* Dijon: Victor Lagier, 1824.

Cova, Anne, and Bruno Dumons. *Femmes, genre et catholicisme: Nouvelles recherches, nouveaux objets.* Lyon: Religions, sociétés et acculturation (RESEA): Laboratoire de recherche historique Rhône-Alpes (LARHRA, UMR 5190), 2012.

Cristiani, Léon. *Marie-Pauline Jaricot: L'Esprit et l'Eglise.* Lyon: Editions du Chalet, 1961.

Curtis, Sarah A. *Civilizing Habits: Women Missionaries and the Revival of French Empire.* New York: Oxford University Press, 2010.

Darche, Jean François Frédéric. *Vie très complète de Sainte Philomène, vierge et martyre protectrice du Rosaire vivant.* Paris: Régis Ruffet, 1867.

Darnton, Robert. *The Great Cat Massacre: And Other Episodes in French Cultural History*. New York: Basic Books, 2009.

Davidson, Denise Z. *France after Revolution: Urban Life, Gender, and the Newsocial Order*. Harvard Historical Studies 155. Cambridge MA: Harvard University Press, 2007.

———. "Making Society 'Legible': People-Watching in Paris after the Revolution." *French Historical Studies* 28, no. 2 (April 1, 2005): 265–96.

Davis, Natalie Zemon. "City Women and Religious Change in Sixteenth-Century France." In *Society and Culture in Early Modern France: Eight Essays*, 65–96. Palo Alto: Stanford University Press, 1975.

Day, Barbara Ann. "Napoleonic Art (1830–1835): From the Religious Image to the New Secular Reality." PhD, University of California, Irvine, 1986.

Deboick, Sophia. "Céline Martin's Images of Thérèse of Lisieux and the Creation of a Modern Saint." In *Saints and Sanctity*, edited by Peter Clarke and Tony Claydon, 376–88. Studies in Church History, vol. 47. Suffolk: Boydell & Brewer, 2011.

Deboick, Sophia Lucia. "Image, Authenticity and the Cult of Saint Thérèse of Lisieux, 1897–1959." PhD, University of Liverpool, 2011.

Delessert, Benjamin Jules Paul, and Gérando, Baron de. *Les bons exemples: Nouvelle morale en action*. Paris: Simon Bacon, 1858.

Delumeau, Jean. *La religion de ma mère: Les femmes et la transmission de la foi*. Paris: Cerf, 1992.

Denby, David J. *Sentimental Narrative and the Social Order in France, 1760–1820*. Cambridge: Cambridge University Press, 2006.

Desan, Suzanne. "Gender, Radicalization, and the October Days: Occupying the National Assembly." *French Historical Studies* 43, no. 3 (2020): 359–90. https://doi.org/10.1215/00161071-8278435.

———. *Reclaiming the Sacred: Lay Religion and Popular Politics in Revolutionary France*. Ithaca NY: Cornell University Press, 1990.

———. "The Role of Women in Religious Riots during the French Revolution." *Eighteenth-Century Studies* 22, no. 3 (1989): 451–68. https://doi.org/10.2307/2738896.

Descouvemont, Pierre, and Helmuth Nils Loose. *Sainte Thérèse de Lisieux: La vie en images*. Paris: Orphelins apprentis d'Auteuil, 1995.

Despland, Michel. "To Interpose a Little Ease: Chateaubriand on Christianity and the Modern World." *Religion & Literature* 21, no. 2 (1989): 19–44.

Diaconoff, Suellen. *Through the Reading Glass*. Albany: State University of New York Press, 2005.

Diefendorf, Barbara B. "Give Us Back Our Children: Patriarchal Authority and Parental Consent to Religious Vocations in Early Counter-Reformation France." *Journal of Modern History* 68, no. 2 (June 1, 1996): 265–307. https://doi.org/10.1086/600767.

"Divini Amoris Scientia (October 19, 1997) | John Paul II." Accessed March 27, 2019. https://w2.vatican.va/content/john-paul-ii/en/apost_letters/1997/documents/hf_jp-ii_apl_19101997_divini-amoris.html.

Dolan, Albert H. *Roses Fall Where Rivers Meet: A Description of the Little Flower Shower of Roses.* Carmelite Press, n.d.

Dolan, Frances E. "Why Are Nuns Funny?" *Huntington Library Quarterly* 70, no. 4 (December 1, 2007): 509–35. https://doi.org/10.1525/hlq.2007.70.issue-4.

Dollen, Charles. *Charity without Frontiers: The Life-Work of Marie-Pauline Jaricot.* Collegeville MN: Liturgical Press, 1972.

Doussin, Jean-Pierre. *Petite histoire des images pieuses: Mémento à l'usage des collectionneurs.* 4th ed. Basse-Goulaine: Chez l'auteur, 2017.

Douyère, David. "L'image de piété chrétienne, objet-support de la croyance? Communiquer la foi par l'image, de l'imprimé au numérique." *Recherches en communication* 38 (2012): 29–46.

Duchartre, Pierre Louis, and Rene Saulnier. *L'imagerie parisienne: L'imagerie de la rue Saint Jacques.* Paris: Grund, 1944.

Duchesne, Philippine, and Chantal Paisant. *Philippine Duchesne et ses compagnes; Les années pionnières, 1818–1823: Lettres et journaux des premières missionnaires du Sacré-Coeur aux Etats-Unis.* Paris: Cerf, 2001.

Dupanloup, Félix. *Avertissement à la jeunesse et aux pères de famille sur les attaques dirigées contre le religion par quelques écrivains de nos jours.* Paris: Blanchard, 1863.

Eco, Umberto. "Towards a Semiotic Inquiry into the Television Message." *Working Papers in Cultural Studies* 3 (1972): 103–21.

Eichner, Carolyn J. *Surmounting the Barricades: Women in the Paris Commune.* Bloomington: Indiana University Press, 2004.

Encyclopédie de la prédication contemporaine: Recueil de conférences, sermons, panégyriques, discours de circonstances, etc. etc. Sermons pour octaves du Saint-Sacrement et du Coeur de Jésus, et pour Triduum de l'Adoration perpétuelle et des quarante-heures . . . Marseille: Mingardon, 1884.

Engbers, Susanna Kelly. "With Great Sympathy: Elizabeth Cady Stanton's Innovative Appeals to Emotion." *Rhetoric Society Quarterly* 37, no. 3 (2007): 307–32.

Fallon, Robert. *Messiaen Perspectives 1: Sources and Influences.* New York: Routledge, 2016.

Farwell, Beatrice. *The Cult of Images: Baudelaire and the Nineteenth-Century Media Explosion*. Seattle: University of Washington Press, 1977.

Fessenden, Tracy. "The Problem of the Postsecular." *American Literary History* 26, no. 1 (February 5, 2014): 154–67.

Fisher, Philip. *Hard Facts: Setting and Form in the American Novel*. New York: Oxford University Press, 1987.

Flaubert, Gustave. *The Complete Works of Gustave Flaubert*. Edited by Ferdinand Brunetière and Robert Arnot. Vol. 2. New York: Walter J. Black, 1904.

———. *Madame Bovary*. Paris: Flammarion, 1986.

Fleury, Claude. *Catéchisme historique: Contenant en abrégé, l'histoire sainte et la doctrine chrétienne*. Hovius, 1805.

———. *Catechisme historique: Contenant en abrégé l'histoire sainte et la doctrine chrétienne*. Duprat-Duverger, 1810.

———. *Catéchisme historique: Contenant en abrégé l'histoire sainte et la doctrine chrétienne*. New. Perpignan: J. Alzine, 1814.

———. *Catechisme historique: Contenant en abrégé l'histoire sainte & la doctrine chrétienne*. Lebatard, 1815.

———. *Catechisme historique: Contenant en abrégé l'histoire sainte & la doctrine chrétienne*. Paris: Delalain, 1831.

———. *Catechisme historique: Contenant en abrégé l'histoire sainte & la doctrine chrétienne*. Paris: Gaume, 1834.

———. *Catéchisme historique: Contenant en abrégé l'histoire sainte et la doctrine chrétienne*. Lyon: Perisse Frères, 1852.

———. *Catéchisme historique, contenant en abrégé l'histoire sainte et la doctrine chrétienne*. Lefort, 1816.

———. *Catéchisme historique, contenat en abrégé l'histoire sainte et la doctrine chrétienne*. D. de Busscher, 1821.

———. *Catéchisme historique, contenant en abrégé l'histoire sainte et la doctrine chrétienne*. A. de Chateauvieux, 1833.

———. *Catéchisme historique, contenant en abrégé l'histoire sainte et la doctrine chrétienne*. Perisse frères, 1854.

Ford, Caroline. *Divided Houses: Religion and Gender in Modern France*. Ithaca NY: Cornell University Press, 2005.

Fouilloux, Étienne. "Femmes et catholicisme dans la France contemporaine: Aperçu historiographique." *Clio. Femmes, Genre, Histoire*, no. 2 (November 1, 1995). https://doi.org/10.4000/clio.498.

Fraisse, Geneviève. *Reason's Muse: Sexual Difference and the Birth of Democracy*. Chicago: University of Chicago Press, 1994.

Fraser, Nancy. *Unruly Practices: Power, Discourse, and Gender in Contemporary Social Theory*. Minneapolis: University of Minnesota Press, 2008.

Froberville, Jean-Baptiste Huet de. *Catéchisme des trois ordres, pour les assemblées d'élection*. 1789.

Fuchs, Rachel G., and Victoria E. Thompson. *Women in Nineteenth-Century Europe*. Houndmills, Basingstoke, Hampshire: Palgrave Macmillan, 2005.

Fuhring, Peter, Louis Marchesano, Remi Mathis, and Selbach Vanessa, eds. *A Kingdom of Images: French Prints in the Age of Louis XIV, 1660–1715*. Los Angeles: Getty Research Institute, 2015.

Furlong, Monica. *Therese of Lisieux*. Maryknoll NY: Orbis Books, 2001.

Gans, Eric. *Madame Bovary: The End of Romance*. Woodbridge CT: Twayne, 1989.

Garfitt, Toby. "What Happened to the Catholic Novel?" *French Studies: A Quarterly Review* 66, no. 2 (April 19, 2012): 222–30.

Gaucher, Guy. *The Story of a Life: St. Theresa of Lisieux*. San Francisco: HarperOne, 1993.

Genlis, Stéphanie Félicité de. *De l'influence des femmes sur la littérature française, comme protectrices des lettres et comme auteurs, ou Précis de l'histoire des femmes françaises les plus célèbres*. Paris: Maradan, 1811.

———. *Les veillées du chateau ou cours de morale à l'usage des enfants*. Vol. 1. Lausanne: J. P. Heubach, 1784.

Ghéon, Henri. *Sainte Thérèse de Lisieux*. Paris: E. Flammarion, 1934.

———. *The Secret of the Little Flower*. Translated by F. J. Sheed. London: Sheed & Ward, 1977.

Giacovelli, Cécilia. *Pauline Jaricot: Biographie*. Paris: Mame, 2005.

Gibson, Ralph. *A Social History of French Catholicism, 1789–1914*. New York: Routledge, 1989.

Girard, Alain R., and Claude Quétel. *L'histoire de France racontée par le jeu de l'oie*. Paris: Balland, 1982.

Glénisson, Jean, and Ségolène Le Men. *Le livre d'enfance et de jeunesse en France*. Bordeaux: Société des bibliophiles de Guyenne, 1994.

Glotin, Edouard. *La Bible du Cœur de Jésus: Un livre de vie pour les générations du IIIe millénaire*. Paris: Presses de la Renaissance, 2007.

Goldsmith, Elizabeth C. *Publishing Women's Life Stories in France, 1647–1720: From Voice to Print*. Burlington VT: Ashgate, 2001.

Goldsmith, Elizabeth C., and Dena Goodman, eds. *Going Public: Women and Publishing in Early Modern France*. Ithaca NY: Cornell University Press, 1995.

Gorrée, Georges. *Pauline Jaricot: Une laïque engagée*. Paris: La Colombe, 1962.

Gorres, Ida Friederike. *The Hidden Face: A Study of St. Therese of Lisieux*. San Francisco: Ignatius Press, 2003.

Gouges, Olympe de. *Le Couvent, ou les voeux forcés, drame en trois actes, représenté en deux actes, et remis en trois au Théatre François, Comique et Lyrique, au mois d'octobre 1790*. Paris: Vve Duchesne, 1792.

Goujon, Patrick. *Prendre part à l'intransmissible: La communication spirituelle à travers la correspondance de Jean-Joseph Surin*. Grenoble: Jérôme Millon, 2008.

A Grain of Wheat: Ven. Rose Philippine Duchesne. St. Louis: B. Herder, 1918.

Gray, Francine du Plessix. *Madame de Stael: The First Modern Woman*. New York: Atlas, 2008.

Gréard, Octave. *Éducation et instruction*, 1889.

Greer, Allan. "Colonial Saints: Gender, Race, and Hagiography in New France." *William and Mary Quarterly*, 3rd ser., 57, no. 2 (April 1, 2000): 323–48. http://www.jstor.org/stable/2674478.

Greer, Allan, and Jodi Bilinkoff, eds. *Colonial Saints: Discovering the Holy in the Americas, 1500–1800*. New York: Routledge, 2002.

Guiley, Rosemary. *The Encyclopedia of Saints*. New York: Infobase, 2001.

Guillemon, Martial H. *De l'intelligence et la foi*. Hachette, 1840.

Guillon, Marie-Nicolas-Silvestre. *Modèles de l'éloquence chrétienne en France après Louis XIV, ou Année apostolique composée des sermons des prédicateurs les plus renommés depuis Bossuet, Bourdaloue et Massillon . . . précédée d'un Discours . . . contenant l'histoire abrégée de la prédication en France . . .* Bureau du Moniteur des Villes et des Campagnes, 1837.

Gutermann-Jacquet, Deborah. *Les équivoques du genre: Devenir homme et femme à l'âge romantique*. Rennes: Presses universitaires de Rennes, 2012.

Habermas, Jürgen. *An Awareness of What Is Missing: Faith and Reason in a Post-Secular Age*. Malden MA: Polity, 2010.

——. *The Structural Transformation of the Public Sphere: An Inquiry into a Category of Bourgeois Society*. Cambridge MA: MIT Press, 1991.

Hall, Stuart. *Cultural Studies 1983: A Theoretical History*. Edited by Jennifer Daryl Slack and Lawrence Grossberg. Durham NC: Duke University Press Books, 2016.

Hamelin, Fortunée, and André Gayot. *Une ancienne muscadine, Fortunée Hamelin: Lettres inédites, 1839–1851*. Paris: Émile-Paul, 1911.

Hanley, Sarah. "Engendering the State: Family Formation and State Building in Early Modern France." *French Historical Studies* 16, no. 1 (1989): 4–27. https://doi.org/10.2307/286431.

Harris, Ruth. *Lourdes: Body and Spirit in the Secular Age*. London: Penguin Books, 2008.

——. "The 'Unconscious' and Catholicism in France." *Historical Journal* 47, no. 2 (2004): 331–54. https://doi.org/10.1017/S0018246X04003711.

Harrison, Carol E. "Conversion in the Age of Mechanical Reproduction: Alphonse Ratisbonne in Rome and Paris." *Journal of Modern History* 92, no. 1 (2020): 116–44.

———. *Romantic Catholics: France's Postrevolutionary Generation in Search of a Modern Faith.* Ithaca NY: Cornell University Press, 2014.

Haynes, Christine. *Lost Illusions: The Politics of Publishing in Nineteenth-Century France.* Cambridge MA: Harvard University Press, 2010.

Heller, Deborah. "Tragedy, Sisterhood, and Revenge in *Corinne*." *Papers on Language & Literature* 26, no. 2 (Spring 1990): 15–35.

Hénault-Morel, Thierry. *Louis et Zélie Martin.* Paris: Cerf, 2016.

Hennequin-Lecomte, Laure. *Le patriciat strasbourgeois (1789–1830): Destins croisés et voix intimes.* Strasbourg: Presses Universitaires de Strasbourg, 2011.

Heuer, Jennifer Ngaire. *The Family and the Nation: Gender and Citizenship in Revolutionary France, 1789–1830.* Ithaca NY: Cornell University Press, 2009.

Hollier, Denis. "Incognito." *Revue Des Sciences Humaines* 247, no. Juillet–Septembre (1997): 25–43.

Hopkin, David M. *Soldier and Peasant in French Popular Culture, 1766–1870.* Rochester NY: Boydell & Brewer, 2003.

Hours, Henri. "Autour de la Fondation du Rosaire Vivant." In *Théologie, histoire, et piété mariale: Actes du colloque, Université catholique de Lyon, 1–3 Octobre 1996*, edited by Jean Comby. Lyon: Profac, 1997.

Houssay, Magdeleine, and Abbé Léonard de Corbiac. *Correspondance Frédéric Ozanam et Amélie Soulacroix: Poèmes, prières et notes intimes.* Paris: Desclée De Brouwer, 2018.

Hufton, Olwen. "The Reconstruction of a Church 1796–1801." In *Beyond the Terror: Essays in French Regional and Social History, 1794–1815*, edited by Gwynne Lewis and Colin Lucas. New York: Cambridge University Press, 2003.

Hunt, Lynn. *Inventing Human Rights: A History.* New York: W. W. Norton, 2008.

Hurlburt, Sarah. "Educating Emma: A Genetic Analysis of Reading in Madame Bovary." *Nineteenth-Century French Studies* 40, no. 1 (October 7, 2011): 81–95.

Irlam, Shaun. "Gerrymandered Geographies: Exoticism in Thomson and Chateaubriand." *Modern Language Notes (MLN)* 108, no. 5 (1993): 891–912.

Izzo, Amanda. *Liberal Christianity and Women's Global Activism: The YWCA of the USA and the Maryknoll Sisters.* New Brunswick NJ: Rutgers University Press, 2018.

Jackson, Emily. *A History of Hand-Made Lace: Dealing with the Origin of Lace, the Growth of the Great Lace Centres, the Mode of Manufacture, the Methods of Distinguishing and the Care of Various Kinds of Lace.* New York: C. Scribner's Sons, 1900.

Jaricot, Pauline. *A mes bien-aimées soeurs du diocèse de Grenoble.* Gratianopolis: C. P. Baratier, 1834.

————. *Histoire de ma vie: Autobiographie spirituelle.* Paris: Mame, 2009.

————. *L'amour infini dans la divine Eucharistie: Le Cœur de Jésus, salut de l'Église et de la société.* Lyon: Rusand, 1822.

————. *L'amour infini dans la divine eucharistie: ou Le Coeur de Jésus-Christ, salut de l'Eglise de la société.* Paris: Les libraires associés, 1823.

Jaricot, Pauline, Marie-Monique de Jésus, and Thierry Brac de la Perrière. *Écrits de jeunesse: Père éternel, je vous offre . . .* Paris: Lethielleux, 2010.

Jarvis, Katie L. "The Cost of Female Citizenship: How Price Controls Gendered Democracy in Revolutionary France." *French Historical Studies* 41, no. 4 (October 1, 2018): 647–80. https://doi.org/10.1215/00161071-6953659.

Jauss, Hans. *Toward an Aesthetic of Reception.* Minneapolis: University of Minnesota Press, 1982.

Jedin, Hubert, and John Patrick Dolan. *History of the Church: The Church between Revolution and Restoration.* London: Burns & Oates, 1980.

Johnson, Christopher H. *Becoming Bourgeois: Love, Kinship, and Power in Provincial France, 1670–1880.* Ithaca NY: Cornell University Press, 2015.

Johnson, Penelope D. *Equal in Monastic Profession: Religious Women in Medieval France.* Chicago: University of Chicago Press, 2009.

Jonas, Raymond Anthony. *France and the Cult of the Sacred Heart: An Epic Tale for Modern Times.* Berkeley: University of California Press, 2000.

Jones, Catherine. "Madame de Staël and Scotland: Corinne, Ossian and the Science of Nations." *Romanticism* 15, no. 3 (October 2009): 239–53. https://doi.org/10.3366/E1354991X09000750.

Kaufmann, Michael W. "The Religious, the Secular, and Literary Studies: Rethinking the Secularization Narrative in Histories of the Profession." *New Literary History* 38 (2007): 607–28.

King, Mike. *Postsecularism: The Hidden Challenge to Extremism.* Cambridge: James Clarke, 2009.

Kselman, Thomas. "Claude Langlois's Vision of Nineteenth-Century French Catholicism." *Historical Reflections / Réflexions Historiques* 39, no. 1 (2013): 66–81.

————. *Conscience and Conversion: Religious Liberty in Post-Revolutionary France.* New Haven CT: Yale University Press, 2018.

————. *Miracles & Prophecies in Nineteenth-Century France.* New Brunswick NJ: Rutgers University Press, 1983.

Kyrlezhev, Aleksandr. "The Postsecular Age: Religion and Culture Today." *Religion, State and Society* 36, no. 1 (March 1, 2008): 21–31. https://doi.org/10.1080/09637490701809654.

Lambert, Jules Mathieu. *Le bienheureux Pierre-Julien Eymard: (1811–1868).* Paris: Lecoffre & Gabalda, 1925.

Lamennais, Hugues Felicité Robert de. *Bibliothèque des dames chrétiennes.* Vol. 16. Paris: P. Didot, 1820.

La Minerve francaise par Aignan, Benjamin Constant, Evariste Dumoulin, Etienne, A. Jay, E. Jouy, Lacretelle aine, Tissot . . . Paris: Eymery, 1819.

Landes, Joan B. *Women and the Public Sphere in the Age of the French Revolution.* Ithaca NY: Cornell University Press, 1988.

Lane, Christopher J. "Vocational Freedom, Parental Authority and Pastoral Persuasion in Seventeenth-Century France." *Journal of Ecclesiastical History* 69, no. 4 (2018): 768–84.

Langlois, Claude. *L'autobiographie de Thérèse de Lisieux: Édition critique du manuscrit A.* Paris: Cerf, 2009.

———. *Le Catholicisme au féminin: Les congrégations françaises à supérieure générale au XIXe siècle.* Paris: Cerf, 1984.

———. "Les effectifs des congrégations féminines au XIXe siècle: De l'enquête statistique à l'histoire quantitative." *Revue d'histoire de l'Église de France* 60, no. 164 (1974): 39–64.

Lathoud, David. *La secret des origines de la propagation de la foi.* Vol. 1 of *Marie-Pauline Jaricot.* Paris: Maison de la Bonne Presse, 1937.

———. *Victime pour la France et pour la classe ouvrière.* Vol. 2 of *Marie-Pauline Jaricot.* Paris: Maison de la Bonne Presse, 1937.

Latour, Bruno. *An Inquiry into Modes of Existence: An Anthropology of the Moderns.* Translated by Catherine Porter. Cambridge MA: Harvard University Press, 2013.

Lavabre, Marion. "Sainte comme une image: Thérèse de Lisieux à travers ses représentations." *Terrain: Anthropologie & sciences humaines,* no. 24 (March 1, 1995): 83–90. https://doi.org/10.4000/terrain.3116.

Leflaive, Anne. *Philippine Duchesne.* Paris: Éditions France-Empire, 1965.

Le Gobien, Charles. *Lettres édifiantes et curieuses, écrites des missions étrangères par quelques missionaires de la Compagnie de Jésus.* 13 vols. Paris: N. Le Clerc, 1707.

Le Goff, Jacques, René Rémond, and Philippe Joutard. *Histoire de la France religieuse.* Paris: Seuil, 1991.

Lejeune, Philippe. *Le moi des demoiselles: Enquête sur le journal de jeune fille.* Paris: Seuil, 1993.

Leo XIII (pope). *Exultabat spiritus noster in Deo salutari nostro. . . ,* 1826.

Lerch, Dominique. "En Quoi l'imagerie populaire a-t-elle été une industrie culturelle? Quelques propositions." In *Histoire des industries culturelles en France XIXe–XXè Siècles,* edited by Jacques Marseille and Patrick Eveno, 321–39. Actes du colloque en Sorbonne. Paris: Association pour le développement de l'histoire économique, 2001.

———. "Le Sentiment religieux, objet d'étude scientifique? Après l'histoire littéraire, pour une histoire des object religieux?" In *Un objet religieux et sa pratique: Le chemin de croix portatif au XIXe et XX siècles en France*, edited by Waltraud Hahn. Paris: Cerf, 2007.

Lisieux, Saint Thérèse de. *Correspondance générale*. 2 vols. Paris: Cerf, 1972.

Lyden, John C., and Eric Michael Mazur, eds. *The Routledge Companion to Religion and Popular Culture*. New York: Routledge, 2015.

Lyon, Comte de. *Catéchisme historique de la papauté: Ouvrage destiné à l'instruction des enfans de tout âge*. Chez Petit, 1791.

Lyon-Caen, Judith. *La lecture et la vie: Les usages du roman au temps de Balzac*. Paris: Tallandier, 2006.

Lyons, Martyn. *Readers and Society in Nineteenth-Century France: Workers, Women, Peasants*. London: Palgrave Macmillan, 2001.

Lysaught, M. "Witnessing Christ in Their Bodies: Martyrs and Ascetics as Doxological Disciples." *Annual of the Society of Christian Ethics*, January 1, 2000. http://epublications.marquette.edu/theo_fac/167.

Machen, Emily. *Women of Faith and Religious Identity in Fin-de-Siècle France*. Syracuse NY: Syracuse University Press, 2019.

Mack, Phyllis. *Heart Religion in the British Enlightenment: Gender and Emotion in Early Methodism*. New York: Cambridge University Press, 2008.

———. "Religion, Feminism, and the Problem of Agency: Reflections on Eighteenth-Century Quakerism." *Signs: Journal of Women in Culture and Society* 29, no. 1 (September 1, 2003): 149–77. https://doi.org/10.1086/375679.

Magnien, Aimée G. *Canivets de la collection Gabriel Magnien*. Lyon: Self-published, 1970.

Mahmood, Saba. *Politics of Piety: The Islamic Revival and the Feminist Subject*. Princeton NJ: Princeton University Press, 2012.

Mainardi, Patricia. *Another World: Nineteenth-Century Illustrated Print Culture*. New Haven CT: Yale University Press, 2017.

———. *Husbands, Wives and Lovers: Marriage and Its Discontents in Nineteenth-Century France*. New Haven CT: Yale University Press, 2003.

Mallès de Beaulieu, Madame. *Contes d'une mère à sa fille*. 2nd ed. Vol. 1. Paris: P. Blanchard, 1820.

Mandrou, Robert. *De la culture populaire aux XVIIème et XVIIIème siècles: La Bibliothèque bleue de Troyes*. Paris: Imago, 2000.

Marcoin, Francis. *Librairie de jeunesse et littérature industrielle au XIXe siècle*. Paris: Champion, 2006.

Marcoin, Francis, and Christian Chelebourg. *La litterature de jeunesse*. Paris: Armand Colin, 2007.

Maréchal, Sylvain. *Catéchisme du curé Meslier*. EDHIS, 1790.

Margadant, Jo Burr. *The New Biography: Performing Femininity in Nineteenth-Century France*. Berkeley: University of California Press, 2001.

Margrave, Christie. *Writing the Landscape : Exposing Nature in French Women's Fiction 1789? 1815*. Cambridge, U.K.: Legenda, 2018.

Marion, Jean-Luc. *The Crossing of the Visible*. Palo Alto: Stanford University Press, 2004.

Marso, Lori J. "Defying Fraternity: Woman as Citizen in Germaine de Stael's Corinne, or Italy." *Women's Studies* 28, no. 6 (December 1999): 645–74.

Martin, Celine (Sister Genevieve of the Holy Face). *The Mother of the Little Flower: The Sister of St. Therese Tells Us about Her Mother*. Rockford IL: TAN Books, 2005.

Martin, Louis, and Zelie Martin. *A Call to a Deeper Love: The Family Correspondence of the Parents of Saint Therese of the Child Jesus*. New York: Alba House, 2011.

Martin, Louis-Aimé. *Education des mères de famille ou de la civilisation du genre humain par les femmes*. 2nd ed. Paris: Desrez, 1838.

Martin, Zélie, Louis Martin, Carmel de Lisieux, and Guy Gaucher. *Correspondance familiale*. Paris: Cerf, 2004.

Maryks, Robert A. *A Companion to Jesuit Mysticism*. Vol. 78. Leiden: Brill, 2017.

Maurin, Julia. *Vie nouvelle de Pauline-Marie Jaricot: Fondatrice de la Propagation de la foi et du rosaire vivant*. Paris: V. Palmé, 1892.

Mayeur, Jean-Marie, Charles Pietri, André Vauchez, and M. Venard. *Histoire du christianisme*. Vol. 12, *Guerres mondiales et totalitarismes, 1914–1958*. Paris: Desclée, 1995.

McCartin, James P. "The Sacred Heart of Jesus, Thérèse of Lisieux, and the Transformation of U.S. Catholic Piety, 1865–1940." *U.S. Catholic Historian* 25, no. 2 (2007): 53–67.

McMahon, Darrin M. *Enemies of the Enlightenment: The French Counter-Enlightenment and the Making of Modernity*. New York: Oxford University Press, 2002.

McManners, John. *Church and Society in Eighteenth-Century France*. Vol. 1, *The Clerical Establishment and Its Social Ramification*. Oxford: Clarendon Press, 1999.

Melzer, Sara E., and Leslie W. Rabine, eds. *Rebel Daughters: Women and the French Revolution*. New York: Oxford University Press, 1992.

Merton, Thomas. *The Seven Storey Mountain*. Boston: Houghton Mifflin Harcourt, 1999.

Michelet, Jules. *Du prêtre, de la femme, de la famille*. Paris: Comptoir des Imprimeurs-Unis, 1845.

——— . *Du prêtre, de la femme, de la famille par J. Michelet*. Paris: Hachette, 1845.

———. *Le prêtre, la femme et la famille*. Chamerot, 1862.

———. *Love: ("L'amour.")*. New York: Rudd & Carleton, 1859.

———. *Priests, Women, and Families*. Translated by C. Cocks. London: Longman, Brown, Green, and Longmans, 1845.

———. *Priests, Women, and Families*. Longman, Brown, Green, and Longmans, 1846.

———. *Woman (La Femme)*. New York: Rudd & Carleton, 1866.

Michelet, Jules A., and Edgar Quinet. *Des Jésuites*. 1843.

Mills, Hazel. "'Saintes Soeurs' and 'Femmes Fortes': Alternative Accounts of the Route to Womanly Civic Virtue, and the History of French Feminism." In *Wollstonecraft's Daughters: Womanhood in England and France, 1780–1920*, edited by Clarissa Campbell Orr, 135–50. Manchester: Manchester University Press, 1996.

Mitchell, Harvey. "Resistance to the Revolution in Western France." *Past & Present* 63, no. 1 (May 1, 1974): 94–131. https://doi.org/10.1093/past/63.1.94.

Mitzman, Arthur. "Michelet and Social Romanticism: Religion, Revolution, Nature." *Journal of the History of Ideas* 57, no. 4 (1996): 659–82. https://doi.org/10.2307/3654087.

Moers, Ellen. *Literary Women*. New York: Doubleday, 1976.

Mohr, Sr Marie Helen. *St. Philomena: Powerful with God*. Charlotte NC: TAN Books, 1953.

Monaque, Antoine. "L'illustration dans les abécédaires imprimés par les Deckherr à Porrentruy et Montbéliard (1810–1860)." *Bibliothèque de l'École des Chartes* 158, no. 1 (2000): 151–67.

Mongin, Hélène. *Louis et Zélie Martin: Les saints de l'ordinaire*. Paris: Editions de l'Emmanuel, 2008.

Montfort-Howard, Catherine. *Literate Women and the French Revolution of 1789*. Birmingham AL: Summa, 1994.

Mooney, Catherine M. *Philippine Duchesne: A Woman with the Poor*. New York: Paulist Press, 1990.

Moses, Claire Goldberg. *French Feminism in the 19th Century*. Buffalo: State University of New York Press, 1985.

Muchembled, Robert. *Culture populaire et culture des élites dans la France moderne*. Baton Rouge: Louisiana State University Press, 1985.

Muller, Eugène. *La morale en action par l'histoire*. Paris: Hetzel, 1881.

Munkácsy, Mihály. *Christ before Pilate*. Paris: C. Sedelmeyer, 1886.

Naïdenoff, Georges. *Pauline Jaricot*. Paris: Médiaspaul, 1986.

Neal, Diana. "The Beautiful Death of Thérèse of Lisieux and the Sufferings of the Tubercular Self." *New Blackfriars* 78, no. 915 (1997): 218–29.

Neill, Thomas Patrick. *They Lived the Faith: Great Lay Leaders of Modern Times.* Milwaukee: Bruce, 1951.

Nodier, Charles. *Œuvres de Charles Nodier.* Lorme: Eugène Renduel, 1820.

Nongbri, Brent. *Before Religion: A History of a Modern Concept.* New Haven CT: Yale University Press, 2015.

Notice sur Sainte Philomène, vièrge et martyre et neuvaine en son honneur. Lyon: J. M. Barret, 1839.

Nouvel alphabet de la vie des saints. Montbéliard: Deckherr frères, 1845.

Offen, Karen. *European Feminisms, 1700–1950: A Political History.* Palo Alto: Stanford University Press, 1999.

Ogden, Emily. *Credulity: A Cultural History of US Mesmerism.* Chicago: University of Chicago Press, 2018.

Olier, Jean-Jacques. *Catéchisme chrétien pour la vie intérieure.* Rusand, 1822.

———. *Catéchisme de la vie intérieure.* Paris: Gaume, 1835.

Outram, Dorinda. "Le langage mâle de la vertu: Women and the Discourse of the French Revolution." In *The Social History of Language,* edited by Peter Burke and Roy Porter. Cambridge: Cambridge University Press, 1987.

Paisant, Chantal. *Litanie pour une nonne défunte.* Paris: Cerf, 2003.

Parent-Lardeur, Françoise. *Les cabinets de lecture: La lecture publique à Paris sous la Restauration.* Paris: Payot, 1982.

———. *Lire à Paris au temps de Balzac: Les cabinets de lecture à Paris, 1815–1830.* Paris: Éd. de l'École des Hautes Études en Sciences Sociales, 1981.

Paskow, Jacqueline Merriam. "Rethinking Madame Bovary's Motives for Committing Suicide." *Modern Language Review* 100, no. 2 (April 1, 2005): 323–39.

Pasture, Patrick, Jan Art, and Thomas Buerman, eds. *Gender and Christianity in Modern Europe: Beyond the Feminization Thesis.* KADOC Studies on Religion, Culture and Society. Leuven: Leuven University Press, 2012.

Paulmier, Abbé. *Le chrétien de l'évangile par opposition au chrétien du jour.* Paris: Gaume, 1841.

Peel, Ellen. "Contradictions of Form and Feminism in *Corinne ou l'Italie.*" *Essays in Literature* 14, no. 2 (Fall 1987): 281–98.

Pellegrin, Nicole. "Les vertus de 'l'ouvrage': Recherches sur la féminisation des travaux d'aiguille (XVIe–XVIIIe siècles)." *Revue d'histoire moderne et contemporaine (1954–)* 46, no. 4 (1999): 747–69.

Pérennès, François Marie. *Dictionnaire de biographie chrétienne, présentant la vie . . .* Self-published, 1851.

Pérez, Ashley Hope. "Against 'Écriture Féminine': Flaubert's Narrative Aggression in 'Madame Bovary.'" *French Forum* 38, no. 3 (2013): 31–47.

Petitot, Hyacinthe. *Sainte Thérèse de Lisieux: Une renaissance spirituelle*. Paris: Édition de la Revue des jeunes, 1952.

Pettegree, Andrew, and Matthew Hall. "The Reformation and the Book: A Reconsideration." *Historical Journal* 47, no. 4 (2004): 785–808.

Piat, Stéphane-Joseph. *The Story of a Family: The Home of St. Thérèse of Lisieux (The Little Flower)*. Charlotte NC: TAN Books, 1994.

Pinker, Steven. *Enlightenment Now: The Case for Reason, Science, Humanism, and Progress*. New York: Viking, 2018.

Pirotte, Jean. "Images de dévotion du XV siècle à nos jours: Introduction à l'étude d'un 'média.'" In *Imagiers de Paradis*. Bastogne, Belgium: Musée en Piconrue, 1990.

————. "Les images de dévotion, témoins de la mentalité d'une époque, 1840–1965." *Revue d'histoire de la spiritualité* 50 (1974): 479–505.

————. "L'imagerie de dévotion aux XIXème et XXème siècles et la société ecclésiale." In *L'image et la production du sacré: Actes du colloque de Strasbourg, 20–21 janvier 1988*, 233–49. Paris: Méridiens Klincksieck, 1991.

Popiel, Jennifer J. *Rousseau's Daughters: Domesticity, Education, and Autonomy in Modern France*. Durham: University of New Hampshire Press, 2008.

Poupelier, Claude-Amand-Napoléon. *Abrégé de la vie de Sainte Philomène: Suivi d'une notice sur le pèlerinage de Sainte Philomène a Neuville-sur-Seine (Aube)*. Troyes: Anner-André, 1854.

Priest, Robert D. "Reading, Writing, and Religion in Nineteenth-Century France: The Popular Reception of Renan's *Life of Jesus*." *Journal of Modern History* 86, no. 2 (2014): 258–94. https://doi.org/10.1086/675502.

Pucci, Suzanne R. "Snapshots of Family Intimacy in the French Eighteenth Century: The Case of *Paul et Virginie*." *Studies in Eighteenth-Century Culture* 37, no. 1 (May 15, 2008): 89–118.

Quantin, Henri, and Alice Quantin. *Zélie et Louis Martin: Les saints de l'escalier*. Paris: Cerf, 2004.

Racaut, Luc. *Hatred in Print: Catholic Propaganda and Protestant Identity during the French Wars of Religion*. New York: Routledge, 2017.

Rearick, Charles. "Symbol, Legend, and History: Michelet as Folklorist-Historian." *French Historical Studies* 7, no. 1 (1971): 72–92. https://doi.org/10.2307/286107.

Records of the American Catholic Historical Society of Philadelphia. Vol. 13. Philadelphia: American Catholic Historical Society of Philadelphia, 1902.

Reddy, William M. *The Invisible Code: Honor and Sentiment in Postrevolutionary France, 1814–1848*. Berkeley: University of California Press, 1997.

————. *The Navigation of Feeling: A Framework for the History of Emotions*. New York: Cambridge University Press, 2001.

Renneville, Sophie. *Correspondance de deux petites filles: Ouvrage propre à former de bonne heure les enfans au style épistolaire*. Paris: Belin, 1811.

Richards, I. A. *Practical Criticism*. London: Kegan, Paul, Trench, 1930.

Robinson, Philip. "Virginie's Fatal Modesty: Thoughts on Bernardin de Saint-Pierre and Rousseau." *Journal for Eighteenth-Century Studies* 5, no. 1 (March 1, 1982): 35–48.

Robo, Etienne. *Two Portraits of St. Therese of Lisieux*. Chicago: H. Regnery, 1955.

Rogers, Rebecca. *From the Salon to the Schoolroom: Educating Bourgeois Girls in Nineteenth-Century France*. University Park: Pennsylvania State University Press, 2008.

Rosenbaum-Dondaine, Catherine. *L'image de piété en France, 1814–1914*. Paris: Musée Galerie de la Seita, 1984.

Rousseau, Jean-Jacques. *Emile; or, On Education*. Translated by Allan Bloom. New York: Basic Books, 1979.

Sackville-West, Vita. *The Eagle and the Dove: A Study in Contrasts: St. Teresa of Avila, St. Therese of Lisieux*. New York: Doubleday, Doran, 1944.

————. *The Eagle and the Dove*. London: Bello, 2012.

Saint-Jérôme. *Mois du Sacré-Coeur de Jésus*. Poussielgue-Rusand, 1840.

Saint-Pierre, Bernardin de. *Oeuvres complètes: Paul et Virginie. La chaumière indienne. Le Café de Surate. Voyages en Silésie. Eloge de mon ami. Voyages de Codrus. Le vieux paysan polonais. Parallèle de Voltaire et de J.-J. Rousseau. Des caractères hiéroglyphiques et du tribunal d'équité en Egypte*. Paris: Armand-Aubrée, 1834.

Samuels, Maurice. "Illustrated Historiography and the Image of the Past in Nineteenth-Century France." *French Historical Studies* 26, no. 2 (2003): 253–80. https://doi.org/10.1215/00161071-26-2-253.

Samuels, Shirley. *The Culture of Sentiment: Race, Gender, and Sentimentality in 19th-Century America*. Edited by Shirley Samuels. New York: Oxford University Press, 1992.

Santonja, Blanca. "Mary Berry and Her Religious Sensibilities." Unpublished, 2017.

Savart, Claude. "A la recherche de l''art' dit de Saint-Sulpice." *Revue d'histoire de la spiritualité* 52 (1976): 265–82.

Schloesser, Stephen. *Jazz Age Catholicism: Mystic Modernism in Postwar Paris, 1919–1933*. Toronto ON: University of Toronto Press, 2005.

Schmitt, Jean-Claude. *Les saints et les stars: Le texte hagiographique dans la culture populaire: Études*. Paris: Editions Beauchesne, 1983.

Schor, Naomi. "Triste Amérique: Atala and the Postrevolutionary Construction of Woman." In Melzer and Rabine, *Rebel Daughters*, 139–56.

Schwartz, Vanessa R., and Jeannene M. Przyblyski. *The Nineteenth-Century Visual Culture Reader*. London: Psychology Press, 2004.

Scott, Joan Wallach. *Sex and Secularism*. Princeton NJ: Princeton University Press, 2017.

Scott, Michael. *Struggle for the Soul of the French Novel*. Washington DC: Catholic University of America Press, 1989.

Seeley, Paul. "O Sainte Mère: Liberalism and the Socialization of Catholic Men in Nineteenth-Century France." *Journal of Modern History* 70, no. 4 (December 1, 1998): 862–91.

Sepinwall, Alyssa Goldstein. *The Abbé Grégoire and the French Revolution: The Making of Modern Universalism*. Berkeley: University of California Press, 2005.

Serna, Pierre. *La République des girouettes: Une anomalie politique: La France de l'extrême centre*. Seyssel: Editions Champ Vallon, 2005.

Simon, Aloïs. *Le cardinal Sterckx et son temps (1792–1867)*. 2 vols. Wetteren: Scaldis, 1950.

Smart, Annie. *Citoyennes: Women and the Ideal of Citizenship in Eighteenth-Century France*. Newark: University of Delaware Press, 2013.

Smith, Bonnie G. *Ladies of the Leisure Class: The Bourgeoises of Northern France in the Nineteenth Century*. Princeton NJ: Princeton University Press, 1981.

Smith, Terry. *Impossible Presence: Surface and Screen in the Photogenic Era*. Chicago: University of Chicago Press, 2001.

Spaas, Lieve. "*Paul et Virginie*: The Shipwreck of an Idyll." *Eighteenth-Century Fiction* 13, no. 2 (2001): 315–24. https://doi.org/10.1353/ecf.2001.0043.

Spencer, Philip Herbert. *Politics of Belief in Nineteenth-Century France: Lacordaire, Michon, Veuillot*. New York City: Grove Press, 1953.

Spininger, Dennis J. "The Paradise Setting of Chateaubriand's *Atala*." PMLA 89, no. 3 (1974): 530–36.

Staël, Anne-Louise-Germaine de. *Corinne or Italy*. Translated by Avriel H. Goldberger. New Brunswick NJ: Rutgers University Press, 1987.

———. *Corinne; ou, L'Italie*. Paris: Victor Lecou, 1853.

———. *De l'Allemagne*. Paris: Didot Frères, 1845.

———. *Des circonstances actuelles qui peuvent terminer la Révolution et des principes qui doivent fonder la République en France*. Edited by Lucia Omacini. Paris: Librairie Droz, 1979.

———. *Oeuvres complètes*. Paris: Firmin Didot, 1838.

Stendhal. *The Red and the Black: A Chronicle of 1830*. Translated by Horace B. Samuel. London: Kegan Paul, Trench, Trubner, 1916.

Stevenson-Moessner, Jeanne. "Elizabeth Cady Stanton, Reformer to Revolutionary: A Theological Trajectory." *Journal of the American Academy of Religion* 62, no. 3 (1994): 673–97.

Stewart, Joan Hinde. *Gynographs: French Novels by Women, 1750–1800*. Lincoln: University of Nebraska Press, 1993.

Surkis, Judith. *Sexing the Citizen: Morality and Masculinity in France, 1870–1920*. Ithaca NY: Cornell University Press, 2011.

Tackett, Timothy. *The Coming of the Terror in the French Revolution*. Cambridge MA: Belknap Press, 2015.

Taveneaux, Evelyne. *La piété en dentelles: Les images de dévotion et leurs dentelles, 1830–1910*. Nancy: Presses universitaires de Nancy, 1992.

Taylor, B., and S. Knott. *Women, Gender and Enlightenment*. Springer, 2005.

Taylor, Charles. *A Secular Age*. Cambridge MA: Harvard University Press, 2007.

Taylor, Thérèse. "Images of Sanctity: Photography of Saint Bernadette of Lourdes and Saint Thérèse of Lisieux." *Nineteenth-Century Contexts* 27, no. 3 (September 1, 2005): 269–92. https://doi.org/10.1080/08905490500416229.

Tesnière, Albert. *Somme de la prédication eucharistique: La sainte communion*. Tourcoing: Bureau de la Revue eucharistique, 1904.

Thérèse, Soeur Geneviève de la Sainte-Face et de Sainte. *La mère de Sainte Thérèse de l'Enfant-Jésus, 1831–1877: Souvenir filial*. Lisieux: Carmel de Lisieux, 1954.

Treadwell, James. *Autobiographical Writing and British Literature, 1783–1834*. New York: Oxford University Press, 2005.

Tricot, Claude, and Raymond Zambelli. *Le mariage et la transmission par la famille, les parents de Thérèse de Lisieux dans la cité d'aujourd'hui*. Paris: Guibert, 2004.

Trouille, Mary Seidman. *Sexual Politics in the Enlightenment: Women Writers Read Rousseau*. Albany: State University of New York Press, 1997.

Turgis, Vve. *Catalogue des estampes et lithographies publiées par Vve Turgis, éditeur*. Paris: Lacrampe, 1844.

———. *Catalogue des estampes et lithographies publiées par Vve Turgis, éditeur*. Paris: De Soye et Cie, 1851.

Turin, Yvonne. *Femmes et religieuses au XIXe siècle: Le féminisme "en religion."* Paris: Nouvelle Cité, 1989.

Ulrich, Laurel Thatcher. "Vertuous Women Found: New England Ministerial Literature, 1668–1735." *American Quarterly* 28 (1976): 20–40.

Valantasis, Richard. *The Making of the Self: Ancient and Modern Asceticism*. Eugene OR: Wipf, 2008.

Vallois, Marie-Claire. "Exotic Femininity and the Rights of Man: Paul et Virginie and Atala, or the Revolution in Stasis." In Melzer and Rabine, *Rebel Daughters*, 178–97.

Vallois, Marie-Claire, and Betsy Wing. "Voice as Fossil Madame de Staël's *Corinne, or Italy*: An Archaeology of Feminine Discourse." *Tulsa Studies in Women's Literature* 6, no. 1 (1987): 47–60. https://doi.org/10.2307/464159.

Van de Walle, Etienne. *The Female Population of France in the Nineteenth Century: A Reconstruction of 82 Départements*. Princeton NJ: Princeton University Press, 1974.

Van Kley, Dale K. "Christianity as Casualty and Chrysalis of Modernity: The Problem of Dechristianization in the French Revolution." *American Historical Review* 108, no. 4 (October 1, 2003): 1081–104. https://doi.org/10.1086/ahr/108.4.1081.

Van Ossalaer, Tine. "'From That Moment On, I Was a Man!': Images of the Catholic Male in the Sacred Heart Devotion." In *Gender and Christianity in Modern Europe: Beyond the Feminization Thesis*, edited by Jan de Maeyer, Leen Van Molle, Tine Van Osselaer, and Vincent Viane, 121–35. Leuven: Leuven University Press, 2012.

Vattimo, Gianni. *After Christianity*. Translated by Luca D'Isanto. New York: Columbia University Press, 2002.

Verhoeven, Timothy. "'A Perfect Jesuit in Petticoats': The Curious Figure of the Female Jesuit." *Journal of Jesuit Studies* 2, no. 4 (September 30, 2015): 624–40.

Verjus, Anne, and Denise Davidson. *Le roman conjugal: Chroniques de la vie familiale à l'époque de la Révolution et de l'Empire*. Seyssel, France: Champ Vallon, 2011.

Vincent-Buffault, Anne. *The History of Tears: Sensibility and Sentimentality in France*. New York: Macmillan, 1991.

Vinken, Barbara. "Wounds of Love: Modern Devotion according to Michelet." *Clio* 36, no. 2 (2007): 155–76.

Vircondelet, Alain. *Le monde merveilleux des images pieuses*. Paris: Hermé, 1988.

Waddy, Helena. *Images of Faith: Expressionism, Catholic Folk Art, and the Industrial Revolution*. Athens: University of Georgia Press, 1991.

Walch, Agnès. *La spiritualité conjugale dans le catholicisme français: XVIe–XXe siècle*. Paris: Cerf, 2002.

Walker, Lesley H. *A Mother's Love: Crafting Feminine Virtue in Enlightenment France*. Lewisburg PA: Bucknell University Press, 2008.

Waller, Margaret. "Being René, Buying Atala: Alienated Subjects and Decorative Objects in Postrevolutionary France." In Melzer and Rabine, *Rebel Daughters*, 157–77.

———. *The Male Malady: Fictions of Impotence in the French Romantic Novel*. New Brunswick NJ: Rutgers University Press, 1993.

Wandelaincourt, Antoine-Hubert. *L'ami des moeurs, de l'état, et de la religion: Ouvrage dans lequel on établit les principes propres à perfectionner l'humanité et à rendre les etats florissants, en dirigeant vers le bien l'homme, considéré soit indiv-iduellement, soit en société, soit relativement à la religion.* Self-published, 1803.

Wang, Ban. "Writing, Self, and the Other: Chateaubriand and His Atala." *French Forum* 22, no. 2 (1997): 133–48.

Ward, Graham. "How Literature Resists Secularity." *Literature and Theology* 24, no. 1 (2010): 73–88.

Wiedemeier, Kurt. *La religion de Bernardin de Saint-Pierre.* Fribourg: Éditions Universitaires, 1986.

Wilkinson, Kate. *Women and Modesty in Late Antiquity.* New York: Cambridge University Press, 2015.

Williams, Abigail. *The Social Life of Books: Reading Together in the Eighteenth-Century Home.* New Haven CT: Yale University Press, 2017.

Wolff, Cynthia Griffin. "Emily Dickinson, Elizabeth Cady Stanton, and the Task of Discovering a Usable Past." *Massachusetts Review* 30, no. 4 (1989): 629–44.

Worley, Sharon. "The Gentle Art of Persuasion: Ethical Aesthetics and Themes of Liberty and Nationalism in Germaine de Staël's Corinne and Political Pro-paganda during the Napoleonic Wars." *International Journal of the Humanities* 6, no. 3 (June 2008): 175–82.

Woshinsky, Barbara R. *Imagining Women's Conventual Spaces in France, 1600–1800: The Cloister Disclosed.* New York: Routledge, 2016.

Würtz, (Abbé) Jean Wendel. *Supersititions et prestiges des philosophes ou les démonolâtres du siècle des lumières.* Lyon, 1817.

Yver, Colette. *Marie-Pauline de Jésus Christ.* Paris: Editions Spes, 1937.

Index

Italicized figure numbers refer to illustrations following page 96.

Bossuet, 42
Bouasse-Lebel, 98, 127, 131–34, 203, 216,
  260n149; publications of, *figs. 1–3,
  6, 10, 11, 13, 15, 17–20*
Bourbons, 32
Brezé, M. Armand de, 71–72
Brochier, Father, 155
Browning, Elizabeth Barrett, 96

Caen, 56, 111
Calhoun, Craig, 10
Calvinism, 53, 57, 58
Cana, 38
canivets, 104, 107, 108, 117, 203, 255n33,
  255n34
Carmelites, 54, 107, 147, 224, 225
Carron, Guy-Toussaint-Julien, 43–45,
  48, 53, 58, 59, 69, 203, 243n88
Catechism for the Interior Life, 40
Catechism of the Diocese of Poitiers, 39
*Catechism of the Diocese of Saint-
  Claude*, 39
*Catechism or Familiar Instruction on
  the Principal Points of the Christian
  Religion*, 33–34
catechisms: content of, 32–36, 240n20,
  240n26; influence on popular literature, 43, 44, 47–48, 174; on marriage, 37–41, 205; as prizes, 272n29;
  publication and promotion of, 17,
  32–34, 153, 240n24; women's and
  girls' reading of, 24, 31, 60, 67. *See
  also* education; literature
Catherine (saint), 212
Catholic Church: calendars of, 116;
  on celibacy, 55, 60, 120, 274n58;
  confiscation of property of, 147;
  control of reading material, 30, 32;
  conversions to, 53, 57, 58; Doc-

tors of, 3, 225, 277n18; femininity
  of, 5–8, 15–17, 29, 233n41; history
  of education in, 137; images in, 1,
  100, 106, 117; importance of catechisms in, 32–36; Jaricot family's
  work for, 170–71, 174; literature
  supporting, 46–47, 138, 170, 175,
  176, 188, 212; practices in Revolutionary era, 17–19, 25, 26, 121, 129–
  30, 144, 149, 153, 180–81, 199, 200,
  201, 209–10; Sacred Heart of Jesus
  devotion in, 4; saints defined by,
  102; seventeenth-century ideals of,
  42–43; teachings about laws of, 38;
  threats to, 17, 124, 128, 131, 152, 223,
  228; women's roles in, xiii, 14, 17, 23,
  124, 169, 170, 197, 231n2; workers'
  commune for, 191
Cecilia (saint), 122, 123
celibacy: as condition of faith, 202, 228;
  in literature, 38, 39, 44, 48, 49, 55, 58,
  59, 76, 78, 83, 84, 96; and married
  life, 50, 59, 203, 207; objections to,
  60, 130, 142–43; religious and political views of, 19, 140, 195, 197; of
  saints and martyrs, 120, 217; widows'
  commitment to, 51; women's preference for, xiii, 22, 55–57, 139, 141, 159,
  160, 166, 171, 185, 187, 198, 201–2, 206.
  See also sexuality; virginity
Certeau, Michel de, 31, 81
Chantal, Baron of, 49
Chantal, Jeanne Françoise (saint), 42,
  49, 147; biography of, 212; devotional lifestyle of, 52, 54; educational
  model of, 144; interpretation of
  Sacred Heart, 128; widowhood of, 51
Chantal, Mother Marie de: as role
  model, 56

Chardin, 110

charity: Martin family's works of, 213; Pauline Jaricot's works of, 170, 174, 183, 188, 190, 191; promotion through games, 114; promotion through literature, 71–72; Rose-Philippine Duchesne's provision of, 149, 150; spiritual growth through, 42, 44; women's commitment to, 50, 53, 56, 165, 272n33. *See also* poverty

Charles Letaille, 121, 127

Charles X, 143

Chartres, 210

chastity. *See* celibacy

Chateaubriand, François-René: associates of, 45; exile of, 83; influence of, 25, 64, 79, 80, 81, 180; on influence of images, 101; on influence of *Paul et Virginie*, 75–76

children: abandonment by mothers, 52–53; as consumers, 200–201, 214–15; education of, 36–37, 56, 109–10, 129, 137, 153, 263n62; experiences of Revolutionary era, 169; family obligations of, 160, 217–18; games for, 110–12, 114–16; holy cards distributed to, 117–18; literature intended for, 68–70; as object of marriage, 39–40, 205–6, 207; portrayals in literature, 74, 75; Zélie Guérin Martin's devotion to, 208–9, 213–15, 217

China, 59

Christianity: association with sentimentality, 66, 80; conversions to, 55, 57, 58, 172; education about, 34–35, 137, 201; feminine ideals of, 120; in French culture, 25, 172; heroic models of, 212–13; political conno-

tations of, 90, 123, 129, 132, 133, 169, 180–81; promotion through literature, 47, 75–76, 81, 84, 88, 94, 96; sacrifice and suffering for, 161, 163, 164, 195, 210–11, 213, 216–17

Christmas (1886), 225

"Chronicle of 1830" (Stendhal), 141

Civil Constitution (1791), 32

Claire d'Albe (Cottin), 25, 86–87, 91, 183

clergy: attitudes toward Sulpician art, 125–26; authority over women, 21, 140; distribution of holy cards, 117; influence on women, 29, 30, 129, 134, 157–58, 167; literature intended for, 44; loyalty oaths of, 17, 44; married men as, 51; objections to missionary society, 173; oversight of publications, 32; Pauline Jaricot's cooperation with, 170, 172, 179; population in France, 165; purchase of religious images, 131; on religious instruction, 33; during Revolutionary era, xi, xii, 18, 149, 151, 175, 199, 201, 243n89; violence against, 210. *See also* religious vocations

Cloistered Victims (Monvel), 140

Cohen, Margaret, 11, 62, 74

Coleman, Charly, 9

Comédie Française, 183

Commune, 210

Communion. *See* Eucharist

Concordat of 1801, 18, 33, 165, 199

Congregation of the Visitation: criticism of, 167; Duchesne family at monastery of, 144–47; foundress of, 52, 54; Léonie Martin's desire to join, 217; Marie-Louise Guérin with, 202, 204, 206; Martin children's education under, 212, 215;

Congregation of the Visitation (*cont.*)
restoration of monastery, 154, 155;
Revolution's effect on, 148; and
Sacred Heart devotion, 156. *See
also* nuns
Constantine, 101
consumer culture: images in, 98, 108–
10, 116–19, 125, 256n57, 257n85; read-
ing in, 31, 64; sentimental ideals of,
64, 97, 98, 122, 125, 224, 228; wom-
en's religious life within, xiii, 27, 121,
199, 217; Zélie Guérin Martin's par-
taking of, 200–201, 214–19. *See also*
modern world
convents, 112, 140–42, 148, 154, 189. *See
also* nuns
Corinne (Staël), 25, 89, 90–96
Corinthians, 39, 195
Correspondence of Two Little Girls
(Renneville), 69
Cottin, Sophie, 25, 85–86
Coudrin, Pierre, 201
Council of Trent, 6, 16, 38
Counter Reformation, 100
Couvin, 100
Curé d'Ars. *See* Vianney, Jean (saint)
Curtis, Sarah, 8, 231n2, 234n48

Dames de la Miséricorde, 263n45
Daughters of Charity, 54, 202
Daughters of Faith, 156
Daumier, Honoré, 30
death: absence of religion in, 218–19; of
children during Revolutionary era,
169; exile as form of, 81, 87–88; as
game subject, 111, 113; in literature,
81, 82, 87, 90, 92, 94–96; Rose-
Philippine Duchesne's acceptance

of, 149; symbols of, 117. *See also*
martyrdom
Deists, 144
Denby, David, 11
Denis (saint), 255n40
dentelle mécaniques, 107
Desfeuilles, 101
Diocletian, 120, 122, 123
divorce, 113. *See also* marriage
Doctors of the Church, 3, 225, 277n18
Dogmatic and Moral Catechism, 39–40,
47, 205
Dominicans, 188
Dopter, 109
Dosithée, Sr. *See* Guérin, Marie-Louise
(Elise)
Duchesne, Amélie, 145, 150–51
Duchesne, Charlotte-Euphrosine, 145,
158–62
Duchesne, Pierre-François, 143, 144,
146, 147, 149, 150, 151, 264n79
Duchesne, Rose-Euphrosine (Perier), 144
Duchesne, Rose-Philippine (saint):
ambitions of, 147–48; care of family
members, 149–50, 158–61; comparison to Pauline Jaricot, 170,
171, 175, 180; comparison to Zélie
Martin, 197, 205, 218, 219, 276n126;
devotional lifestyle of, 4, 137–39,
143–47, 151–52, 156–57, 160–62, 195,
221, 228; education of children, 153;
influences on, 147; missionary trip
to North America, 137–38, 261n3,
261n6; order of, 20, 261n11; restoration of convent, 154–55; visits to
imprisoned, 263n45; writings of,
26, 139, 195, 261n9
Dupanloup, Félix, 125, 134

Ecclesiastes, 46
Edgeworth, Maria, 69
Edict of Nantes, 42
Edifying Lives of Young Girls (Carron), 46
education: as game subject, 115; through images, 100, 102, 110–12, 117, 118; of marriageable women, 145; mothers responsible for, 129, 198; for poor, 172; reading material for, 68–74, 77–78; during Revolutionary era, 152, 200, 201; Rose-Philippine Duchesne's role in, 137, 147, 153, 158, 160; of women religious, 130, 137, 141–42, 144, 201–2. *See also* catechisms
England, 44, 57, 91, 92, 94
Enlightenment, 19, 32, 140, 178
Epinal, 109, 110, 121
Eucharist: association with Sacred Heart, *fig. 14*, 174, 178, 185, 186, 187, 192, 201, 267n27; images of, 100, 102, 105, 133; marriage as priority over, 53. *See also* First Communion
Evenings of Adolescence, 69

families: Christian ideals in, 213; correspondence within, 139, 208; financial support from, 154; as game subject, 112, 113, 114; in literature, 47, 55, 63, 71, 73, 85, 140; love and marriage in, 204–5, 208–9, 261n5; religious instruction in, 36; religious practices of during Revolutionary era, 17–18, 148; saints' roles in, 121, 122; separation from, 26, 52–54, 57–58, 122–23, 138, 141, 144–47, 150–51, 157, 159–66, 184; social mobility of, 200; women's

role in, 21, 22, 31, 49, 50, 142, 143, 145, 149–51, 158–59, 166, 169, 195; Zélie Guérin Martin's devotion to, 208–9, 216–17. *See also* marriage; motherhood
feminism, 8–9, 234n49
First Communion, 36, 41, 144, 145, 158, 240n26. *See also* Eucharist
Fitch, Marie-Anne, 57–58
Flaubert, Gustave, 24, 61, 64–65, 67, 75, 273n49
Fleury, Claude, 34–36, 37, 40, 47, 203, 272n29
flowers, 104, 111. *See also* lilies; pansies; roses
Forced Vows (Gouges), 140
Ford, Caroline, 120, 222, 228
Fosse Moisson, Anne-Jeanne Victoire de la, 56
Fouilloux, Étienne, 231n2
Fourvière, 191
France: attitudes toward religion in, xi, 231n2; Carmelites introduced in, 54; children's experiences in, 169; feminism in, 8; idioms of sentimentality in, 13–14, 132; image production and consumption in, 98–100, 103, 110, 119–20, 131; Marie-Félice des Ursins in, 49; Marie Guyard's departure from, 53; missionary work in, 148, 152, 190, 201; post-Revolutionary Church in, 18, 129–30, 137, 175, 177, 180–81; postwar atonement in, 172, 175, 177, 181, 185, 226, 227; reading practices in, 42, 44, 62, 66–67, 188; religious images in, 104, 108, 109; religious instruction in, 33, 44–45; religious vocations in, 165, 166; Sacred Heart

France (*cont.*)
  devotion in, 128, 129; saints and martyrs in, 119, 122; social mobility in, 200; St. Thérèse esteemed in, 197; women's devotional work in, 6, 10, 14, 23; women's rejection of marriage in, 22, 25
Frances of Rome, 212
Franco-Prussian War, 210, 226, 227
French Restoration, 34, 86, 107, 200, 262n33
French Revolution: attitudes toward women during, 19, 81, 93; clerical opposition to, 43–44; divorce laws from, 113; effect on religious vocations, 148, 154, 169; effects on families, 143, 197, 199–200; as game subject, 110, 111; masculine emotions during, 5; popular literature during, 62, 83, 87, 88; religious images after, 117; religious instruction during and after, 35, 44, 137; religious practices during era of, xi, 17–18, 107, 128, 129, 144, 172, 176–77, 180–81, 201, 221; Rose-Philippine Duchesne's work during, 148–49, 263n42; social control after, 31, 32, 90; women's devotional work during and after, 6, 17, 22, 25, 139, 140, 141, 152, 165
The Friend of Adolescents (Berquin), 68–69

Gallican tradition, 33, 175
Game of Civility, 114
Game of Fortune, 114
Game of Life Stages, figs. 8–9, 113–14
Game of the Goose, 110–13

games, 110–17, 215
Gartland, Bishop, 131, 260n145
Gautier, Léon, 126
Gazette universelle de Lyon, 174
Genesis, 37
Geneva, 58
Genius of Christianity (Chateaubriand), 30, 64, 76, 79, 80, 82
Genlis, Stéphanie Félicité de, 68, 70, 87, 88
Géricault, Théodore, 108–9, 116, 127
Germany, 109, 255n34
Ghéon, Henri, 2, 3, 27
girls. *See* women and girls
girouettes, 200
Golden Legend, 102, 121
Gondy, Charlotte Marguerite de, 53
Gonzaga, Aloysius (saint), 105, 159, 164
Gospel, 59. *See also* Bible
Gouges, Olympe de, 140
Grâne, 148, 149, 151, 162
Greer, Allan, 59–60
Gregory XVI, Pope, 120, 189
Grenoble: criticism of Rose-Philippine Duchesne in, 155, 156, 157; Duchesne family in, 143, 145, 148, 149, 150, 162; religious education in, 144, 153; Rose-Philippine Duchesne's writings in, 139
Guérin, Céline, 208–9, 211, 215
Guérin, Isidore (brother of Zélie), 202, 208–9, 211, 215, 272n30
Guérin, Isidore (father of Zélie), 199, 200, 201, 208, 273n45
Guérin, Louise-Jeanne, 200, 272n25
Guérin, Marie-Louise (Elise) 201, 202, 204, 208, 273n45
Gutenberg, 100

Guyard, Marie (saint), 42, 51, 52–54, 138, 147–48

Habermas, Jurgen, 10, 11, 12
hagiographies: about Philomena, 119; images from, 102, 106; influence on women, 24, 31, 55, 59–60, 72, 225; intent of, 70, 71; popularity of, 42, 43; publication and promotion of, 32, 43; tone of, 26, 170, 174, 238n136, 239n137, 243n89
Harlay, Catherine de, 55
Harris, Ruth, 8
Harrison, Carol, xii, 9, 21, 231n2
Hazay, Jeanne Pinczon du, 48, 52
Helen (saint), 101, 117
Heller, Deborah, 95
Henrici, Catherine, *fig. 4*, 58, 59
heroism: in literature, 30, 59, 70, 71, 72; of married women and mothers, 52, 53, 195; of missionary work, 261n4; qualities of, 58, 59, 124, 218, 219; through self-abnegation, 54–55, 203; sentimentality associated with, 4, 122, 124, 209, 224, 228, 274n76; Thérèse's aspiration to, 225, 227, 228; women's identification with, 12, 13, 14, 23, 24, 26, 27, 169, 170, 171, 190, 212–13, 221
Historical Catechism (Fleury), 34–37, 40, 47
Hiu, Madam Candide, 59
holy cards, *figs. 6–7, 10–22*; connotations of, 106–7, 117–18, 133–35, 258n96; content of, 102–3, 255n23; decorative features of, 103–5, 107, 125; images on, 98, 105, 120, 127, 222, 223, 227; mass production of, 107–

8, 116, 117, 121, 188; sentimental style of, 131–32; of St. Philomena, *figs. 10–12*, 190
Holy Days, 23, 38, 56, 212
Holy Week, 94
Hopkins, David, 106, 109
Hotel-Dieu, 188, 271n125
Huysmans, Joris-Karl, 125–26, 232n4

images: decorative features of, 103–5, 125; influence of, 97, 117–19, 212; of Philomena, *figs. 10–12*, 121; proliferation of, 98–101, 107–8, 116, 119–20, 256n57; as signs of spirituality, 218–19; of St. Thérèse, *fig. 1*, 1–2, 115, 126, 222, 227, 278nn32–33; of suffering, exile, and martyrdom, *fig. 7*, 135; textual features of, 101–3, 131–32; of women and girls, 115
Imitation of Christ (Kempis), 103
Imperial Academy of Sciences, Arts, and Literature, 111
Imperial Army, 200
Imperial Catechism (Napoleon), 33, 240n24
Imperial government, 203
Incarnation, Marie de l'. *See* Guyard, Marie (saint)
Infinite Love in the Divine Eucharist (Jaricot), 170, 174–80, 185, 186, 188, 267n27
Instructive Game of Flowers, 111
Introduction to the Devout Life (Sales), 42
Isaac, 53, 242n59
Italy, 90–95, 119, 148, 188, 273n36. *See also* Mugnano, Italy; Naples
Izzo, Amanda, 9

Leo XIII, Pope, 170
Letaille, Charles, 121, 127, 134; publications of, *figs. 7, 12, 14, 16, 21, 22*
letter writing: of Euphrosine Jouve, 163–64; within families, 139, 207–8; by missionaries, 172; of Pauline Jaricot, 170, 188; of Rose-Philippine Duchesne, 150–51, 160, 162; as sentimental outlet for women, 12, 26; significance of, 195, 271n2; of Zélie Guérin Martin, 196, 198, 199, 207–8, 211–15. *See also* writing
The Life of the Venerable Mother Marie of the Incarnation, 147
lilies, 104, 111, 119, 121, 123. *See also* flowers; pansies; roses
Lisieux, 207, 208, 215. *See also* Thérèse (saint)
literature: forms of didactic, 69–70; as gift, 215; and images, 100–103, 106, 108, 109, 117, 118, 123–24, 127, 131–32, 255n23, 258n91; influence on women, 24, 29–31, 46–47, 59–60, 65–66, 183, 213, 242n73; Jouve and Duchesne families' interest in, 264n79; marriage and family in, 41, 115–16; "nonfiction," 70, 71; political implications of, 30, 31, 33, 35, 47, 77, 85, 89–90; popularity of spiritual, 42, 43, 44, 188, 212, 222; post-Revolutionary influence of, 24, 45, 174, 176, 177; publication of morally acceptable, 32, 63; religious vocational life in, 140–42, 170; self-improvement through, 67–68, 77–78, 212. *See also* Bible; catechisms; novels; writing
Literature Considered in Its Relation to Social Institutions (Staël), 63

lithography, 108–9, 116, 117
Little Ladies Lottery, 115
Little Lottery of Strengths and Weaknesses, 114–15
Lives of the Just among Christian Virgins (Carron), 46, 55
Lives of the Just in Ordinary Conditions (Carron), 243n88
Lives of the Just in the State of Marriage (Carron), 44, 46, 47, 48, 56, 59
Louisiana Territory, 137, 138, 261n3
Louis-Philippe (king of France), 143, 200
Lourdes grotto, 222
love: catechetical teachings about, 41–42, 241n52; as game subject, *fig. 9*, 113–15; language of, 167, 170; in Martin and Guérin families, 207–9; Pauline Jaricot's writing about, 180, 182, 184, 187, 192. *See also* marriage
Loyola, Ignatius (saint), 105. *See also* Jesuits
Lucy (saint), 255n40
Lumague, Marie, 51
Lutherans, 100
Lyon: clergy expelled from, 179; instability in, 148; Jaricot family in, 171; men's religious practices in, 239n1; Pauline Jaricot's life and work in, 26, 169, 175–76, 188, 191, 192, 271n125; Reparatices of the Heart of Jesus in, 172
Lyons, Martin, 30, 42

Mack, Phyllis, 8
Mâcon, bishop of, 19
Madame Bovary (Flaubert), 64–65, 75, 80, 273n49
Le Magasin Pittoresque, 109

Mahmood, Saba, 7, 9
Mahomet II, 58, 59
Malines, archbishop of, 118
Marchant, Jacques, 100
Marillac, Louise de (saint), 48, 52–54
marriage: attitudes toward, 19–25, 43, 51–55, 97, 120, 123, 138, 144, 162, 166, 171, 184–85, 190, 214, 217, 238n133, 261n5; Church's view of, 14, 37–41, 195–96, 205–6; devotional lifestyle within, 27, 49–51, 59, 197–99, 202–7; as game subject, *fig. 9*, 110, 112–15; images of, 98; Josephite, 207–8, 274n58; in literature, 25, 46–49, 55, 58, 63, 74, 84, 86–88, 140–41, 212; Rose-Philippine Duchesne resistance to, 145–46; Sacred Heart devotion as, 137, 161, 187; spirituality of, 16, 38–39, 42. *See also* families; love
Marso, Lori, 95
Martin, Fanie, 204
Martin, Léonie, 212, 217
Martin, Louis: business of, 27; charitable works of, 213, 216; family of, 199, 200; joking about wife's materialism, 214; marriage of, 204, 205, 206, 207, 242n61; sentimentality of, 207, 274n60
Martin, Louis-Aimé, 143
Martin, Marie, 214, 215–17, 272n33
Martin, Marie-Azélie (Zélie) Guérin: attitude toward suffering, 210–13, 216–17, 276n126; background of, 199–201, 272n25; business of, 203–4, 207–8, 272n30, 273n42, 273n45; death of, 207; devotional lifestyle of, 4, 196, 198, 212–13, 221, 228; education of, 201–2, 272n29; health of, 202, 208; letters of, 27, 196–97, 272n30;

marriage and family of, 203–9, 215–16, 222, 242n61; reading of, 212
Martin, Pauline, 210, 215, 217, 218
Martin, Pierre-François, 205
Martin, Thérèse. *See* Thérèse (saint)
martyrdom: as act of heroic piety, 24, 88, 122; images of, 135, 255n40; in literature, 58, 80–83, 89; missionary name suggestive of, 173; Rose-Philippine Duchesne's acceptance of, 149; women's identification with, 27, 120, 152, 166, 169, 170, 223. *See also* death
martyrs: bones of, 119; contemporary appeal of, 123, 124; images of, 101, 105, 106, 120, 121; during Revolution, 180; stories about, 138, 152, 181
Mary: feast days of, 212; images of, *fig. 6*, 100, 101, 102, 115, 131–32, 255n26; marriage of, 206, 274n58; prayers to, *fig. 18*, 203, 210; as spiritual mother and protector, *fig. 17*, 57
masculinity: in Catholic Church, 6, 7, 15, 233n41; in literature, 89, 94, 95; in postsecular scholarship, xii, 11–12; sentimentality associated with, 5; visual representations of, 126; women's roles shaped by, xi, 10–11, 20–21, 238n120. *See also* men
Mass, Catholic, 17, 53, 126, 129, 157, 182, 199
men: administration of mission society, 174, 267n22; authority over women, 29–31, 66–68, 76–78, 90, 93, 95, 96, 124, 125, 130, 134, 167, 174, 191, 192, 196, 197, 239n1; as Doctors of the Church, 277n18; feminine images of, 133; heroism of, 72; literature intended for, 44, 67, 82; marriages of holy, 49, 51; political

interests of, 90; religious vocations of, 165; role in Catholic instruction, 36–37, 241n44; women's intellectual relationships with, 54. *See also* masculinity

Mercure de France, 104, 105

Merton, Thomas, 2, 3, 27

Michelangelo, 94

Michelet, Jules: anticlericalism of, xii; criticism of nuns, 26, 142; criticism of sentimental art, 126; on Jeanne Chantal's spiritual devotion, 52; opposition to celibacy, 60; opposition to Sacred Heart devotion, 130; on value of women, 166–67; on women's literary influences, 29, 32, 42, 43; on women's role in the Church, xi, 6, 19–23, 134, 135, 156, 192, 239n1

Miracle of Saint Philomena, 120

Miraculous Medal, 175

Miramion, Madam de, 51, 52

missionaries, *fig.* 22; naming of, 173; Pauline Jaricot's promotion of, 26, 170, 171, 172, 185; Picpus's promotion of, 201; Rose-Philippine Duschene's promotion of, 137, 138, 261n6, 261nn3–4; stories about, 30, 147, 148, 152, 181, 239n6, 263n42

modern world: critique of *Corrine* in, 95–96; as distraction and moral threat, 111–12, 214–19, 275n110; in literature, 75, 88, 89; path to sainthood in, 123, 190, 197, 226, 228; Pauline Jaricot's life in, 171, 179–88, 192–93; preservation of faith in, 169–70, 173–78, 199; qualities of, xii, 12–13, 185; religious images in, 123–24, 127, 131–33, 223; Rose-

Philippine Duchesne's detachment from, 148; women's roles in, 10–12, 14–15, 80, 81, 89, 90, 93, 135, 190–91, 222, 234n48; Zélie Guérin Martin's life in, 197, 198, 206–10, 213–19. *See also* consumer culture; secularism

Molière, 32

Montbéliard, 121

Montmorency, Henry, Duke of, 49

Monvel, Boutet de, 140

morality: games supporting, 113, 114, 115; images to enforce, 100, 110–12; in literature, 32, 63, 67–73, 85, 87–90; women as agents of, 89, 92, 96

Morality in Action (Bérenger), 69–71, 203

Morals of Adolescence, 69

motherhood: difficulties of, 160, 163, 195–96, 198–99, 206, 218; duties of, 129, 198; education supporting, 137; ideals of, 242n69; images of, 98; literature geared toward, 45, 115–16; pride in, 215–16; service to God through, 202–3; St. Philomena's role in, 190; value in French culture, 25, 166; as widows' priority, 51; women's rejection of, 52–54. *See also* families

Mugnano, Italy, 119, 122

Naples, 189

Napoleon: catechism of, 33, 240n24; Duchesne family's opposition to, 143; images of, 111, 115, 116; lace preference of, 203; life under rule of, 169, 200; relationship to Church, 18, 90, 154; on women's societal influence, 89

Napoleonic Code of 1804, 113

Pietà, 102
pilgrimages, 101–2, 129, 152, 171, 188, 189, 210
Pius VII, Pope, 171, 174, 176
Pius IX, Pope, 191, 255n25
Poitiers, 201
Pommélie, Suzanne de la, 53
popes, 100, 101, 188, 210
postsecularism, 9–13. *See also* secularism
poverty, 44, 184, 191–92, 202, 212. *See also* charity
The Practice of Everyday Life (Certeau), 31
prayers, 101–3, 106, 122, 130, 153, 172, 187–90
priests. *See* clergy
Priests, Women, and Families (Michelet), 20, 22–23, 42, 142
Proverbs, 69

Quinet, Edgar, 239n1

Racine, 32
The Raft of the Medusa (Géricault), 108
Ragecourt, Marguerite de, 50–51
Raphael, Archangel, *fig. 3*, 40
Rebecca, 242n59
The Red and the Black (Stendhal), 141
Reddy, William M., 4, 11, 166, 176, 180, 181
Régis, Francis (saint), 105, 148, 149, 152–53, 159, 171, 263n62
religion: as artistic subject, 108–9, 126; femininity of, xi–xiii, 5–10, 13, 15, 17, 80, 81, 126, 195, 231n2, 237n109, 259n124; games emphasizing, 112–13; images relating to, 100, 116; literature concerned with, 66, 67; objections to women in, 20; polit-

ical connotations of, xi, 18, 49, 50, 90, 118, 119, 130, 133, 134, 140, 144, 175, 178, 188, 201, 210, 231n2, 243n89; within secular culture, 97–98, 107–10, 116–19, 123–24, 127–31, 133–35, 148, 156–58, 218, 257n85, 257n87; sentimentality associated with, 5, 10, 13, 14, 21–22, 65, 89, 134
Religious of the Sacred Heart: activities of, 107; authority of, 20; convent in Rome, 189; criticism of, 167; education by, 130, 142; Euphrosine Jouve's desire to join, 159, 161; founder of, 188, 261n11; portrayals in literature, 141; Rose-Philippine Duchesne with, 26, 137, 139, 148, 156, 157, 261n11. *See also* nuns
Religious of the Sacred Hearts of Jesus and Mary (the Picpus), 201, 272nn24–25
religious vocations: comparison with domestic life, 93–95, 203, 206, 212, 217, 218; of Martin family, 197, 211; objections to, 140–42, 146, 147, 156–67; popularity of, 120, 121, 124–25, 142; Rose-Philippine Duchesne's dedication to, 145, 153, 154; value of women in, 56–57, 161, 195–96; women's choice of, 107, 138, 139, 144, 166, 180–82, 185, 187, 202. *See also* clergy; laymen; laywomen; nuns
Renan, Ernst, 242n73
René (Chateaubriand), 82
Renneville, Sophie, 69
Reparatices of the Heart of Jesus, 172
reparation, 171–73, 175, 178, 185, 187–88, 191, 223–26, 228. *See also* atonement
Rerum Novarum (Pope Leo XIII), 170
Richelieu, Cardinal, 71

Rivet, Father, 155
Robespierre, 87, 149
Robineau, Madeleine, 49–50
Romans, France, 148–51
Romantic genre, 87
Rome, 49, 90, 93–94, 120, 189, 191
rosary, 17, 129, 188
roses, *fig. 1*, 104, 227. *See also* flowers
Rousseau, Jean-Jacques, xii, xiii, 4–5, 45, 62, 86, 128, 268n51
Rousseau's Daughters (Popiel), 68
Rue Saint-Jacques, 100, 108
Rue Saint-Sulpice, 108, 131, 259n118

Sackville-West, Vita, 2, 3
sacraments, 17, 34, 36, 38, 39, 40, 186–87, 189
Sacred Heart: images of, *figs. 2, 7, 13–15, 22,* 102, 105, 116, 127–28, 132–33, 164, 224, 255nn26–27; interpretations of devotion to, 103, 127–31, 202, 226–27; missionary name suggestive of, 173; pamphlet about, 174; Pauline Jaricot's devotion to, 175, 177, 178, 186, 189, 192, 267n27, 268n49; political connotations of, 18, 25, 127, 132–33, 185, 201; post-Revolutionary significance of, 172, 178; promotion of devotions to, 24, 138, 255n25; scholarship on, 9, 14; women's devotions to, xiii, 15, 16, 17, 21, 137, 155–56, 178
Sainte Marie-d'en-Haut, 144–48, 154–56, 158–60
sainthood: paths to, 198, 212, 218, 228; Thérèse's aspiration to, 225–26; Zélie Guérin Martin's desire for, 199, 211, 217, 219. *See also* hagiographies; saints

Saint-Jacques images, 100
Saint-Just, 152, 155
Saint Philomena Receiving the Palm of Martyrs, 120
Saint Philomena Thrown into the Tiber, 120
saints: characteristics of, 102, 105–6, 118, 119, 127–28, 153–54; families of, 197; images of, 100–102, 105, 116, 118, 119, 121, 255n40; literature about, 159; relationships to, 106, 107, 123–24; veneration of, 120–21. *See also* hagiographies; sainthood
Saint-Vallier, 172
Sales, Francis de (saint): biblical citation by, 242n59; educational model of, 144; idealism of, 42; interpretation of Sacred Heart, 128; on marriage, 41, 42; as mentor to spiritual women, 54, 58, 262n29; on use of images, 100, 102
Sarah, 40, 205
Satan, 103
Savannah GA, bishop of, 131, 260n145
Savoye-Rollin, Jacques Fortunat, 145, 149, 263n45
Schor, Naomi, 76, 81
Scott, Joan, xi, 7, 15
sea, *figs. 16–19,* 132, 260n149
Second Empire, 143, 203
secularism, 9, 10, 15, 33, 217, 223, 228. *See also* modern world; postsecularism
self-discipline: catechetical teachings about, 40–41, 44, 47; families as obstacles to, 53; heroism of, 54–55, 72, 203; in language and literature, 60, 71; "practices" of, 213; promotion through games, 114; through reading, 68; of Rose-Philippine Duchesne, 139; of saints, 105, 123, 124

self-improvement, 67–68, 77–78, 212

Sénard, Marie-Antoine Jules, 65, 87

sentimentality: and Christianity, 66; in consumer culture, 199; in discourse of Church, xiii, 7, 23; feminization of, 2–5, 11–16, 21, 25, 26, 80–81, 195, 259n145; historical perceptions of, 4–5, 13–14, 223, 224; images of, 97, 98, 99, 122; inspiration through, 26–28; in language and literature, xii, xiii, 44, 61, 65, 85, 127, 166, 170, 174–75, 179–80, 183, 190, 207–9, 218, 221–22, 228, 274n60, 274n76; of married women and mothers, 197, 198, 209; and religious vocations, 160, 162–63, 165, 181; of Rose-Philippine Duchesne, 151, 152; of the Sacred Heart, 128, 130, 178, 191; of Sulpician art, *fig. 2*, 1, 125, 133, 134; tears as expression of, 179, 268n50. *See also* novels

Serna, Pierre, 200

Sévigné, Madame de, 32

sexuality, 40–41, 73–78, 81, 84, 87, 88. *See also* celibacy

Sibyls, 94

silk workers, 172, 187, 191

Sisters of St. Vincent de Paul. *See* Daughters of Charity

Sistine Chapel, 94

social order. *See* modern world

Society for Good Books, 32, 60, 188, 240n18

Society for the Propagation of Faith, 173–74, 191, 267n22

Society of Jesus. *See* Jesuits

Soldier and Peasant (Hopkins), 106

Solomon, 37, 54

Spaas, Lieve, 76

Spiritual Combat (Sales), 42

spirituality, 16, 38–39, 41–43

Spiritual Recreation, 112–13

Staël, Anne-Louise-Germaine de, 25, 63, 89, 96

Stations of the Cross, 112

Stendhal, 61, 130, 141–42

Stephen (saint), 101, 117

Stewart, Joan, 61

Stories of Adolescence, 69, 71

Story of a Soul (St. Thérèse), 222

The Story of My Life (Jaricot), 178–80, 186

Story of Sainte Marie (Duchesne), 148, 155

St. Peter's Basilica, 93–94

St. Pierre, Bernardin de, 24, 73, 76, 79

Sulpician art, *figs. 2, 10–11, 19–20, 22*; criticism of, 125–26, 134, 232n4; as holy cards, *figs. 6–7, 10–22*, 127, 222; place of production, 259n118; popularity of, 126, 131, 256n57; subject matter of, 1, 125, 133, 135, 210, 212, 224, 278nn32–33

Surkis, Judith, 19

Tales of the Castle (Genlis), 68

Taylor, Charles, xii

tears, 179, 268n50

Tekakwitha, Kateri (saint), 57

Ten Commandments, 34, 38

Theresa of Avila (saint), 100, 102, 224

Thérèse (saint): aspirations of, 225–26; as Doctor of the Church, 3, 225, 277n18; illness of, 217; images of, *fig. 1*, 1–2, 115, 126, 227, 278nn32–33; influences on, 27; mother of, 197, 207; perceptions of, 2–3, 14, 224–25; popularity of, 1–2, 222–23, 224, 232n21; spirituality of, 226–29

Third Republic, 111

Three Christian Heroines, or Edifying Lives of Three Young Women (Carron), 44–46
Timothy, 196
Tobias, *fig. 3*, 40, 205
Tobit, book of, 40, 205, 224, 242n61
Tricalet, Marie-Elisabeth, 50
Trinitarian doctrine, 38
True Cross, 101
Turgis, 109, 120, 121, 122, 124, 127, 133
Turks, 58
typhoid epidemic, 149

Ulrich, Laurel Thatcher, xi, xiii
unsectarian, 10, 235n60
Ursins, Marie-Félice des, 49
Ursuline order, 53, 54, 112–13, 138, 147. *See also* nuns

Varin, Father, 156, 264n68
Veronica (saint), 115
Vianney, Jean (saint), 188, 189
virginity, 243n88. *See also* celibacy
Vobalamma, Indian Princess, 55, 57
volonté, 128
Voyage to Cythera, 113

Walch, Agnès, 38
Walker, Lesley, 115
widows, 48, 50, 51, 56, 60, 71, 195, 212
women and girls: as authors, 63, 66; autonomy and individualism of, xi–xiii, 12–15, 20, 22–28, 31, 61, 64, 65, 67, 72, 78, 84–86, 89, 90, 92, 95–97, 107, 128–29, 134, 135, 138–41, 166, 205, 218, 222, 234n48, 235n59; in catechisms and literature, 37, 38, 72, 75–76, 81, 140–42; as consumers and subjects of images, 99; emotional nature of, 5, 8, 11, 15–16, 19–22, 27, 63, 66, 89, 90, 126, 165, 166, 180, 195; games for, 112–15; holy cards owned and produced by, 103–5; influence of literature on, 29–30, 41–50, 59–60, 64–69, 75, 77, 84–85, 242n69; limitations of, 80–83, 85, 89–93, 98, 126, 143–44, 157, 171, 178, 195–97, 237n109; lives of single, 203, 272n33; role in Catholic Church, 7–10, 16–19, 22, 124–25, 165–66, 197, 233n41, 277n18; spirituality of, 42–43, 51, 56, 58, 119–22, 157, 212; treatment in Guérin family, 200–201
writing, 26, 139, 221–22. *See also* autobiographical writing; journals; letter writing; literature
Würtz, Abbé Jean Wendel, 171, 174, 175, 178, 183

Xavier, Francis (saint), 147, 152
Xenophon, 115

Young Christian Heroines (Carron), 44